THE BEGINNING AND THE END

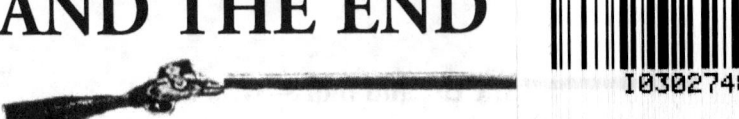

The Civil War Story of Federal Surrenders Before Fort Sumter and Confederate Surrenders after Appomattox

Dayton E. Pryor

HERITAGE BOOKS
2009

HERITAGE BOOKS
AN IMPRINT OF HERITAGE BOOKS, INC.

Books, CDs, and more—Worldwide

For our listing of thousands of titles see our website
at
www.HeritageBooks.com

Published 2009 by
HERITAGE BOOKS, INC.
Publishing Division
100 Railroad Ave. #104
Westminster, Maryland 21157

Copyright © 2001 Dayton E. Pryor

All rights reserved. No part of this book may be reproduced or transmitted in any form or by any means, electronic or mechanical, including photocopying, recording or by any information storage and retrieval system without written permission from the author, except for the inclusion of brief quotations in a review.

International Standard Book Numbers
Paperbound: 978-0-7884-2007-8
Clothbound: 978-0-7884-8273-1

For my Grandsons

James Jordan Nichols
Jesse Louis Nichols
Grant Jordan Pryor

TABLE OF CONTENTS

AUTHOR'S NOTES
VII

INTRODUCTION
VIII

HISTORICAL BACKGROUND
XIII

PART ONE
THE SURRENDER OF FEDERAL FORTS AND OTHER EVENTS THAT CULMINATED IN THE CONFEDERATE CAPTURE OF FORT SUMTER.

CHAPTER 1
THE BEGINNING: CASTLE PINCKNEY
DECEMBER 1860-JANUARY 1861.

MAJOR ANDERSON'S ORDERS-THE IMPORTANCE OF FORT SUMTER-PRESIDENT BUCHANAN'S POLICY-FORTY MUSKETS-THE PALMETTO REPUBLIC-ANDERSON MOVES TO FORT SUMTER-THE FIRST OVERT ACT-THE SOUTH CAROLINA COMMISSIONERS-THE STAR OF THE WEST-A TRUCE PENDING SURRENDER-SIX MORE STATES SECEDE.

1

CHAPTER 2
MORE FEDERAL FORTS ARE SURRENDERED:
JANUARY-FEBRUARY 1861.

GEORGIA: A FORT AND AN ARSENAL-FORT PICKENS AND THE NAVY YARD-THE FORTS AT THE KEYS-THE COUNTY FISHERY COMMISSIONER-ALABAMA, LOUISIANA AND MISSISSIPPI-NORTH CAROLINA AND ARKANSAS-FORT SUMTER AS REAL ESTATE-TWIGGS SURRENDERS IN TEXAS-MCCULLOCH TAKES THE ALAMO-THE FIRST PRISONERS OF WAR.

55

THE STORY OF CIVIL WAR SURRENDERS.

CHAPTER 3

THE C. S. GOVERNMENT PREPARES FOR WAR: FEBRUARY-MARCH 1861.

THE MONTGOMERY CONVENTION-THE CONFEDERATE CONSTITUTION-STRATEGY AND PROBLEMS-CONGRESS LEGISLATES AN ARMY-THE CONFEDERATE WAR DEPARTMENT-CONFEDERATE FINANCE-CONFEDERATE POSTAL SERVICE-CONFEDERATE DIPLOMACY-THE VIRGINIA PEACE CONFERENCE.

96

CHAPTER 4

THE U. S. GOVERNMENT SEEKS A POLICY: FEBRUARY-MARCH 1861.

THE SITUATION AT FORT SUMTER-THE CONFEDERACY TAKES CHARGE-THE LINCOLN ADMINISTRATION-THE THREE CONFEDERATE COMMISSIONERS-THE PROBLEM OF THE FORTS-SOME TALK OF SURRENDER-THE U. S. ARMY AND NAVY-MILITIAS AND VOLUNTEERS-THE STATUS QUO AT FORT PICKENS.

134

CHAPTER 5

FORT SUMTER SURRENDERS: APRIL 1861.

A DECISION: RELIEVE BOTH FORTS-THE FORT PICKENS OPERATION-THE FORT SUMTER OPERATION-BEAUREGARD STOPS ALL SUPPLIES-THE CONFEDERATES OPEN FIRE-"I AM WILLING TO EVACUATE THIS FORT"-LINCOLN CALLS FORTH THE MILITIA-THE FINAL FOUR STATES SECEDE.

167

THE BEGINNING AND THE END.

PART TWO
APPOMATTOX AND AFTER.

CHAPTER 6
LEE SURRENDERS IN VIRGINIA: APRIL 9, 1865.
THE FINAL CAMPAIGN BEGINS-THE CONFEDERATE CONGRESS ADJOURNS-PETERSBURG AND RICHMOND-THE BATTLE OF FIVE FORKS-THE CONFEDERATES ABANDON THEIR CAPITAL-TOWARD DANVILLE, THEN TOWARD LYNCHBURG-GRANT INITIATES NEGOTIATIONS-LEE DECIDES TO SURRENDER-THE TWO GENERALS MEET-CONDITIONS ARE AGREED TO-THE GOVERNMENT MOVES TO DANVILLE-THE GUERILLA CHIEF MOSBY-THE ARMY'S WORK IS NOT FINISHED.

207

CHAPTER 7
JOHNSTON SURRENDERS IN NORTH CAROLINA: APRIL 26, 1865.
SHERMAN ADVANCES TO GOLDSBORO-RALEIGH IS SURRENDERED-JOHNSTON CONFERS WITH DAVIS-A SUSPENSION OF HOSTILITIES-THE BENNETT HOUSE MEETING-MEMORANDUM, OR BASIS OF AGREEMENT-THE GENERALS AWAIT A DECISION-STONEMAN'S CAVALRY RAID-APRIL 26: SURRENDER AT LAST-SCHOFIELD BEGINS RECONSTRUCTION-THE NEED FOR A POLICY.

255

CHAPTER 8
SURRENDERS IN ALABAMA, GEORGIA AND FLORIDA: APRIL-MAY 1865.
CANBY ASSAULTS SPANISH FORT-FORT BLAKELY FALLS-WILSON'S EXPEDITION-THE CAPTURE OF SELMA-THE SURRENDER OF TAYLOR-WILLFUL DESTRUCTION OF AMMUNITION-FROM MONTGOMERY TO WEST POINT-THE ARSENAL CITY OF COLUMBUS-COBB SURRENDERS MACON-CROXTON REJOINS THE CORPS-VODGES AWAITS INSTRUCTIONS-JONES SURRENDERS AT TALLAHASSEE-PRESIDENT DAVIS IS CAPTURED.

292

The Story of Civil War Surrenders.

Chapter 9
Surrenders West of the Mississippi: May-July 1865.
Pope Plans an Offensive-Thompson Surrenders in Arkansas-Kirby-Smith Holds Out-Guerilla Warfare Ends-A Commander without an Army-The Flight to Mexico-War with the Confederate Indians-War with the Plains Indians.

340

Chapter 10
The End: On the Water April-December 1865.
The Battle of Palmito Ranch-The Plight of the Prisoners-The Sultana Disaster-The Scapegoat: Captain Wirz-All the Prisoners Go Home-Civilian Prisoners-Runners and Raiders-Finale in the Aleutians-Slavery Abolished, the Nation Endures.

373

Notes on Sources
405

Bibliography
408

Index
419

The Beginning and the End.

Author's Notes

Over the years, in reading about the Civil War, similarities in descriptions of people, places and battles caused me to wonder who was copying from whom. It eventually became obvious that writers often based their descriptions on common sources, especially *Battles and Leaders* and the *Official Records of the Union and Confederate Armies in the War of the Rebellion.* The 128 volumes of the *Official Records,* packed with the reports and correspondence of the Union and Confederate armies, is an essential source for any study of the war. Quotations, except where another attribution is given in the text, are from *The Official Records.* There is no use of "sic" to point out variant spellings, grammatical mistakes, or even substantive errors in these quotations. What you read is exactly what the writers wrote, back in the 19th Century.

Numbers are sometimes reported differently in different sources. Those most commonly accepted, or consistent with known facts, have been used. Population figures cited are from the Census of 1860, but the number of people in particular places varied during the war. Accurate numbers for the Confederates in the final months of the war are difficult to find because after-action reports were seldom completed, and records were often lost. Moreover, the count of men present for duty varied enormously because of casualties, illness, and the large number of deserters, many of whom left in search of food and supplies, but sooner or later rejoined their commands.

A few notes about language usage:

- Although the words "black," "colored," "African" and even "men of color" and "A.D."(African Descent) appear in contemporary sources, the term "African-American" does not. The most common term for people of sub-Saharan ethnicity was "Negro," so that is the term used in this book.

- The term "states' rights" is a modernism: Americans in the 19th Century spoke of "state rights."

The Story of Civil War Surrenders.

Introduction

In the popular mind, and as a practical matter, the Civil War began when Confederate forces attacked Fort Sumter on April 12, 1861, and ended when General Robert E. Lee surrendered to General Ulysses S. Grant at Appomattox Court House on April 9, 1865. In fact, these events marked neither the actual beginning nor the ultimate end of the conflict. From a legal standpoint, the war may be said to have begun when President Abraham Lincoln declared a state of insurrection on April 15, 1861, and called upon the state militias to suppress it, or when the Confederate States declared a state of war with the United States on May 6, 1861. It formally ended when President Andrew Johnson proclaimed the nation at peace on May 29, 1865. (Except in Texas, where he did not proclaim peace until August 20.)

This book is about military affairs in general, and surrenders in particular. Much that was military in character happened between the election of Lincoln in November 1860 and the attack on Fort Sumter. The seceding states took possession of nearly a hundred Federal forts, arsenals, ships and civil facilities, for the most part in January 1861, before the Confederacy existed. Civil War books typically refer to pre-Sumter surrenders, evacuations and preparations in a sentence or less; but their significance deserves fuller treatment, which this book provides. In describing the end of the war, books tend to conclude with Lee's surrender. This was only the first by a Confederate army, and involved the fewest men. Following the subsequent surrenders of Johnston in North Carolina, Taylor in Alabama, and Kirby-Smith in the Trans-Mississippi, were a number of interesting events related to guerillas, Indians, prisoners of war and encounters at sea.

Part One deals with the surrender of Federal forts and other events that culminated in the Confederate capture of Fort Sumter. Chapter One portrays the situation in Charleston, South Carolina's decision to leave the Union, the occupation of Fort Sumter by U. S. troops, the seizure by the secessionists of three forts and the arsenal in Charleston, the firing of the first shots in January, and the secession of six more states. Chapter Two describes how the states that were about to secede took possession of scores of Federal forts, arsenals and other property, and the surrender of a large part of the U. S. Army in Texas. Chapter Three covers the formation of the Confederacy in February and March of 1861. It characterizes the Confederate Constitution and describes the organization of the C. S. military, acquisition of munitions, and financial arrangements. Chapter Four deals with events between Lincoln's inauguration and the attack on Fort Sumter. It includes an analysis of the situations at Fort Sumter, Fort Pickens, and the Florida Keys forts, and the condition of the armed forces of the United States and the Northern states. Chapter Five examines the decisions of the new Republican administration, operations in support of Fort Pickens and Fort Sumter, the surrender of Fort Sumter, Lincoln's declaration of a state of insurrection, and the secession of the final four states.

Part Two explores the extended series of Confederate surrenders at and after Appomattox Court House. It begins with chapter Six, which explains the circumstances leading to Lee's surrender of the Army of Northern Virginia, and presents the terms of that surrender in considerable detail. It also considers the limited military alternatives available to the Confederacy as the government gradually collapsed. Chapters Seven, Eight and Nine cover events that occurred in the eleven weeks that followed Appomattox, and the combat that continued, at various levels of intensity, especially in Alabama. Warfare with guerillas in the spring of 1865, the possibility of war with France over Mexico, surrenders in the Indian Territory, and war on the plains are each examined briefly. Chapter Ten tells the story of the last battle fought along the Rio Grande, the homeward movement of prisoners of war, the fate of the remaining Confederate sea raiders, and the firing of the last shot in Alaskan waters in June of 1865.

From the Old French *sur + rendre*, to give back or yield, comes the English word surrender, meaning to relinquish possession or control on demand or compulsion, or to give up to an enemy. The concept of surrendering has existed since pre-historic times, with varying consequences for those who did. Slavery was a likely result, as was death, though either prospect nullified the desirability of surrendering. It is useful to distinguish between the two types of surrender: that of individuals or small groups, and that of whole commands or places. In the first, which we might call

The Story of Civil War Surrenders.

the "hands up" surrender, one man at a time, or several together, cry "I surrender" and raise their arms, preferably with their hands open so as not to be thought to be concealing a weapon. In the second type of surrender, a whole formation or a fort is yielded by the commander, and formal terms are usually agreed upon and put in writing. We might call this the "white flag" surrender, since it is customary in this method to indicate one's intentions by displaying a white cloth. The commander who yields may present his sword to the victor, and there may be a formal handing over of rifles, cannons, ammunition and flags. In both types of surrender, the men doing the surrendering are very likely to become prisoners of war.

Not all prisoners voluntarily surrender. Some do not surrender at all: they are captured against their will by being overwhelmed. Since prisoners are an important source of intelligence, combatants sometimes deliberately allow themselves to be captured in order to deliver false information. In modern warfare, the common practice of armies (though not always of guerillas) has been to accept surrenders, and to hold the persons surrendered as prisoners of war. As prisoners, it is expected they will be treated in a humane way. Provided with more or less adequate food, clothing, shelter and medical care, protected from harassment and injury, and allowed to communicate with their families. Civil War prisoners were handled in three ways. They were: exchanged, a prisoner of one side for a prisoner of the other; paroled, released on their written word that they would not again take up arms until they were exchanged; or imprisoned, held in long-term prison camps until they were exchanged, paroled, or died.

By commonly accepted (though unwritten) rules of war, an officer has a moral obligation to surrender the men under his command when there is no longer any reasonable prospect of avoiding defeat and death, but not to do so when that is not the case. In actual combat, this is a matter of close judgment, and depends on the nerve, training and experience of the commander. One can plausibly believe that the Confederacy reached the point of "no reasonable prospect" on July 4, 1863: Vicksburg had been occupied, giving the Union complete control of the Mississippi River, and the Army of Northern Virginia had been decisively defeated at Gettysburg. The number of its men under arms was

The Beginning and the End.

declining, the strength of the Union forces was growing, the people of the South were suffering severe economic privation, and there was little likelihood of foreign intervention.

Why then did the Confederacy not surrender? Several possible answers come to mind: the Confederate leadership recognized or admitted to none of these circumstances, their commitment to Southern independence remained undiminished despite these circumstances, they hoped that Lincoln would not be re-elected and that the anti-war sentiment in the North would lead to a negotiated settlement. Surrenders, nevertheless, were hardly novel experiences for the Confederates, who suffered them frequently between May 1861 and May 1865. That they were able to sustain the struggle for four years, despite steady losses in men and geography, indicates how fervently devoted they were to the principles for which they were fighting.

Only a few of the scores of Southern cities surrendered were ever retaken. Winchester, Harpers Ferry and Manassas changed hands a number of times, and for varying periods the Confederates reoccupied Fredericksburg, Baton Rouge, Jacksonville, Galveston and some smaller places. Nevertheless, the accumulated losses, and Union occupation of large parts of all of the seceded states except Texas, including virtually all of the Atlantic coast and the Mississippi River, did not lead the Confederate government to any overt consideration of national surrender. Indeed, in a government committed to strict interpretation of the Constitution, and devoted to state rights, there were no clear means by which surrender could be accomplished, even if the leaders had desired to do so. They did not.

The reader should bear in mind that the Federal surrenders up to and including Fort Sumter, and all of the Confederate surrenders in 1865, occurred without guidance from their respective national governments. As the secession crisis intensified, Buchanan and his secretaries of war failed to give direction to the U. S. commanders in the field. This was especially true of Fort Sumter, the focus of political attention; no oversight was provided to Anderson even after Lincoln became president. Because the Army of Northern Virginia was surrounded, Lee surrendered it without authority from Davis, with whom he could not communicate; but because he could not do so, he declined to surrender the remaining C. S. armies. Davis was unable to control those forces except, intermittently, for Johnson's. As a result, when all of the other generals surrendered, they did so without the approval of Confederate authorities. In both the beginning and the end of the Civil War, the central authorities were unwilling or unable to control events.

The Historical Background essay that follows is intended for readers who are unfamiliar with the incidents and issues that led up to the Civil War: the question of sovereignty, the nullification controversy, the slavery dilemma, constitutional and other arguments about secession, differences between North and South, the election of 1860, President Buchanan's position, and Congressional attempts to find a compromise. Those who are knowledgeable about the sources of the conflict may prefer to begin reading at Chapter One.

The Beginning and the End.

Historical Background

The United States was confounded by a Constitutional crisis in December of 1860: Was the Federal Union permanent, or was each state a sovereign entity in a compact from which it could withdraw at will? The question arose when a South Carolina convention voted to secede. The secession of that state, promptly followed by six others, was caused by profound disagreements over slavery, which had been an issue since the adoption of the Federal Constitution in 1787. The issue remained quiet for several decades, but became increasingly contentious in the decades between 1820 and 1860. Forces favoring the limitation or abolition of slavery, mainly in the North, became more assertive, while states in which it was sanctioned by law, mainly in the South, became more defensive. The slave states of the cotton South gradually convinced themselves that they had a reason to secede from the free states of the Union. They had previously convinced themselves that they had a right to do so. Did they have that right?

The question, which had occasionally arisen during the first seventy-one years of the nation's history, was rooted in the means of governance of the British North American colonies. Legal authority was based on 17th and 18th century charters, with the King unquestionably sovereign. By 1775, the people of the thirteen colonies, convinced that their constitutional rights as Englishmen had been hopelessly abrogated, began to think of themselves as "Americans" and to speak of the colonies as their "country." Collectively, they declared themselves independent, and took up arms. The King resisted, so the colonies formed an alliance to coordinate a defense against the Monarch. Joining together in a "Continental Congress," they created a Continental Army. *The Articles of Confederation and Perpetual Union* (1777), with each state having one vote, was the instrument on which the power to govern was based.

The Story of Civil War Surrenders.

On September 3, 1783, the signing of the Treaty of Paris ended the prolonged war between the Americans and Britain. Britain recognized as sovereign and independent "the United States of America," composed of the thirteen former colonies and the territory east of the Mississippi River. Did sovereignty pass to the collective whole with which the treaty had been negotiated, or to the individual states? A popularly elected assembly or lower house had governed each of the colonies, and (except in Pennsylvania) a council or upper house, with governors appointed by the Crown in royal colonies and elected by the assemblies in the others.

Independent of control by Britain, the royal charters no longer applied, so each of the states had to create a plan of government. They adopted written constitutions, based mainly on the unwritten British constitution – an amalgam of ancient charters, legislation and common law traditions, to which they added a number of important innovations. While proceeding independently in their efforts, the states vigorously exchanged ideas. There was common agreement that the form of government should be a republic -- that is, elected by men who owned land or other property. There should be two legislative bodies as well as an executive and a judiciary, and power should be structured so as to avoid the excesses of both democracy and aristocracy. The process was completed in all thirteen states between July 1775 and April 1777. In some states, the constitutions were regarded as interim arrangements, in hopes that the dispute with Britain could be resolved short of American independence. None of the states declared themselves to be, or thought of themselves as, independent nations.

The Articles of Confederation soon proved to be an unsatisfactory basis for the general government. In 1787, the Continental Congress called for a convention of the states "to render the constitution of the federal government adequate to the exigencies of the union." While there was broad agreement about the need for better definition of the powers of the general government, there was intense disagreement about the proper nature and extent of those powers. Meeting in secret sessions, the delegates abandoned the Articles and laboriously crafted a new Constitution. They debated, among other issues, whether the improved government should be "federal" or "national" in nature. Treaties regulate relations among sovereign states. The word "federal" is derived from the Latin word for treaty, "foedus." It suggests, therefore, an agreement among separate entities. National, on the other hand, is derived from the Latin "natus," meaning birth, and suggests a common place of belonging.

Reaching agreement on a new form of government required extensive compromises. Two of these, both dealing with voting power, were to have momentous consequences. One was creation of an upper house, or Senate, in which each state, regardless of size, had two members. The other was counting each slave as three-fifths of a person in determining a state's number of members in the House of Representatives. The word "slavery" was not actually used in the Constitution, but the existence of the practice was implicitly recognized. The terms "other persons" and "such persons" in Article I, and "Person held to Service or Labour" in Article IV, refer to slaves:

> [I, Section 2] Representatives . . . shall be apportioned among the several States which may be included within this Union, according to their respective Numbers, which shall be determined by adding to the whole Number of free Persons, including those bound to Service for a Term of Years, and excluding Indians not taxed, three fifths of all other Persons.
>
> [I, Section 9] The Migration or Importation of such Persons as any of the States now existing shall think proper to admit, shall not be prohibited by the Congress prior to the year [1808].

[IV, Section 2] No Person held to Service or Labour in one State, under the laws thereof, escaping into another, shall, in Consequence of any Law or Regulation therein, be discharged from such Service or Labour, but shall be delivered up on the Claim of the Party to whom such Service or Labour may be due.

Thus the Constitution dealt with the matter only by providing that each slave counted as three-fifths of a person for the purpose of determining a state's number of members in the House of Representatives, by allowing for an eventual end to the slave trade, and by requiring that owners of slaves escaping to another state be able to recover them. (However, the Ordinance of 1787, which established a government for the territory west of the Ohio River, provided that "slavery and involuntary servitude shall be forever prohibited" in that territory). After debating for four months, the convention produced, in September 1787, a document that established an effective governmental structure, yet was sufficiently ambiguous to allow the delegates to agree to it. The Continental Congress submitted it to conventions in the thirteen states, where enough members satisfied themselves that it was, on balance, acceptable, and ratified it.

Just as the delegates had disagreed about the Constitution's content, there were soon disagreements about its interpretation. The basic dispute was between "nationalism" and "state rights." Where did political power ultimately reside? It was not rationally or legally possible that both the nation (if there were such a thing) and the states could be sovereign. It must be one or the other. The proponents of the two views, exemplified by Thomas Jefferson ("state") and Alexander Hamilton ("nation"), began contending during the first administration of President George Washington. Then as now, neither side was consistent in its position, and the

The Beginning and the End.

situation is confused by the fact that those who espoused the "national" view called themselves Federalists.

The principle did not become critical until war with France threatened in 1798. In order to limit anti-government activity, Congress passed the Alien and Sedition Acts. They made it unlawful to speak or write "with the intent to defame" or to bring "into contempt or disrepute" the president or Congress. Ten men were convicted under the acts, provoking public opposition. The Kentucky legislature responded by passing a resolution, written by Jefferson, protesting the acts as an unconstitutional usurpation of power. The United States, declared the resolution, was a compact among sovereign states, each of which had "an equal right to judge for itself." This created a great deal of dissension. In 1799, a New Hampshire resolution contended that only the federal judiciary could decide constitutional issues. Fortunately, the Alien and Sedition Acts were repealed in 1800, but the opposing views became one of the main issues in that year's election. (In 1803, the Supreme Court ruled in Marbury v. Madison that the court was the final arbiter of the constitutionality of laws).

The issue remained dormant for a dozen years, until the United States declared war on Britain in June of 1812. The putative causes were the British Orders in Council interfering with American shipping, and the impressments of American seamen by British warships. It was also based on the desire of much of the public to invade Canada, and join it to the United States. The New Englanders, however, were vigorously against the war, partly for commercial reasons and partly because they were opposed to geographic expansion. (They regarded the Louisiana Purchase of 1803 as unconstitutional, since the Constitution delegated no power to the Federal government to expand the United States by buying land. President Jefferson, who held to the state-rights view and was a strict constructionist, nevertheless decided to seize the opportunity to double the size of the country). Some Federalists in

New England talked of seceding from the Union and negotiating a separate peace with Britain. A convention met in Hartford at the end of 1814 and proposed seven Constitutional amendments that would have redressed their grievances. However, the war ended the next month, and no action was taken.

When the issue again arose, it brought the nation perilously close to hostilities. Various Federal laws promoting development of industry and interstate commerce had been passed under what was called the American System. Nationalistic in concept, it was antithetical to state rights. In 1828, Congress enacted a tariff bill, widely known as the "Tariff of Abominations," that protected manufacturers from foreign imports. Generally favored in the North, it was widely disliked in the agricultural states, especially in the South. Vice-president John C. Calhoun of South Carolina adamantly opposed it and anonymously authored a book forcefully stating the doctrine of nullification, that is, the right of any state to refuse to obey or enforce a Federal law to which it did not assent. President Andrew Jackson favored state rights, but did not believe those rights encompassed disobedience to the laws of the United States. He declared his position unambiguously in a famous toast: "Our Federal union — it must be preserved."

A modified protective tariff was passed in 1832, eliminating some of the "abominations" but retaining high duties on iron and textiles. On November 24, South Carolina declared the tariff "Unauthorized by the Constitution of the United States, null, void, and no law, not binding upon this State, its officers or citizens." It forbade Federal officers from collecting duties within the state after February 1, 1833. The state legislature promptly adopted measures to implement nullification, including secession if the Federal government attempted to enforce collection of the duties.

President Jackson dispatched two revenue cutters to Charleston and sent General Winfield Scott there with orders to strengthen the defenses at Fort Moultrie and Castle Pinckney. On

The Beginning and the End.

December 10, 1832, Jackson, who had been re-elected the previous month, issued a proclamation to the people of South Carolina. He said that nullification was based on the strange proposition that a state might retain its place in the Union and yet be bound only by whichever laws it chose to obey. He went on:

> Whether it be formed by compact between the States, or in any other manner, it is a government in which all the people are represented, which operates directly on the people individually, not upon the States. Each state having parted with so many powers as to constitute, jointly with the other States, a single nation, cannot possess any right to secede, because such secession does not break a league but destroys the unity of a nation.

Jackson, reluctant to employ force, nevertheless asked Congress for authorization to use the army and navy to compel the collection of duties in South Carolina. Seeking compromise, Senator Henry Clay of Kentucky proposed a revised tariff bill "to prevent the destruction of the political system, and to arrest civil war and restore peace and tranquility to the nation." It reduced duties over ten years to 20 percent of value and was acceptable to Calhoun and other tariff opponents. The Force Bill and the Tariff Bill were both enacted on March 1, 1833, and the confrontation over nullification was averted. The broader question of state rights was only temporarily in remission. Jackson accurately predicted: "the next pretext will be the Negro, or slavery question." The issue arose again in 1850, and was again temporarily contained by the five-point compromise of that critical year. However, the diametrically opposed positions, "state" versus "nation," remained, and the intensity with which they were supported grew. No judge or jury existed that could decide the matter in a way that was acceptable to both sides: the issue seemed to be irreconcilable.

Those who espoused the "state" view, mainly in the South, were prepared to leave the Union. They held that the source of political power resided in each state. The states, they said, not the whole people, had ratified the Constitution. Each of the original states, when it ceased to be a colony, became sovereign and independent. They continued to possess every power and jurisdiction not expressly delegated to Congress in the Constitution, which was a compact among the states. Each state entered into the compact independently, and could separate itself simply by canceling its ratification. Jefferson Davis described the Federal government as "the agent of the States in their foreign relations" and as "an umpire between the States in their relations one to another." Beyond the Constitution was the inherent right of revolution against an oppressive government. Southern conservatives, however, were reluctant to champion secession in revolutionary terms.

Those who embraced the "nation" view, mainly in the North, were prepared to defend the Union. They held that the Constitution devised by the 1787 Convention had created a "more perfect union" that could not be dissolved merely by one or more of the member states deciding to withdraw. "We, the People of the United States" had indeed ratified the Constitution, through their delegated representatives. The intent was clearly to establish a perpetual Union, endowed with all the powers essential to sovereignty. In the articles of the Constitution that defined legislative, executive and judicial functions, the framers provided a way for new states to be added to the Union, but none by which states could leave. The alternative to a sovereign American nation would be anarchy and an end to the stability of republican government. Beyond the Constitution was the prerogative of every government for self-preservation.

The Beginning and the End.

The existence of slavery in the United States was the consequence of two-and-a-half centuries of history that began with the first British settlement. After the introduction of African slaves in Virginia in 1619, slavery expanded rapidly in the South. The Africans seemed to adapt well to the performance of physical labor in the warm climate and soon became the basic human resource for the production of sugar, cotton and tobacco, and for all kinds of manual work. Even in the North, where slavery became less prevalent that in the South, it was an important source of labor. By 1750, slaves were 10 percent of New York City's population. Often used by their owners in agricultural and manufacturing, they were also hired out as day-workers, just as firms today supply employers with "temps." The end of slavery in the North began when Vermont outlawed it in 1777 and the Massachusetts Constitution of 1780 excluded it. By 1804, it had been terminated, or was in the process of being terminated, in all states north of the Mason-Dixon line.

Motivated by Christians who regarded the practice as immoral, and free laborers who resented the wage competition of slaves, a movement gradually emerged to end slavery nationally. In the South, the prospect that slavery might ultimately be extinguished was perceived as a serious threat. Just over 30 percent of families owned slaves (though most owned only a few), and they feared the destruction of the labor basis of their economy and of the social system that defined the relationship of the two races. They were also anxious about the possibility that Southerners who did not own slaves might gradually come to oppose slavery.

In 1820, this contentious political, economic and moral issue was, it was widely hoped and believed, resolved by the Missouri Compromise. At the time, there were twenty-two states, eleven free and eleven slave. An agreement was reached in Congress that forever prohibited slavery in the territories north of latitude 36* 30' (the southern border of Missouri), admitted Maine as a free state in 1820, and admitted Missouri as a slave state in 1821. Over the next two decades slavery was abolished elsewhere: by Mexico in 1829, by Britain in 1833, and by France in 1848.

In America, however, the issue festered with increasing virulence during the 1840s and 1850s. A series of accommodations dealt with the status of slavery in the territories and in new states, and related events influenced attitudes and positions. Among the most notable were:

- Texas Statehood. After Mexico abolished slavery, but exempted the Province of Texas, American settlers there decided to secede rather than give up their right to slavery, which they expected eventually to lose. They declared themselves independent in 1836. This led to a dispute about admitting Texas to the United States as a slave state. It was admitted in 1845, precipitating war with Mexico, which had never recognized the independence of Texas.

- The Wilmot Proviso. This 1846 amendment to a Mexican War appropriations bill declared (quoting the Northwest Ordinance): "neither slavery nor involuntary servitude shall ever exist" in the territories. Though not adopted, it heightened tension over the slavery issue and was attached unsuccessfully to many other bills.

- Acquisition of more than 500,000 square miles of territory from Mexico. In 1848, the United States became a transcontinental republic when it purchased, for $18,250,000, land that eventually became six states and parts of two others. The two sections of the country divided sharply over what the status of slavery was to be in this new territory.

- The Compromise of 1850. By mid-century eighteen states had been added, nine free and nine slave. This compromise consisted of five parts: admission of California as a free state;

THE BEGINNING AND THE END.

organization of the New Mexico and Utah territories with no restrictions on slavery but with provision for "squatter sovereignty;" settlement of the Texas boundary claims; prohibition of the slave trade (but not slavery) in the District of Columbia; and a Fugitive Slave Act giving the Federal government exclusive jurisdiction.

- Publication of *Uncle Tom's Cabin, or Life Among the Lowly.* This melodramatic novel, which appeared serially in 1851, and as a book the following year, forcefully depicted the evils of slavery. Read by millions of Americans and foreigners, it focused public attention on the issue and provoked an outraged response in the South.

- The Kansas-Nebraska Act. Introduced in 1854 and passed three years later, after rancorous debate and much modification, this bill repealed the 36* 30' provision of the Missouri Compromise, and provided for "popular sovereignty" in the territories by leaving decisions about slavery up to the voters after the territory became a state.

- The Republican Party. The gradual collapse of the Whig Party and the sectional split of the Democratic Party were accompanied by the formation of the Free-Soil Party. It held that Congress had both the right and the duty to prohibit slavery in the territories. This became the Republican Party, which ran John C. Fremont for the presidency against Democrat James Buchanan in 1856.

- Dred Scott vs. Sandford. In 1857, an activist Supreme Court held that Negroes were of an "inferior order," possessed no rights, and could not be citizens. More broadly, it ruled that the provision of the Missouri Compromise barring slavery north of 36* 30' was unconstitutional, and that Congress had no power to legislate regarding slavery except to protect the property rights of slave owners.

- John Brown's Raid. The October 1859 attack at Harpers Ferry, Virginia shocked the slave states. The Southerners saw the raid not simply as the act of a few fanatics, but with some justification, as part of a Northern abolitionist plan to promote "servile" uprisings.

After the invention of the cotton gin in 1793, slavery gradually but steadily became fundamental to the economy of the South, since it was, or was believed to be, essential to cotton production. Moreover, like tobacco, cotton tends to wear out the ground in which it grows. This meant that new land had to be acquired so that the cultivation of cotton could expand. To Southerners, therefore, extension of slavery in the territories seemed almost as important as preservation of slavery where it existed. They were apprehensive that legal constraints would gradually diminish, and eventually eliminate, the right of property in slaves -- which they came to regard as a social good, even as the will of God. They were, in addition, anxious about the potential violence and cost of slave rebellions. This fear was aggravated by the aggressive behavior of Northern abolitionists during John Brown's raid. Their salvation seemed to lie in an independent, slave-holding nation.

Underlying the conflict over slavery were a number of important differences between the sections. These differences strengthened the Southerners' desire to become a separate nation. Many Southern opinion-makers entertained the strong belief that theirs was a culture not only different from, but superior to, that of the North. True, the sections shared five things in common: the English language, the republic they created when they freed themselves from Britain, a legal system based on the common law, the British ethnicity of the white people, and the Protestant religion. But many of these were changing. From the 1840s

The Beginning and the End.

onward, for instance, as the republic was becoming more democratic, large numbers of Irish and German immigrants were bringing with them Catholicism, ethnic diversity, and the German language. Few of these immigrants settled in the South, where they would have to compete with slave labor.

Other disparities so effectively divided the country into two distinct societies that the two largest religious denominations, the Methodists and the Baptists, split into Northern and Southern branches. The economy of South Carolina, Georgia and the Gulf Coast states was relatively stable and mainly agricultural, with cotton, tobacco, rice and sugar as the principal crops. New Orleans was the only large city. The climate was markedly milder and the way of life more leisurely, at least for the well-to-do planters who supplied the social and political leadership, committing them to the maintenance of things as they were. The three-quarters of the population that did not own slaves earned a modest living on small, isolated farms, were often illiterate, and feared that freedom for the slaves would depress them even further. There was also, of course, the great demographic difference: almost half of the South's population was composed of people of mainly African descent. While regarding their own society as harmonious, religious and conservative, Southerners considered Northerners to be mercenary, heretical and, worst of all, abolitionist.

The expanding Northern economy was a diverse mixture of agriculture, manufacturing, commerce and finance. There were several large cities and many textile-producing mill towns. Farms grew wheat and hemp, and bred hogs, horses and mules. Natural resources included coal, iron and copper, while gold and silver from the West provided both coinage and specie to exchange for imports. The North was beginning to export timber, grains and other foods. The transportation system of turnpikes, canals and railroads accommodated the east-west flow of goods, firmly uniting the Northeast with the Northwest. Education was more highly valued in the North (where many of the Southern gentry attended college), public schools were numerous, and a greater proportion of the population was literate. People were more amenable to change and interested in using the new machinery that was being invented. Their view of the South was that it was backward, poor, inefficient and decadent.

As a result of these many differences, and the persistent controversy over slavery, the urge to create a Southern Nation was strong. Cotton was America's principal source of foreign exchange, and because Southerners thought it was essential to the economies of the North and of Europe, they believed that cotton was "king," and that it would enable them to thrive independently. The cotton-kingdom states felt confident that those just to the north would join this Southern Nation: Arkansas, Tennessee and North Carolina certainly, Missouri, Kentucky and Virginia probably. Beyond that, the trade that flowed North-South along the Mississippi River would promote good relations with the states of the Northwest. While those states might never join, they seemed more likely to ally themselves with it than with the Northeast.

Expansion to the west and south seemed possible; New Mexico and California might well choose to join; Cuba, northern Mexico and even parts of Central and South America might be acquired. Most Southerners assumed that they could either peacefully separate themselves from the North or easily win any armed struggle that might result from secession. Few admitted, or even realized, the great risk involved: if they tried and failed to establish a Southern Nation, the outcome might be not the preservation of slavery but what they feared most - the end of it.

Not all Northerners viewed the Southerners' desire to leave the Union as threatening. There were those who even thought it would be desirable, and who would be content to let the slave states go. Others believed that, if some of the states seceded, not many years would pass before they would seek readmission. Still others dreaded the possibility that owners of slaves would be allowed to bring them into the free states, making slave ownership a property right everywhere (as the Supreme Court's Dred Scott decision implied), and thereby threatening free labor. Many people were simply tired of the dispute over slavery, which they regarded as morally corrupt and an affront to Christianity, and they desired its abolition. The abolitionists aggressively used every means to promote freedom for the slaves.

Abolition was not supported by Northern merchants who profited from the cotton trade, bankers who provided credit to Southern planters, or textile manufacturers for whom cotton was their raw material. Other people discounted the economic importance of cotton: the total value of the South's cotton crop, while large, was less than that of the North's hay crop. (Hay, the fuel of horses, was the gasoline of those times, even though steam was providing a growing share of power). Most importantly, however, many Northerners realized that the present prosperity and future growth of the United States depended on the existence of a large market throughout which goods could freely move - a connected, national economy. A majority of these people were therefore strongly committed to preservation of the Union, and were willing and prepared to use force to prevent secession. In both the North and South, it seemed certain that the institution of slavery must, and would, either expand or die. No basis had been found, nor was it ever found, on which these fundamental differences could be peacefully resolved within the Union.

By 1860, public attention was concentrated on two specific issues, neither of which was of substantial immediate significance. One was the recovery of runaway slaves. The Fugitive Slave Act of 1850 empowered Federal marshals to act when local sheriffs refused to do so. Citizens could be compelled to serve on posses to recover runaways, real and alleged, who were denied the right to a jury trial or even to give evidence. In an effort to thwart the marshals, many of the free states attempted a form of nullification by enacting personal liberty laws. However, Northern indignation at the fugitive law gradually subsided, some of the personal liberty laws were repealed, and opposition was minimal except in New England. Besides, the number of escaped slaves was small.

The other issue was that of the extension of slavery into the territories. As viewed by Northerners, this meant the existing territories, especially New Mexico (which included present Arizona), where its economic viability was likely to be limited by climate and other conditions. (In 1860, there were only forty-six slaves in all of the territories). To the Southerners, however, it also meant other, potential territories, farther south, that might be acquired. Moreover, Southerners insisted on being able to take their property wherever they chose, so the issue was one of principle as well as of practice.

Slavery policy reached a crisis in the election of 1860. Its outcome set in motion horrific events that not only abolished slavery, but also determined that America was to be one nation, indivisible, rather than two or more fragments. The crisis arose because the fundamental tenet of the Republican Party was that "the normal condition of all of the territory of the United States is that of freedom." Owners of slaves, especially in the lower South, believed that the election of the Republican Party candidate, if it should occur, would seriously menace their right to possess Negroes as property. Their only credible remedy would be to form a separate nation in which slavery was secure.

The composition of Congress changed somewhat after Oregon was admitted in 1859. There were then eighteen free states and fifteen slave states, and sectional differences intensified in the 1860 session. The North pressed for legislation supporting economic development while the South was consumed by doctrinal insistence on the preservation of slavery and its extension into the territories.

The Beginning and the End.

In 1859 and 1860, Southern legislators were barely able to prevent passage of three measures involving the disposition of Federal public lands. One was a homestead bill, under which any person could become the owner of 160 acres. It passed in both the House (where all but one of the votes in favor were from the North, and all but one of those against were by members from slave states), and the Senate, but President James Buchanan vetoed it. A second bill, for the building of a railroad between the eastern United States and the Pacific coast, to be financed mostly by subsidies in the form of grants of public lands and government bonds, was blocked in the Senate. The third bill, which also failed of enactment, was for grants of public lands to the states for the support of agricultural and mechanical colleges. (These and related measures were enacted within two years after the delegations of the seceded states left Congress).

On April 23, 1860, the Democratic Party convention, meeting in Charleston, culminated in a split that presaged what was in store for the nation. The Southern delegates, determined to provide security for their property, demanded that a "slave code" be included in the platform. Despite their commitment to state rights, they insisted that the right of slave owners to take their property into the territories be guaranteed by the Federal government, rather than leaving the matter to the territorial legislatures. When this move failed, forty-nine delegates from eight states walked out. Various motives seem possible: the hope of throwing the election into the House of Representatives, or of forcing the supporters of Illinois Senator Stephen A. Douglas to make concessions, or of assuring a Republican victory and thus setting the stage for secession. More likely, members acted individually on the basis of personal tendencies, without regard to the possible consequences.

The Republican Party convention gathered in Chicago on May 16. Although Senator William H. Seward of New York seemed most likely to be selected, the nomination went to Abraham

Lincoln of Illinois. He was considered electable partly because he had condemned slavery without advocating radical action against it. His political experience was limited to a single term in Congress, but in so short a time he had made few enemies. His views were relatively well known because of the widely publicized debates between him and Douglas in the 1858 race for an Illinois seat in the U. S. Senate. After the nomination of Lincoln, the divided Democrats held two separate conventions. The Northern Democrats chose Douglas while the Southern Democrats nominated Vice-president John C. Breckinridge of Kentucky. The Constitutional Union party nominated a fourth candidate, John Bell of Tennessee.

The 1860 campaign, both North and South, was characterized by excitement and contention. The Republican platform, which was more specific than most such documents, affirmed "the right of each state to order and control its own domestic institutions." Lincoln clearly stated his dedication to preserving the Union as well as his opposition to the extension of slavery into the territories, while vowing not to interfere with slavery where it existed. But Southerners remembered that in the 1858 debates Lincoln, paraphrasing Jesus, had said:

> A house divided against itself cannot stand. I believe this government cannot endure permanently half slave and half free. I do not expect the Union to be dissolved -- I do not expect the house to fall -- but I do expect it will cease to be divided. It will become all one thing, or all the other. Either the opponents of slavery will arrest the further spread if it, . . . or its advocates will push it forward until it shall become alike lawful in all the States, . . .

The Southerners, many of whom genuinely feared the Republicans, became despondent and tense as they realized that Lincoln was certain to carry nearly all of the free states. The character of their fear can perhaps be understood from the rumor that the vice-presidential candidate, Hannibal Hamlin of Maine, was part Negro. Moreover, widespread stories of slave insurrections, made credible by memories of Nat Turner's rebellion and John Brown's recent raid, caused near hysteria. Instances of arson and murder were attributed to slaves, and several whites as well as slaves were lynched or beaten. Volunteer military companies, some destined soon to fight the Union, were organized for protection against the slaves.

Southerners had talked of secession for years, and speakers during the election vociferously advocated that the slave states leave the Union in the event of a Republican victory. Support for secession was widespread, even though it is likely that a majority of the population opposed immediate action. This support was not limited to slave owners, who were a minority of the white population. Non-owners, especially in areas where Negroes outnumbered whites, were deeply concerned that the end of slavery would mean the end of racial barriers and thus of white supremacy. Those who opposed secession were branded "submissionists."

That the people of the thirty-three states sensed the importance of the 1860 election is evidenced by the fact that votes were cast by 82 percent of those eligible, a proportion exceeded only once (1876) in American history. On November 6, Lincoln was the victor with 39.9 percent of the popular vote, but in ten of the fifteen slave states he was not even on the ballot. He won 180 electoral votes, consisting of all of the votes of seventeen of the eighteen free states and half of the votes of the eighteenth. The two Democratic candidates shared 47.5 percent of the popular vote: Douglas won 29.4 percent and Breckinridge 18.1 percent. Between them, however, they received only 84 electoral votes. John Bell of Kentucky, running on the Constitutional Union ticket, received 12.6 percent of the popular vote and 39 electoral votes. The Democrats remained in control of Congress, but Lincoln, candidate of the party dedicated to preventing the spread of slavery into the territories, and unquestionably committed in the longer term to its elimination, had won the presidency. It appeared certain that some of the slave states would attempt to leave the Union.

With the election of a Republican president, the right of a state to secede was aggressively asserted throughout the slave states. The ominous question was: If a state were to test this right by actually seceding, would the remaining states peacefully allow it to do so, or would they resist by force? Definitive resolution could no longer be postponed, but President Buchanan was determined to postpone it. A lawyer from Lancaster, Pennsylvania, he was a "dough-face," a Democrat sympathetic to the South. His political experience was considerable: he had served in both the House and the Senate and had been ambassador to both Britain and Russia. He had excellent analytical skills, a conservative view of affairs, and believed in a strict interpretation of the Constitution. While the Constitution did not provide, as he interpreted it, for a state to secede from the Union, neither did it provide for the use of force by the Federal government to prevent a state from seceding. As president, he was empowered to enforce the laws against individuals, but not against states.

According to Buchanan, Lincoln's election "accomplished the triumph of the anti-slavery over the slaveholding States, and established two geographical parties, inflamed with hatred against each other." He hoped to preserve the Union, but he doubted that it could survive the shock of civil war. He had, he said, repeatedly and solemnly "warned his countrymen of the approaching danger, unless the agitation of the North against slavery in the South should cease." The potential danger became real on November 10, 1860, when the South Carolina legislature, which was in session in order to choose presidential electors (it was the only state where that was not done by popular vote), called a convention to meet on December 17.

Faced with the near certainty of at least one state leaving the Union, Buchanan desperately wanted to avoid a crisis and to leave decisive action to the new administration that would take office on March 4. He thought that his sole alternative, absent any authorization from Congress, was to defend government property. In his view, the lawful means available to a president to carry out his duties were strictly limited. Only Congress could empower the executive to use force. *The Act of 1795* authorized the president to call out the militia "whenever the laws of the United States shall be opposed . . . in any state by combinations too powerful to be suppressed by the ordinary course of judicial proceedings, or by the power vested in the marshals." In addition, an 1807 law empowered the president to use military force for any lawful purpose, but only defensively. During the nullification crisis in 1833 a so-called Force Bill had authorized President Jackson to collect the customs at Charleston "either on land or on board any vessel," but the power had not been used, and the act had expired.

On December 3, Buchanan transmitted, to the lame-duck session of the 36th Congress, his final state-of-the-union message. He began by observing the South had been wronged by "the incessant and violent agitation of the slavery question throughout the North, for the last quarter of a century. . ." He said this agitation was perpetuated by the press and handbills, by abolition sermons and lectures, by state and county conventions, and by speeches in Congress. The problem, he thought, could be simply resolved:

> How easy would it be for the American people to settle the slavery question forever, and to restore peace and harmony to this distracted country! They, and they alone, can do it. All that is necessary to accomplish the object, and all for which the slave States have ever contended, is to be let alone and

permitted to manage their domestic institutions in their own way. As sovereign States, they and they alone are responsible before God and the world for the slavery existing among them.

Buchanan continued that "the election of one of our fellow-citizens to the office of President does not of itself afford just cause for dissolving the Union." Better to wait, he advised, for some "overt and dangerous act." The president executes, but does not make, the laws, and there was no probability of passage of an act to impair the right of property in slaves. Moreover, the Supreme Court had decided that slaves, as property, were protected by the Constitution. He then explained:

> In order to justify secession as a constitutional remedy it must be on the principle that the federal government is a mere voluntary association of States, to be dissolved at pleasure by any one of the contracting parties. . . . Such a principle is wholly inconsistent with the history as well as the character of the federal Constitution. . . . It was intended to be perpetual, and not to be annulled at the pleasure of any one of the contracting parties. . . . The framers never intended to implant in its bosom the seeds of its own destruction, nor were they at its creation guilty of the absurdity of providing for its own dissolution.

Having argued forcefully against the right of secession, Buchanan addressed the matter of executive responsibility, noting that he was bound "to take care that the laws be faithfully executed." But what if there were events over which he had no control? He was powerless in South Carolina because all the federal officers there had resigned. The same obstacle did not apply to collection of the customs. If the collector in Charleston were to resign, the president could appoint a successor to perform that duty. As to United States property in South Carolina, this has been purchased for a fair equivalent, by the consent of the legislature of the State, for the erection of forts, magazines, arsenals, &c., and over these the authority 'to exercise exclusive legislation' has been expressly granted by the Constitution to Congress. It is not believed that any attempt will be made to expel the United States from this property by force; but if in this I should prove to be mistaken, the officer in command of the forts has received orders to act strictly on the defensive.

Buchanan declared that as president he had, apart from execution of the laws, no authority to decide what the relations between South Carolina and the United States should be. It was his "duty to submit to Congress the whole question in all its bearings." He posed the critical question: "Has the Constitution delegated to Congress the power to coerce a state into submission which is attempting to withdraw or has actually withdrawn from the [United States]?" His answer was no, the power to make war against a state was "not among the specific and enumerated powers." Even if the power existed, would it be wise to use it to preserve the Union? No again, because "in the fraternal conflict a vast amount of blood and treasure would be expended, rendering future reconciliation between the States impossible." Dissolution of the Union could be averted by passing an "explanatory amendment," that would "forever terminate the existing dissensions, and restore peace and harmony among the States." He proposed that it

> be confined to the final settlement of the true construction of the Constitution on three special points: 1. An express recognition of the right of property in slaves in the States where it now exists or may hereafter exist. 2. The duty of protecting this right in all the common Territories . . . until they shall be omitted as States into the Union, with or

without slavery, as their constitutions may prescribe. 3. A like recognition of the right of the master to have his slave, who has escaped from one State to another, 'delivered up' to him. . . .

Buchanan believed this "appeal ... would be received with favor by all the States." However, neither the secessionists, nor the unionists reacted favorably to the message. The secessionists objected because the president argued against the right of secession, and because he indicated his intention to collect the revenues at Charleston. From the point of view of the Republicans, to whom the "explanatory amendment" was unacceptable, it was virtually an abdication in favor of dissolution of the Union.

Congress responded to the president's message with a desperate but futile attempt to find a means of averting secession. To do that, it must resolve the sectional antagonisms that more than forty years of political effort had failed to settle. This attempt was made even though many Southerners no longer sought compromise, and many Northerners were opposed to it. On December 4, by a vote of 145 to 38, the House of Representatives agreed to the appointment of a special Committee of Thirty-three, one member from each state, to consider "so much of the President's message as relates to the present perilous condition of the country." On December 6, the Senate (from which the South Carolina senators had resigned on November 9) agreed to the appointment of a Committee of Thirteen, to which it referred that part of the message relating to "the agitated and distracted condition of the country, and the grievances between the slave-holding and non-slave-holding states."

On December 18, the Senate referred to the committee an omnibus package of six Constitutional amendments and four resolutions, proposed by Senator John J. Crittenden of Kentucky. It was prefaced by the statement that "it is the desire of Congress, as far as its power will extend, to remove all just cause for the popular discontent and agitation which now disturb the peace of the country, and threaten the stability of its institutions." The most important of the six amendments would have extended to the Pacific the Missouri Compromise line (which had been repealed in 1857), with "slavery of the African race . . . recognized as existing" south of that line. This just might have been acceptable to the Republicans if it had applied only to territory then held, but because it encompassed all territory ever to be acquired it directly conflicted with the main plank of the Republican platform.

The second, third and fourth of the amendments provided that "Congress shall have no power" to abolish slavery in places under its exclusive jurisdiction within slave states; or to abolish slavery in the District of Columbia so long as it exists in Virginia and Maryland, and without the consent of "the inhabitants," or to prevent members of Congress from bringing slaves with them; or to hinder transportation of slaves from one state to another. The fifth proposed amendment required Congress to compensate an owner for "full value" when a marshal failed to arrest a fugitive slave because of violence or intimidation, and reserved the right of the United States to sue the county to "recover from it, with interest and damages, the amount paid."

The last provided that "No future amendment of the Constitution shall affect the five preceding articles" and two other specified clauses, and added that "no amendment shall be made to the Constitution which shall authorize or give to Congress any power to abolish or interfere with slavery." To many people, the idea of prohibiting amendments to the Constitution seemed illogical (could not that amendment later be amended?) as well as undesirable. After four days of meetings the first two resolutions of the Crittenden proposal were agreed to, but nothing else, and the compromise required that the entire package be adopted. On December 24, Senator Seward made, with Lincoln's approval, the final Republican offer: the Constitution not to be altered to allow Congress to abolish slavery in the states, the fugitive slave law to be amended to grant jury trials, and the state legislatures to be asked to repeal certain laws regarding personal rights. Only the first was acceptable to Senator Jefferson Davis of Mississippi and the other Southerners. The committee therefore reported on December 31 that it had "not been able to agree upon any general plan of adjustment." The Senate had failed.

Thomas Corwin of Ohio chaired the House committee. Even though several members refused to serve, the group was awkwardly large. It too considered and rejected the idea of extending the Missouri Compromise line, then proposed to admit New Mexico as a state immediately (to by-pass the territorial issue) with an implicit understanding that it would be a slave state but that slavery would probably not succeed there. On January 14, the committee submitted a majority report (though it no longer represented a majority, since many of the Southern members had by then resigned) and seven minority reports. About a dozen resolutions were adopted, many of them similar to the Crittenden proposals, but none were considered by the Senate.

As 1861 began, the nation was indeed imperiled. South Carolina had seceded; its senators and congressmen had resigned. Six other states had called conventions that were certain to result in their secession. Both houses of Congress had attempted to find some basis on which to satisfy the Southerners, but no new alternatives were available: the conceivable options had all been exhausted in the previous forty years. Buchanan, convinced that secession was illegal, but that only Congress had the power to deal with it, was resolved to take no action.

Lincoln, who remained largely silent in Springfield, Illinois, replaced him on March 4. Privately, however, the president-elect assured Southern friends that he would not interfere with the interstate slave trade or with slavery in the Southern states. He was even willing to support a Constitutional amendment to forever prohibit Federal interference with slavery. On December 15, in response to a request that he make a public statement on several issues, he wrote to John A. Gilmer of North Carolina:

> As to the state [personal liberty] laws . . . I really know very little of them. I have never read one. If any of them are in conflict with the fugitive slave clause, or any other part of the constitution, I certainly should be glad of their repeal; . . . On the territorial question, I am inflexible, . . . On that, there is a difference between you and us; and it is the only substantial difference. You think slavery is right and ought to be extended; we think it is wrong and ought to be restricted. For this, neither has any just occasion to be angry with the other.

On December 20, he stated the other issue on which he claimed, and proved, to be inflexible: "That the Federal Union must be preserved."

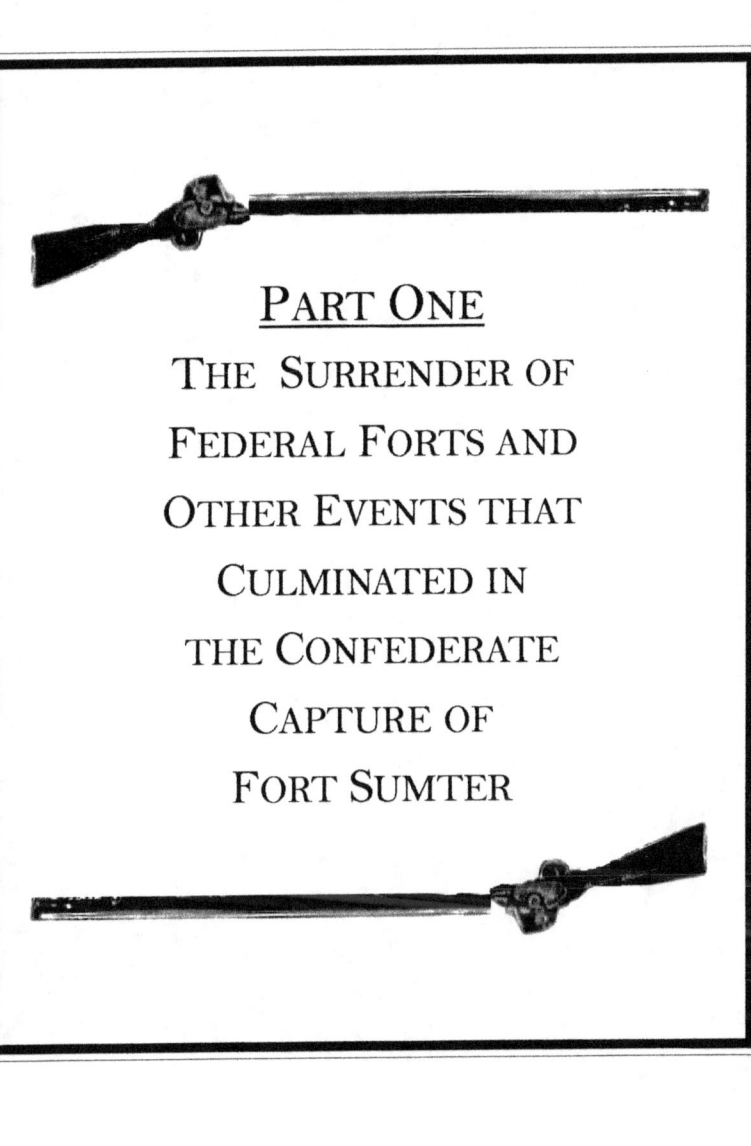

Part One

The Surrender of Federal Forts and Other Events that Culminated in the Confederate Capture of Fort Sumter

Chapter 1

The Beginning: Castle Pinckney
December 1860-January 1861

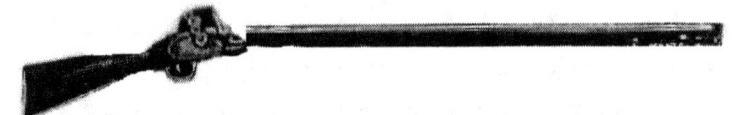

Major Anderson's Orders

U. S. military property at Charleston, South Carolina consisted of four forts and an arsenal. Fort Moultrie, on Sullivan's Island, a sand spit north of the harbor entrance, had been established during the War for Independence. A masonry fort with fifteen-foot high walls, to the top of which sand had drifted during years of neglect, it mounted fifty-five guns and had three brick barracks that could house 500 men. In 1860, it was the only fort that was garrisoned. On a shoal south of the harbor entrance stood unfinished Fort Sumter. Construction began in 1829 on this pentagonal brick structure with walls five feet thick and nearly fifty feet high. It was designed for 146 guns in three tiers, and a garrison of 650 men. The construction that was in progress was being performed under the direction of the Corps of Engineers.

Southwest of the harbor entrance, on James's Island, was Fort Johnson. On that site, which had been fortified as early as 1704, stood a four-sided structure made of bricks and palmetto logs, and several barracks. Defense of the inner harbor was provided by the smallest of the forts, Castle Pinckney, a half-round brick structure on a three-and-a-half acre island. It was manned only by an ordnance sergeant who lived there with his family, and whose duty it was to insure that the harbor lighthouse, which was inside the fort, was lit. Since the fort was only half a mile from the Charleston wharves, its guns could bear on the city itself. The original purpose of the forts was to protect the harbor against enemy ships, but now, as the South Carolinians contemplated secession, they regarded the Federal forts as a threat.

The bar, a submerged ridge outside the harbor entrance that was about four miles long, was an obstacle to ships of deep draft and thus provided some protection, especially at low tide. There were four ways by which ships could approach Charleston. Using the Main Ship Channel, which followed the shore northward along Morris Island, a vessel from the south could turn west just beyond Fort Sumter to enter the harbor. Using the Maffitt Channel, a vessel coming from the northeast could follow the shore of Sullivan's Island and turn west beyond Fort Moultrie to gain entrance. There were also two nearly parallel channels that approached Charleston from the east-southeast: the North Channel and, just south of it, the Swash Channel. The guns of the two outer forts covered all of these approaches, while Castle Pinckney and Fort Johnson defended the inner harbor.

On November 11, 1860 Major F. J. Porter, the assistant adjutant-general of the U. S. Army, completed an inspection of the Charleston fortifications and submitted his report to his superior in Washington, Colonel Samuel Cooper (who resigned four months later to join the Confederacy). Porter said that, under the command of Lieutenant Colonel John L. Gardner, Fort Moultrie was garrisoned by Companies E and H of the First Artillery, and the regimental band. There were present seven officers and seventy-three enlisted men, of whom eleven were in arrest and confinement, and four were sick. Porter expressed his concern:

> The unguarded state of the fort invites attack, if such design exists, and much discretion and prudence are required on the part of the commander to restore the proper security without exciting a community prompt to misconstrue actions of authority. . . . All could have been easily arranged several weeks since, when the danger was foreseen by the present commander. Now much delicacy must be practiced. The garrison is weak, and I recommend that a favorable opportunity be taken to fill up the companies with the best-drilled recruits available.

He noted that Fort Sumter was incomplete, and that

> No arms are here, and I doubt if they would be serviceable in the hands of workmen, who would take the side of the stronger force present. Unless it should become necessary I think it advisable not to occupy this work so long as the mass of engineer workmen are engaged in it. The completion of those parts essential for the accommodation of a company might be hastened.

As to Castle Pinckney, Porter said, since the quarters and magazine required repairs, "I would not recommend its occupation."

There was also an arsenal in Charleston, where Ordnance Captain F. C. Humphreys was in charge. On November 10, less than a week after the election, Humphreys wrote to the Chief of Ordnance, Colonel H. K. Craig, saying:

> I received an order from Colonel Gardner, commanding troops in the harbor, to issue to him all the fixed ammunition for small-arms (percussion caps, primers, &c.) at this arsenal, such a step being advisable, in his estimation, for the better protection of the property in view of the excitement now

existing in this city and State. . . . I proceeded to obey [his order] on the afternoon of the 8th.

A captain had come from Fort Moultrie with a detachment to load the stores, including several barrels of powder, onto a schooner, Humphreys said, but

> the shipment of them was interfered with by the owner of the wharf until the city authorities could be notified, and there were but three or four cart-loads on board. I considered it best that they should be reconveyed to the magazine until something definite should be determined, which was done.

Humphreys wished to avoid an incident, and he decided not to make the transfer even after the mayor, when told of the shipment, did not object. Craig referred the message from Humphreys to the Secretary of War, John B. Floyd, with the remark that "I am not aware by what authority Colonel Gardner undertook to give such an order." Two days later Humphreys notified Craig that "In view of the excitement now existing in this city and State, and the possibility of an insurrectionary movement on the part of the servile [slave] population, the governor has tendered . . . a [South Carolina Militia] guard, of a detachment of a lieutenant and twenty men for this post, which has been accepted." On November 20, Ordnance Colonel Benjamin Huger arrived to take command of the arsenal.

Colonel Gardner was concerned about insurrection by secessionists, and not, as the governor claimed to be, by slaves. Gardner warned that seizure of the forts could only be prevented by reinforcement of the garrison. This is not what Secretary Floyd wanted to hear. A former governor of Virginia, Floyd believed, along with many others, in the right of a state to secede, but doubted that it was desirable to do so. He decided to address the situation by assigning Major Robert Anderson, a fifty-five-year-old

The Beginning and the End.

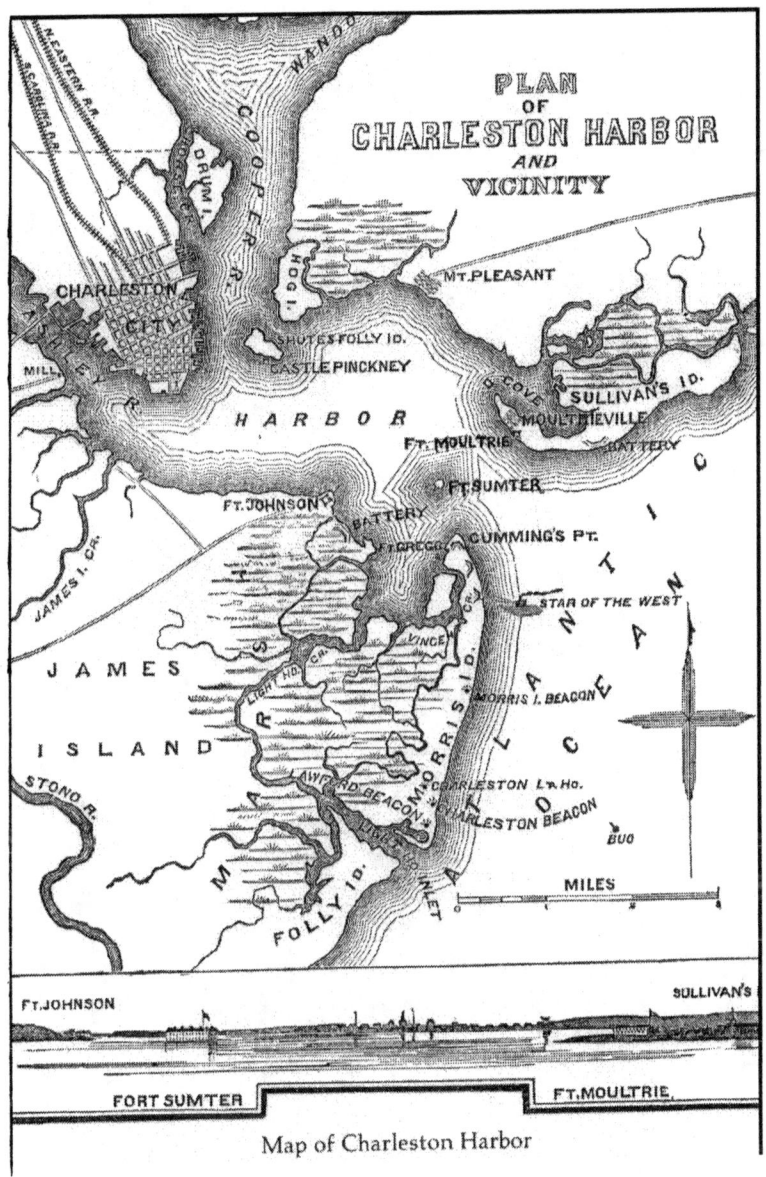

Map of Charleston Harbor

artillery officer, to Charleston with instructions to avoid a confrontation. Anderson's wife was from Georgia and the couple had recently owned a plantation and slaves. He was a close friend of Senator Jefferson Davis, a fellow Kentuckian who had been a plebe during Anderson's senior year at West Point, from which he graduated in 1825. Although Anderson's sympathies were indeed with the South, Floyd failed to appreciate that he was also a staunch and loyal Unionist, deeply committed to his duty as a regular army officer.

On November 15, he received orders: "Major Robert Anderson, First Artillery, will forthwith proceed to Fort Moultrie, and immediately relieve Bvt. Col. John L. Gardner, lieutenant-colonel of the First Artillery, in command thereof." Anderson was stationed in New York City, where General-in-Chief Winfield Scott, under whom he had served in the Mexican War, had his office. Before leaving for Charleston he went to see Scott. The old general advised him that, since he would have very few men, he should concentrate them at one place, preferably Fort Sumter. Anderson reached Charleston on November 21.

Fort Moultrie, which was designed to repel ships attempting to enter the harbor, was indefensible from the landward side, from which any attack now would undoubtedly come. The same was true of Fort Johnson. Work on the Charleston forts, which had been resumed in August 1860, was being continued under the direction of Corps of Engineers Captain John G. Foster, who had arrived on November 11. He soon reported that he had 260 hired men on the job. Of these, 115 were at Fort Moultrie, where Foster was exerting himself "to make it so defensible as to discourage any attempt to take it." A wet ditch was being built, the guns were carefully positioned, and he planned to erect a tower for sharpshooters on the guardhouse.

The Importance of Fort Sumter

On November 23, Anderson began numbering his reports to Cooper, so that if one was missing, it might indicate that the mail was being intercepted. In this lengthy first report, Anderson told Cooper that he had inspected the forts of the harbor. He described the work in progress at Fort Moultrie, where there were hillocks within 400 yards of the wall "which offer admirable cover to approaching parties, and would be formidable points for sharpshooters." But the engineers were energetically improving the situation, so that

> When the outworks are completed, this fort, with its appropriate war garrison, will be capable of making a very handsome defense. . . . The garrison now in it is so weak as to invite an attack, which is openly and publicly threatened. We are about sixty, and have a line of rampart of 1,500 feet in length to defend. If beleaguered, as every man of the command must be either engaged or held on the alert, they will be exhausted and worn down in a few days and nights.

He then addressed the condition of Fort Sumter. He said that all the guns would be mounted in about seventeen days, that the fort was ready to comfortably accommodate one company, and more on a temporary basis, and that the four magazines were completed and in excellent condition. He then appraised the situation:

> This work is the key to the entrance of this harbor; its guns command [Fort Moultrie], and could soon drive out its occupants. It should be garrisoned at once. Castle Pinckney, a small casemated work, perfectly commanding the city of Charleston, is in excellent condition . . . It is, in my opinion, essentially important that this castle should be immediately

occupied by a garrison, say, of two officers and thirty men. The safety of our little garrison would be rendered more certain, and our fort would be more secure from an attack by such a holding of Castle Pinckney than it would be from quadrupling our force. The Charlestonians would not venture to attack this place when they knew that their city was at the mercy of the commander of Castle Pinckney.

Anderson said that he was anxious "to avoid collision with the citizens of South Carolina," but added that "The clouds are threatening, and the storm may break upon us at any moment." He "most earnestly entreat[ed] that a re-enforcement be immediately sent" to Fort Moultrie, plus at least two companies to Fort Sumter and Castle Pinckney. He concluded:

> With these three works garrisoned as requested, and a supply of ordnance stores . . . I shall feel that, by the blessing of God, there may be a hope that no blood will be shed, and that South Carolina will not attempt to take these forts by force, but will resort to diplomacy to secure them. If we neglect, however, to strengthen ourselves, she will, unless these works are surrendered on her first demand, most assuredly immediately attack us. I will thank the Department to give me special instructions, as my position here is rather a politico-military than a military one.

Cooper wrote on November 24 to say that "The Secretary of War desires that you will communicate . . . the present state of your command" and that he wanted to know whether "it might be advisable to employ reliable persons, not connected with the military service, for purposes of fatigue and police." Anderson responded on November 28, again emphasizing:

> security from attack would be more greatly increased by throwing garrisons into Castle Pinckney and Fort Sumter

than by anything that can be done in strengthening the defenses of [Fort Moultrie]. There are several intelligent and efficient men in this community, who, by intimate intercourse with our Army officers, have become perfectly well acquainted with this fort, its weak points, and the best means of attack. There appears to be a romantic desire urging the South Carolinians to have possession of this work . . .

As to hiring reliable persons for fatigue and police duties, Anderson said:

> I doubt whether such could be obtained here. They would certainly be of great assistance to us. The excitement here is too great. Captain Foster informs me that an adjutant of a South Carolina regiment applied to him for his rolls, stating that he wished to enroll the men for military duty. The captain told him that they had no right to do it, as the men were in the pay of the United States Government.

In a clear statement of where he believed he and his men should be, one that foreshadowed the move he made a month later, he said,

> If I had been here before the commencement of expenditures on this work, and supposed that this garrison would not be increased, I should have advised its withdrawal, with the exception of a small guard, and its removal to Fort Sumter, which so perfectly commands the harbor and this fort.

Anderson had heard talk in the city that heavy guns could, if needed, be obtained within two days, and supposed they would be brought from Fort Pulaski, near Savannah. His immediate concern was that none of Fort Sumter's guns be mounted, so that they could not be used against Fort Moultrie.

Anderson wrote to Cooper on December 1, saying "things look more gloomy," that there was great excitement in the city, and that a state militia officer had said that the citizens were not going to allow men or stores to enter any of the forts. He had also heard "that attempts have been made, by offers of heavy sums, to induce men at Old Point Comfort to join a Southern army." But he added that he knew of no attempts "to tamper with our men, who thus far cheerfully perform the arduous and ceaseless duties imposed upon them . . ."

Things must have seemed gloomy indeed to Anderson when he received Cooper's note of December 1, in response to his request for reinforcements. Cooper said that Colonel Huger had been ordered to Washington and that before he left, Anderson should confer with him "on the matters which have been confided to each of you." He then got to the point:

> The increase of the force under your command, however much to be desired, would, the Secretary thinks, judging from the recent excitement produced on account of an anticipated increase, as mentioned in your letter, but add to that excitement, and might lead to serious results.

On December 9, Anderson pointed out to Cooper that, when South Carolina seceded, he believed that "their first act will be to take possession of [Fort Sumter]." He could be driven from Fort Moultrie if that fort were in hostile hands, and even wondered whether it might not be prudent,

> to cause the ammunition . . . to be destroyed or rendered unserviceable. . . . Fort Sumter is a tempting prize, the value of which is well known to the Charlestonians, and once in their possession, with its ammunition and armament and walls uninjured and garrisoned properly, it would set our Navy at defiance, compel us to abandon this work, and give them the perfect command of this harbor.

The War Department sent Major Don Carlos Buell to Charleston to tell Anderson what he should do in the event of being attacked. After the two officers discussed the situation, Major Buell wrote, on December 11, a memorandum of the instructions he had given to Anderson:

> You are carefully to avoid every act which would needlessly tend to provoke aggression; and for that reason you are not, without evident and imminent necessity, to take up any position which could be construed into the assumption of a hostile attitude. But you are to hold possession of the forts in this harbor, and if attacked you are to defend yourself to the last extremity. The smallness of your force will not permit you, perhaps, to occupy more than one of the three forts, but an attack on or an attempt to take possession of any one of them will be regarded as an act of hostility, and you may then put your command into either of them which you may deem most proper to increase its power of resistance. You are also authorized to take similar steps whenever you have tangible evidence of a design to proceed to a hostile act.

On December 13, Foster reported to Lieutenant Colonel R. E. DeRussy, who at the time was commanding the Corps of Engineers:

> A strict night watch is maintained, and during the daytime a man stands at the gate to prevent interested persons entering and inspecting the fort and its arrangements for defense. This latter precaution I have found to be necessary on account of numbers of men connected with the military, who came for the purpose of obtaining knowledge to use against the defenders of the fort in case of a collision with the Government. I have given the same instructions to Lieutenant Snyder, at Fort Sumter...

Like Anderson himself, and officers at other army posts, Foster added a plea for "I would respectfully, but strongly, urge that more definite instructions be given me for my guidance." Over the next four months, ad hoc policy would be made, often by junior officers, while two administrations procrastinated in the absence of a consistent strategy.

On one small matter Cooper gave instructions, though not clear ones. Anderson had asked what to do about South Carolina authorities who were attempting to enroll, in state forces, men employed by the Corps of Engineers to work on the forts. The adjutant-general told Anderson, "you will, after fully satisfying yourself that the men are subject to the enrollment, and have been properly enrolled under the laws of the United States, and of the State of South Carolina, cause them to be delivered up or suffer them to depart." Following this garbled answer were detailed instructions about how to defend against hostile forces approaching the fort from the surrounding sand hills.

President Buchanan's Policy

Buchanan's cabinet was divided on the question of whether a state had a Constitutional right to secede, but there was more agreement that the government had the right to defend Federal property. This was the opinion of seventy-five-year-old Winfield Scott, general-in-chief of the U. S. Army for nineteen years. A hero of the War of 1812 and the Mexican War, he had run unsuccessfully for the presidency as the Whig Party candidate in 1852. He suffered from gout and other illnesses and, because he weighed 300 pounds, was unable to mount a horse. His headquarters was in New York City, away from the politics of Washington.

As early as October 29, 1860 Scott had written (in the third person) his "Views suggested by the imminent danger of a disruption of the Union by the Secession of one or more of the Southern States." He submitted this unusual document to the president and the secretary of war. It began with a scenario involving the break up of the Union into four "confederacies," for each of which he not only defined borders, but nominated a capital city. It then advised the president that (as a political matter) secession was legal and the Constitution did not provide for the use of force to preserve the Union against an exterior, as distinct from an interior, state. Nevertheless, he believed that (as a military matter) the Federal forts should be defended:

> From a knowledge of our Southern population it is my solemn conviction that there is some danger of an early act of rashness preliminary to secession, viz., the seizure of some or all of [eight] forts. In my opinion all these works should be immediately so garrisoned as to make any attempt to take any one of them, by surprise or coup de main, ridiculous. . . . With the army faithful to its allegiance, and the navy probably equally so, and with a Federal Executive, for the next twelve months, of firmness and moderation — moderation being an element of power not less than firmness — there is good reason to hope that the danger of secession may be made to pass away without one conflict of arms, one execution, or one arrest for treason.

Scott realized that the meager armed forces of the United States were ill prepared to cope with even so limited a mission as defending the forts. At the beginning of 1861, to protect the thirty-one million people living in three million square miles of territory, the army had 16,375 soldiers - 1,116 officers and 15,259 enlisted men - of whom 14,663 were present for duty. (The president was, however, authorized to increase the number to 18,626). The men were assigned to 198 line companies, 183 of which were deployed in scores of locations scattered throughout the western states and territories, acting as security forces between settlers and Indians. The rest garrisoned the coastal forts and the twenty-three arsenals. The men of the Corps of Engineers were engaged in surveying railroad routes, constructing fortifications and military roads, and assisting navigation in harbors and rivers. The navy, which had no overall commander, comprised about 8,000 men and forty-three vessels, only nine of which were steam-powered. Thirty of these ships were on foreign stations. There was doubt about the loyalty of many of the regular officers, and in fact, when the crisis came, 27 percent of the officers in the army and 15 percent of the navy officers resigned to join the Confederate forces. Most of the enlisted men - the majority of whom were foreign born - stayed in Federal service.

On December 8, as Congress sought some way to defuse the rapidly deteriorating situation, five members of the South Carolina Congressional delegation called on President James Buchanan at the White House. In view of the certain outcome of the secession convention scheduled to meet in just nine days, their purpose was to discuss the best means of avoiding a hostile collision over the forts at Charleston. Buchanan had determined not to disturb the military arrangements there as long as U. S. troops were not molested. To avoid a misunderstanding, the president suggested that the prospective secessionists reduce to writing what they had said, which they did:

> In compliance with our statement to you yesterday, we now express to you our strong convictions that neither the constituted authorities, nor any body of the people of the State of South Carolina, will either attack or molest the

United States forts in the harbor of Charleston, previously to the action of the Convention; and we hope and believe not until an offer has been made, through an accredited representative, to negotiate for an amicable arrangement of all matters between the State and the Federal Government, provided that no reenforcements be sent to these forts, and their relative military status shall remain as at present.

They said they made this statement on their own, without any authority binding their state, but expressed confidence that it would be sustained by the convention when it met. Buchanan, a cautious man, questioned the word "provided," in case it might be construed as an agreement on his part not to reinforce the forts. That, he said, was a commitment he was not empowered to make. Nevertheless, within three weeks the Southerners would consider that he had made a pledge, and that he had broken it.

Forty Muskets

To understand an event that sheds light on the ambivalent policy of the Federal government, we need to go back to October 31, when Colonel Craig wrote to Secretary Floyd:

> There is at Fort Sumter . . . a considerable quantity of ammunition, &c., and it has been suggested by the Engineer officer in charge of the work that a few small-arms be placed in the hands of his workmen for the protection of the Government property there might be a useful precaution. If the measure should . . . meet with the concurrence of the commanding officer of the troops in the harbor, I recommend that I may be authorized to issue forty muskets to the Engineer officer.

Floyd endorsed this "Approved." Craig sent a copy to Gardner, asking his "views as to the expediency or propriety," and telling him to have the weapons issued if he approved of the measure. Gardner replied that he saw no objection to the propriety. He said,

> while I do not apprehend that any attempt upon the United States works here will receive the countenance of the State or city authority, it is by some thought that a tumultuary force may be incited by the feeling of the time . . . this possibility makes it incumbent on me to provide as far as I may against it, and forty additional musketeers would then to desirable. . The arms need not be delivered to the men selected by the Engineer officer till the occasion should actually obtain. The workmen in charge of the property are bound on principles of common law to defend it against purloiners . . .

As for expediency, that was "quite another question." Gardner noted that there were then about 109 workmen at Fort Sumter, most of them of "foreign nativity," and he was suspicious of them. When questioned about how they would be inclined in the event of secession, they replied that they were indifferent, but "intimated that the largest bribe would determine their action." The engineer officer would have to keep the arms:

> beyond the physical possibility of being taken from him by the untrustworthy . . . [otherwise] this large body of laborers may . . . unrestrainedly deliver up the post and its contents on a bribe or demand. Meanwhile they cannot be moved outside of that isolated island post, which has not a foot of ground beyond the walls of the fort.

Gardner concluded that "the only proper precaution . . . is to fill these two companies with drilled recruits (say fifty men) at once, and send two companies from Old Point Comfort to occupy respectively Fort Sumter and Castle Pinckney." Craig sent this reply to Floyd with an endorsement that "... it is probable that the issue has not and will not be made without further orders."

On November 30, Foster, who had arrived in the area three weeks prior, told Colonel DeRussy that, in carrying out the work at Castle Pinckney, he was endeavoring to "secure a proper protection to the property of the United States." In order to do that, he said,

> It will be indispensable that I have the men instructed, to a certain extent, in the service of the guns, and also in the manual of arms, if I can arrange with Colonel Huger to have the requisite number of muskets sent from the arsenal. I shall also have Lieutenant G. W. Snyder take up his quarters in Fort Sumter, and give like instructions to fifty picked men, in whom I can place reliance in case of an emergency.

On December 2, Foster requested of DeRussy:

> that application may be made to the War Department to have Colonel Huger, Ordnance Corps, issue to me four boxes of muskets (smooth-bores), with percussion caps for sixty rounds. Fifty of these muskets are required for Fort Sumter and fifty for Castle Pinckney. The cartridge boxes and belts are not absolutely necessary . . . Colonel Huger, who I consulted upon the subject of the muskets, said he could not issue them without authority from Washington . .

Foster planned to arm those workmen that he thought could be relied upon to resist an attack by a mob (though not by the militia). The request was referred to Floyd, who endorsed it "Action deferred for the present."

On December 3, Foster assigned thirty men to work at Castle Pinckney. Anderson lent Lieutenant Jefferson C. Davis (no relation to the Mississippi senator) to be in command in the absence of an engineer officer. Foster, who assiduously kept the Corps of

The Beginning and the End. 17

Engineers informed, both of his activities and of the local situation, wrote at length to DeRussy again on December 4, saying he had changed his mind about the "state of feeling" of the workmen:

> I do not now judge it proper to give them any military instruction, or to place arms in their hands; at least that is the case with reference to Fort Sumter. I do not think that any of them will go so far in the defense of public property as to fight an armed body of the citizens of this State. I ascertained this for the first time to-day, of the men in Fort Sumter, where I had been confident that I could rely in any emergency, at least upon the Baltimore mechanics, about fifty in number. . . . The men in Castle Pinckney . . . being picked men, may prove to be more reliable. But the feeling here in regard to secession is become so strong that almost all are entirely influenced by it. I therefore judge it best to suspend all idea of arming them at present.

Foster went on to say that he had exercised great prudence and taken every precaution, so that if any overt act should occur, "no blame can properly attach to me." He continued with an accurate, pragmatic assessment of the situation:

> I regret, however, that sufficient soldiers are not in this harbor to garrison these two works. The Government will soon have to decide the question whether to maintain them or to give them up to South Carolina. If it is decided to maintain them, troops must instantly be sent, and in large numbers. . . . The plan of the leaders in this State appears to be, from all that I can see and hear, first, to demand the forts of the General Government, after secession, and then, if refused, to take them by force of arms.

On December 17, Foster, without consulting Anderson as troop commander, drew forty muskets from the arsenal on the basis of the October 31 requisition for exactly that number. He did this because the ordnance sergeants at the forts had requested that they be issued weapons. The next day he wrote to DeRussy about the matter. He said that Captain Humphreys had written to him to say that a South Carolina militia general named Schnierle had come to the arsenal and told him that Colonel Huger had assured the governor that no arms would be removed from the arsenal. Humphreys said, "The shipment of the forty muskets, &c., has caused intense excitement," and that, according to the general, "some violent demonstration is certain unless the excitement can be allayed." Humphreys wanted Foster to bring the muskets back because he had "pledged my word that they shall be returned by tomorrow night." Foster told DeRussy that he had not been informed by Huger of such a commitment, nor did he have any official knowledge of it. What he did know was that he had a proper order for precisely forty muskets, and that he needed them to protect government property. He wrote:

> To give them up on a demand of this kind seems to me as an act not expected of me by the Government, and as almost suicidal under the circumstances. It would place the two forts under my charge at the mercy of a mob.... I must say plainly that I have for some days arrived at the conclusion that unless some arrangement is shortly made by the Congress, affairs in this State will arrive at a crisis and a conflict between the Federal forces and the troops of this State [will] be a not improbable event.

Foster replied to Humphreys that he knew nothing of a commitment by Huger, but that

> an order was given to issue forty muskets to me, that I actually required them to protect the property of the Government against a mob, and that I have them in my

possession. To give them back now, without proper authority, would subject me to blame if any loss should occur which might be prevented by keeping them. I am willing to refer the matter to Washington. I am very sorry to be obliged to disappoint you.

On December 19, Foster sent a telegram to the Ordnance Department stating, "I received from the arsenal on the 17th the forty old muskets ordered to be issued to me on November 1. There is some little talk about it, and I am asked to return them. Shall I return them or keep them?" The day after Foster withdrew the muskets, Anderson reported to Cooper the details of the work being done at Fort Moultrie, and added his answer to Foster's question. "We are busily at work erecting traverses, defilading our work, increasing the height of our walls, and securing protection for our men and guns by means of barrels filled with sand." Then he said that, because the matter was likely to be reported in letters and newspapers, he thought he ought to explain that Foster "had obtained yesterday from the Charleston Arsenal forty muskets for Fort Sumter and Castle Pinckney." Foster had received a letter from Humphreys saying that the removal of the muskets had produced great excitement. "I told Captain Foster," Anderson wrote, "that my instructions were that I was not to do anything calculated to produce excitement, and that . . . I would certainly advise him to return them. He left me stating that he would do so"

On the same day, Foster, an officer who understood his responsibilities, again reported to DeRussy, saying that he "was actuated in all that I did by a sincere desire to remove all causes of irritation, so that if the extremists are disposed on violent measures they must force the issue themselves." He told him -- so that the colonel could disapprove if he so wished -- that he planned to connect a powerful battery "with the magazine at Fort Sumter, by means of wires stretched across under water from Fort Sumter to Fort Moultrie, and to blow up Fort Sumter if it is taken by an armed force. . . . I regard a complete state of preparations as the surest safeguard against attack."

Foster now learned the result of the referral of the matter to Washington. At 2:00 A.M. on December 20, he received a telegram from Floyd, saying that "If you have removed any arms, return them instantly." Foster telegraphed back, "I received forty muskets from the arsenal on the 17th. I will return them in obedience to your order." He then reported to Debussy, "the order of the Secretary of War of last night I must consider as decisive upon the question of any efforts on my part to defend Fort Sumter and Castle Pinckney. The defense now can only extent to keeping the gates closed and shutters fastened, and must cease when these are forced." The forty muskets were returned.

Foster then received another letter from Humphreys, saying that there was a rumor that twenty men had been transferred to Fort Sumter. The governor was asking for a denial. The rumor was untrue, but Foster said he could not accede to the request that he write to the governor of South Carolina to deny it. "As the governor of a State that has by an ordinance today decided to secede from the Union, I cannot, I conceive, properly communicate with him in matters of this kind, except through the Government in Washington."

The Palmetto Republic

Foster's statement was his recognition that South Carolina had just seceded, the culmination of a series of events in that state that had begun on the day following the election. On November 7, the foreman of the Grand Jury of the U. S. District Court in Charleston announced that "In these extraordinary circumstances, the Grand Jury respectfully decline to proceed with their presentments." The Honorable Andrew G. Magrath, judge of the court, then resigned, followed by the district attorney and the collector of the port. The mechanism for enforcing Federal law in South Carolina ceased to exist. The state's junior senator, James Chesnut, resigned on November 10; the senior senator, James H. Hammond, followed suit on the next day. South Carolina was no longer represented in the U. S. Senate.

A month earlier, on October 5, anticipating the outcome of the presidential election, Governor William H. Gist had sent a confidential circular letter to the governors of the other cotton states, seeking their commitment to join his state in secession. He said that South Carolina would call a convention if Lincoln were elected, and "If no other state takes the lead, South Carolina will secede (in my opinion) alone, if she has any assurance that she will be soon followed by another or other States; otherwise it is doubtful." He asked for their views and advised that the states act together. Only Florida responded encouragingly, but leaders throughout the South considered the matter of whether, and by what means, they might secede, and Gist gradually received reliable assurances.

In order to choose presidential electors (South Carolina was the only state in which they were not popularly elected), Gist had called a special session of the legislature for November 5. The legislature remained in session after the election, and on November 9 voted to call a convention to meet on January 15, 1861,

> for the purpose of taking into consideration the dangers incident to the position of the State in the Federal Union . . . and the measures which may be necessary and proper for providing against the same, and thereupon to take care that

the Commonwealth of South Carolina shall suffer no detriment.

Delegates to the Convention were to be chosen on December 6 by the less than ten percent of the population included in "All persons qualified and entitled . . . to vote for members of the legislature." The act provided that from among those qualified to vote, "All free white male citizens of the State of the age of twenty-one and upward" were eligible for election to a seat. The legislature then reconsidered the date on which the convention was to meet and advanced it by a month, to December 17. On that day the delegates gathered in the First Baptist Church in the state capital, Columbia. On the fourth ballot they elected David F. Jamison as permanent president.

The members were overwhelmingly in favor of leaving the Union, as was most of the white populace. But before taking any action, they considered adjourning because of an outbreak of smallpox. Some of the steadier members pointed out that this would indicate irresolution in the face of danger, so they went by train to Charleston, where they reconvened on December 18 in Institute Hall. A committee was appointed to prepare an ordinance of secession, while others members were assigned to the Committee on Relations with the Slaveholding States of North America. On December 20, the convention delegates moved to the larger St. Andrew's Hall where, at 12:45 P. M., they voted to secede by 169 to 0:

> We, the people of the State of South Carolina, in convention assembled, do declare and ordain . . . that the Ordinance adopted by us in convention on the 23rd day of May, in the year of our Lord 1778, whereby the Constitution of the United States was ratified, [is] hereby repealed, and the union now subsisting between South Carolina and other

states under the name of the United States of America is hereby dissolved.

Church bells pealed, all business was suspended, and people were wildly jubilant. South Carolina was now the Palmetto Republic, "separate and independent." The convention proceeded to establish a cabinet and the other offices of a national government, and declared that the governor (as he was still called) had the power to make war. They considered the Federal forts and other property within the state to be in violation of their sovereign territory.

The more thoughtful among them realized that the act of secession was likely to lead to war because president-elect Lincoln, while willing to leave slavery alone where it existed, was unequivocally committed to preserving the Union. The Palmetto Republic's 291,388 white inhabitants (there were also 402,406 slaves and 9,914 free blacks) did not deceive themselves into thinking that they alone could prevail against the United States. They believed that if there were to be a war over secession, it would not be between the United States and the Palmetto Republic, but between the United States and the Southern Nation. In the secession convention it was moved that all fifteen slave states be invited to a convention, in Montgomery, Alabama, to establish a Southern confederacy. Their call for this convention declared:

> South Carolina desires no destiny separate from yours. To be one of a great slave-holding Confederacy, stretching its arms over territory larger than any power in Europe possesses . . . United, we must be a great, free and prosperous people. . . . We ask you to join in forming a Confederacy of slave-holding States.

On December 24, the newly elected Governor, Francis W. Pickens, owner of a large number of slaves, issued a *Declaration of the Immediate Causes which Induce and Justify the Secession of South Carolina from the Federal Union.* Like so many documents that were to be written in the months and years ahead, it explained the reasons for separation at great length, and concluded:

> The Government of the United States is no longer a Government of Confederate Republics, but of a consolidated Democracy. It is no longer a free Government, but a despotism . . . the People of South Carolina, by our delegates in Convention assembled, appealing to the Supreme Judge of the world for the rectitude of our intentions, have solemnly declared that the Union heretofore existing between this State and the other States of North America, is dissolved, and that the State of South Carolina has resumed her position among the nations of the world as a separate and independent State, with full power to levy war, conclude peace, contract alliances, establish commerce, and do all other acts and things which independent States may of right do.

The state's four Congressmen resigned on Christmas day.

Anderson Moves to Fort Sumter

When Major Buell returned to Washington after his mission to Fort Sumter, he gave Floyd a copy of his memorandum to Anderson. The secretary endorsed it on December 21, and showed it to the president. Both men saw that the order authorized Anderson to move to Fort Sumter under certain conditions, but neither thought those conditions would arise. Buchanan was, however, bothered by the phrase "to the last extremity." Told to soften it, Floyd wrote a letter to Anderson and sent it by a messenger who arrived at Fort Moultrie on December 23. It said:

In the verbal instructions communicated to you by Major Buell, you are directed to hold possession of the forts in the harbor of Charleston, and, if attacked, to defend yourself to the last extremity. Under these instructions, you might infer that you are required to make a vain and useless sacrifice of your own life and the lives of the men under your command, upon a mere point of honor. This is far from the President's intention. You are to exercise a sound military judgment on this subject. . . . If [the forts] are invested or attacked by a force so superior that resistance would, in your judgment, be a useless waste of life, it will be your duty to yield to necessity, and make the best terms in your power.

On December 20, DeRussy wrote to Floyd in response to questions that had been raised by the House Committee on Military Affairs. He ended by saying:

Of all the fortifications in the harbor of Charleston, Fort Sumter must be looked upon as by far the most important, and it is now in condition, as regards its state of preparation, to resist any attack that will be made upon it, provided it is furnished with a proper garrison.

After dark on the day that South Carolina declared itself to be independent, the watchman at Fort Sumter saw a steamer, showing no lights, approach and take soundings. It remained near the fort most of the night. Several hours later a steamer reconnoitered around Castle Pinckney. When hailed by the watchman as to what they wanted, a voice from the vessel replied "You will know in a week." The following night two steamers ominously kept watch around Fort Sumter. The South Carolinians recognized, of course, that it would make good sense militarily for the Federal troops to move to Fort Sumter and, therefore, meant to prevent it, if attempted. Governor Pickens ordered the militia to keep watch on the waters around the forts and assigned two guard boats, the *Nina* and the *General Clinch*, to that duty. He also sent watchers to Fort Monroe, Virginia and the Norfolk Navy Yard to alert him of any movement of reinforcements from those places.

Anderson, who had all along regarded Fort Sumter as the most defensible place available, was convinced that the nightly approaches by the boats were tangible evidence of hostile intent. Acting on his own initiative, but consistent with the orders given to him by Buell and by Floyd's subsequent message, he decided to move his men and their dependent women and children to Fort Sumter. Forty-eight of its guns were mounted and there were 40,000 pounds of powder in its magazines. It was the only one of the four forts that could possibly be held. From it, if possessed by the South Carolinians, the Federal force could easily be driven from Fort Moultrie.

Anderson intended to move on Christmas but was prevented by heavy rains, so the transfer was made on the evening of December 26. He told no one of his plan until it became necessary to involve several officers. In the afternoon he arranged for three small schooners to transfer the wives and children, and enough provisions for several months, to Fort Johnson, explaining that he was preparing to defend against an attack on Fort Moultrie. The officer in charge of the boats was to head for Fort Johnson, but not to land until he heard two signal guns, and then to come to Fort Sumter. At dusk, half the men boarded rowboats and headed for Fort Sumter. Captain Abner Doubleday, commander of Company E and the senior officer under Anderson, described the movement of his men in his post-war book *Reminiscenses*.

> Every thing being in readiness, we passed out of the main gates, and silently made our way for about a quarter of a mile to a spot where the boats were hidden behind an irregular pile of rocks, which originally formed part of the sea wall.

There was not a single human being in sight as we marched to the rendezvous, and we had the extraordinary good luck to be wholly unobserved. We found several boats awaiting us, under charge of two engineer officers, Lieutenants Snyder and Meade. They and their crews were crouched down behind the rocks, to escape observation. In a low tone they pointed out to me the boats intended for my company, and then pushed out rapidly to return to the fort. Noticing that one of the guard-boats was approaching; they made a wide circuit to avoid it. I hoped there would be time for my party to cross before the steamer could overhaul us; but as among my men there were a number of unskillful oarsmen, we made but slow progress, and it soon became evident that we would be overtaken in mid-channel. It was after sunset, and the twilight had deepened, so that there was a fair chance for us to escape. While the steamer was yet afar off, I took off my cap, and threw open my coat to conceal the buttons. I also made the men take off their coats, and use them to cover up their muskets, which were lying alongside the rowlocks. I hoped in this way that we might pass for a party of laborers returning to the fort. The paddle wheels stopped within about a hundred yards of us; but to our great relief, after a slight scrutiny, the steamer kept on its way. In the meantime our men redoubled their efforts, and we soon arrived at our destination.

It was good luck for all concerned, because two of Fort Moultrie's guns were trained on the guard boat, ready to fire on it if it interfered with the troops. With the full moon up, the boats brought over the rest of the men, the signal guns were fired, and the families and supplies on the schooners sailed to Fort Sumter. On landing, the troops were greeted by cheers from the fifty-five civilian workmen who favored the Union, but fixed their bayonets to control the sixty secession sympathizers, some of whom had pistols and who chose to leave in the schooners. Additional trips were made the next morning to bring over ammunition and more food, but some supplies and personal belongings had to be left behind.

Late on the night of the December 26, from Fort Sumter, Anderson wrote to Cooper that "I have just completed, by the blessing of God, the removal to this fort of all my garrison, except the surgeon and [eleven] men. . . . I left orders to have all the guns at Fort Moultrie spiked, and the carriages of the 32-pounders destroyed. . . . The step which I have taken was, in my opinion, necessary to prevent the effusion of blood." The next morning at 11:45, with the band playing and the garrison on parade, Anderson raised his colors over the fort.

On its morning rounds, the guard boat saw Federal soldiers on the ramparts of the fort and steamed into the city with the news. Anderson's action was regarded as a breach of what the secessionists believed to be a commitment by Buchanan not to alter the status quo. Pickens sent an aide to demand that Anderson return his troops to Fort Moultrie. Anderson replied, "I cannot and will not go back." Foster went into Charleston "to negotiate a draft on New York to pay off the workmen employed on Fort Moultrie. I saw that an attack was to be made somewhere to-night, and also that it would not be safe for me to go to town again for some time."

THE FIRST OVERT ACT

Floyd, incredulous and outraged when he heard of the move early the next day, telegraphed to Anderson:

Intelligence has reached here this morning that you have abandoned Fort Moultrie, spiked your guns, burned the carriages, and gone to Fort Sumter. It is not believed, because there is no order for any such movement. Explain the meaning of this report.

Anderson promptly replied:

The telegram is correct. I abandoned Fort Moultrie because I was certain that if attacked my men must have been sacrificed, and the command of the harbor lost. I spiked the guns and destroyed the carriages to keep the guns from being used against us. If attacked, the garrison would never have surrendered without a fight.

In a more detailed letter to Cooper, Anderson explained, "many things convinced me that the authorities of the State designed to proceed to a hostile act." He described the visit by the governor's aide, Colonel Johnston Pettigrew, who had told him "that there was an understanding between [Pickens's predecessor, Gist] and the President that no reenforcements were to be sent to any of these forts, and particularly to this one, and that I had violated this agreement." Anderson had told the aide that he had not been reenforced and that "as the commander of this harbor, I had a right to move my men into any fort I deemed proper." If the president had made an agreement, Anderson had not been informed of it. Anderson and his men remained in the fort until it was attacked and surrendered fifteen weeks later.

Pickens was immediately and severely criticized by an alarmed and indignant population for not having occupied Fort Sumter when he had the chance. His counselors now pressured him to wait no longer. Even though the legislature had not authorized military action, he issued orders for the immediate seizure of the three forts. But before they could be carried out, the first Federal property to come into the hands of South Carolina was not the result of action by the state. The U. S. revenue cutter *William Aiken* -- a vessel of what we now call the Coast Guard -- was stationed in Charleston. It's commander, Captain N. L. Coste, had told the executive officer, Lieutenant John Underwood, that he was determined not to serve under Lincoln and that he planned to resign when South Carolina seceded, leaving Underwood in charge. In the event, however, on the afternoon of December 27, without resigning and thus in violation of his oath of office, he turned the vessel over to the secessionists. The crew left the ship and went north.

To seize Castle Pinckney, Pickens sent Colonel Pettigrew with 150 militiamen -- three companies of the Washington Light Infantry and the Meagher Guards. The fort was on an island called Shutes Folly, just at the mouths of the Ashley and Cooper Rivers. Pettigrew's party, on the *Nina*, could be seen approaching the long wharf that stretched into the harbor from the southwest side of island. Lieutenant Richard K. Meade of the Corps of Engineers, who had arrived on December 10, was in charge of the thirty laborers and four mechanics who were working at the fort. Meade, West Point 1857, although a Virginian who was in sympathy with the South and who resigned a few months afterward to join the Confederacy, was indignant at the attempted intrusion and had the gate barred. The militia charged down the dock, trying unsuccessfully to reach the gate before it was closed. The workmen, whom Foster had hoped would be of help in an emergency such as this, stayed out of the way. The militiamen used ladders to scale the walls and entered the fort without a shot being fired. Pettigrew told Meade that he was seizing Castle Pinckney in the name of Governor Pickens.

The only other U. S. soldier there was Ordnance Sergeant Skillen. His fifteen-year-old daughter Kate is said to have wept as the secessionists lowered the U. S. flag and raised one with a white star on a field of red -- borrowed from the *Nina*, since no one had thought to bring along the official Palmetto flag. Told by an officer that she need not be afraid, she replied: "I am not afraid. I am crying because you put that miserable rag up there." A problem immediately arose: were the two Federal soldiers captured in the fort to be considered prisoners of war? If so, it would imply that there was in fact a war. Following a lengthy discussion, Meade and the mechanics were allowed to go to Fort Sumter after Pettigrew promised that the sergeant and his family would be treated properly. The place was of little importance -- besides the twenty guns, it consisted of a two-story barracks, a warehouse for Corps of Engineers equipment, and a lighthouse. What was significant was that the secessionists now held, for the first time, a U. S. fort. Doubleday called it "the first overt act of the Secessionists against the Sovereignty of the United States."

Colonel Charles Allston and Lieutenant Colonel Wilmot G. DeSaussure were dispatched to Fort Moultrie, to put the guns there into condition for use in defense of the harbor. Their force of 225 militiamen from the German, Lafayette, Marion and Washington artillery companies arrived at Sullivan's Island on the *Nina* and the *General Clinch* in the dark at 7:30 P.M. on December 27. The men were reluctant to enter the empty fort, fearing that it might have been mined (it was not). Eventually one of the colonels and several men went in and planted the Palmetto flag in the ground -- the flag staff having been cut down. The Federal troops had burned the gun carriages when they evacuated, but DeSaussure and Allston had their men at work the next day building replacements and getting the fifty-six captured guns ready to be fired: nineteen 32-pounders, sixteen 24-pounders, two 12-pounders, four 6-pounders, ten eight-inch Columbiads, four 24-pounder howitzers, and a ten-inch seacoast mortar. Doubleday later explained:

Out of the mouth of each gun hung a white string. As many of the guns had been kept loaded for a considerable length of time, these strings had been tied by me to the cartridges, in order that the latter might be pulled out and sunned occasionally, as a precaution against dampness. The Carolinians imagined that these strings were arranged with a view to blow up the guns the moment anyone attempted to interfere with them, and each soldier, as he passed, avoided the supposed danger.

The second Federal property, Fort Moultrie, was now in the possession of South Carolina. It was to play an important role in the April bombardment of Fort Sumter.

The next day, April 28, a detachment under Captain Joseph Johnson, Jr. reached James Island and occupied Fort Johnson. This deserted strong point consisted of a two-story building to house post headquarters and officer's quarters, a barracks for enlisted men, half a dozen smaller structures, and a number of gun emplacements. All were in poor condition. There was, however, a large and useful supply of fuel. The third and last of the Federal forts had been taken.

To prepare for a Federal counter-attack, Pickens told his chief engineer to choose a location on Morris Island for a battery of two 24-pounder guns (to which a third was soon added) to cover the Main Ship Channel. He then sent Major P. F. Stevens, commandant of the Citadel Academy, with forty of his cadets to man the battery. Ninety men of the Vigilant Rifles were sent to protect and assist the artillerymen. Two companies of the First Infantry Regiment, the German Rifles and the Zouave Cadets, were sent to Cummings Point. Colonel Allston, whose role in the Fort Moultrie operation was completed, took the 32nd Infantry

Regiment farther south to establish batteries to protect the entrances to the bays and rivers.

Meanwhile, Pickens ordered Colonel John Cunningham of the 17th Infantry Regiment to "take entire possession" of the U. S. arsenal, on the bank of the Ashley River. In doing so Cunningham was to "state distinctly that you do this with a view to prevent any destruction of public property that may occur in the present excited state of the public mind, and also as due to the public safety." Once in possession he was to inventory the stores and the condition of the arms. Pickens expected that there would be no difficulty, but if there was, the colonel was to use "no more force that may be absolutely necessary, and with the greatest discretion and liberality to Captain Humphreys, who is at perfect liberty to remain in his present quarters."

Humphreys, whose command consisted of fourteen enlisted men, notified the Ordnance Bureau by telegraph on December 28 that "A body of South Carolina military now surround the arsenal, outside, however, of the inclosure, but denying ingress or egress without countersign. The officer in command denies any intention of occupancy, and the United States flag is undisturbed. I await instructions." In a message the next day, he said that the post was "to all intents and purposes in the possession of the South Carolina troops." He was going to make a formal protest and ask that the troops be removed. If this was not done, he would consider the arsenal to be in the hands of the secessionists and would "haul down my flag and surrender."

The militiamen he referred to were those who had been assigned to the arsenal six weeks earlier, ostensibly to guard against a slave insurrection, but actually to prevent the transfer of munitions to the Federal forts. When Cunningham arrived on December 30 with a detachment of the Union Light Infantry, he presented a message dated 10:30 A.M.: "I herewith demand an immediate surrender of the U. S. Arsenal at this place and under your charge, and a delivery to me of the keys and contents of the arsenals, magazines, &c. I am already proceeding to occupy it with a strong-armed detachment of troops. I make the demand in the name of the State of South Carolina." Humphreys replied:

> I am constrained to comply with your demand for the surrender of this arsenal, from the fact that I have no force for its defense. I do so, however, solemnly protesting against the illegality of this measure in the name of my Government. I also demand, as a right, that I be allowed to salute my flag, before lowering it, with one gun for each State now in the Union (32), and that my command be allowed to occupy the quarters assigned them until instructions can be obtained from the War Department.

Humphreys asked the Ordnance Bureau what disposition he was to make of his men. While waiting for an answer, he spent several days getting vouchers for the arms, ammunition and other property for which he was responsible. (The value of the property was later estimated to be $400,000). As soon as the secessionists signed for it, they issued it to their troops. Losses consisted of two field guns, seven howitzers, 1,115 pistols and 21,308 muskets. "Myself and men and our families are very unpleasantly situated," Humphreys reported, "and we are in actual danger from accident when so many inexperienced persons are [handling] loaded arms. Our movements are watched and restricted, and I would earnestly request that we be moved elsewhere." The War Department sent the men to the nearest arsenal, at Augusta, Georgia.

By the end of the day on December 30, ten days after the state had seceded from the United States, Pickens had control of three forts, the arsenal, the branch Treasury, the customs house, the post office, and the Corps of Engineers office, where there were maps and drawings of the harbor forts. The South Carolina authorities possessed all the properties of the U. S. Government property within the state except one: Fort Sumter.

THE SOUTH CAROLINA COMMISSIONERS

While these events were taking place, Buchanan and his divided cabinet struggled to find a coherent policy. At the beginning of December the cabinet consisted of three Northerners, two men from border slave states, and two from cotton states. Three were Unionists, three secessionists, and one a non-entity. Secretary of the Treasury Howell Cobb of Georgia, Secretary of War John B. Floyd of Virginia, and Secretary of the Interior Jacob Thompson of Mississippi believed in the right of a state to secede. A different view was held by Secretary of State Lewis Cass of Michigan, Attorney-General Jeremiah Black of Pennsylvania, and Postmaster-General Joseph Holt of Kentucky. Secretary of the Navy Isaac Toucey of Connecticut was a man without opinions.

The cabinet soon began to change. On the day Buchanan sent his message to Congress, Cobb resigned, effective December 8, followed by Thompson, in both cases because they disagreed with the president's position that secession was illegal. Cass submitted his resignation on December 12. Floyd, who had been involved in a scheme related to army supply contracts, in which $870,000 in bonds was stolen, was asked by Buchanan for his resignation. In tendering it, Floyd gave as his reason that the president had refused to order Anderson to withdraw from Fort Sumter.

On December 31, Buchanan named Holt to replace Floyd, and Horatio King of Maine became postmaster-general in place of Holt. Black took Cass's place as secretary of state and Edwin M. Stanton of Ohio replaced Black as attorney general. Philip F. Thomas of Maryland briefly filled the post of secretary of the treasury, which was then taken by John A. Dix of New York. The post of secretary of the interior was left vacant. As 1861 began, the six department heads were all strong Unionists, who forced the president to follow a more energetic policy. General Scott, who had been by-passed by Floyd, was now included in the decision-making process. The assistant secretary of state, W. H. Trescot of South Carolina, was a close friend of Buchanan and continued to see and influence him after handing in his resignation, effective December 17.

The South Carolina convention appointed three commissioners: Robert W. Barnwell, James H. Adams, and James L. Orr. They arrived in Washington on December 26,

> to treat with the Government of the United States for the delivery of the forts, magazines, light-houses, and other real estate . . . within the limits of South Carolina; and also for an apportionment of the public debt, and for a division of all other property held by the Government of the United States as agent of the confederated States of which South Carolina was recently a member; and generally to negotiate . . . for the continuance of peace and amity between this commonwealth and the government at Washington.

On December 27, the news arrived by telegraph of Anderson's move. Trescot and two Southern Senators went to the White House and informed the president, who was as yet unaware of what had happened. They urged him to order Anderson to return to Fort Moultrie, but Buchanan refused to commit himself.

At 2:30 P.M. on December 28, the three commissioners and Trescot called on Buchanan. The president explained that he was receiving them as "private gentlemen," rather than as representatives of a government, but that he was willing to communicate to Congress any proposition they might have to make. They presented a copy of the ordinance of secession by which South Carolina "declared her perfect sovereignty and independence." Following this, they said,

> It would also have been our duty to have informed you that we were ready to negotiate with you . . . to inaugurate our new relations as to secure mutual respect, general advantage, and a future of good will and harmony . . . But the events of the last twenty-four hours render such an assurance impossible.

Until the president could explain those events in a manner satisfactory to the commissioners, they were forced to "suspend all discussion." That is, they were terminating the negotiations which had not been started, and in which Buchanan was unwilling to participate. They then urged the president not to order Anderson to return, but instead to immediately withdraw from Charleston harbor all the U. S. troops, since they were "a standing menace" which "threatens speedily to bring to a bloody issue questions which ought to be settled with temperance and judgment."

A week after they seceded, the South Carolinians were threatening war. This was too much even for the pacific and indecisive Buchanan. Had Governor Pickens not seized the other forts, it is possible he might have ordered the garrison to return, but now there was no place for Anderson and his men to go. Buchanan prepared a draft reply to the commissioners, which was considered by the cabinet on December 29. All but Toucey thought it conceded too much, so Attorney-General Black, assisted by Holt and Stanton, wrote a memo detailing what they thought it would be appropriate for the president to say. They also recommended that two warships be promptly sent to Charleston. Buchanan incorporated some, but by no means all, of the cabinet members' suggestions in his lengthy reply to the commissioners on December 31.

He began by citing parts of his December 3 state-of-the-union message, reiterating his lack of authority and submitting the whole question to Congress, which "alone possess the power, as to prevent the inauguration of a civil war . . ." Land had been purchased from the state, he reminded them, for the building of forts over which the Federal government had exclusive jurisdiction. As to their contention that he had made a pledge regarding the forts, he pointed out that he had met on December 8, before secession, with four members of the South Carolina Congressional delegation and discussed the situation. A memorandum had been made of what they said, which was that South Carolina would not attack the forts "provided that no reinforcements shall be sent into those forts, and their relative military status shall remain as at present." He had not, he said, sent any reinforcements, nor had he authorized any change in "relative military status."

Buchanan enclosed a copy of Buell's memorandum of December 11 and said that Anderson had "acted upon his own responsibility and without authority" unless he had evidence of hostile intent. He said that he had at first thought of commanding Anderson to return, but South Carolina had immediately seized two Federal forts, as well as the customs house and post office. With regard to withdrawing the troops before negotiations could begin, the president stated unequivocally: "This I cannot do; this I will not do. Such an idea was never thought of by me in any contingency." He concluded with the following observation, "while it is my duty to defend Fort Sumter . . . against hostile attacks, from whatever quarter they may come, I do not perceive how such a defence can be construed into a menace against the city of Charleston."

On January 1, the commissioners replied with a combination legal brief and political diatribe that was even longer than the president's. After reiterating previous arguments, they declared: "Major Anderson waged war. No other words will describe his action," and that he had done so "without the slightest provocation." As to the alleged agreement, they insinuated that the president was not telling the truth. "By your course you have probably rendered civil war inevitable," they said. The letter was read in the cabinet meeting on January 2 and was then endorsed "This paper, just presented to the President, is of such a character that he declines to receive it." The mission of the three commissioners was ended. The encounter was nothing more than the exchange of legalistic arguments having no realistic bearing on the matter in dispute. Buchanan, influenced by his now mainly Unionist cabinet, began to take a firmer stand. Anderson's move was widely applauded in the North, and the House of Representatives passed a resolution of approval by a vote of 124 to 53. Sentiment for strong action in the face of South Carolina's seizure of the forts was growing.

On December 30, General Scott, starting to take an active policy role even before he knew that Floyd was gone, wrote directly to the president. He asked whether, "without reference to the War Department and otherwise, as secretly as possible, [he might] send two hundred and fifty recruits from New York Harbor to re-enforce Fort Sumter. . . . It is hoped that a sloop of war and cutter may be ordered for the same purpose as early as tomorrow." Buchanan agreed, but because of his personal sympathy with the Southerners he wished, incredibly, to delay action for several days as a courtesy to the commissioners. Nevertheless, the Federal government was finally about to take action: men and supplies would soon be on their way.

The *Star of the West*

At the cabinet meeting on January 2, after South Carolina had seized the three forts and the arsenal, and after the reply of the commissioners had been rejected, Buchanan decided to support Fort Sumter. Scott had already sent, on December 31, an order to the commander of Fort Monroe at Old Point Comfort, Virginia:

> Prepare and put on board the sloop-of-war Brooklyn, as soon as the latter can receive them, four companies, making at least two hundred men, destined to re-enforce Fort Sumter. Embark with said companies twenty-five spare stands of arms, complete, and subsistence for the entire detachment for ninety days. . . . Manage everything as secretly and confidentially as possible. Look to this.

The *U. S. S. Brooklyn*, commanded by Captain David G. Farragut, was a twenty-five-gun steamer that was more than capable of dealing with the still-weak secessionist batteries. But before it was ready to sail, Scott had second thoughts. The warship's draft might be too deep for it to cross the bar, and he had qualms about reducing the garrison at Fort Monroe, the most important of the U. S. forts. Instead, he proposed to send a commercial vessel carrying 200 recruits from the Governor's Island depot at New York -- recruits who could just as easily have replaced the men ordered from Fort Monroe. The commercial sidewheeler *Star of the West*, commanded by Captain John McGowan, was chartered for $1,250 a day. Its draft was less than the *Brooklyn's*, and it might be less likely to provoke a reaction from the secessionists. But it would be unable to attack the batteries or to defend itself. Buchanan reluctantly, and mistakenly, accepted the change. An unarmed merchant ship with raw recruits, rather than a warship with experienced troops, was sent to relieve Fort Sumter.

On January 5, a junior officer was assigned to deal with the delicate situation. Lieutenant Charles R. Woods of the Ninth U. S. Infantry received orders to proceed, with three officers and the recruits, to Charleston. In a vain attempt to maintain secrecy, the ship was cleared for New Orleans. It left the wharf at 5:00 P.M. that day, and the troops were put on board after dark from tugboats in the river. If Scott thought the *Star of the West* would be able to sail with greater secrecy than the *Brooklyn*, he badly deluded himself. The newspapers in New York, Washington and Charleston published accounts of the mission, and Governor Pickens was further alerted by messages from sympathizers in Washington.

Only Anderson, the commander of the fort, was unaware of what was happening. A message to him from the assistant adjutant-general, Lieutenant Colonel Louis Thomas, sent by mail on January 5, failed to arrive in time. Had he received it, Anderson would have known that a relief ship was coming with 200 men and that "should a fire [of guns be opened], likely to prove injurious upon any vessel bringing re-enforcements or supplies, or upon tow-boats within the range of your guns, they may be employed to silence such fire." Thomas, perhaps explaining why he had resorted to the mail in this critical situation, told Anderson to "be upon your guard against all telegrams, as false ones may be attempted."

Meanwhile, in his Report No. 15 to Cooper on December 31, five days after the move to Fort Sumter, Anderson, apparently in an optimistic and confident mood, conveyed more than he probably intended:

> . . . the South Carolinians show great activity in the harbor today. . . . this afternoon about 80 soldiers, with wheelbarrows, barrels, &c., and some draught horses, were landed on Morris Island. . . . The more I reflect upon the matter the

> stronger are my convictions that I was right in coming here. . . . .Thank God, we are now where the Government can send us additional troops at its leisure. To be sure, the uncivil and uncourteous action of the governor in preventing us from purchasing anything in the city will annoy and inconvenience us somewhat; still, we are safe. . . . we can command this harbor as long as our Government wishes to keep it.

It was certainly a mistake on Anderson's part to tell the Buchanan administration that he could be reinforced "at leisure," and the significance of the news about being unable to purchase supplies locally was overlooked in Washington. As a result of the receipt of this message on January 5, a last-minute attempt was made to recall the *Star of the West*, but it had already sailed. The *Brooklyn*, hurriedly dispatched from Norfolk, failed to arrive in time to be of help. But the ship could not have provided support in any case, since the captain was ordered not to cross the bar.

The *Star of the West* sailed south in fine weather and arrived off Charleston at 1:30 A.M. on January 9. Arms and ammunition were issued to the men, who were then sent below decks. The regular navigation lights around Charleston had been extinguished, but a light was visible at Fort Sumter. When a sentinel ship lying near the channel saw the *Star of the West*, it steamed away, firing rockets as it went. In his report, Lieutenant Woods described what happened:

> As soon as we had light enough we crossed the bar, and steamed up the main ship channel. This was on the first of the ebb tide, . . .We proceeded without interruption until we arrived within one and three-quarter miles of Forts Sumter and Moultrie – they being apparently equidistant – when we were opened on by a masked battery near the north end of Morris Island. This battery was about five-eights of a mile

distant from us, and we were keeping as near in to it as we could, to avoid the fire of Fort Moultrie.... We went into the harbor with the American ensign hoisted on the flag staff, and as soon as the first shot was fired a full-sized garrison flag was displayed at the fore, but the one was no more respected than the other. We kept on, still under the fire of the battery, most of the balls passing over us, one just missing the machinery, another striking but a few feet from the rudder, while a ricochet shot struck us in the fore chains, about two feet above the water line, and just below where the man was throwing the lead. The American flag was flying at Fort Sumter, but we saw no flag at Fort Moultrie, and there were no guns fired from either of these fortifications.

The shots that hit the ship came from the Morris Island battery manned by Citadel cadets, who fired seventeen rounds from their three guns. Anderson, observing all this but taken by surprise, pondered what to do. His orders were to act only defensively, and he was acutely aware, after the storm raised by his move to Fort Sumter, that any aggressive action he might take could bring on hostilities. He ordered the guns manned, but the Morris Island battery was beyond their range. As the *Star of the West* came closer, several shots were fired from Fort Moultrie, but fell well short of the ship. Fort Sumter's guns could easily have reached that fort, but Anderson did not bring them into action. Captain McGowan and Lieutenant Woods, in a dangerous situation, without supporting fire and with several vessels approaching from the harbor, made the critical decision not to try to land the troops and supplies. The *Star of the West* turned and steamed away, and the relief force was back in New York on January 12. The attempt to support Anderson was a fiasco. The actions of the Buchanan administration had been inept and ineffective, and the first shots of the Civil War had been fired.

Reaction to this event, including Anderson's failure to open fire on the secessionists, varied. Anderson, uninformed of what had been attempted, had been reluctant to engage in an exchange of gunnery, but the officers and men at the fort, including several of their wives, were distressed that the fort had failed to return the fire. In Charleston, it was seen as an indication that the Federals were unwilling to fight. It hardened the position of those who wanted to attack the fort at once. In the North, outrage was the consequence of this rebellious insult to the flag. Buchanan was severely criticized. Many in the government and the public believed that he should have declared that South Carolina had started a war, and that he should have taken action in reprisal.

The ignominious failure of the attempt inspired Elias Hasket Derby of Boston, a former director of the Boston and Bangor Steamboat Company, to make a suggestion. He wrote on January 16 to the secretary of the navy (with copies to the president and the general-in-chief) with an idea "derived from actual experiments upon mail-clad steamers abroad."

> My plan is to purchase at once in New York a common propeller of 400 tons burden . . . drawing when laden 8 or 10 feet of water. I would then protect her from end to end by a coat of mail composed of two sheets of boiler iron of five-eighths of an inch thickness. . . . She would then be impervious to balls fired from 32-pounders at a distance of a quarter of a mile, and passing, as she might, the batteries of Fort Moultrie and Morris Island at a distance of more than half a mile, could pass them in perfect safety. . . . the steamer laden with 200 troops and stores for six months could deliver her cargo under the walls of Fort Sumter uninjured.

Derby provided considerable detail ("that the bolts be placed . . . 6 inches apart, have a washer of 4 inches square around them . . .") and thought the total cost, including "ten or twelve cannon," would be $60,000. In support of his scheme, he noted "one of the balls fired at the *Star of the West* actually recoiled from the plank on the ship's side." None of the three persons he addressed chose to follow up on his concept. Other schemes, however, would soon be proposed.

A Truce Pending Surrender

As the *Star of the West* sailed away, Anderson called a council of his officers. They were divided as to whether or not to close the port by firing warning shots at commercial vessels. After heated discussion they chose to send an officer into the city with a letter demanding to know if the ship had been fired upon with the governor's sanction. It said:

> Two of your batteries fired this morning upon an unarmed vessel bearing the flag of my Government. As I have not been notified that war has been declared by South Carolina against the Government of the United States, I cannot but think that this hostile act was committed without your sanction or authority. . . . I . . . notify you, if [this act] be not disclaimed, that I must regard it as an act of war, and that I shall not, after a reasonable time for the return of my messenger, permit any vessel to pass within range of the guns of my fort.

After consulting with his council, Pickens handed the officer his reply. It was a lengthy document, much like a political speech in character. It told Anderson that he had "not been fully informed . . . of the precise relations which now exist between [the U. S. government] and the State of South Carolina." It said that Buchanan had understood that sending any reinforcements would be regarded as an act of hostility. South Carolina's position was that "To repel such an attempt is too plainly its duty to allow it to be discussed." Moreover, Anderson's occupancy of Fort Sumter had been the first act of hostility. Anderson must be the judge with regard to closing the harbor, but "it is not perceived how far the conduct which you propose to adopt can find a parallel in the history of any country, or be reconciled with any other purpose of your Government than that of imposing upon this State the condition of a conquered province."

The governor realized that South Carolina was not yet prepared for war, and that the commerce of Charleston could in fact be shut off by Fort Sumter's guns. He ordered four officers to "consider and report the most favorable plan for operating upon Fort Sumter, so as to reduce that fortress." They concluded that the fort could be taken by "incessant bombardment" and "slow starvation." So it proved to be, three months later. Meanwhile, anticipating that Buchanan might now decide to send warships to relieve the fort, Pickens had four hulks, loaded with stone and intentionally sunk to partially block the Main Ship Channel, making it difficult for ships to enter even when guided by pilots who knew the exact location of the hulks. On January 11, in hopes of convincing Anderson to give up, he sent his secretary of state, former federal judge and future governor Andrew G. Magrath, and his attorney general, Colonel Isaac W. Hayne, to call on Anderson. They handed him a letter from Pickens:

> I have thought proper, under all the circumstances of the peculiar state of public affairs . . . to appoint [two] members of the Executive Council . . . to present to you considerations of the gravest public character, and of the deepest interest to all who deprecate the improper waste of life, to induce the delivery of Fort Sumter to the constituted authorities of the

State of South Carolina, with a pledge on its part to account for such public property as is under your charge.

Anderson was not about to "deliver" the fort. But rather that strait-forwardly saying no, he replied that it was a matter for the government to decide and suggested that Pickens send a representative to Washington. The governor, undeterred by the failure of the three commissioners who had just returned, accepted the idea. In effect, an indefinite truce would now begin. This was acceptable to Pickens because it would afford South Carolina time to strengthen its batteries for the bombardment of the fort. For Anderson, it avoided, or at least delayed, a crisis that might provoke civil war. Pickens designated Hayne to go to see Buchanan with a letter from the governor saying Hayne was sent "to demand the surrender of Fort Sumter . . . to the constituted authorities of the State of South Carolina . . . because of my earnest desire to avoid bloodshed, which a persistence in your attempt to retain the possession of that fort will cause."

On January 14, Foster reported to General Joseph G. Totten, the chief engineer,

> the facilities for mail communication between the fort and the city of Charleston have been restored by order of Governor Pickens. The arrangement is for one of my boats to receive the mail at Fort Johnson, wither it is to be brought every day at 12 o'clock, and to deliver the mail from the fort at the same time.

He noted that the South Carolinians were hard at work on Fort Moultrie, and he could observe a force of about 700 men drilling on the island. Living conditions for the people in the fort were poor. "The weather since the command has occupied the fort has been very bad, and the whole force, including the camp followers, have been suffered to quarter in the officers' quarters." Food and other supplies could be purchased in Charleston, but the Southerners, to help depress the morale of the men in the fort, made it difficult for them to obtain whiskey and tobacco, a serious matter in an age when most men drank and chewed in earnest.

Meanwhile, the president and his cabinet, now composed of Unionists, were still unable to conceive of any plan of action. Their effort had failed to re-supply the soldiers, dependents and workmen isolated in a seceded state that had seized three forts and an arsenal. Other states were seceding and likewise taking possession of forts and arsenals. There were rumors that Washington was in danger of seizure by secessionist sympathizers from Maryland and Virginia. Fearing the loss of the Federal capital, and all that that might mean, Scott appointed Colonel Charles P. Stone to organize the militia and volunteers to help the few regulars to defend the city. Buchanan took the only action of which he was capable: more words. On January 8, as the *Star of the West* approached Charleston, he sent a prolix special message to Congress, repeating much of his state-of-the union message. He said that "the prospect of a bloodless settlement" was fading, and that he "had no right to make aggressive war upon any State." It was his province, he said, "to execute and not to make the laws. It belongs to Congress, exclusively, to repeal, to modify, and to enlarge their provision, to meet exigencies as they may occur." But, he added with emphasis,

> *the right and the duty to use military force defensively against those who resist the federal officers in the execution of their function, and against those who assail the property of the federal government, is clear and undeniable. . . .*

"I commend the question to Congress, as the only human tribunal, under Providence, possessing the power to meet the existing emergency." Among all his verbiage was the simple message that secession was a problem for Congress to solve. As president he could do nothing, and for the next eight weeks that is essentially what he did.

Hayne called at the White House on January 13, but the president declined to see him, asking that all intercourse between them be in writing. On the advice of Jefferson Davis and others, Hayne did not deliver the letter from Pickens. Instead, a series of discussions began that continued inconclusively for weeks. Both the secessionists and the president considered this to be an advantage, since each one wished for delay, though for different reasons.

Six More States Secede

From the time of the Democratic Party's divided nominating conventions, it had appeared obvious to Southern leaders that the Republican candidate — to them, the Black Republican candidate -- would win the election. They believed that the threat to slavery would then be so great that they would have no alternative but to leave the Union. The perplexing question was how to go about doing that. One way was for the slave states to act in concert, calling a convention at which they would secede together. The problem with this was that the delegates, in consideration of the pro-Union sentiment in much of the South, might delay action indefinitely and thus defeat the purpose of the secessionists. The other way was for one state to take the lead, with the others to follow as quickly as possible. That state would almost certainly be South Carolina, where commitment to secession was high, and had been so for nearly thirty years. There would be an added advantage to this approach if the bordering slave states — particularly Tennessee, North Carolina and Virginia — did not secede at once. They would provide a buffer zone between the states that had left the Union and the presumably hostile Northern states.

South Carolina took the lead, confidently expecting that it would be only the first of many states to do so. This expectation was soon proved to be valid. Within two weeks, Mississippi became the second state to leave the union. As early as November 14, Governor John J. Pettus summoned the legislature to a special session and asked it to call a convention to consider secession. The election of delegates was closely contested by men who held a wide variety of views, but the majority of those elected (85 percent of whom owned slaves) were for immediately leaving the Union. They met at Jackson on January 7. Two attempts were made to delay secession: until at least four other states had seceded, or until the people could approve in a special election. Both motions were defeated, 25 to 74 and 29 to 70. On January 9, the convention voted to secede by 84 to 15. It created a state army and appointed Jefferson Davis, one of Mississippi's U. S. Senators who was about to resign, its major general. The state's population of 791,305 included 436,631 slaves. At 55 percent of the total, this was the second highest proportion of slaves in any state.

Florida Governor Madison S. Perry called for an election on December 22 of delegates to a convention to meet at Tallahassee on January 3. Half of the seventy-one men chosen were farmers or merchants, and fifty-one held slaves. Only 10 percent were natives of Florida. Sentiment for cooperation was fairly strong, but there was little unionism. The only real question was whether the state should succeed on its own, or together with others. The convention heard speeches by representatives from Alabama, South Carolina and Virginia. An attempt was made to wait until Georgia and Alabama had seceded, and also to allow a vote by the people, but both moves were defeated, 27 to 42 and 26 to 41. On January 10, the convention voted 62 to 7 to leave the Union.

Florida was to be the Confederacy's smallest state in population, with only 140,424 people, 44 percent of whom were slaves. It was the site of the only three forts located in Confederate territory that remained in Union hands throughout the Civil War.

In Alabama, Governor Andrew B. Moore, a strict constructionist, refused to call a convention until after the presidential electors cast their ballots on December 5, but made it known that there would be an election on December 24, followed by a meeting of a convention on January 7 in Montgomery. Conservatives and unionists were strong in the northern part of the state, while secessionists predominated in the middle and south. The 100 delegates, seventy-nine of whom owned slaves, were narrowly divided. South Carolina's commissioner addressed the delegates, and the governor told them that Alabama's commissioners to the other slave states reported that secession by them was imminent. After defeat of an attempt to refer the matter to the people, an ordinance of secession, together with an invitation to other slaveholding states to meet at Montgomery on February 4, was introduced. This passed on January 11, by a vote of 61 to 39. Alabama was the second most populace of the cotton states with 964,201 people, 45 percent of whom were slaves.

As soon as Georgia Governor Joseph E. Brown learned of Lincoln's election, he asked the legislature to call a convention and to approve $1,000,000 for military expenditures. On November 20, the lawmakers enacted a bill for an election on January 2, and a convention on January 16 at Milledgeville. Some candidates favored separate state action, some joint secession, and some were conditional unionists. Just over 50,000 votes were cast for secessionists and about 37,000 went to cooperationists. Of the 301 delegates, 86 percent were slaveholders. A resolution was offered that a series of demands be made to the northern states: if not met, the southern states would secede. This impractical proposal was carried, 166 to 130, but not implemented. Instead, a committee of seventeen was appointed to draft an ordinance of secession, which was adopted on January 19 by a vote of 208 to 89. Georgia was important to the Confederacy-to-be because of its strong economy and because it had the largest population of the seven states: 1,057,286 people, of whom 44 percent were slaves. The convention elected ten delegates to the Montgomery convention and then addressed such matters as new courts and postal service.

Louisiana was less secessionist than the other states, partly because the tariff protected its sugar producers, but attitudes began to change after Lincoln's election. Governor Thomas O. Moore called the legislature into session on December 10. It set January 7 for election of delegates and January 23 for a convention to meet at Baton Rouge. Of the 130 members, 39 percent were planters or farmers and 30 percent were lawyers. Here, too, there was a dispute over whether the state should secede on its own or in concert with other states, but an ordinance of immediate secession was moved. One member offered an amendment that the other states be invited to a convention at Nashville on February 25 to determine what amendments to the U. S. Constitution were necessary. It failed to carry, 24 to 106. On January 26, by a vote of 113 to 17, the convention declared that "the Union . . . is hereby dissolved. . . . Louisiana is in full possession and exercise of all those rights of sovereignty which appertain to a free and independent state." Its population was 708,002, 47 percent of whom were slaves, and its principal city, New Orleans, was by far the largest in the South.

Texas Governor Sam Houston was opposed to secession and ignored demands that he call a convention. On their own, a group of men committed to secession issued an address to the people calling for election of delegates to a convention, to meet on January 28 at Austin to consider relations with the federal government.

Houston called the legislature into session and recommended that it not recognize the convention, but the legislators nonetheless did so, providing only that its actions be subject to a vote of the people. (It was the only state of the seven to allow for popular ratification). Just over 40 percent of the delegates were lawyers, 32 percent were farmers, and 72 percent owned slaves. On the second day, with commissioners from South Carolina and Georgia present, a motion that "Texas should separately secede from the Union" carried by 152 to 6. An ordinance of secession was then offered, and on February 1, the convention voted to secede by 166 to 7. The voters endorsed the ordinance on February 23 by a margin of three to one, and it became effective on March 2. Texas constituted fully one-third of the land area of the Confederacy. It had a population of 604,215, of whom slaves constituted 30 percent, the smallest proportion in the seven states.

More than a month before the inauguration of Lincoln, seven states had declared themselves to be no longer part of the United States. The totals of the votes in the conventions, which had been hastily convened and were unrepresentative of the populations, were 863 for secession and 174 against. Only in South Carolina was there no opposing vote. The total number of people in the seven states was 4,969,141, of whom 47 percent were slaves (2,312,352) or free Negroes (36,811). The foreboding question, North and South, was whether the eight bordering states, with their population of 7,271,152 (23 percent of whom were slaves) would also secede or would remain loyal to the Union.

Early in January 1861, the unscrupulous but ingenious Democratic mayor of New York City, Fernando Wood, proposed, perhaps with tongue in cheek, that the city also secede, become a city-state, and benefit as a center of trade between the North and South. "Why should not New York City, instead of supporting by her contributions in revenue two-thirds of the expenses of the

United States, become also equally independent? As a free city, with but nominal duty on imports, her local government could be supported without taxation upon her people." His real purpose, of course, was to try to separate the city from New York State, which he called a "venal and corrupt master." Nothing came of it, and he changed his position completely after the surrender of Fort Sumter.

Sea Battery at Ft. Moultrie

Chapter 2

More Federal Forts Are Surrendered January-February 1861

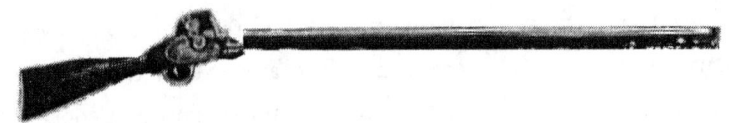

Georgia: A Fort and an Arsenal

Shortly after the seizure by South Carolina of Castle Pinckney and Fort Moultrie at the end of December, similar military actions occurred throughout the six other states that were about to secede. Each state considered that it was, or was about to be, sovereign and independent. All public property within its borders belonged to it, rather than to what they considered to be a foreign power. In disputing the ownership of Federal property, there was neither legal precedent nor practical guidance. In each case, the land on which the Federal forts stood had been ceded to the Federal government. Did the states have the right to re-possess that land? If so, did they have an obligation to compensate the Federal government for the property?

Today, the matter would be so complex as to defy consideration, but in those simpler times the problem concerned only military posts: forts, barracks, arsenals, armories, and navy yards, and civil facilities: customs houses, revenue cutters, sub-treasuries, mints, and post offices. At the beginning of 1861 there were sixty-one Federal forts. Most were either large coastal forts built since 1820, or small frontier posts. There were twenty-eight arsenals and armories. The difference between the two was that weapons were manufactured and repaired at arsenals, while they were stored at armories used mostly by state militias. The arsenals and armories contained 525,948 muskets, 91,933 rifles and 4,167 artillery pieces. The states held that each fort, arsenal, armory or civil facility should be possessed by the state in which it was located.

In the first week in January, even before delegates to secession conventions were elected, and before any except South Carolina had seceded, the states began to take possession of Federal forts and other property. Sometimes this was done by local citizens acting spontaneously, and sometimes by militias at the command of the state governor. These events constituted both an emotional reaction to Lincoln's election and a rational preparation for war if it should come. All of the properties were taken without opposition. Those actions that were taken in states before they seceded, states which were therefore still part of the United States, were clearly insurrectionary in nature. State governors and committed secessionists, however, considered the actions necessary in order to prevent Federal troops from reinforcing the forts.

When news of Anderson's move to Fort Sumter reached Georgia, Governor Brown realized that the Federal government might attempt to reinforce Fort Pulaski. This fort, located on Cockspur Island at the mouth of the Savannah River, commanded the river's two channels. Begun in 1829, it was named for Count Casimir Pulaski, who aided the American cause in the War for Independence. It was a moated, five-sided structure, similar in shape to Fort Sumter. Designed for 140 guns, only twenty were mounted and none were serviceable. It was the first post to which Corps of Engineers Lieutenant Robert E. Lee was assigned after his graduation from West Point in 1829. Because of its location, men and supplies could easily be delivered to the fort by sea. As long as it was in Federal hands, Georgia's only large port would effectively be closed.

Brown went to Savannah on January 2 and conferred with city officials. Action had already occurred there the night before when a number of armed civilians boarded the revenue cutter *J. C. Dobbin*. The commander promptly surrendered the vessel. The next day Brown, as commander-in-chief of the Georgia militia, ordered the First Volunteer Regiment, under Colonel A. R. Lawton, "to take possession of Fort Pulaski . . . and to hold it against all persons, to be abandoned only under orders from me or under compulsion of an overwhelming hostile force." All the local militia companies were eager to participate in this assignment, and a force of 134 men was assembled from the Chatham Artillery, the Savannah Guards, and the Oglethorpe Light Infantry. They went down the river by boat on the morning of January 3.

At the fort there was no resistance by Ordnance Sergeant Walker, the only soldier there, and he was allowed to remain in his quarters. The citizens of Savannah applauded the governor's action, though more serious-minded men protested that he had acted illegally, without the legislature's authorization. Crowds cheered his train as it passed through small towns as he returned to Milledgeville, the capital. The day after Fort Pulaski was taken, the volunteer companies of Macon asked Brown if he would sanction their going to South Carolina, but he declined, pending the action of the convention, which was to meet on January 6.

Captain William H. Whiting, a North Carolinian who was the U. S. Army engineer officer in charge at Savannah, had been absent at Fort Clinch, Florida, and returned to the city on January 6. He notified the chief engineer, General Joseph G. Totten, that he had found Fort Pulaski occupied by Georgia troops but he had been "received with great civility." He said he had sent Sergeant Walker to the Oglethorpe Barracks and discharged the fort's single employee. The telegraph, he said, was in the hands of the state government and he was not permitted to send any message of a military or political nature. Then as now the Corps of Engineers was responsible for river-and-harbor projects, and Whiting reported that "As to the Savannah River improvement, no interference with the property belonging to the appropriation [of funds] has been attempted, nor is any at present anticipated. I have therefore directed the discharge of all employees except a watchman."

On January 19, the Georgia convention voted to secede, and Brown prepared to defend the state's new independence by force of arms. Besides Fort Pulaski, the only other military installations in Georgia were the barracks at Savannah and the arsenal at Augusta, 130 miles up the Savannah River. Captain Arnold Elzey of the Second U. S. Artillery, a Maryland native, commanded a small garrison there. It was increased to eighty men on January 10 when the ordnance detachment from the Charleston arsenal, which had been seized, unexpectedly arrived. Elzey protested this move. "It was injudicious and impolitic, added much to the excitement in Augusta . . . the people believing it to be a reinforcement to my command." On January 23, the governor, accompanied by his aide-de-camp, Henry R. Jackson, called on Captain Elzey and asked him to withdraw his men from the state. When Elzey (who later resigned to join the Confederacy) refused, Colonel Alfred Cumming, commanding the Augusta militia, was ordered to prepare to use force. The Oglethorpe Infantry, the Clinch Rifles, the Irish Volunteers, the Montgomery Guards, the Richmond Hussars, and the Washington Artillery were mustered.

Elzey then received a written demand for surrender, backed by some 600 or more troops. An answer was expected by 9:00 A.M.

the next day, January 24. About 1:00 A.M. Elzey received a telegram from Secretary of War Holt:

> The governor of Georgia has assumed against your post and the United States an attitude of war. His summons is harsh and peremptory. It is not expected that your defense shall be desperate. If forced to surrender by violence or starvation, you will stipulate for honorable terms and a free passage by water with your company to New York.

Elzey then had his adjutant write to Jackson asking for an interview with the governor "for the purpose of negotiating honorable terms of surrender." Brown arrived at Elzey's quarters about 10:00 A.M. and they agreed on the following:

> (1) The flag to be saluted and lowered by the United States troops. (2) The company to be marched out with military honors and to retain its arms and company property. (3) The officers and soldiers to occupy quarters until removed beyond the limits of the State, and to have the use of the post transportation to and from the city and in the neighborhood, and the privilege of obtaining supplies from the city. (4) The public property to be receipted for by the State authorities, and accounted for upon adjustments between the State of Georgia and the United States of America. (5) The troops to have unobstructed passage through and out of the State by water, via Savannah.

After a salute of thirty-three guns, the stars and stripes were lowered and the flag of Georgia, a red star on a white field, was raised. The secessionists were now in possession of 20,000 muskets, other small arms, two howitzers, two cannons and a large supply of ammunition. Shortly afterwards Brown demanded control of the Oglethorpe Barracks in Savannah and then occupied the U. S. Mint at Dahlonega. The coastal lighthouses, essential to shipping, were not interfered with.

FORT PICKENS AND THE NAVY YARD

The first move against Federal property in Florida was seizure of the Apalachicola arsenal, near the village of Chattahoochee (population 1,904). U. S. Ordnance Sergeant E. Powell reported by telegraph on January 6, "The arsenal has been taken possession of by the State this morning, 7 o'clock. My forces too weak to defend it. I have refused keys of magazine and armory. Answer, with instructions." He followed this with a letter, enclosing a copy of the orders that had been issued to a Colonel Dunn by Governor Perry: "I hereby authorize and empower you to raise a company of picked men and proceed to the Apalachicola River and seize and possess the arsenal, arms, ammunition, stores, buildings, and other property now in possession of the General Government, and retain the same subject to my orders. You are requested to act with secrecy and discretion." Sergeant Powell soon decided to yield the keys, and the state of Florida thus obtained 800,000 cartridges and 50,000 pounds of gunpowder.

State troops occupied Fort Marion at St. Augustine the following day. This was a square, moated, brick-and-masonry structure with extended bastions at the corners. The only man on duty there, Ordnance Sergeant Henry Douglas, sent a report to Colonel Craig on January 7, describing the event and expressing an opinion:

> I am obliged to perform what is to me a painful duty, viz, to report to the Chief of Ordnance that all the military stores at this place were seized this morning by the order of the governor of the State of Florida. A company of volunteer soldiers marched to the barracks and took possession of me,

and demanded peaceable possession of the keys of the fort and magazine. I demanded them to show me their authority. An aide-de-camp of the governor showed me his letter of instructions authorizing him to seize the property, and directed him to use what force might be necessary. Upon reflection I decided that the only alternative for me was to deliver the keys, under protest, and to demand a receipt for the property. One thing certain, with the exception of the guns composing the armament of the water battery, the property seized is of no great value. The gentleman acting under the governor's instructions has promised to receipt to me for the stores.

Further north, on Amelia Island, was Fort Clinch. Intended to guard the entrance to Cumberland Sound, through which the Amelia and Saint John rivers flow into the Atlantic, it was an unfinished, pentagonal, masonry structure. Designed for seventy guns, there was not even one in the fort. It was easily occupied by the Florida militia.

A great deal more important than these places were the facilities at Pensacola. Both Fort Pickens and the Warrington Navy Yard would soon be threatened. The yard, on the west bank of the river seven miles southwest of the town (population 2,876), was the best ship repair facility on the Gulf of Mexico. It had a dry dock, workshops, and a supply of materials, and employed 120 white men and eighty Negroes. It was commanded by Captain James Armstrong and garrisoned by a detachment of eighty sailors and thirty-eight marines, for whom there were 100 muskets and 3,000 rounds of ammunition. The yard was unfortified, surrounded only by a brick wall two feet high. Its protection against assault from the sea was provided by three army forts. Two of these, Forts Barrancas and McRee, were shore batteries on the mainland southwest of the yard. The forty-six men of Company G, First U. S. Artillery were stationed at nearby Barrancas Barracks. The company captain, a Southern sympathizer, was away on leave, so Lieutenant Adam J. Slemmer was in command, assisted by Lieutenant Jeremiah H. Gilman. No troops were stationed at Fort Pickens, which was located on the tip of Santa Rosa Island, two miles to the south, on the outer side of the harbor entrance.

On January 7, a rumor was heard that troops from Florida and Alabama were on the way to seize the installations. Captain Armstrong was unable to decide what to do in the absence of any instructions from Washington. Lieutenant Slemmer, after some hesitation, clearly understood his responsibilities, moved his powder supply to a more secure location, and mounted a guard. On January 9, he received orders from General Scott:

> The General-in-Chief directs that you take measures to do the utmost in your power to prevent the seizure of either of the forts in Pensacola Harbor, by surprise or assault — consulting first with the Commander of the Navy Yard.

That night about twenty men tried to enter Fort Barrancas, and quickly fled when they were fired upon. These shots, on the same day that the *Star of the West* was hit off Charleston, were the first fired by Federal forces.

Slemmer consulted Armstrong, who had received similar orders from the navy, and they agreed that the only defensible place was Fort Pickens. Though it was in poor condition, it commanded the harbor entrance: defense of the harbor was the purpose for which it and similar coastal forts had been built. It was in the shape of a pentagon, bastioned at each of the corners. With walls forty feet high and twelve feet thick, it was surrounded by a dry ditch and flanking out-works. Designed to mount 252 guns in two tiers, 201 were in place. In the magazines were 8,000 shot and shell, 500 rounds of canister, and 12,000 pounds of powder. It was supposed to be defended by 1,260 men in wartime. The fort was beyond the range of the guns of the two mainland batteries and could easily be reinforced from the sea.

Armstrong at first agreed to send the steamer *U. S. S. Wyandotte* to transfer the artillery troops, but backed out at the urging of the yard executive officer, Commander Edward Farrand (who shortly resigned to join the Confederacy). However, on January 10 (the day Florida seceded), Armstrong changed his mind after a meeting in which Lieutenant Gilman reminded him of his commitment. The next morning he ordered Lieutenant Commanding O. H. Berryman of the *Wyandotte* to "render to the commanding officer of the storeship *Supply* aid and assistance in the delivery with all possible dispatch to Fort Pickens of provisions which he has been ordered to land there . . ." After a delay caused by engine problems and a dense fog, the *Wyandotte* towed a lighter and two small boats, loaded with men, guns, ammunition, tools and 22,000 pounds of powder, across the bay to Fort Pickens. The day after that it made another trip with firewood, food and supplies for five months. The *Supply* also provided some provisions to the fort. More than 20,000 pounds of powder that could not be moved was dumped into the river. Slemmer asked Armstrong to send the marines and more supplies to the fort. Instead, he sent thirty seamen, without arms or equipment or even extra clothing.

On January 12, an estimated 500 militia troops, five companies from Alabama and two from Florida, armed with muskets but without artillery, arrived at the navy yard. The commander of this battalion, Colonel Lomax, demanded that Armstrong surrender. The force available at the yard consisted of the marines under Captain Josiah Watson, and fifty ordinary men (thirty having been sent to Fort Pickens). There were two dozen cannon, but they were mounted only to fire salutes, and were not mobile. Afloat there were, on the *Wyandotte* and the *Supply*, whose crews totaled 110 men, eight guns which could be brought within range of the road on which the secessionists approached. But in the five days since he had learned that the secessionists were coming Armstrong had, it was later found, taken "no precautions of any character . . . looking to a defense of the yard." He had, however, ordered the commander of the *Supply* to take his ship to Vera Cruz, Mexico if the yard was lost. Armstrong decided that resistance was futile and notified navy secretary Toucey by telegraph:

> Commissioners appointed by the governor of Florida, with a regiment of armed men at the gate, demanded the surrender of this navy yard, after having previously taken possession of the magazines. I surrendered the place and struck my flag at half past 1 o'clock p. m. this day.

Armstrong was "regarded [as] a prisoner of war, and . . . placed on his parole of honor . . . not to bear arms against the State of Florida." This clearly implied that a state of war existed between Florida and the United States. Armstrong later complained, "I had no specific instructions to guide me. I was not advised of the intended policy of the Government in dealing with these troubles." Since Buchanan's policy was to have no policy, the same frustrating situation was experienced by scores of U. S. Army and Navy officers in late 1860 and early 1861.

Several hours after the yard was taken, the Florida state commissioner, Colonel William H. Chase, demanded the surrender of the fort in the name of the state governors. Slemmer, whose attitude differed from that of Armstrong, answered, "I am here by authority of the President of the United States and I do not recognize the authority of any governor to demand the surrender of United States property — a governor is nobody here." Several men were seen near the fort the following night and were fired upon. Governor Moore of Alabama was seriously alarmed over the strategic implications of Federal possession of Fort Pickens. On January 13, he expressed the opinion that "the possession of all the fortifications commanding the entrance to and the harbor of Pensacola is of the [greatest] importance to the safety of the seceding States on the Gulf of Mexico. No other place on the Gulf is safe while the Federal troops hold possession of the commanding fortifications at Pensacola." He had already sent the Second Alabama Volunteer Regiment to Pensacola in support of the Florida militia, and expected Mississippi to do the same. He now urged the colonel of the regiment to attack the fort, telling him not to "uselessly expose the lives of your troops" but emphasizing that the importance of taking the fort may "render a sacrifice necessary."

No attack was made, even after Colonel Chase made a second demand for surrender on January 15. Slemmer again refused, saying:

> It is our duty to hold our position until such a force is brought against us as to render it impossible to defend it, or until the political condition of the country is such as to induce us to surrender the public property in our keeping to such authorities as may be delegated legally to receive it. . . . however, we must consider you the aggressors, and if blood should be shed that you are responsible therefor.

To be prepared against possible attack, Slemmer strengthened the guard.

On January 29, after the *U. S. S. Brooklyn* sailed with troops and supplies, a notice of truce was sent from Washington to Slemmer and the naval commanders at Pensacola. It was the result of an agreement between Secretaries Holt and Toucey and Florida officials Chase and Stephen Mallory (soon to be Confederate secretary of the navy). Their message:

> In consequence of the assurances received from Mr. Mallory . . . that Fort Pickens would not be assaulted . . . you are instructed not to land the company on board the *Brooklyn* unless said fort shall be attacked or preparations shall be made for its attack. The provisions necessary for the supply of the fort you will land. . . . Your right . . . freely to communicate with the Government by special messenger . . . will remain intact.

Two weeks later the Confederate government was formed. Its leaders wished to avoid a confrontation over the fort, in hopes that there would be a peaceable conclusion to secession. When the *Brooklyn* arrived on February 9, Slemmer refused to allow the reinforcements to land. The situation was thus stabilized, and Fort Pickens remained in Union hands throughout the Civil War.

Armstrong, who was in Washington by January 26, asked Toucey to have a court of inquiry convene, and look into the "facts and circumstances" of the capture of the navy yard. The court found that:

> Commodore Armstrong was culpable in not taking any precautionary measures for the defense of his post . . . he had such a force under his command as should have induced a resistance on his part against the forces brought against him . . . having determined not to defend the yard, there was no reason why he should not have carried his men, with such public property as he could remove, to Fort Pickens, and what he could not remove have destroyed.

This finding resulted in his court martial for (1) neglect of duty, and (2) disobedience of orders and conduct unbecoming an officer. Found guilty of both charges, he was sentenced to be suspended from duty for five years, and to be reprimanded by the Secretary of the Navy.

THE FORTS AT THE KEYS

The Federal forts at the tip of Florida were of critical importance because they controlled the passage of ships between the Gulf of Mexico and the Atlantic Ocean. The year after Spain ceded Florida to the United States in 1821, the U. S. Navy established a base for ships and the U. S. Army built the Key West Barracks. When Florida became a state in 1845, the naval base was shifted to Pensacola and the Corps of Engineers began construction of two forts. The first was Fort Zachary Taylor at Key West, built on a sandy shoal several hundred yards from shore. In the shape of a trapezoid, it measured 255 feet on the seaward side and 495 feet on the landward side. There were four bastions, and emplacements for 106 guns.

Construction of the second, Fort Thomas Jefferson, was begun the following year on Garden Key, one of a cluster of seven coral reefs called the Dry Tortugas, seventy miles west of Key West and 100 miles north of Havana. A lighthouse had been built there in 1825 as a navigation aid for ships passing around the tip of Florida. The largest of all U. S. forts, it occupied most of the sixteen-acre key. It was six sided, with a bastion at each angle, and a perimeter of half a mile. The walls were eight feet thick and thirty feet high. It was designed for 450 guns, placed in three tiers, and was to be garrisoned in wartime by 1,500 men, but none were there in late 1860.

A few days after the election, on November 10, Captain Montgomery C. Meigs of the Corps of Engineers wrote to General Scott from Fort Jefferson, arguing for troops to be sent to the fort. He described the trip south that he had just completed; the conditions he found at the Dry Tortugas, where he had arrived two days earlier; and the fact that taking control of U. S. forts and other property was already being considered by aspiring secessionists:

> I found on some parts of the route a very strong feeling of hostility to the Union.... At Key West the question has been discussed as to the effect of a demand by the Governor of Florida for the possession of the U. S. public works. This is enough to show that such a demand is regarded as within the range of possibilities. Resistance to the inauguration or to the administration of a Republican President has been openly discussed.... There is danger, however, that a few ardent, desperate men, seeing the great fortifications of Pensacola, of Key West, of this harbor — the key of the Gulf — unoccupied by troops, may emulate the fame of Ethan Allen.... At this place, Fort Jefferson, there is not a single gun, and I doubt whether among the seventy or eighty persons, white and black, employed or permitted on the island half a dozen fowling pieces could be found.... both this place and Fort Taylor are at the mercy of a party which could be transported in a fishing smack. What a disgrace such an assault, if successful, would inflict on our Government.

On January 12, 1861, after forts had been seized in South Carolina, Georgia and Florida, Captain E. B. Hunt of the Corps of Engineers, in charge of construction at Key West, wrote to Captain John M. Brannan, First Artillery, who commanded the small garrison there. Hunt told Brannan that he would soon be discharging most of his mechanics and laborers and lacked the means of guarding the fortification. "I deem it my duty to call upon you to make [secure] the military custody of Fort Taylor." On January 14, before learning of the action taken by the Florida convention on the 10th, Brannan reported to army headquarters that, "in consequence of the recent seizure by unauthorized persons of several forts and arsenals in the Southern States, I have placed my entire command [forty-four men] in Fort Taylor for the purpose of protecting it." He noted that he had not received an answer to a message he had sent on December 11 to the adjutant general in which he said, "the present condition of affairs in this State indicates very clearly that Florida, by the act of her people, will secede from the Federal Government. I have reliable information that as soon as the act is committed an attempt will be made to seize upon Fort Taylor. I therefore request instructions what I am to do." The following day Brannan, now aware that Florida had left the Union, sent another message:

> In consequence of the secession of this State and the seizure of the forts and arsenals in other Southern states, I have moved my command to Fort Taylor, and will defend it to the last moment against any force attempting to capture it. I have four months' provisions and 70,000 gallons of water, but we cannot stand a siege against any organized army, and therefore should be re-enforced immediately. Two vessels of war should be stationed here to protect the entrance to the harbor and prevent a landing beyond the range of my guns. Mail facilities having ceased through Florida, all orders for this post should be sent via Havana from New York through the American consul.

The naval commander, Captain T. A. Craven, in the steamer *U. S. S. Mohawk*, was prepared to use his vessels to protect the forts, saying that "The importance of the posts . . . can not be overestimated, commanding as they do the commerce of the Gulf of Mexico." But he was ordered by the Navy Department to return to his cruising station.

Captain Meigs, in charge of construction and maintenance at Fort Jefferson, was also in command of the fort since there was no garrison there. A loyal officer who was later promoted to general and commanded the U. S. Quartermaster Corps, he wrote to DeRussy on January 15. After describing what he had done to prepare the fort against attack, he again made the case for a garrison, as he had done earlier in his letter to Scott. (Elsewhere he expressed the view that the government seemed possessed by "palsy"):

I have closed nearly 200 openings in the scarp wall, taken up several bridges which gave easy access to the work, put up a draw bridge and a gate at the postern, and brought the work into a condition which would enable a small force with guns and supplies to hold it. . . . Should the War Department under its new head adopt a new policy . . . the location of a proper force, military and naval, at the Tortugas Harbor would effectually close the ports of the Gulf coast, and . . . no more convenient point for collecting the duties due upon goods entering the ports of Texas, Louisiana, Alabama, Mississippi, and Florida exists. Unless it is soon occupied by the United States in proper force, I have no doubt that it will be seized by the parties who have shown so much more energy and promptness than those [in Washington].

The County Fishery Commissioner

As the army advanced its military preparations, a civil matter arose in the form of a conflict with the Monroe County fishery commissioner. Meigs wrote to Brannan on January 17 that an official had arrived with the sheriff to collect license fees from fishing smacks in the harbor. Several of the boats, with captains from other states, had been compelled to pay $210 for each smack over thirty tons. The fees were exacted when the smacks called at Key West to clear the U. S. customs house. Meigs believed the fees to be illegal because it was "an invasion of the jurisdiction of the United States for any officer of Florida to attempt to execute process in the Tortugas, which have been ceded by the State of Florida to the United States." He felt it was his duty to protect the vessels from "seizure or molestation." To do this he needed guns, and asked Brannan for a loan of six flanking guns and six heavy casement guns, in case Florida secessionists from Pensacola should attack the fort.

Meanwhile, on January 10, Major Lewis G. Arnold of the Second U. S. Artillery left Fort Independence at Boston aboard the steamer *Joseph Whitney* with four officers and sixty-two enlisted men. On January 18, he notified Cooper that he had arrived at Fort Jefferson and "garrisoned and assumed command of the post, in accordance with the instructions of the General-in-Chief. . . . I would respectfully inquire if Fort Jefferson is a double-ration post? If not, I request that it be announced as such in orders from the War Department." On January 23, enclosing a letter from Meigs regarding placement of the guns that had just been received from Fort Taylor, Arnold reported more substantively:

> I found on my arrival here, notwithstanding the energetic, well-directed, and highly-commendable efforts of Captain Meigs, the Engineer in charge, that Fort Jefferson could not be successfully defended from a judiciously-planned and concerted attack with a formidable force without having each front of the work and each bastion armed with artillery.

He had sent Meigs (on the latter's advice) to Key West to obtain additional guns. Meigs had returned with "six 8-inch columbiads and four field pieces and an ample supply of ammunition." Arnold now thought that he was "in position to make a strong defense, most probably to hold this important position — the key of the Gulf — against any force that is likely to be brought against it."

Meigs wrote to Totten on January 19 to say that Arnold had arrived the previous day and taken command of the post. He said there was "sufficient magazine space, well sealed and bomb-proof," for the small supply of ammunition Arnold had brought. "The work is now secure to the United States, and I trust that its flag once raised upon these walls will never again be lowered." He had learned, he said, that Florida had seceded, and the Governor had "seized all the U. S. property within his reach." He told Totten about the civil problem with the state: how fishermen had told him that the sheriff had instructions from the Florida authorities to "arrest and carry to Key West one fishing vessel — a schooner — and the master of another" and that "another vessel was off the buoy, supposed to have come to assist the sheriff in seizing the vessels and citizens. . . ." He continued:

> Under these circumstances, having . . . assured myself that from the crews of the fishing vessels in the neighborhood I could in case of actual attack obtain the assistance of thirty men loyal to the Union, I chartered a fast-sailing smack and despatched her to Key West with the letter to Captain Brannan. . . . I knew that he had in Fort Taylor a surplus of field artillery and more heavy guns than he could possibly need for defense.

He sent his letter on the *Joseph Whitney*, which was returning north, and enclosed a copy of his last letter. He had sent that by way of Havana, and he thought the copy was likely to arrive before the original.

On January 26, Brannan sent another message to Cooper, again noting that he had not yet received any answer to his letter of December 11:

> I have to report that no demonstration has been made upon this fort to date. There is no apprehension from the population of Key West, but I have no doubt that a force will soon appear at any moment from the mainland. If my company was filled up to a hundred men, and a sloop of war stationed in this harbor, there would be no danger of any successful attack, or even an attempt at present. The defenses are improving daily.

Brannan sent a message to army headquarters by the *Mohawk* on January 31. He acknowledged receipt of orders saying that he was to transfer his company to Fort Taylor and be on guard against surprise or assault, and that Major Arnold was coming with a company to garrison Fort Jefferson. He continued:

> There are about sixty men, mechanics and laborers, on the work, who are willing to take the fate of it, and assist in defending the same. I require at least fifty more muskets for these men. . . . The powder is not the best, and the supply of ammunition is limited except for the heavy guns. . . . I have sent a requisition to [the Ordnance Department]. The fort is being put in a very good state of defense by Captain Hunt, and will be in short time able to stand an attack very successfully. With a vessel of war in the harbor a landing could be easily prevented. I transferred to Major Arnold six 8-inch columbiads, with seven hundred shells; two 6-pounder and two 12-pounder howitzers, with a small supply of ammunition for the latter; 10,000 pounds of powder. He has all his guns mounted and in position, and is stronger than I am, as he cannot be attacked by land. We have communication with each other every few days. . . . I would suggest that a paymaster be ordered here to pay the troops. Last payment to October 31.

Small but adequate garrisons had now been moved into the two forts, which could easily be re-supplied by ships. They were secure because they could be successfully attacked only by a seabourne force of considerable strength, and the seven states, singly or together, did not possess such a capability. Later, the Confederacy was never able to develop one. Both Fort Taylor and Fort Jefferson remained in Federal hands throughout the Civil War.

Alabama, Louisiana and Mississippi

The Mount Vernon arsenal in Alabama contained 20,000 stand of arms, 150,000 pounds of powder, and large amounts of other munitions. It was seized on January 4 by state troops on orders from Governor Andrew B. Moore. Ordnance Captain Jesse L. Reno, expressing concern for his men's pay and his own career, reported to his superior:

> This arsenal was taken possession of by four companies of volunteers from Mobile at daylight this morning. I did not make, nor could I have made, any resistance, as they had scaled the walls and taken possession before I knew anything about the movement. The governor has demanded all the public property, and his men now have entire possession of the arsenal. I telegraphed to you today for orders as to what disposition is to be made of the enlisted men and myself. . . . The men have not been paid, and I fear that now there is no prospect of it at present. . . . As it was impossible for me to hold this place with my seventeen men, I trust that the Department will not hold me responsible for this unexpected catastrophe.

Moore wrote a lengthy letter to Buchanan on January 4 justifying the seizure of Federal property. He explained that a convention was to assemble on January 7 and that he was convinced it would "withdraw the State of Alabama from the Government of the United States." This, he said, was "made necessary by the conduct of others." He continued that he had "received such information as left but little, if any, room to doubt that the Government . . . was about to re-enforce those forts and put a guard over the arsenal." This being the case, "it was but an act of self-defense," and he hoped thereby "to avoid and not to provoke hostilities."

At the entrance to Mobile Bay were two forts. On the western side, at the tip of Dauphin Island, was Fort Gaines. Begun in 1821, it was five-sided with corner blockhouses, and walls twenty-two feet high. On the eastern side of the entrance, at the end of a long peninsula, was Fort Morgan. Completed in 1834, it was a regular five-pointed star designed by one of Napoleon's engineers. The ordnance sergeant at Fort Morgan wrote to the adjutant general on January 5 that "I have been superseded by Colonel Todd, of the Militia of Alabama, and he took and receipted for all of the property belonging to the Ordnance Department and fort. I wait for orders...." At Fort Gaines, Lieutenant C. B. Reese said that on January 18, he had been "about to send all the hands off on a steamer chartered for the purpose [when] Colonel Todd, of the State militia, arrived there in a small boat with four or five officers" and took possession. The revenue cutter *Lewis Cass* was surrendered to Alabama officials on January 30.

On the latter date, Moore wrote to the president of the Alabama Senate, reviewing the situation. He concluded by saying:

> In all I have done I have had due regard to the public safety and economy. I trust that the securing of the forts and arsenal, with a very large amount of arms, ammunition, &c., and the probable prevention of a large expenditure of money and blood under the circumstances, will be a sufficient justification of my acts in taking and securing them without the authority of law.

In Louisiana, the election for convention delegates was held on January 7. The following day the city celebrated the anniversary of the battle of New Orleans, and Governor Thomas O. Moore ordered the militia to mobilize, with the stricture that "The rules and regulations and Articles of War now in force in the Army of the United States shall regulate ... the organization and discipline of troops enrolled or called into the service of the state." The units called up included the Louisiana Legion, the Louisiana Grays, the Louisiana Guards, the Sarsfield Rifles, the Crescent Rifles, the Orleans Cadets, the Washington Artillery, the Yagers, and the Chasseurs.

Moore had decided to seize Federal property, even though the state had not yet seceded. On January 10, Major Paul Theard, with a force of seventeen officers, 151 men and four musicians went down river on the steamboat *Yankee* to Fort St. Philip, on the east bank of the Mississippi near its mouth. Henry Dart, who was keeper of the fort with the help of a dozen slaves, wisely offered no resistance. Theard then crossed to Fort Jackson, where Sergeant H. Smith turned over the keys under protest. Both of the down-river defenses of New Orleans were now controlled by the secessionists. Fort Pike, guarding the eastern entrance to Lake Pontchartrain, was also easily taken.

Up river, at Baton Rouge, seven companies of militia gathered on January 10 near the arsenal, which was commanded by Major Joseph Haskins. A regular army artillerist, he had lost an arm in the Mexican War. The garrison consisted of sixty artillerists and twenty ordnance men. Presented with a written demand by Colonel Braxton Bragg to surrender the post, Haskins ordered his men to load four cannons with grapeshot and said he would sooner lose his other arm and be damned than surrender to "that lot of ragamuffins." Negotiations indicated, however, that while Haskins would not, as a matter of pride, yield an artillery post to infantry, he might find it honorable to do so to a superior force of guns. So the Washington Artillery and other reinforcements were summoned from New Orleans. When they arrived the next day, Haskins signed an agreement with Moore, then marched his troops through most of the town on the way to the steamboat landing, his band playing "The Girl I Left Behind Me." The arsenal contained

50,000 small arms, four howitzers, twenty pieces of heavy ordnance, and 30,000 pounds of powder. The naval hospital below New Orleans was taken possession of on January 14. The remaining Federal properties in New Orleans - the branch mint, which had $880,000 on hand, the customs house, and the revenue schooner *Washington* - were taken over on January 31.

The only Federal installation in Mississippi was Fort Massachusetts. On Ship Island, twelve miles south of Gulfport, it guarded one of the entrances to New Orleans. It was a brick structure, begun in 1856 when Jefferson Davis was secretary of war and still unfinished. Engineer Lieutenant Frederick Prime wrote to Totten on January 30 to report that a body of army men, saying they were acting on their own responsibility, visited Fort Massachusetts on the morning of January 13, but went away. Another armed party came in the afternoon, and left ten men, who made no attempt to interfere with operations. A third body arrived on January 20, and took forcible possession of the works and engineer property. He noted that the engineer property on Dauphin Island had been seized on January 18, and added that he believed that these actions had been carried out without authority from the governor. He was wrong: Governor Pettus had ordered the fort seized eleven days after Mississippi seceded. He renamed it Fort Twiggs.

North Carolina and Arkansas

Although North Carolina did not secede until four months later, rebellious citizens took possession of Federal property soon after South Carolina declared its independence. On December 31, residents of Wilmington wired Governor John W. Ellis for permission to occupy Fort Caswell, on Oak Island at the mouth of the Cape Fear River, but he refused. There was no garrison at this post, which dated from 1825, but local people were afraid it would be reinforced. A delegation went to Raleigh the next day to try to convince Ellis. The governor said there was no legal basis for such an act, and again refused to sanction it.

Two dozen men from Wilmington then organized the Cape Fear Minute Men. When a rumor circulated on January 8 that a ship with fifty men and eight guns was on its way to Fort Caswell, Major John J. Hendrick started down the river with the Minute Men. They reached Smithville (present Southport) very early on the morning of January 9. Here, on the west bank of the river four miles above Fort Caswell, was Fort Johnson. There had been a fort on this site since 1745. The land was ceded to the Federal government in 1794, and a brick and masonry fort built in 1804. Its only occupant was Ordnance Sergeant James Reilly, who described what happened:

> I have the honor to report herewith that this post has been taken possession of this morning at 4 o'clock a.m. by a party of the citizens of Smithville, N. C. They came to my door at the time above stated and demanded the keys of the magazine of me. I told them I would not give up the keys to any person with my life. They replied that it was no use to be obstinate, for they had the magazine already in their possession, and that they had a party of twenty men around it, and were determined to keep it if not by fair means, they would break it open. I considered a while and seen it was no use to persevere, for they were determined to have what ordnance stores there was at the post. I then told them that if they would sign receipts for me for the ordnance, and ordnance stores at the post I would give it up to them. (There was no alternative left for me but to act as I did). They replied that they would do so. The receipt was signed and [they] left fifteen men in charge of the post; the remainder proceeded to take Fort Caswell, which is in their possession by this time. I do not know what arrangement Ordnance Sergeant Dardingkiller made with them.

The scenario was repeated at Fort Caswell, at which only two guns, both unusable, were mounted. When the news reached Raleigh, Ellis sent an officer with orders that the forts be immediately returned to the Federal government. They were evacuated on January 14. Ellis informed Buchanan of what had happened; he asked for, and got, assurances that the forts would not be garrisoned. They remained in Union hands until April 15, the day on which Lincoln called on North Carolina for troops to help suppress the insurrection. Ellis thought this call a violation of the law, refused, and again took possession of Forts Caswell and Johnson. The state seceded five weeks later.

There was a large U. S. arsenal at Fayetteville. In October 1860, the mayor, fearing a raid similar to the one that had just occurred at Harpers Ferry, Virginia, asked the War Department to send troops "for the protection of the arms and ammunition." A small detachment was assigned to the arsenal. After Lincoln's election, Ellis, recognizing that the situation had changed, asked Floyd to remove the soldiers as "notoriously unnecessary."

Arkansas, like North Carolina, had not seceded, but it was a slave state, inclined to the Southern cause. On January 28, Governor Henry M. Rector wrote to the commander of the Little Rock arsenal, Captain James Totten of Company F, Second U. S. Artillery. He said:

> The U. S. Arsenal at this place will be permitted to remain in the possession of the Federal officers until the State, by authority of the people, shall have determined to sever their connection with the General Government, unless, however, it should be thought proper to order additional forces to this point; or, on the other hand, an attempt should be made to remove or destroy the munitions of war in said arsenal.

Governor Rector wanted assurances that neither of these things would be done. He also wanted, he said, to "prevent a collision between the sovereign people of Arkansas and the Government troops." In reply, Totten said that he understood that "the troops under my command were ordered here at the request of some of the members of Congress from this state," though he had never been told for what reasons. In any case, he said, "I cannot give your excellency any assurances as to what instructions may in future be issued regarding this arsenal and the Federal troops now stationed here," but added that no such orders had yet been issued.

Captain Totten sent copies of Rector's letter, and his reply to it, to Cooper in Washington. He expressed the opinion that "most positive and unequivocal instructions are called for, in order that I may not mistake the intentions of the administration regarding the matter at issue. I believe there is trouble ahead for this command, and that by the 4th day of March decided action will be absolutely imperative." Like officers and sergeants elsewhere, he felt a desperate need for clear orders from a government whose chief executive was vacillating indecisively. On February 6, he told Cooper that "companies of armed citizens from various sections of this State have already arrived, and it is said there will soon be five thousand here for the express purpose of taking this arsenal. Instructions are urgently and immediately asked."

Hardly was that message on its way when General T. D. Merrick of the Arkansas militia appeared with another letter from Rector. It said that "a large force of citizens" was on its way to take the arsenal. This action was not authorized by him, the governor said, but he would fail in his duty if he did not interpose his authority to prevent a collision between the people and the troops. "I therefore demand in the name of the State the delivery of the possession of the arsenal and munitions of war under your charge to the State authorities, to be held subject to the action of the convention to be held on the 4th of March." Totten sent a copy of this to Cooper with a brief letter stating,

> I am perfectly in the dark as to the wishes of the administration, from the want of instructions how to meet such a crisis as at present. If I had positive orders to cover the case in point I should obey them implicitly; but I have

nothing whatever, within my knowledge, indicative of the course the Government wishes its agents to pursue, and I am therefore left to act as my judgment and my honor as a Federal officer dictate.

Totten then prepared his reply to Rector. Before responding, he said, there were three points on which he was anxious to learn official answers, "explicit and detailed." First, would the governor take charge of the arsenal and munitions in the name of the U. S. government and hold them until legally absolved? Second, would he guarantee to the garrison, including its public and private property, unmolested passage through the state? Third, would he guarantee the right of marching away "with all the honor due them as Federal officers and soldiers who do not surrender their trust, but simply evacuate a post for want of instructions from their superiors?" The next day the governor said that "after mature reflection" he accepted the three propositions, provided that no cannon were taken away, and that the troops not be stationed elsewhere in Arkansas. Totten and his men "retired" from the arsenal at noon on February 8 and went into camp on the banks of the Arkansas River.

Fort Sumter as Real Estate

While Federal forts passed into the possession of secessionists throughout the South, legal arguments continued to be exchanged between officials in Charleston and Washington. Hayne remained in Washington, where he wrote to Buchanan on January 31 regarding Fort Sumter. Secretary Holt replied to the letter on February 6. The position that had been stated two weeks earlier by Governor Pickens of South Carolina, Holt noted, seemed to have been modified by new instructions to Hayne on January 26, which said:

If it be so that Fort Sumter is held as property, then as property, the rights, whatever they may be, of the United

> States can be ascertained; and for the satisfaction of these rights the pledge of the State of South Carolina you are authorized to give.

Hayne had then, in his January 31 letter to the president, expressed what Holt called the "full scope and precise purport" of his instructions:

> I do not come as a military man to demand the surrender of the fort, but as the legal officer of the State — its attorney general — to claim for the State the exercise of the undoubted right of eminent domain, and to pledge the State to make good all injury to the rights of property which arise from the exercise of the claim. . . . The proposition now is that her (South Carolina's) law officer should, under authority of the governor and his council, distinctly pledge the faith of South Carolina to make such compensation in regard to Fort Sumter and its appurtenances and contents, to the full extent of the money value of the property of the United States delivered over to the authorities of South Carolina by your command. . . . an attack upon it would scarcely improve it as property, whatever the result, and if captured it would no longer be the subject of account.

After his review of Hayne's brief, Holt stated what he made of it:

> The proposal, then, now presented to the President is simply an offer . . . to buy Fort Sumter and contents as property of the United States, sustained by a declaration in effect that if she is not permitted to make the purchase she will seize the fort by force of arms. As the initiation of a negotiation for the transfer of property between friendly governments this proposal impresses the President as having assumed a most unusual form.

Before making comprehensive comments to Hayne, Holt noted that the president (who was a thorough and competent lawyer) had "investigated the claim on which it professes to be based." He then stated:

> The title of the United States to Fort Sumter is complete and incontestible. . . . It has absolute jurisdiction over the fort and the soil on which it stands. This jurisdiction consists in the authority to "exercise exclusive legislation" over the property referred to, and is therefore incompatible with the claim of eminent domain . . . South Carolina can no more assert the right of eminent domain over Fort Sumter than Maryland can assert it over the District of Columbia. . . . The President . . . has no constitutional power to cede or surrender it. The property of the United States has been acquired by force of public law. . . . the governor is too familiar with the Constitution of the United States . . . not to appreciate at once the soundness of this legal proposition.

Holt went on to conclude, "Fort Sumter is in itself a military post, and nothing else," built to protect the city of Charleston and the commerce of its harbor. Its small garrison, still there for that purpose, can hardly "compromise the dignity or honor of South Carolina, or become a source of irritation to her people." The president, Holt said, has made clear that he intends to hold possession of the fort as public property, which it is his duty to protect and preserve. "The forbearing conduct of his administration for the last few months should be received as conclusive evidence of his sincerity." If the authorities of South Carolina should assault Fort Sumter and plunge the country into civil war, Holt said, upon them must rest the responsibility for the consequences.

One wonders whether Holt offered this sincerely, or whether, with tongue in cheek, he was being subtly derisive of Hayne's suggestion of buying the fort. That suggestion may in itself have been merely a legal gambit in what was becoming an enigmatic chess game. In any case, the legal arguments of each side, whatever their merits might have been judged to be by an impartial court, were of no practical effect. People of the South were determined to leave the Union, and increasingly confident of their right to do so. People of the North denied that right, and were equally determined that the Union should be preserved.

TWIGGS SURRENDERS IN TEXAS

At San Antonio, seventy-one-year-old General David E. Twiggs, fourth-ranking officer in the U. S. Army, was in command of the Department of Texas. On December 13, he wrote to General Scott: "I think there can be no doubt that many of the Southern States will secede from the Union. The State of Texas will be among the number. . . . What is to be done with public property in charge of the Army?" On December 27, he wrote again, this time to the adjutant general, asking the same question. The next day he received, through Scott's aide, a reply to his letter of the 13th. (It typically took two weeks for mail to travel between San Antonio and Washington). The general-in-chief was less than helpful:

> Probably the policy of the Government in regard to the forts and depots within the limits of seceding states will have been clearly indicated before events can have caused a practical issue to be made up in Texas. The General does not see at this moment that he can tender you any special advice, but leaves the administration of your command in your own hands, with the laws and regulations to guide, in the full confidence that your discretion, firmness, and patriotism will effect all of the good that the sad state of the times may permit.

Every few days Twiggs wrote again. "There is no time to lose," he said. Then, "I respectfully asked for instructions." On January 15, he notified Scott of a decision. "I am placed in a most embarrassing situation. I am a Southern man, and all these States will secede. . . . As soon as I know Georgia has separated from the Union I must, of course, follow her. I most respectfully ask to be relieved in command of this department on or before the 4th of March."

On January 20, Texas Governor Sam Houston, who was opposed to secession, wrote to Twiggs, saying that he believed that "an effort will be made by an unauthorized mob to take forcibly and appropriate the public stores and property to uses of their own." If Twiggs needed assistance in resisting an attack, he was authorized to call on the mayor and citizens of San Antonio for help. Twiggs sent a copy of the letter to Cooper and informed him that he would "after secession, if the governor repeats his demand, direct the arms and other property to be turned over to his agents." He said that he had repeatedly asked for instructions, and he explained "The troops in this department occupy a line of some twelve hundred miles, and some time will be required to move them to any place. I ask again, what disposition is to be made of them?"

Twiggs issued orders to the post commanders. He told them what Governor Houston had said about the "unauthorized mob" and instructed them to "take the most stringent measures to guard the public stores, and [to] arm two 6 pounders with fixed ammunition, and have them in readiness for immediate service." The infantry company at Camp Verde, and two companies from Fort Clark, were to come to San Antonio, though the Fort Clark order was countermanded a few days later.

On January 28, orders were issued relieving Twiggs of command and replacing him with Colonel Carlos A. Waite of the First U. S. Infantry, who was at Camp Verde. Three days later Scott finally despatched instructions to Twiggs. He was to "take immediate measures for replacing the five companies of artillery on the Rio Grande and put them in march for Brazos Santiago, to which place a steamer will be sent to bring them out of Texas. The light companies will take their guns and equipments, but will leave their horses."

On February 1, the Texas convention adopted an ordinance of secession. The next day they named delegates to the Southern convention about to meet in Montgomery, Alabama, and formed a twenty-two-man Committee on Public Safety with broad powers. This committee delegated four of its members to negotiate with Twiggs about "the public arms, stores, munitions, etc." under his control. The four men arrived in San Antonio on February 8. The next day Twiggs appointed three of his officers to act as a military commission to discuss the demands of the Texans with them. The two sets of commissioners held a series of meetings and exchanges of letters that continued over seven days. Various points were gradually agreed upon before the Texans took action. The officers turned their minutes over to Twiggs, who then dealt personally with the situation. Twiggs learned of the acceptance of his resignation on February 15, but Colonel Waite had not yet arrived in San Antonio to replace him, so he continued to exercise command. He did not want to make any decision until March 2, when the results of the election would make the state's secession official.

McCulloch Takes the Alamo

The secessionists, however, declined not to wait that long. They feared that the U. S. Government would (as in fact it did) replace Twiggs with an officer whose loyalty was certain. They appointed Colonel Ben McCulloch, a Mexican War hero and Indian fighter, to raise a cavalry force, and he soon enlisted 400 volunteers. In camp at Salado Creek, near San Antonio, they were joined by 150 members of the Knights of the Golden Circle, a secret organization dedicated to expanding slavery into the New Mexico territory, California, and northern Mexico, and to annexing Cuba. Other men joined the force, and by February 15 about a thousand had assembled. In the pre-dawn hours, they rode into San Antonio and demanded the surrender of the U. S. Army compound, which consisted of the barracks, the arsenal, the ordnance building, the commissary depot and the Alamo. Surgeon E. H. Abadie, the post medical director, described what happened:

The Beginning and the End.

> In the night, or a little before day, of the 16th, some 1,200 or 1,500 Texan troops, commanded by Maj. Ben. McCulloch ... quietly took possession of the arsenal and arms, quartermaster and commissary property at this depot, and demanded its unconditional surrender by General Twiggs. After a stormy conference between the department commander and the commissioners, who had been here with their demands since the 8th instant, the general has acceded to their demands, and the two companies of United States troops marched out of the town in the afternoon and went into camp until arrangements could be made to transport them to the coast.

Company I of the First U. S. Infantry and Company A of the Eighth U. S. Infantry left, while the men of the post headquarters and the band remained in town. Lieutenant Colonel William Hoffman of the Eighth Infantry, who had assumed command of the post on February 11, wrote in his report of March 1:

> Soon after the receipt of the order relieving General Twiggs, and placing Colonel Waite in command of the department, it was reported that a body of State troops were being collected to come into town to take possession of the property by force. To meet such a state of things I inquired of the general commanding under what circumstances I should use ball cartridges. He replied, under no circumstances ... but on reflection I deemed it best to have them loaded, and told the general I would understand his orders to give me this latitude. ... Soon after 4 o'clock ... I heard the corporal of the guard report to the officer of the day that in consequence of a demand by a large force that he should surrender he had withdrawn his guard from the depot.

In the midst of all this, Colonel Robert E. Lee arrived in town from Fort Mason, but took no part in the events. He had just been relieved of command of the Second U. S. Cavalry and ordered to

Washington. There, two months later, he appears to have been unofficially offered, but resigned rather than accept, command of the U. S. Army.

On February 16, a letter addressed to the Officer in Command of the Department of Texas (apparently the commissioners knew that it was no longer Twiggs), said: "You are required, in the name of and by the authority of the People of the State of Texas, in Convention assembled, to deliver up all military posts and public property held by or under your control." Getting no prompt reply, they wrote the next day, saying, "we again demand the surrender" of public property. Twiggs now wrote to them saying:

> I will direct the positions held by the Federal troops to be turned over to the authorized agents of the State of Texas, provided the troops retain their arms and clothing, camp and garrison equipage, quartermaster's stores, subsistence, medical, hospital stores, and such means of transportation of every kind as may be necessary for an efficient and orderly movement of the troops from Texas, prepared for attack or defense against aggression from any source.

On February 18, the day before Waite's arrival, Twiggs, although retired and no longer in actual command, agreed to nearly everything the secessionists asked for. He balked only at giving up the artillery. "As to the condition of surrendering the guns of the light batteries," he wrote, "that, you must see, would be an act which would cast a lasting disgrace upon the arms of the United States. . . . I am sure you will not insist in a demand which I am not at liberty to grant." Other points of the surrender agreement were that everything was to "remain in status quo" until March 2; that no movement, change of position, or concentration of troops was to take place, and that none of the arms, ordnance, and military stores were to be disposed of. The troops were to march in detachments of not more than 200 men, separated by three days march, to the Gulf Coast, and from there to be transported north by ship. Twiggs signed the agreement on the day that Jefferson Davis was inaugurated as provisional president of the Confederacy.

THE FIRST PRISONERS OF WAR

The agreement covered five regiments: First, Third and Eighth Infantry, Second Cavalry, and First Artillery. The men of the thirty-four companies of these regiments constituted one-seventh of the entire strength of the U. S. Army. The property surrendered was estimated to have a value of more than $1,300,000, not counting the twenty-two forts, and consisted of 35,000 stands of arms, seventy artillery pieces, ammunition, horses, wagons, and supplies. The revenue cutter *Dodge* was seized at Galveston.

On March 1, in Washington, Secretary Holt issued General Orders No. 5:

> By the Direction of the President of the United States, it is ordered that Brig. Gen. David E. Twiggs, major-general by brevet, be, and is hereby, dismissed from the Army of the United States, for his treachery to the flag of his country, in having surrendered, on the 18th of February, 1861, on the demand of the authorities of Texas, the military posts and other property of the United States in his department and under his charge.

Twiggs reportedly threatened to challenge Buchanan to a duel in retaliation.

When Waite arrived to take command, he found that there was no way to revoke the agreement. His men were "stationed at different camps or posts in small garrisons, and spread over a very large extent of country. To concentrate a sufficient number to make a successful resistance, after the Texans had taken the field, was not practicable." He began making arrangements for transports to embark the men at Indianola, on Matagorda Bay, and at Brazos Santiago, at the mouth of the Rio Grande. He reported the total number of people to be moved as 2,684. This included 102 officers, 2,343 enlisted men, 136 laundresses and 103 officers' servants. He asked the commissioners to communicate with the Louisiana government to see if that state would allow some of his command to travel up the Mississippi River. He established a camp twenty miles west of Indianola at Green Lake, the only place where he could find sufficient fresh water and good grazing.

On February 23, the citizens of Texas voted, 46,129 to 14,697, to ratify secession, which became effective on March 2. In anticipation, the Confederate government sent General Earl Van Dorn to command the Department of Texas, with orders to "prevent the movement of the United States troops from the State of Texas." On February 28, he arrived in San Antonio and, in violation of the February 18 agreement, arrested the U. S. soldiers who had not yet left.

As they had been ordered to do, the companies on the frontier began leaving their posts and moving to their assigned ports. On March 12, Fort McIntosh was evacuated and the command marched to Fort Brown. This post was in turn abandoned on March 20. Police from Brownsville took possession of the fort until the arrival of state troops. On the same day, Fort Duncan was evacuated. The process continued until all of the forts were controlled by the Texas convention.

On April 13, the day that Fort Sumter surrendered, Major C. C. Sibley arrived at Green Lake with three companies of the Third Infantry. He was told that he would be transported on *the Star of the West*, which was lying off the coast, with four other companies - two from the First Infantry and two from the Eighth, which arrived four days later. Sibley promptly marched the seven companies, with thirty-five women and children in wagons, to the wharf at Indianola.

On April 18, the baggage, equipment and stores were stowed on two steam lighters, which had been engaged to take the troops out to *the Star of the West*. When they got into the bay, however, they found that the ship had disappeared (it had, they later learned, been captured) so they had to return to the wharf. Three days later Sibley managed to charter two small schooners, *Horace* and *Urbana*. The men had to unload the cargo of one of them, which took a day and a night. On April 23, they got under way in weather that was so bad, and the ships were so loaded, that the captains could not sail across the bay into the Gulf of Mexico.

A third schooner was chartered, but before they could get started again, three steamers appeared, carrying an estimated 800 Confederate soldiers positioned behind cotton bales, with General Van Dorn on board. "I was obliged to capitulate under the most favorable terms which I could obtain," Sibley said. The terms, signed at Salurnia on April 25, were, in fact, quite favorable. Officers must give their paroles, and soldiers their oaths, not to bear arms against the Confederate States of America, unless exchanged. Their arms, equipment and public property must be given up before they boarded the transports to return to the United States "by way of Galveston and up the Mississippi River." They went, in fact, to New York, where they arrived a month later, on May 31.

The last U. S. troops remaining in Texas consisted of a 320-man battalion of six companies of the Eighth Infantry, under Colonel I. V. D. Reeve. These soldiers were the garrisons of Forts Bliss, Davis and Quitman. As they marched toward San Antonio, believing themselves under the terms of the February 18 agreement, they learned that a force under Van Dorn was between them and that city. On the night of May 8 they camped at San Lucas Spring, a strong defensive position. The command was by then reduced, through sickness and desertions, to ten officers and 270 men.

In the morning, an officer arrived under flag of truce and demanded their surrender, saying that the Texan force was "overwhelming." Reeve was unconvinced and, with the agreement of Van Dorn, sent a lieutenant into the Confederate lines to estimate their strength. He returned with a comprehensive report:

at least 1,200 and possibly 1,500 men (later ascertained to be 1,400; the lieutenant's estimate was accurate) and four pieces of artillery. Reeve saw the situation as desperate:

> With this force before me, odds of about five to one, being short of provisions, having no hope of re-enforcements, no means of leaving the coast, even should any portion of the command succeed in reaching it, and with every probability of utter annihilation in making the attempt, without any prospect of good to be attained, I deemed that stubborn resistance and consequent bloodshed and sacrifice of life would be inexcusable and criminal, and I therefore surrendered.

Van Dorn decided to hold the men as prisoners of war until he received instructions from Montgomery. The men were permitted to march to San Antonio, where their arms were taken and they went into camp along the river. They were, said Reeve, "treated, in the circumstances of our capture, with generosity and delicacy." Altogether, 815 men become prisoners of war in Texas. Waite and some of the other officers were paroled, but the rest were held for nearly two years before being exchanged.

During January and February, the seceding states took possession of a total of forty-nine Federal forts, camps, barracks and arsenals, plus a navy yard and hospital. These ranged in size from large forts at seaports, designed for hundreds of guns and thousands of defenders, to small posts on the plains that consisted of nothing more than a house for officers, tents for the men, a corral for the horses, and a flag pole. In addition to the military installations, the seceding states seized dozens of customs houses, courthouses, sub-treasuries and mints, as well as six revenue cutters. The physical character of the places taken by the secessionists was not the essential point. What mattered was that Buchanan, who had declared to Congress in early December his intention to defend the public property "against hostile attacks from whatever quarter," had not done so, nor had he attempted to recover any of the places or any of the soldiers that had been lost. The volatile situation was his legacy to the new president.

U. S. MILITARY POSTS OCCUPIED OR ABANDONED BEFORE THE SURRENDER OF FORT SUMTER

SOUTH CAROLINA

Castle Pinckney	December 27
Fort Moultrie	December 27
Charleston Arsenal	December 31
Fort Johnson	January 2

GEORGIA

Fort Pulaski	January 3
Augusta Arsenal	January 24
Oglethorpe Barracks	January 26
Fort Jackson	January 26

FLORIDA

Chattahoochee Arsenal	January 6
Fort Marion	January 7
Fort Clinch	January 8
Fort McRee	January 12
Fort Barrancas	January 12
Barrancas Barracks	January 12
Pensacola Navy Yard	January 12

LOUISIANA

Baton Rouge Arsenal	January 10
Baton Rouge Barracks	January 10
Fort Jackson	January 11
Fort St. Philip	January 11
Fort Pike	January 14
Naval Hospital	January 14
Fort Macomb	January 28

ALABAMA

Mt Vernon Arsenal	January 4
Fort Morgan	January 5
Fort Gaines	January 18

MISSISSIPPI

Fort Massachusetts	January 20

ARKANSAS

Little Rock Arsenal	February 8
Napoleon Ordnance Depot	February 12

TEXAS

San Antonio Arsenal	February 16
San Antonio Barracks	February 16
Camp Adams	February 18
Camp Cooper	February 21
Brazos Santiago	February 21

TEXAS (Cont.)

Camp Colorado	February 26
Fort Chadbourne	February 28
Fort Belknap	February ?
Camp Verde	March 7
Ringgold Barracks	March 7
Fort McIntosh	March 12
Camp Wood	March 15
Camp Hudson	March 17
Fort Inge	March 19
Fort Lancaster	March 19
Fort Clark	March 19
Fort Duncan	March 20
Fort Brown	March 20
Fort Bliss	March 31
Fort Mason	March 31
Fort Quitman	April 5
Fort Davis	April 13
Fort Stockton	April ?

Also taken over were the revenue cutters *William Aiken, J. C. Dobbin, Lewis Cass, Washington* and *Henry Dodge*, as well as customs houses, post offices, sub-treasuries and mints.

Twiggs surrendered the Texas forts on February 18. Subsequent dates indicate when the posts were occupied or abandoned.

Chapter 3

The Confederacy Prepares for War
February-March 1861

The Montgomery Convention

Each seceded state regarded itself as independent, a sovereign nation in its own right, free to make and enforce its own laws and pursue its own policies. But there was also a deeply held commitment to the concept of a Southern Nation, equal to the United States and to all other countries. These two ideas were inherently contradictory. The conflict between them, never resolved, was a substantial impediment to the conduct of the war, which these "independent" states were forced to fight, in an attempt to uphold secession. Though they would have preferred to be part of a reconstituted United States that guaranteed slavery to any state that wished to have it, and in any territory or state that might be added, they quickly formed themselves into a "confederated" Southern Nation.

Eleven days after South Carolina seceded on December 20, it sent representatives to the other slave states with a proposal for a Convention and a plan for establishing a Southern confederacy. When Alabama seceded it offered its capital, Montgomery, a city of 4,341 whites and 4,502 blacks, as a meeting place. All six of the states that had seceded by the end of January responded. When the delegates assembled on February 4 (to be joined a month later by representatives from Texas), each state was represented by a number of men equal to the number of congressmen and senators to which it was entitled in the U. S. Congress. However, it was agreed that each state would cast only one vote. Of the fifty delegates, none were popularly elected: all were chosen by their state legislatures or secession conventions. Over half had been members of those conventions. There were forty-two lawyers, and half of the delegates had served in the U. S. Congress. Secessionists outnumbered cooperationists and unionists by just over three to two.

The Convention chose Howell Cobb as its presiding officer. A capable leader with an excellent grasp of the parliamentary process, Cobb had been elected to the U. S. House of Representatives when he was twenty-eight years of age, and became Speaker at thirty-four. After serving as Governor of Georgia, he became Buchanan's secretary of the treasury, resigning on December 8, 1860 over the issue of secession policy. Owner of a thousand slaves, he disliked slavery and had once been a strong Unionist. Despite some contention between the more democratic members and those of an aristocratic bent, within three days the Convention successfully completed its objective and adopted a Provisional Constitution. Article VI, Section 2 addressed the matter of relations with the states remaining in the Union:

> The Government hereby instituted shall take immediate steps for the settlement of all matters between the States forming it and their other late confederates of the United States in relation to the public property and public debt at the

time of their withdrawal from them; these States hereby declaring it to be their wish and earnest desire to adjust everything pertaining to the common property, common liability, and common obligations of that Union, upon the principles of right, justice, equity and good faith.

Laws of the United States that were not in conflict with the Provisional Constitution were to remain in force. The Provisional Constitution was to serve as the organic law of the Confederacy for one year, or until a permanent Constitution was adopted. The Convention was to act as the Congress until one could be elected under the provisions of the permanent Constitution.

On February 8, the Convention declared the autonomy of the Provisional Government of the Confederate States of America. The following day, by a vote of 6 to 0, Congress elected Jefferson Davis of Mississippi as provisional president. The fifty-two-year-old Davis, born in Kentucky, had graduated from West Point in 1828, and served for seven years as a lieutenant in the U. S. Army. After ten years as a civilian, he returned to the military during the Mexican War as commander of a volunteer regiment, the First Mississippi Rifles, fought in the battles of Monterrey and Buena Vista, and was seriously wounded. Davis was a U. S. Senator from Mississippi from 1847 to 1851. In the administration of President Franklin Pierce (1853-57), he served effectively as secretary of war. His accomplishments included increasing the size of the army, improving its staff organization and sending observers to the Crimean War to learn new military tactics. He was again in the Senate from 1857 to 1861, resigning on January 21, 1861 after his state seceded.

Davis was an intelligent man with polished manners, noted for his graceful oratory. When he received word of his election he was at Brierwood, his cotton plantation below Vicksburg. He had hoped to be made commander of the Confederate army, but gracefully accepted the presidency and set out for Montgomery, where he was inaugurated on February 19. In his address, he touched more than once on the possibility of war - which was only eight weeks in the future - when he said,

> If we may not hope to avoid war, we may at least expect that posterity will acquit us of having needlessly engaged in it. . . . If, however, passion or the lust of dominion should cloud the judgment or inflame the ambition of those [Northern] States, we must prepare to meet the emergency and to maintain by the final arbitrament of the sword the position which we have assumed among the nations of the world. . . . [If] the integrity of our territory and jurisdiction be assailed, it will but remain for us, with firm resolve to appeal to arms and invoke the blessings of Providence on a just cause. . . . For purposes of defense the Confederate States may, under ordinary circumstances, rely mainly upon their militia, but it is deemed advisable in the present condition of affairs that there should be a well-instructed and disciplined army, more numerous than would be required on a peace establishment.

For a man charged with the exceedingly difficult task of integrating six (soon to be seven, later eleven) independent states, Davis had notable faults. He tended to be obstinate, failed to heed the counsel of others, often lacked practical judgment, and could not establish good relationships with other senior members of the government. Moreover, his evaluation of subordinates was often faulty, and he was overly supportive of personal favorites. He was genuinely dedicated to the concept of state rights, and asserted in his inaugural address, "delegated powers are to be strictly construed." His practical attitude changed as he assumed leadership of the Southern Nation, and he began to think in terms of national rather than state interests. Davis gradually came to see the need to centralize power in the Confederate government as a means of effectively managing the war by which the right of the Southern Nation to exist could be established. This is not the place to explore the two models of government, but the reader should be aware of the contradiction, and its effect on preparations for the expected war of independence.

Alexander H. Stephens, aged forty-nine, was elected provisional vice-president, even though he, along with many others, had voted against the secession of his home state of Georgia. After graduating from the University of Georgia he read law and practiced in his home county. He served in the state legislature and in the U. S. House of Representatives, where he joined with a member from Illinois, Abraham Lincoln, in opposing the Mexican War. He was scholarly and introspective, and tended to view matters more theoretically than practically.

The cabinet posts were identical with those of the United States except that there was no secretary of the interior, since such an office suggested interference in the affairs of the states. By political design (and at some cost in effectiveness) the presidency and the cabinet posts were filled by men from all seven states. Of the six secretaries, five were lawyers and three were foreign born.

The secretary of war was an Alabama lawyer with no military experience named Leroy P. Walker. He was born near Huntsville in 1817, and attended the Universities of Alabama and Virginia. A promoter of secession, he was a delegate to the 1860 Democratic convention, and led the walkout of his delegation when the platform failed to demand support for slavery in the territories. Though energetic and confident, he proved to be the wrong man for the job, and resigned within six months. He was in charge of mobilization in the eight weeks before the attack on Fort Sumter.

Stephen R. Mallory of Florida, a forty-nine-year-old native of Trinidad, attended the Moravian school in Nazareth, Pennsylvania and then read law. He was elected to the U. S. Senate in 1851, and became chairman of the committee on naval affairs. In that position, he supported naval modernization, especially the building of ironclad ships. He was confirmed as secretary of the navy on a 5 to 2 vote, with the Florida delegation voting against him because he had advised against attacking Fort Pickens. Davis had offered similar advice. Both men hoped at the time to avoid armed confrontation with the Federal government.

Robert Toombs was named to the key post of secretary of state. Born in Georgia in 1810, he graduated from Union College in New York and studied law at the University of Virginia. After serving seven years in the U. S. House of Representatives, he spent ten years in the Senate. He was not an ardent radical, and had accepted the Compromise of 1850. Intelligent, honest and generous, he was lacking in self-control.

For secretary of the treasury, Davis chose Christopher G. Memminger of South Carolina. A month after his birth in the Duchy of Wurttemberg (present Germany) in 1803, his father had been killed in battle, and his mother brought him to the United States. When he was five, she too died and he was placed in an orphanage. A trustee sent him to the University of South Carolina, from which he graduated when only fourteen. He studied law, specialized in banking and commerce, and served in the state legislature for twenty years. He was competent and industrious, but somewhat morose, slow to make friends, and unable to placate men of opposing views. In the Convention, he served as chairman of the committee that wrote the Constitution.

The attorney general was Judah P. Benjamin of Louisiana. Born on the island of Saint Croix in 1811, he graduated from Yale University, and became a successful and wealthy lawyer in New Orleans. Since the scope of the job was narrow, he was also assigned the functions performed by the secretary of the interior in the United States. A versatile man with a strong personality, he later served the Confederacy as secretary of war and secretary of state.

Davis first asked two Mississippians to be postmaster-general and both declined the honor. He then approached John H. Reagan of Texas, who had to be asked three times before he agreed to accept. Born in Tennessee in 1818, Reagan attended Maryville College, moved to Texas when he was twenty-one, and read law there. Elected to the U. S. House of Representatives in 1857, he resigned when Texas seceded in 1861. He remained in his post to the very end of the Civil War, and was the only cabinet member still with Davis when the president was captured in May of 1865.

THE CONFEDERATE CONSTITUTION

The permanent Constitution was adopted on March 11. By April 2, Secretary of State Toombs was able to declare that it had been ratified by the necessary five states, and that is was "now the fundamental law of the Confederate States." This Constitution was nearly identical to that of the United States, but with a number of important differences, starting with the preamble (changes shown here in italics):

> We, the people of the Confederate States, *each State acting in its sovereign and independent character*, in order to form a *permanent government*, establish justice, insure domestic tranquillity, and secure the blessings of liberty to ourselves and our posterity — *invoking the favor and guidance of Almighty God* — do ordain and establish this Constitution for the Confederate States of America.

They substituted "a permanent government" for "a more perfect union." They omitted "to promote the general welfare" and "to provide for the common defense" - but inserted defense elsewhere. The invocation of God was indicative of the deeply held belief of the Southerners that the Deity was on their side. Indeed, they believed that God had created the white race to be superior and the Negro race to be inferior and that, consequently, slavery was obedience to God's will.

Like the U. S. Constitution, Congress was given the power to regulate commerce, but this was not to be construed to include "the power to . . . appropriate money for any internal improvement intended to facilitate commerce," except for aids to navigation. Congress had the power:

> (9) To lay and collect taxes, duties, imposts, and excises, for revenue necessary to pay the debts, provide for the common defense, and carry on the Government . . . but no bounties shall be granted from the treasury; not shall any duties or taxes on importations from foreign nations be laid to promote or foster any branch of industry.

As for the Post Office, after March 1, 1863, its expenses were to be "paid out of its own revenues." Congress could "appropriate no money from the treasury except by a vote of two-thirds of both houses." Simple majorities were sufficient if the money was requested by the president, or was to pay for Congress's own expenses.

With regard to military affairs, Congress was given the power

> (11) To declare war, grant letters of marque and reprisal, and make rules concerning captures on land and water. (12) To raise and support armies . . . (13) To provide and maintain a Navy. (14) To make rules for the government and regulation of land and naval forces. (15) To provide for calling forth the militia to execute the laws of the Confederate States; suppress insurrections, and repel invasions. (16) To provide for organizing, arming, and disciplining the militia and for governing such part of them as may be employed in the service of the Confederate States; reserving to the States, respectively, the appointment of the officers, and the authority of training the militia according to the discipline prescribed by Congress.

Unlike the U. S. Constitution, the Confederate States Constitution, specifically mentioned slavery. It provided that

> The importation of negroes of the African race, from any foreign country, other than the slaveholding States or Territories of the United States, is hereby forbidden . . . Congress shall also have power to prohibit the introduction of slaves from any State not a member of, or Territory not

belonging to, this Confederacy. No . . . law denying or impairing the right of property in negro slaves shall be passed.

If the Confederate States acquired new territory (expansion into northern Mexico and acquisition of Cuba were contemplated), "the institution of negro slavery, as it now exists in the Confederate States, shall be recognized and protected" therein. Three-fifths of each slave continued to count as one person for the purpose of apportioning representation. (South Carolina soon proposed an amendment— never adopted— that would have made each slave count as a whole person).

The article dealing with the executive contained two notable differences. One was that the president and vice-president were to serve a six-year term and were not eligible to be re-elected. The other was that the president had what we now call the line-item veto. As in the U. S. Constitution, the president was "commander-in-chief of the army and navy of the Confederate States, and of the militia of the several States, when called into the actual Service of the Confederate States."

Integrated into the C. S. Constitution were the first ten amendments to the U. S. Constitution, commonly called the Bill of Rights. Like its source document, it was silent with regard to nullification and secession. It declared that the Constitution, and laws and treaties made pursuant to it, were "the supreme law of the land." Amendments required a vote of only two-thirds of the states, rather than the three-quarters specified in the U. S. Constitution. In summary, the Confederacy substantially retained the U. S. Constitution, but with two important economic exceptions: it protected slavery and prohibited facilitation of commerce.

STRATEGY AND PROBLEMS

Now that the Southern Nation had been born, organizing for war was the priority task facing the Confederate leaders.

They assumed that, if war came, it would be defensive, and the Confederacy intended to fight. The Southerners firmly believed that they would prevail in defense of their home territory and institutions. But there were two alternatives to a defensive strategy that might serve as a means of compelling the Federal government to conclude peace. One was offensive warfare, an invasion of the North, starting with seizure of Washington. The arguments against this were that the Confederacy lacked the required military resources, especially if a sustained campaign should prove to be necessary, and that the Northerners would have the advantage of fighting on their home territory. The alternative was guerilla warfare (which was considered again in 1865). But this was clearly not a way to establish a Southern Nation, and was inconsistent with the traditions and experience of its West Point-trained leaders. Military thinking (in both the North and the South) was based on the experience of the Mexican War, which involved small armies operating independently. The need for command and control of large formations was not understood, nor was the importance of the execution of a coordinated plan recognized.

The assumption was nearly universal that the war would be short. As the Confederate leaders conceived the situation, either the North would easily be defeated by the intrinsic superiority of Southern soldiers, or the people of the North would lack the sustained will to fight a prolonged war. They were confident that the Confederate government would be recognized and aided by Britain, France and other foreign powers. The basis for this was their belief that the economies of those countries were heavily dependent on cotton supplied by the South.

In fighting a defensive war, whether short or long, the Confederacy faced several difficult strategic problems. The most obvious was that the Northern states had a numerical advantage in manpower. The eighteen free states had a population of 22,340,000, which was steadily growing through immigration. The population of the seven Confederate states consisted of 5,450,000 whites.

There were also 3,654,000 Negroes, all but a few of whom were slaves. In the still uncommitted eight border states, there were 5,419,000 whites, 3,950,500 slaves and 250,800 free Negroes. The Confederates realized that the future depended greatly on which of these states would support secession and which would support the Union. Without these states, the South was outnumbered four to one in men available for military service. Slaves were an essential source of labor, but much of this labor was devoted to growing cotton, which was of critical importance for earning foreign exchange but of little value for making war. Although there were skilled mechanics throughout the South (including slaves and free Negroes), there were not the numbers required for rapid development of industrial capacity.

As to military equipment and supplies, the South produced inadequate amounts to fight a war. Ten times as many manufactured goods were produced in the North, fifteen times as much iron, thirty times as many shoes, thirty-three times as many firearms, twenty-five times as many railroad locomotives. No steel at all was made in the Confederacy, and what limited manufacturing facilities there were existed mainly to support agriculture. Seizure of the Federal arsenals yielded 190,000 firearms, but many of these were obsolete. The seven state governments controlled about 300,000 weapons of uneven quality. It was not anticipated, as in fact happened, that when war came these governors, zealous in their independence, would many times not allow firearms to be taken out of their states. It was clear that imports would have to be relied on for modern rifles.

Many of the natural resources needed for manufacturing munitions either did not exist, or had not been exploited. While there was iron in Alabama, copper, tin and zinc were scarce, as were sulphur and nitrates. There were limited supplies and sources of such materials as leather, rubber, paper, coffee, salt and medicines. What was abundant was cotton: in 1860 the South produced 4,200,000 bales of it. Much of the land used to grow cotton would have to be shifted to the production of food, since the South was dependent on the states of the Northwest for grain and other agricultural products. Some of the labor, mostly slave, devoted to cotton could be applied to food crops as well as to manufacturing and to construction of fortifications and railroads.

The South's geography presented both advantages and disadvantages. Of the 563,678 square miles of the seven states, less than half was east of the Mississippi River: Texas alone comprised 47 percent of the total and Louisiana west of the river about 7 percent. There were no mountains to speak of, and the rivers -- particularly the Mississippi -- might be as advantageous to invaders as to defenders. If the Union could command the Mississippi (as in fact it did by July of 1863), the Confederacy would be literally cut in half.

Railroads, the only means of covering the vast distances involved with any speed, were of limited capacity. To begin with there were, in the seven states, barely 5,000 miles of track. Georgia had the most with 1,420, South Carolina had 973, and the other five states together had 2,649 miles. The gauge of track in the six states east of the Mississippi was five feet, but in North Carolina and Virginia, which were expected to eventually join, it was a problematic four feet, eight and a half inches. It was five feet, six inches west of the Mississippi, but that was less of a handicap since trains could not cross the river. What was of more significance was that the lines were mostly short and not connected, and there were many gaps. In Augusta, for example, 600 yards separated the two lines that served the city, so goods moving through had to be hauled by wagon from one to the other. All of the lines were single track, with only occasional sidings for passing, which limited the volume of traffic the lines could carry. Bridges were mainly of wood and therefore vulnerable to fire, so they could be easily destroyed. The South had some capacity to produce rails, and railroad companies made their own cars, using wheels and axles from foundries in Augusta and Cartersville, Georgia. But the only locomotives made in the South were built in Richmond, and it was uncertain whether Virginia would secede. Many of the engineers and other skilled railroaders were Northerners, and could be expected, in case of war, to return (as in fact they did) to the loyal states.

There were 2,507 miles of coastline, but more than half of it was accounted for by Florida, where the only useful ports were Jacksonville on the Atlantic and Pensacola on the Gulf of Mexico. In the 287 miles of South Carolina and Georgia coast, there were two main ports, Charleston and Savannah, each with rail lines running in three directions. Goods leaving or arriving at the smaller ports, which were not served by railroads, had to be transported by riverboats or wagons. The task of blockading, while it would not be easy, would be less difficult than the total miles of coastline would suggest.

The South lacked both merchant vessels in which to ship cotton, one of the only sources of foreign exchange with which to purchase arms, and naval vessels to protect incoming cargo, to defend against a Union invasion and to attack Union commerce. The North had a navy and, more importantly, extensive capability to build ships, including yards, materials and technology, which the South completely lacked except for the Navy Yard at Pensacola. The Confederates believed that, if there were to be a naval blockade, European nations would not recognize it and would bring in munitions and other supplies, and take out cotton, in their own vessels. (When war began, Lincoln promptly declared a blockade of the Confederate coast).

While not recognized by the Southerners, there were potential disadvantages in their mental attitudes, four of which bear reflection. One was their over-confidence in perceived Southern superiority, not only culturally, but also in terms of military prowess. If war came, it was believed that it would be short— a matter of months— thanks to the Southerners' innate ability to whip their weight in wildcats. Another attitudinal problem was their obsession with state rights. A successful war against the United States would require a high degree of national unity and centralized control, which could probably not be achieved. The historian Frank Owsley has suggested that an epitaph for the Confederacy might read "Died of State Rights." A third was their conservative outlook, which led to some reluctance to capitalize on the advantages offered by new technology. The North, when war came, was more successful in employing railroads, the telegraph, rifled cannon, repeating carbines, aerial balloons, photography, etc. Finally, there was the opposition to government economic assistance, exemplified by the Constitutional prohibition of the use of funds "to promote or foster any branch of industry." When war came, victory would depend on the rapid expansion of the South's munitions industry.

CONGRESS LEGISLATES AN ARMY

On February 20, the Provisional Congress began to implement the actions implied in President Davis's inaugural address by passing *An Act to Provide for Munitions of War*. It authorized the president or the secretary of war to "make contracts for the purchase and manufacture of heavy ordnance and small arms; and of machinery for the manufacture or alteration of small-arms and munitions of war, and to employ the necessary agents and artisans for these purposes; and to make contracts for the establishment of powder mills and the manufacture of powder." The following day came *An Act to Establish the War Department*. The secretary was to "have charge of all matters and things connected with the Army, and with the Indian tribes within the limits of the Confederacy."

More legislation came from Congress, as was necessary in the course of establishing a new nation. On February 26, it produced *An Act for the Establishment and Organization of a General Staff*. The staff was to consist of four departments, each headed by a colonel: adjutant and inspector general; quartermaster general; commissary general; and medical. Two days later, two additional laws were passed. The first was *An Act to Raise Money for the Support of the Government and to Provide for Defense*, authorizing the president to borrow up to $15,000,000. The other was *An Act to Raise Provisional Forces.* This bill, "to enable the Government of the Confederate States to maintain its jurisdiction over all questions of peace and war," directed the president "to assume control of all military operations in every State." It authorized him to receive from the states the arms and munitions of war acquired from the United States, and to receive into Confederate service those forces now in the service of the states "in such numbers as he may require, for any time not less than twelve months." These forces could be received, by companies, battalions or regiments, to form a part of the Provisional Army of the Confederate States, and were to "have the same pay and allowances as may be provided by law for volunteers."

As more bills followed, they became longer, more complex, and greatly detailed. Two more comprehensive pieces of military legislation were enacted on March 6. One was *An Act to Provide for the Public Defense*. It declared that "in order to provide speedily forces to repel invasion," the president was authorized "to ask for and accept the services of any number of volunteers, not exceeding 100,000, who may offer their services, either as cavalry, mounted riflemen, artillery, or infantry ... to serve for twelve months." The militia, when called into service, could not be compelled to serve for more than six months. Volunteers were to furnish their own clothes and, if mounted men, their own horses, and were to be armed by the states from which they came. The bill provided that "For horses killed in action volunteers shall be allowed compensation according to their appraised value at the date of muster into service." Then more details: "The President may limit the privates in any volunteer company, according to his discretion, at from sixty-four to one hundred." Almost as an afterthought the act had a naval component: the president was authorized "to purchase or charter, arm, equip, and man such merchant vessels and steamships or boats as may be found fit or easily converted into armed vessels, and in such numbers as he may deem necessary for the protection of the sea-board."

The other bill, extremely lengthy with thirty-one sections, was *An Act for the Establishment and Organization of the Army*. It provided for one corps of engineers, one corps of artillery, six regiments of infantry, one regiment of cavalry, and staff departments. The act spelled out the pay rates, with interesting differentials. For example: brigadier generals were to receive $301 a month. Colonels in the engineers, artillery and cavalry were to be paid $210, while those in the infantry were to be paid $195. Sergeants in the engineers, artillery and cavalry received $34 but infantry sergeants received $31. For privates, the pay was $13 in the engineers, $12 in the cavalry, and $11 in the artillery and infantry. Officers received, in addition, $9 for every five years of service in the U. S. Army. The act also defined tables of organization. Again, for example:

> Sec. 5. The corps of artillery, which shall also be charged with ordnance duties, shall consist of one colonel, one lieutenant-colonel, ten majors, and forty companies of artillerists and artificers; and each company shall consist of one captain, two first lieutenants, one second lieutenant, four sergeants, four corporals, two musicians, and seventy privates. There shall be one adjutant, to be selected by the colonel from the first lieutenants, and one sergeant-major, to be selected from the enlisted men of the corps. The President may equip as light batteries, of six pieces each, such of these companies as he may deem expedient, not exceeding four in time of peace.

The act authorized four brigadier generals, and provided that all C.S. Army officers be "appointed by the President, by and with the advice and consent of Congress." Congress had to approve every officer in the regular army -- though not in the volunteer regiments of the states. No officer was to be appointed until he had passed an examination satisfactory to the president, who had discretionary power to postpone this examination for one year. Vacancies up to the rank of colonel were to be filled by seniority. The act provided that "the rank and file shall be enlisted for a term not less than three nor more than five years."

Articles of War were adopted by the simple expedient of copying those of the U. S. Army, substituting the word "Confederate" wherever the word "United" appeared. A ration — the food for one soldier for one day — was to be the same in the C. S. Army as in the U. S. Army. Specifically, it was to be three-quarters of a pound of pork or bacon, or one-and-a-quarter pounds of fresh or pickled beef; eighteen ounces of bread or flour, or twelve ounces of hard bread, or one-and-a-quarter pounds of corn meal. In addition, for every 100 men, there were to be eight quarts of peas or beans, or ten pounds of rice; six pounds of coffee; twelve pounds of sugar; four quarts of vinegar; one-and-a-half pounds of tallow, or one-and-a-quarter pounds of adamantine, or one pound of sperm candles; four pounds of soap, and two pounds of salt.

There was no general-in-chief: the commanders of the regional departments all reported to the president. Davis appointed Samuel Cooper to the post of adjutant general. Born in New Jersey in 1798, Cooper had graduated from West Point in 1820, thirty-sixth in a class of forty. He had been a colonel in the U. S. Army and served as adjutant general until his resignation in March. Married to an aristocratic Virginian, his sympathies were with the South. Davis promoted him to full general when that rank was created in May, and he played an important role throughout the Civil War in strategy development and control of forces, but never held a command because of his age. By date of rank he was the Confederacy's senior general, followed in order by Albert S. Johnston (killed in action at the battle of Shiloh), Robert E. Lee, Joseph E. Johnston and Pierre G. T. Beauregard.

THE CONFEDERATE WAR DEPARTMENT

Forming reliable armed forces for the Confederacy out of disparate pieces and sovereign states was the daunting task that fell to Secretary of State Walker. Unfortunately, his personal characteristics and abilities were inadequate to meet this challenge. Davis, who had a military education, combat experience, and service as secretary of war, not surprisingly chose to take an active role in the work of the C. S. War Department, immersing himself in administrative details. The effect of this behavior is reflected in the fact that in the course of the four-year conflict six, often-frustrated men served as Confederate secretaries of war. In the late winter of 1861, Walker and Davis energetically set about creating the army together. Davis described the struggle to procure gunpowder and the ingredients needed to make it:

> We had no powder-mills, no depots of powder, and beyond the small supply required for sporting purposes, our local traders had no stock on hand. Very little saltpeter was purchasable in our markets. Sulphur had been recently employed in the clarification of sugar-cane juice, and thus a considerable amount of it was found in New Orleans. Prompt measures were taken to secure a supply of sulphur, and parties were employed to obtain saltpeter from the caves, as well as from the earth of old tobacco-houses and cellars; and artificial niter beds were made to provide for prospective wants. Of soft wood for charcoal there was abundance, and thus materials were procured for the manufacture of gunpowder.

On February 21, Davis plunged into the minutia of arming the new nation, demonstrating his inclination to participate directly in this task. He wrote to naval Captain Raphael Semmes, authorizing him to contract for machinery and munitions, and made specific suggestions: "Of the proprietor of the Hazard Powder Company, in Connecticut, you will probably be able to obtain cannon and musket powder, and also to engage with him for the establishment of a powder mill at some point in the limits of our territory." Drawing on his knowledge as a former secretary of war, Davis told Semmes where he might find machines for making caps and friction primers and for grooving muskets and heavy guns, and who to contact about "the most improved machinery for the manufacture of rifles, intended for the Harper's Ferry Arsenal." He suggested that Semmes seek "the most improved shot for rifled cannon" and possibly obtain "a few of the 15-inch guns like the ones cast at Pittsburgh."

According to the Confederate Constitution, the militias of the states could be called into the service of the Confederate government, but the militias were in no better shape in the South than they were in the North. The policy of the U. S. Government for decades had been to rely on a very small regular army, to be supported in time of need by the state militias. Congress had consistently been unwilling to appropriate enough funds so that the militias could be properly armed, and they were for the most part untrained, poorly organized, and not prepared to fight. It was now necessary for the Southern states to strengthen their militias by obtaining more and better arms and equipment, including heavy weapons, and to improve their training and organization. The states were asked to supply certain numbers of men, armed and equipped to serve, and to send them to designated places. Against Walker's wishes, the term of enlistment was limited by law to twelve months. Men who joined as individuals, however, and who were equipped by the Confederacy, rather than the states, were enlisted for the duration. In the spate of enthusiasm for the cause, more men answered the call than could be equipped.

The Provisional Army, consisted of two parts: the militiamen, who were enrolled for twelve months, and the volunteers, enlisted for the duration. There was also, on paper at least, a regular army. It was, however, comprised mainly of 750 officers: generals with Confederate, as distinct from state, commissions, and most of the officers who had resigned from the U. S. Army to join the Confederacy. Surviving records suggest that there were only about 1,000 enlisted men in the regulars. The fighting, when it came, was done entirely by the volunteer and militia regiments.

To equip the Southern army with the materials of war, Walker established ordnance, quartermaster and commissary bureaus. Major Josiah Gorgas was appointed chief of the Ordnance Bureau, with responsibility for furnishing the army with the weapons of war. This included setting up manufacturing plants in the South and acquiring munitions from abroad. He was a West Point graduate, class of 1845. Born in Pennsylvania, he married a woman from Alabama. Before resigning as a captain in the U. S. Army to serve the Confederacy, he had commanded the Frankfort Arsenal in Philadelphia. Davis appointed him to the ordnance office without having met him, solely on the basis of his fifteen years of military experience. He was, in effect, the only professional ordnance officer available, but his selection was a stroke of good luck: Gorgas proved to be highly competent. Since his resignation was not effective until April 2, he had barely taken up his duties in Montgomery by the time of the attack on Fort Sumter.

The only foundry in the Confederacy capable of making cannon was at Rome, Georgia. If the border states should decide to join, the foundries at Memphis and Nashville would be gained. The prize was Richmond, Virginia, where the Tredegar Iron Works was located. Its proper name was Joseph R. Anderson & Co. Anderson, a West Point graduate, employed 800 workers, many of them slaves. Tredegar had produced guns for the U. S. Army since the 1840s, but was not currently doing so because the plant was not using the Ordnance Department-approved Rodman method of casting. Anderson found ready customers in the state governments of Alabama, Georgia, Mississippi and South Carolina. Tredegar delivered fifty-six cannon in the winter of 1861: thirty-five heavy guns, fourteen field guns and seven seacoast mortars. Many of these were arrayed against Fort Sumter.

Thirteen miles above Richmond on the James River was the Bellona Foundry, which also had produced for the U. S. Army, but like Tredegar, had not adopted the Rodman method. In February 1860, Secretary of War Floyd allowed Bellona to resume production on forty-six guns, the balance of a suspended 1857 order. When war began, twenty-three of these had been completed, but none had been delivered, as intended, to Fort Monroe. The importance of these two foundries is indicated by the fact that, of 2,300 cannon produced in the South during the Civil War, half were made at Richmond.

When war began, the Confederacy could muster a total of about 2,150 cannon. A large number of these came from the seized U. S. forts and arsenals, and were mostly heavy guns for coastal defense. About 400 smoothbore field guns - many of which were obsolete and nearly useless - were in the hands of the state militias and military academies, or came from the arsenals or the Texas forts. The largest single source of armaments was the Gosport Navy Yard at Norfolk, which was seized on April 20, when Virginia seceded. The weapons found here proved to be of little use to the Ordnance Bureau in February and March because they were still under Union control.

Captain Semmes had been sent North to buy whatever weapons he was able to find, but Davis realized that the sources exploited there would cease to be available as soon as war began. He hoped that the shortage of munitions could be overcome by purchases from European countries, especially Britain. William L. Yancey sailed for London in March, with the dual mission of persuading Britain to recognize the Confederacy, and to obtain arms in exchange for cotton. He was disappointed in both. In 1833, the British had abolished slavery in their dominions and colonies, so Yancey found Queen Victoria's government reluctant to recognize a slave power. He also learned that there were more than half a million bales of cotton in British warehouses, and that cotton bought from the Southern states for fourteen cents a pound was being profitably sold to New England textile mills for as much as sixty cents a pound. He was, however, able to purchase 10,000 rifles.

Yancey was joined by a thirty-year-old West Pointer named Caleb Huse. On extended leave from the U. S. Army, he was serving as commandant of cadets and professor of chemistry at the University of Alabama. On April 1, Secretary Walker informed him that Davis had designated him to go to Europe to purchase arms and other military supplies. Huse went to New York. Unable to sail from there when the war began, he made his way to Montreal and thence to London. He was told that funds would be made available through Fraser, Trenholm & Co. When he called on the London Armory Company, the only private firm manufacturing rifles with interchangeable parts, a U. S. Army officer was there ahead of him. The man was waiting for instructions from Washington (which would have to come by ship because the trans-Atlantic cable was not yet in operation), and he placed an order for only 1,300 rifles. Huse then made a deal for "all its output of arms," and the company supplied Enfield rifles to the Confederacy throughout the war. Several of the states sent representatives to obtain munitions in Europe, but their efforts were uncoordinated, and in some cases even competitive with those of the Confederate government.

Chief of the Quartermaster Bureau was Lieutenant Colonel Abraham C. Myers, a South Carolina native who graduated from West Point in 1833. He was a man who knew and adhered to the regulations, but who could be innovative when the circumstances required. His job was to furnish the army with the vast array of supplies it needed: uniforms, shoes, socks, hats, blankets, tents, cooking pots, utensils, axes, spades, picks, soap, etc. Davis named one of his friends, Lucius B. Northrup, also a South Carolina native, to be chief of the Commissary Bureau, with the rank of lieutenant colonel. His task, which proved to be well beyond his capabilities, was that of feeding the army. He accomplished little before the war began, and proved to be a man with grave limitations for so important an assignment.

Mallory, meanwhile, began to organize a Confederate navy, starting with no vessels except those seized from the United States, and with no shipyards in which to build them. He continued his interest in armor-plated ships, formed during his experience as a U. S. Senator, and he conceived of a fleet of such vessels to overcome the numerous wooden ships of the U. S. Navy. He also promoted the idea of fast, lightly armored ships to attack the commerce of the North, and this eventually proved to be the real strength of Confederate sea forces. But neither of these ideas extended beyond the planning stage in the period before the attack on Fort Sumter.

Confederate Finance

To the German immigrant Memminger fell the formidable task of finding the cash and credit with which to finance a war. This responsibility was complicated by several circumstances. One was the fact that, although there were banks throughout the South, Southerners depended heavily on Northern and foreign banks for financing. The other was that the capital of the Southern economy, primarily agrarian, was composed mainly of slaves and land. Although data are not readily available for the early period of the Confederacy, a C. S. Treasury report dated July 24, 1861 provides estimates of the value of property in the eleven seceded states. ("Investments" includes stocks, bonds, merchandise and cash).

Negro slaves	$2,142,634,200	46%
Real estate	1,949,306,915	42%
Investments	540,219,386	12%
Total	$4,632,160,501	100%

Since the proportion of slaves was higher in the original seven, slaves must have constituted at least 50 percent of the capital in those states. With another 40 percent of its assets in land, the South enjoyed little liquidity.

The Convention/Congress passed *An Act to Establish the Treasury Department* on February 21. The secretary's duties included (1) collecting public revenues, (2) establishing government credit, (3) proposing a budget, (4) implementing an accounting system, (5) granting warrants for money paid into and issued by the treasury, (6) executing the sale of public property, and (7) preparing reports to the president and Congress. In addition to the secretary there was a comptroller, an auditor, a register, a treasurer, and an assistant to the secretary. On March 15, Congress added a second auditor, specifically for the War Department. Many of these positions were filled by former employees of the U. S. Treasury, who brought with them essential knowledge and copies of forms and regulations. These officials, with thirty-one clerks and four messengers, conducted their business in the Commerce Building in Montgomery. The offices had hardly opened when a colonel appeared with an order from Davis to provide money for equipping a hundred men. Memminger went to a local bank and arranged for a small amount of money on his personal credit.

The money that had been seized at the Federal sub-treasuries and mints was immediately available to the Confederate as a source of funds. On March 5, Memminger issued a circular letter to all U. S. officials residing in the South. He told them they were immediately to pay to the treasury all sums in their control belonging to the United States. The first receipts came from the New Orleans mint: $389,267 in coins and bullion. Operation of the mints was not suspended until May 14, at which time, the treasury received an additional $68,370 from New Orleans and $23,716 from the Dahlonega, Georgia mint. There being a lack of gold and silver bullion, the mints were not needed by the Confederacy to produce coins, but they were valuable as a source of nitric acid. The Confederate treasury realized $718,249 from seized customs and depository funds.

Helpful as these immediate monetary resources were, they were not renewable. Memminger faced the difficult question of how to provide long-term revenues for the new nation. He preferred taxation, but this was not seriously considered as a source until nearly a year later. Southerners were averse to direct taxes on property and transactions. Besides, there was no system in existence for collecting taxes other than customs duties, and establishing one would require time. The leadership asserted that separation from the Union would probably be peaceable and that, if there should be a war, it would be short and the expenses not great. So the Confederate government believed that a fiscal policy that relied on customs receipts and loans, with the possibility of a limited amount of fiat money, would be adequate.

The tariff was almost the only source of revenue to the U. S. Government, and its tariff laws remained in force in the Confederacy. While the Confederacy intended to use customs duties in a way that maximized income, it did not wish to protect selected industries. Many (though not all) of the states advocated free trade. On February 18, Congress passed an act providing that, interestingly, "the State of Texas be and is hereby exempted from the operation of the tariff laws," and:

> the following articles shall be exempt from duty and admitted free . . . : Bacon, pork, hams, lard, beef, fish of all kinds, wheat and flour of wheat and flour of all other grains, Indian corn and meal, barley and barley flour, rye and rye flour, oats and oat meal, gunpowder and all materials of which it is made, lead in all forms, arms of every description, and munitions of war and military accouterments, percussion caps, living animals of all kinds; also all agricultural products in their natural state.

The reason for exempting war materials is clear. But Congress also recognized that, since agriculture in the Confederate states was concentrated in cotton, tobacco, and sugar, much of their meat and grain and many of their horses and mules were "imported" from states farther north. On March 15, Congress levied an *ad valorem* duty of 15 percent on iron, coal, paper, lumber and cheese. The next day it legislated that "a duty of five cents per ton, to be denominated Light Money, shall be levied and collected on all ships or vessels which . . . may enter the seaports of the Confederate States."

Most individual customs collectors continued to perform their jobs, but were told that by April 1 the expenses of collection had to be reduced by 50 percent, mainly by employing fewer people in the task. At the same time, however, the customs bureau needed to add personnel when interior customs posts had to be established because imports now entered not only via the seaports, but also down the Mississippi River and across the borders from Tennessee and North Carolina.

Loans were the favored means of finance, and from the start the Confederacy relied heavily on borrowing. On February 8, as the new government was being formed, the Alabama state assembly approved a loan of $500,000, the first money the treasury received. On February 28, the Congress passed *An Act to Raise Money for the Support of the Government and to Provide for the Defense of the Confederate States of America.* It provided for the issuance of stocks or bonds in the amount of $15,000,000, payable on September 1, 1871. Interest at 8 percent was to be paid semi-annually, in specie. The Confederacy could, after giving three months notice, "pay up any portion" on September 1, 1866. The certificates were issued in four denominations: $1,000, $500, $100 and $50. Effective August 1, 1861, a duty of one-eighth of a cent per pound was to be collected on all raw cotton exported, and this revenue was pledged for the payment of the interest and principal of the loan. When the loan was repaid, the export duty would cease. As things worked out, this tax did not remotely meet expectations: throughout the war it raised a mere $30,000. A sinking fund was to be established, but never was, since there was no revenue to put into it.

Purchasers of the bonds were required to make an initial payment of 6 percent in specie, with the balance due by May 1. This proved to be a problem: many banks had suspended specie payments, so there were few gold and silver coins in circulation. Notes of those banks still redeeming in specie remained at par, but the public applied a 2 to 4 percent discount to notes of the others. Memminger therefore decided to accept bank notes at whatever the exchange rate was for those notes. He then wrote to the presidents of banks that had suspended payment and asked that they redeem in specie all notes used to subscribe to this 15-Million-Dollar Loan, as it was commonly called. The banks agreed to do so. About half of the bonds were sold by June, and all by November, partly to individuals, but more extensively to banks. Nearly 40 percent of the issue was sold in New Orleans.

The number of coins and the amount of bullion were severely limited because nearly all gold and silver had to be sent to Europe to buy war materials. Congress passed a law declaring the U. S. silver coins minted under the acts of 1853 to be legal tender for all debts up to ten dollars, and defining the value of foreign coins - U. S. and Mexican dollars, English sovereigns, Napoleons and five-franc pieces, Spanish and Mexican doubloons, all of which quickly disappeared from circulation. A shortage of currency to meet the everyday needs of the economy soon developed. Hundreds of Southern banks issued their own paper notes, just as did those in the North. But it was soon apparent that there was no reliable parity in the value of these notes.

Memminger was opposed to paper money in general, and to its use by the Confederate government. Circumstances, however, made it necessary for the government to have a means of paying for purchases, so on March 9, Congress passed *An Act to Authorize the Issue of Treasury Notes.* The president was to "cause treasury notes to be issued for such sum or sums as the exigencies of the public service may require, but not to exceed at any given time one million of dollars, and of denominations not less than fifty dollars." They were a short-term expedient and were to be redeemed in one year. If not, they then bore interest at 3.65 percent - one hundredth of a percent per day. These notes were accepted, and sometimes required, in payment of duties and taxes. Considering their large denominations, and because they could only be transferred by endorsement, they were not intended for circulation.

Memminger soon discovered that there were no facilities in the South for printing certificates, nor was any paper available. Supplies of this kind all came from the North or from Europe, and all bank notes and bonds were engraved and printed in New York. The American Bank Note Company agreed to print the bonds and treasury notes, but war broke out before they were ready for shipment and they were confiscated by Federal authorities as contraband of war. The treasury's needs grew rapidly after war commenced, and printing of currency began in June of 1861. An old German lithographer in Richmond engraved the plates and printed, on smuggled stock, the crude pieces of paper that served as the Confederate medium of exchange. By August, notes as small as $5 were being printed as part of a $100-million issue. When the war ended, 57 percent of all taxes paid to the C. S. Government had been satisfied by treasury notes. Even though they were widely used, no legal tender act was ever passed: those opposed to it believed that it was unconstitutional. Later the states themselves issued their own money, and eventually even counties and cities did so. The value of Confederate money became so deflated that, as the war's end approached in March of 1865, one U. S. gold dollar could be exchanged for $70 worth of C. S. Treasury notes.

At the beginning of 1861, thousands of Southern citizens and companies owed money to lenders in the North. This matter was not dealt with until after Fort Sumter. An act was passed on May

21 prohibiting these debtors from paying their creditors during the war. Instead, they were required to pay the sum owed into the Confederate treasury. In exchange, they received certificates bearing the same rates of interest as their loans. These certificates were to be redeemed at the end of the war, when the proceeds were to be used to settle accounts.

While it is beyond the scope of this book to describe financial activities during the war, it is important to note that the treasury was successful in financing foreign purchases of armaments and other military needs. This was done partly with specie and partly with cotton, but mainly through credit obtained from European suppliers and governments. Between what the Confederacy acquired abroad and what it produced at home, it lost no battles for want of enough guns and ammunition.

Confederate Postal Service

Years afterward, John H. Reagan wrote that his objection to accepting the job of postmaster-general was that Southern people were accustomed to good postal service from the U. S. Government, and would become dissatisfied during the time required for the new nation to establish comparable service. "While I would gladly perform my duty to the Confederacy, I did not desire to become a martyr." The establishment of an effective postal service, for the economy in general and for the prospective war in particular, was crucial in three important ways. First, it was the main basis for transmission of information in that pre-electronic age. Second, postal money orders enabled people to safely transfer funds (a means still used today) in that pre-checking age. Third, when war began, it would be a major contributor to the morale of troops by enabling them to keep in touch with their families and to receive food and clothing from home. The Adams Express Company, which provided similar services, was the chief competitor of the postal service. The telegraph was becoming widespread with the growth of the railroads, but it could only transmit words. Mail remained the principal means of moving information and light goods.

On March 6, Reagan began performing his duties. In an upstairs office in the Exchange Hotel, with the help of three clerks, he wrote to the department heads of the U. S. Post Office Department, offering them positions with the Confederate government. Within two weeks many of them accepted and moved to Montgomery. With these managers came the experience and information that enabled Reagan to quickly organize the postal service. They brought copies of forms, records, routes, lists of personnel, and a postal map of Texas — the only one they could obtain. Throughout the seceded states, nearly all the postal employees remained in their jobs. There were openings nevertheless, and filling them proved to be a burdensome nuisance. Reagan had to contend with some difficult patronage problems. To make sure that the growing number of employees understood their jobs, Reagan "organized a school for the purpose of enabling the officers and clerks to qualify themselves for their respective duties." Sessions were conducted from 8:00 to 10:00 each evening. The government rented a three-story building and the staff set to work revising the mail route structure and ordering postal supplies. Bids were sought for mail bags, post office blanks, wrapping paper, twine and sealing wax, circular marking and dating stamps, postage stamps and stamped envelopes, and mail locks and keys, and they were to be submitted by May 1.

A potential problem that loomed from the start was the provision in the Confederate Constitution that the postal service must be self-sufficient by March 1, 1863. The U. S. postal service had never operated without a subsidy in the seventy-two years since it was established. This requirement presented a difficult challenge, which Reagan achieved by adopting a policy of stringent savings. He paid low salaries to employees and accepted only low bids from railroads, steamship companies, and other contractors. Congress helped by abolishing the franking privilege and by raising postal rates to five cents for a half-ounce. On April 25, Reagan invited thirty-five railroad executives to meet with him to explore ways of reducing the cost of rail transportation, which consumed about two-thirds of U. S. postal revenue in 1860. They agreed to cut charges in half and to accept government bonds in payment until the war ended. Reagan ordered that, until he was ready to take over the service,

> The government of the Confederate States will not interfere with any existing contracts entered into between the government of the United States and the present contractors, until it assumes the entire control of its postal affairs. This course is rendered necessary by the utter impracticability of mixing the employees of the two governments in the same service. . . . All postmasters and other employees of the postal service are directed to continue the performance of their duties as such, and render all accounts, and pay all moneys to the order of the government of the United States, as they have heretofore done. . . . We must regard the carrying of our mails at this time by the government as a great public necessity to the people of both governments, resulting from their past intimate political, commercial and social relations. . . . It [is] hoped this course would have beneficial effects. By removing all doubts as to the duty, for the time being, of those engaged in the postal service, and by showing to the government at Washington that so long as it continued to hold itself liable for the mail service in the Confederate States, it should receive all the revenues derived from that service.

On May 13, one week after the Confederacy declared war, the postmaster-general proclaimed that on June 1 he would assume control of all postal facilities in Confederate territory. All stamps and stamped envelopes on hand were to be returned to Washington. Lincoln had promised in his inaugural address on March 4 that "The mails, unless repelled, will continue to be furnished in all parts of the Union," and that promise had been kept. Now, following Reagan's proclamation, U. S. Postmaster-General Montgomery Blair announced that, also on June 1, he would suspend federal mail service in the seceded states.

One of the most difficult problems Reagan faced was finding a source of postage stamps. He ordered "until postage stamps and stamped envelopes are procured for the payment of postage within the Confederate States, all postage must be paid in money." The South had for years censored the U. S. mail by refusing to deliver anti-slavery documents. Although censorship became more prevalent and widespread during the transition period, it is remarkable that continuation and transition of service was accomplished so smoothly. It seems even more remarkable that, by raising rates, reducing costs, and eliminating some routes and services, Reagan was able to make the Confederate postal service self-sustaining from the start.

Reagan was frustrated by the problem of obtaining stamps printed from steel plates, like those used by the United States, until the Confederacy was eight months old. Although he might have obtained such stamps from companies in New York, he wisely decided against that alternative. While his staff sought a supplier, most postmasters collected cash for each letter and hand stamped it. Others made their own "provisional" stamps, mostly type-set, but some from woodcuts or lithographs. Finally, Reagan resorted to the same technology that Memminger had used four months earlier to print money. A Richmond lithographer agreed to mass-produce stamps from rather crude images engraved on stone. The firm could not, however, perforate them, so they had to be cut by scissors. The first stamps, bearing a portrait of Jefferson Davis and a denomination of five cents, went on sale on October 16. They were in various shades of green because of the difficulty in obtaining ink of a consistent color. On November 6, Reagan issued a blue, ten-cent stamp with a portrait of Thomas Jefferson. He never was able to obtain stamped envelopes.

CONFEDERATE DIPLOMACY

Recognition by the European powers was virtually essential to the successful creation of a Southern Nation. To that end, William L. Yancey, Pierre A. Rost, and A. Dudley Mann were sent to Europe as Special Commissioners. On March 16, Secretary of State Toombs prepared instructions that amounted to a legal brief in favor of diplomatic recognition. The three men were scheduled to visit London, then Paris, Brussels and St. Petersburg. They were told to inform those governments that "the several Commonwealths comprising the Confederate States" had left the United States and were now "endowed with every attribute of sovereignty and power necessary to entitle them to assume a place among the nations of the world." The commissioners were to emphasize that in so doing they had not violated any obligations of allegiance, but "merely exercised the sovereignty, which they have possessed since their separation from Great Britain." They were to further emphasis that during the process of separation "order and respect for individual and collective rights have been scrupulously observed."

Having made these arguments, they announced: "The Confederate States, therefore, present themselves for admission into the family of independent nations, and ask for the acknowledgment and friendly recognition which are due to every people capable of self-government and possessed of the power to maintain their independence." Their message was clear. It was the intention of the Confederacy to "propose to negotiate a treaty of friendship, commerce and navigation." Toombs closed with the arguments that Confederate markets would be open to European manufacturers, and that cotton imports from the Confederacy were the source of $600,000,000 worth of what we call GDP. "The British Ministry will comprehend fully the condition to which the British realm would be reduced if the supply of our staple should suddenly fail or even be considerably diminished. A delicate allusion to the probability of such an occurrence might not be unkindly received by the Minister of Foreign Affairs."

In the briefing Toombs gave the C.S. diplomats, he addressed only slightly, inaccurately, or not at all, a number of important matters that would affect European actions. One was the question of whether the Southern Nation was actually capable of defending its independence. While he told the commissioners to suggest "the United States is at this time wholly destitute of the power and means to commence an aggressive war," the British, at least, might think that such power could be (as it was) quickly assembled. Another was what proved to be the great miscalculation: the belief that the supply of American cotton was so critically important to the British economy that the government would have no alternative to recognizing and supporting the Confederacy. A third and delicate issue that Toombs had judiciously avoided was that of slavery, which the British had abolished in 1833. Given the strength of liberalism in Britain and elsewhere, opposition to recognizing a government based on slavery was bound to be strong.

Yet another factor the Confederates failed to consider was that the British Empire, which encompassed one-fifth of the world's population, comprised a conglomeration of countries that were not bound together by anything remotely like the U. S. Constitution. If Britain were to endorse the idea of secession from the well-structured American government, the notion might have appeal for the disparate parts of its loosely amalgamated empire, with dire consequences. There was also the danger to Canada, which had twice in the past been invaded by the Americans. Northern newspapers were already editorializing in favor of incorporating Canada into the United States, and the prospect of that happening must have seemed real when Lincoln's new ambassador arrived and diplomatically informed the British that, if they recognized the Confederacy, the United States would regard it as an act of war.

(The British were unaware, of course, that Lincoln's policy was "one war at a time.")

There was one other "foreign country" with which the Confederacy needed friendly relations: the Indian Territory. This was the area north of Texas and west of Arkansas that became the Oklahoma Territory in 1890, but which was, at that time, independent. It was the homeland of the Five Civilized Tribes -- the Cherokees, Chickasaws, Choctaws, Creeks, and Seminoles -- who had been expelled several years before from the southeastern states. There they owned several thousand Negro slaves. The Indians themselves were alert to what was happening, and as early as February 7, one tribe made clear its position in a declaration sent to the state governors and conventions:

> *Resolved by the General Council of the Choctaw Nation Assembled:* That we view with deep regret and great solicitude the present unhappy political disagreement . . . That in the event a permanent dissolution of the American Union takes place, our many relations with the General Government must cease, and we shall be left to follow the natural affections, education, institutions, and interests of our people, which indissolubly bind us in every way to the destiny of our neighbors and brethren of the Southern States . . .

The Indians soon organized two regiments for service in the Confederate army, and treaties were entered into between the five "nations" and the Confederate government.

THE VIRGINIA PEACE CONFERENCE

The new government in Montgomery anxiously awaited the reaction of the eight states of the Upper South to the formation of the Confederacy. What happened was not encouraging. In late January, five of those states, less committed to slavery than those of the Lower South and with stronger economic ties to the North, called conventions: Arkansas, Missouri,

Tennessee, Virginia and North Carolina. Each state presented the issues, in somewhat different forms, to the voters in February, but the majority in each state opposed secession. The legislatures of the three remaining slave states, Kentucky, Maryland and Delaware, refused to call conventions.

Former President John Tyler of Virginia suggested that there be a meeting of representatives from border states, six slave and six free, "interested in keeping the peace." The General Assembly of Virginia expanded this idea in seven resolutions adopted on January 19. These resolutions were submitted to Congress by President Buchanan on January 28, with a letter describing them as "having in view a peaceful settlement of the exciting questions which now threaten the Union." Buchanan explained that the Virginians had asked that he, and the state authorities, "agree to abstain, pending the proceedings . . . from any and all acts calculated to produce a collision of arms . . ." He was convinced that he did not possess the power to enter into such an agreement. "Congress, and Congress alone, under the war-making power, can exercise the discretion of agreeing to abstain," he said.

The Virginia resolutions invited all "States, whether slaveholding or non-slaveholding, as are willing to unite with Virginia in an earnest effort to adjust the present unhappy controversies . . . so as to afford to the people of the slaveholding States adequate guarantees for the security of their rights, to appoint commissioners to meet on the 4th day of February next, in the city of Washington . . . ." If the commissioners agreed on a plan requiring amendments to the Constitution, they were to communicate the proposed amendments to Congress for submission to the states. It was the opinion of the General Assembly that a modified version of Senator Crittenden's proposals would constitute the basis for adjustment of the controversy acceptable to Virginia. Twenty-one of the twenty-seven states that had not seceded responded to the call, sending 133 delegates to meet in the concert hall annexed to Willard's Hotel. They named

Tyler chairman, then decided that each state would have one vote and that the meetings would be closed to the public.

While the Conference met, president-elect Lincoln arrived in the capital. On February 23, a group of Virginians called on him and asked if he would withdraw the Federal troops from Fort Sumter. He reportedly replied: "Why not? If you will guarantee me the state of Virginia, I will remove the troops. A state for a fort is no bad business." They were, of course, unable to guarantee that Virginia would not secede. Finding a way to keep the Upper South states in the Union was one of Lincoln's most difficult problems. While the people of these states had expressed opposition to secession, they were nevertheless committed to supporting the seceded slave states if the Federal government should attempt to reconstruct them by force. After extensive debate and consideration of a number of alternatives, the final report of the Peace Conference was delivered to Congress on February 27 with the "request that your honorable body will submit it to conventions in the States as Article thirteen of the amendments to the Constitution."

The terms of the proposed amendment were similar to Crittenden's "compromise" of December. The seven sections, several of them lengthy, can be summarized as follows: (1) Slavery to be prohibited in territory north of 36* 30' [that is, extend the Missouri Compromise line to the Pacific], but with the status of slaves in territory south of the line not to be changed, and no law to be passed to hinder taking them to the said territory. (2) No territory to be acquired by the United States without the concurrence of a majority of senators from slave states as well as a majority from free states. (3) The Constitution not to be construed to give Congress the power to regulate, abolish or control slavery in the District of Columbia without the consent of Maryland and the slave owners; but bringing slaves into the District for sale to be prohibited. (4) The Constitution not to be construed to prevent any state from enforcing the delivery of fugitive slaves to their owners.

(5) The foreign slave trade to be forever prohibited. (6) Six specified sections of the Constitution not to be amended without the consent of all the states. (7) The United States to pay full value to the owner of a fugitive slave who could not be recovered because of mob violence or intimidation.

Since adjournment was set for March 3, the day before inauguration of the new president, there was little time for Congress to debate the recommendations. Moreover, because the conference sessions had been secret, there had been no intelligent discussion in the newspapers and the public was, therefore, uninformed. Once the proposals became known, the reaction ranged from neutral to opposed. Strong support was lacking from any source. The Senate, nevertheless, appointed a special committee of five to consider the report.

Chapter 4

The U. S. Government Seeks a Policy
February-March 1861

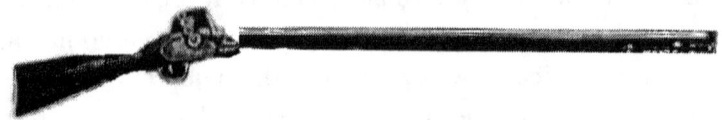

The Situation at Fort Sumter

While the Confederate government organized in Montgomery and the Peace Conference met in Washington, the tense situation in Charleston settled into a routine of sorts. The South Carolina militia held Fort Moultrie, Fort Johnson and Castle Pinckney and the Federal troops remained in Fort Sumter. Since all communication with the War Department was under the control of Governor Pickens, Anderson sealed his letters with red wax to prevent, or at least to expose, tampering with the mail. Outgoing mail was wrapped in a package addressed to the Charleston postmaster and carried to Fort Johnson by boat at noon each day. (Based on the dates on which letters were sent and received, it appears that the time typically required for mail to travel to or from Washington was three days). Pickens was under pressure from the radicals to attack Fort Sumter while the state was still independent. He resisted doing so however, because the state's armed forces were inadequate to successfully undertake such a task. He preferred to wait until the Confederacy could assume military control, thus assuring the support of the other seceded states.

The South Carolina militia, governed by an 1841 law, consisted of groups of poorly trained men, typically without uniforms or weapons. The companies were in many instances nothing more than social clubs. The governor was commander-in-chief of the five divisions, ten brigades and forty-six regiments into which the militia was, at least in theory, organized. Most white males between the ages of sixteen and sixty were required to serve, and those forty-five and under were liable to be called up for three months service. Each company was supposed to meet quarterly for drill, and regiments were to assemble once a year. Company and regimental officers were elected by the men, generals by brigade officers. All officers were supposed to attend a five-day training camp every two years. Many of the officers served in hopes of political advancement rather than because of any commitment to the military.

A committee appointed by the state legislature in 1858 to recommend improvements submitted three reports the following year. None of their suggestions were enacted into law. A year later, as secession approached, and as there was fear that abolitionists might attempt to arouse the slave population, Vigilance Committees were formed to restore the patrol system that was supposed to be conducted by the militia but that was barely functioning. An organization of Minute Men was also formed, partly to maintain order and partly for military duty in case of war. They adopted a blue rosette as an insignia, and the drills and parades of these companies helped to foster support for secession, though not many of these companies ever saw actual service.

The state created an Ordnance Board, to buy munitions and equipment and to survey the coast defenses. On December 17, as the secession convention met, the legislature created an army, consisting of 10,000 men by combining the militia system with a volunteer force. One infantry company was to be enlisted from each militia battalion, and two rifle companies from each militia brigade. A draft was authorized if enough men did not volunteer within thirty days. The governor could call these forces to active duty for up to one year.

Before the law took effect, Anderson moved to Fort Sumter and South Carolina occupied the other three Federal forts. This created an immediate need for troops. On January 1, the state convention (which was acting as a second legislature) authorized the governor to enlist volunteer companies to serve for six months. Pickens raised a regiment of six-month men and appointed Colonel Maxcy Gregg to command it. By February 1 the men were assembled for duty. The convention also authorized a regiment of regulars, to consist of 640 men enlisted for one year. Colonel Richard H. Anderson was put in command. A more permanent regular army was provided for by the legislature when, on January 28, it passed an act for the formation of an infantry regiment, an artillery battalion and a cavalry squadron, the men to be enlisted for three years. In the belligerent atmosphere prevailing in the state it was not difficult to fill the companies.

On January 19, Anderson received a note from David F. Jamison, the Palmetto Republic secretary of war, which said that "an officer of the State [will] procure and carry over with your mails each day to Fort Sumter such supplies of fresh meat and vegetables as you may indicate." Anderson replied stiffly that he had "not represented in any quarter that we were in need of such supplies." Moreover, he expressed concern about the important distinction between the governor doing this "based upon a right" rather than as a "courtesy and civility." If as a right, he said,

> Then I must procure the meat as we have been in the habit of doing for years under an unexpired contract with Mr. McSweeney, a Charleston butcher, who would, I presume, if permitted, deliver the meat, &c., at this fort or at Fort Johnson, at the usual periods for such delivery, four times in ten days.

On what he considered a related matter, he said he was anxious about the women and children who were confined to the fort and who might be exposed to sickness there. He asked that they be permitted to leave on one of the regular steamships.

Meanwhile, the quartermaster-general of the South Carolina militia, Colonel L. M. Hatch, who had been instructed by Secretary Jamison to send food, notified Anderson that there would be "two hundred pounds of beef and a lot of vegetables" on the next day's mail boat. Anderson replied that he felt "compelled to decline the reception of those supplies." Two days later a letter from Jamison informed him that the governor's act was solely a courtesy and that he was indifferent as to the arrangements for supplies, so long as they were carried in a boat "under an officer of the State." As to the women and children, the governor would "afford every facility in his power to enable [Anderson] to remove them from the fort." On February 3, after being delayed several days by a storm, all twenty dependents departed on a steamer for New York.

A letter was sent to Daniel McSweeney on January 24, asking whether he would continue to furnish food for the garrison. If so, he was to "send 184 pounds of fresh beef at a time, at such hour and wherever Quartermaster-General Hatch . . . may advise you." When, three days later, he had received no reply to this, Anderson became concerned that McSweeney was unwilling or unable to fulfill his contract because of pressure from Charleston citizens. He notified Cooper that "up to this moment, we have not derived the least advantage from the Charleston markets," and listed the commissary stores on hand in the fort:

38 barrels pork	37 barrels flour
2 barrels beans	13 barrels hard bread
3 barrels vinegar	1 barrel coffee
½ barrel sugar	3/4 barrel salt
40 pounds soap	10 pounds candles

In his message of January 31, Anderson advised Cooper "the butcher has sent down a supply of fresh beef, with a note . . .

stating that he had not received my note. . . . he will cheerfully send what I require." Anderson was also told by a friend, "the governor is very desirous that we shall receive our supplies regularly."

The army of South Carolina continued to strengthen its fortifications against a possible landing by Federal forces, and to prepare for the bombardment of the Federal garrison if that became necessary. From Fort Moultrie, fourteen guns were aimed at Fort Sumter, 1,900 yards to the southwest. Another fourteen guns were trained on the Maffitt channel. A battery, believed by Foster to contain five guns aimed at Fort Sumter, was placed 300 yards northwest of Moultrie. Foster's estimate of the garrison was 800 men, with several hundred Negroes constructing "merlons, formed of timber, sand bags and earth" and other works to protect the guns and barracks.

Due south of Fort Sumter, at Cummings Point on Morris Island, was a battery of six or eight mortars, protected by shell-proof shelters. Farther south on Morris Island, at a distance of about 2,500 yards and out of sight and range of Sumter, was the battery called Fort Morris. The Federals believed that it now contained four guns, the original two of which had fired on the *Star of the West* on January 9. At Fort Johnson on James Island, 2,300 yards southwest of Sumter, two batteries covered the harbor, one of three guns and the other of three mortars. Laborers were working day and night to strengthen the fortifications protecting these weapons, and new guns were being added from week to week. In his letter of February 5, Anderson told Cooper:

> their engineering appears to be well devised and well executed, and their works, even in their present condition, will make it impossible for any hostile force, other than a large and well-appointed one, to enter this harbor, and the chances are that it will then be at a great sacrifice of life.

While Anderson wrote daily to Cooper, Captain Foster reported every few days to General Totten. In late January, he described Fort Sumter's offensive capabilities. He said that the fort could fire on Fort Moultrie with twenty-five guns: nine eight-inch columbiads and howitzers, eight forty-two-pounders and eight thirty-two-pounders. Cummings Point, at 1,300 yards, was within easy range of Sumter's heavy guns, a total of sixteen of which could fire on it. One evening the artillerymen fired some practice rounds (which the South Carolina batteries regularly did) with a large cannon, a ten-inch columbiad. They calculated that, with a charge of two pounds of powder, they achieved a range of about 2,000 yards. "We are hard at work perfecting the arrangements for defense and offense," Foster told Totten, but his efforts were hampered by serious shortages of fuel and materials.

The Confederacy Takes Charge

Officials in Montgomery assumed control of matters related to occupation of Federal property within the Confederacy, and of all military matters. On February 12, they:

> Resolved in the Congress of the Confederate States of America, That this Government takes under its charge the questions and difficulties now existing between the several States of this Confederacy and the Government of the United States of America, relative to the occupation of forts, arsenals, navy-yards, and other public establishments . . .

To add a sense of greater urgency, the Congress passed a second resolution three days later:

> That it is the sense of this Congress that immediate steps should be taken to obtain possession of Forts Sumter and Pickens . . . either by negotiations or force, as early as practicable, and that the President is hereby authorized to make all necessary military preparations . . .

As part of those preparations Davis, on February 23, appointed Major W. H. C. Whiting to go to Charleston to inspect the works and gain knowledge of the situation there. Davis told Whiting:

> In inspecting the works of the Confederate States you will bear in mind the double relation they may have as works of offense and defense. You will make an inventory of the armament and of the munitions at the forts and in store, noting particularly the different qualities of cannon powder, as indicated by grain. Generally, I desire you to perform all the duties which devolve upon an engineer charged with the examination of works, and the preparation for active operations under circumstances such as those of Charleston, in this emergency.

Four days later Pickens wrote to Davis to tell him that "we feel that our honor and safety require that Fort Sumter should be in our possession at the very earliest moment possible." He said that Major Whiting thought they were devoting too much energy to preparing to attack the fort, and not enough to improving defenses against Federal reinforcement. Pickens said he would await orders from Montgomery, because "we feel that our cause is common, and . . . that we should do nothing to involve all the States united in a permanent war by any separate act of ours . . ." In the weeks that followed he continued to threaten independent action, in order to compel the Confederate government to take Fort Sumter either by negotiation, as Davis and others preferred, or by force.

On March 1, Walker telegraphed to Pickens: "This Government assumes the control of military operations at Charleston, and will make demand of the fort when fully advised." He followed with a letter suggesting that the "earliest moment possible" was some time off:

> Thorough preparation must be made before an attack is attempted, for the first blow must be successful . . . A failure would demoralize our people and injuriously affect us in the opinion of the world as reckless and precipitate. . . . the President has appointed Peter G. T. Beauregard brigadier-general to command the Provisional Forces of this Government in the harbor of Charleston.

The Beginning and the End.   141

On the same day Walker wrote to Beauregard to tell him:

> You will proceed without delay to Charleston and report to Governor Pickens for military duty in that State. You are authorized . . . to raise Provisional Forces for the Confederate States, to receive into the service of this Government such forces as may be tendered or may volunteer, not to exceed five thousand men . . .

The following day Walker sent another letter, telling Beauregard that a credit of $20,000 was being established to meet his "necessities," and added a suggestion: "unless in your opinion it is absolutely necessary . . . decline to receive any cavalry into the Provisional Army, as you are aware the cost of this arm of the service is very heavy, and it is more than probable that [you] will not require this outlay." Cost was on Walker's mind, because he sent to Davis on March 4 an estimate that $2,183,995 would be required for the 5,000 men at Charleston for twelve months, and $6,533,760 for the regular army under the bill then pending in Congress.

Beauregard was a formidable commander. He graduated from West Point in 1838, where Anderson had been his artillery instructor, so the two officers were well acquainted. Beauregard had fought in the Mexican War and afterwards served in the Corps of Engineers, where he gained extensive experience with the army's coastal forts. He arrived on March 3, and energetically continued to strengthen the fortifications. He freed the troops to drill by recruiting more slaves to perform the heavy labor, working them day and night. He began shifting artillery positions to better defend against attack by sea. He improved and added works to Fort Moultrie on Sullivan's Island, Fort Johnson on James Island, and especially the Cummings Point battery on Morris Island, which was closest to Fort Sumter.

The Confederate guns fired regularly to register on the area where relief ships would have to enter the harbor to reach the fort. Within a month, the batteries would be ready to engage both fort and ships. Given the preference for a peaceful solution by both sides, it was widely believed, by the authorities and the public, that no engagement would be necessary. Instead, the secessionists expected, based on statements by Secretary of State Seward and others, that the fort would soon be evacuated.

A report of March 6 to General M. L. Bonham, commanding the Volunteer Forces of South Carolina, stated the organization's current strength. Presumably most of the men were at Charleston, though the report does not say so:

> The number of companies organized and received under the act of the general assembly of 17th December, 1860, is one hundred and four — in the aggregate amounting to 8,835, rank and file, constituting ten regiments of ten companies each. The force is divided into four brigades, constituting one division.

Meanwhile, in Montgomery, the Provisional Congress adjourned on March 16. In five weeks, the representatives of the seven states had established a Constitution, selected leaders, created an army and navy, and provided for the financing of the new nation. As the members left for their homes, the question remained unanswered: Could the Confederate States succeed in separating from the United States without war?

The Lincoln Administration

As the 36th Congress was about to expire, the Senate took up the report of the Virginia Peace Conference. The committee appointed to consider it voted 3 to 2 to present the report to the full Senate without change and with a recommendation to submit the amendments to the states. The two senators in the minority suggested, rather lamely, that the states consider a national convention. The Senate remained in session past midnight and into March 4. Near dawn, with the expiration of the terms of the Senators only hours away, three votes were taken. The first was on an amendment to the Constitution forbidding any future amendment that would give Congress the power to interfere with slavery in the states. It passed by 24 to 12, exactly the two-thirds required. The Peace Conference report was then rejected by a vote of 28 to 7. Finally, the Crittenden plan came to a vote, ten weeks after it had been introduced, and was defeated 20 to 19. The House refused to consider the Conference report, on a procedural rather than a substantive vote: a motion to suspend the rules failed by 93 to 67, fifteen votes short of the necessary two-thirds. However, on February 28, the House had already passed, by 133 to 65, one vote more than the necessary two-thirds, the amendment adopted by the Senate:

> No amendment shall be made to the Constitution which will authorize or give to Congress the power to abolish or interfere, within any state, with the domestic institutions thereof, including that of persons held to labor or service by the laws of the said state.

Congress sent the proposed amendment to the state legislatures for ratification. Two free states, Illinois and Ohio, and one border slave state, Maryland, ratified it. But it was too late, and in any event inadequate, to resolve the conflict.

On March 4, a shattered James Buchanan left office and Abraham Lincoln was inaugurated as the 16th President of the United States. With the impending threat of war, and rumors that violence would interrupt the ceremony, 600 regular and militia troops were assigned to guard Pennsylvania Avenue and the Capitol. Lincoln, in his carefully worded inaugural address, began by saying:

> Apprehension seems to exist among the people of the Southern States that by the accession of a Republican Administration their property and their peace and personal security are to be endangered. There has never been any reasonable cause for such apprehension. . . I do but quote from one of [my] speeches when I declare that "I have no

purpose, directly or indirectly, to interfere with the institution of slavery in the states where it exists. I believe I have no lawful right to do so, and I have no inclination to do so."

He spoke next of the recovery of fugitive slaves, saying that right was plainly written in the Constitution, and that anyone who swore to uphold the Constitution was bound by it. He then turned to his central tenet, preservation of the Union. It was on this point that Lincoln would allow no compromise.

> I hold that . . . the Union of these States is perpetual. Perpetuity is implied, if not expressed, in the fundamental law of all national governments. It is safe to assert that no government proper, ever had a provision in its organic law for its own termination. . . . Again, if the United States be not a Government proper, but an association of States in the nature of contract merely, can it, as a contract, be peaceably unmade by less than all the parties who made it? . . . It follows from these views that no state, upon its own mere motion, can lawfully get out of the Union; that resolves and ordinances to that effect are legally void; and that acts of violence, within any State or States, against the authority of the United States, are insurrectionary or revolutionary, according to circumstances. I therefore consider that, in view of the Constitution and the laws, the Union is unbroken.

It was his duty to see that the laws were faithfully executed in all the States, and in doing this there needed to be no bloodshed or violence.

> The power confided to me will be used to hold, occupy, and possess the property and places belonging to the government, and to collect the duties and imposts; but beyond what may be necessary for these objects, there will be no invasion, no using of force against or among the people

anywhere. . . . The mails, unless repelled, will continue to be furnished in all parts of the Union. . . .

He then addressed those persons who "seek to destroy the Union at all events:"

> Before entering upon so grave a matter as the destruction of our national fabric, with all its benefits, its memories, and its hopes, would it not be wise to ascertain precisely why we do it? . . . All profess to be content in the Union if all constitutional rights can be maintained. Is it true, then, that any right, plainly written in the Constitution, has been denied? I think not. . . . One section of our country believes slavery is right, and ought to be extended, while the other believes it is wrong, and ought not to be extended. This is the only substantial dispute. . . . Physically speaking, we cannot separate. We cannot remove out respective sections from one another, nor built an impassable wall between them. . . . Suppose you go to war, you cannot fight always; and when, after much loss on both sides, you cease fighting, the identical old questions as to terms of intercourse are again with you.

Then, referring to the Constitutional amendment which had just passed both houses of Congress by the necessary two-thirds vote, "to the effect that the federal government shall never interfere with the domestic institutions of the States, including that of persons held to service," he said he had no objection to that being made express and irrevocable, even though he thought it was implied in the Constitution. After urging all Americans to "think calmly and well upon this whole subject," he concluded plaintively:

> In your hands, my dissatisfied fellow countrymen, and not in mine, is the momentous issue of civil war. The government will not assail you. You can have no conflict, without being yourselves the aggressors. You have no oath registered in Heaven to destroy the Government, while I shall have the most solemn one to "preserve, protect and defend it." . . . We

are not enemies, but friends. We must not be enemies. . . . The mystic chords of memory, stretching from every battlefield, and patriot grave, to every living heart and hearthstone, all over this broad land, will yet swell the chorus of the Union, when again touched, as surely they will be, by the better angels of our nature.

The new cabinet members promptly took office following the inauguration. For the crucial post of secretary of war, Lincoln chose Simon B. Cameron, sixty-two, the political boss of Pennsylvania. Cameron had been a "favorite son" candidate at the Republican convention, and represented the protectionist interests of his state. A journalist by trade, he won a seat in the U. S. Senate in 1845, joined the Republican party when it was formed in 1856, and was re-elected for a third senate term in 1857 even though Democrats were in the majority in the Pennsylvania legislature (senators were not yet popularly elected). Corrupt and incompetent, Cameron lasted only ten months.

Gideon Welles, fifty-nine, who attended Norwich Military Academy in Vermont, was named secretary of the navy. A native of Connecticut, he too was a journalist. A former Democrat, he left that party over the slavery issue and helped to organize the Republican Party in New England. During the Mexican War, he served in the administration of President Polk as head of the Navy Department's Bureau of Provisions and Clothing. He was an effective, energetic administrator and was responsible for the rapid expansion of the U. S. Navy.

Nearly as important as Cameron and Welles for purposes of the war that was about to begin was the fifty-three-year-old secretary of the treasury, Salmon P. Chase. A graduate of Dartmouth College, he was a founder of the Free-Soil Party, and later of the Republican Party. Strongly anti-slavery, he exemplified the abolitionist point of view. As a lawyer in Cincinnati, he defended fugitive slaves. His political experience included a term in the U. S. Senate and the governorship of Ohio. He was to finance the Civil War for the Union by issuing "greenbacks," the first legal-tender paper currency.

For secretary of state, Lincoln chose William H. Seward, sixty, of New York. After graduating from Union College he read law, practiced for a few years, then went into politics. An accomplished - and devious - politician, he became governor of New York, and was elected to the U. S. Senate in 1849. At the Republican convention, he was the principal, though unsuccessful, contender for the nomination. Seward felt himself intellectually superior to Lincoln, and believed he should take the reins of government and save the Union. Committed to a policy of conciliation and of avoiding the use of force, he thought that the seceded states, if not further provoked or offended, would eventually return to the Union, especially if the border states did not secede.

Edward P. Bates of Missouri, as attorney-general, represented the border west. Montgomery Blair of Maryland, a member of one of the country's most influential political families, was made postmaster-general. Caleb Smith of Indiana was named secretary of the interior. Sensitive to the potential peril to the Union that would result from support of the Confederate government by Britain and France, Lincoln carefully chose his ambassadors to those two countries. He sent Charles Francis Adams to London and William L. Dayton to Paris. Aging Winfield Scott, physically limited by great weight and poor health, continued as general-in-chief.

THE THREE CONFEDERATE COMMISSIONERS

By remaining in the Union, the Southern states would have been in a better position to maintain their institutions. They certainly would have been able to prevent passage of any legislation proposed by the minority Republicans that was unacceptable to them. They chose instead to try to become a separate nation. Ironically then, as the Southern Democrats abandoned their seats in Congress, the Republicans became the majority party. This majority, however, posed substantial problems for Lincoln, partly because of dissidents within the party, but also because he needed to carefully cultivate the members of both parties from the eight border slave states. In the end, four of those states left the Union.

Jefferson Davis, meanwhile, hoped to avoid armed conflict over the forts. He dispatched three commissioners to Washington to negotiate with the new president: Alfred Roman of Louisiana, Martin Crawford of Georgia, and John Forsyth of Alabama. The first arrived on March 3, the others soon after. They realized they would have to approach Lincoln carefully, both because of the delicacy of the situation and because his personality and his policies were largely unknown, though the latter became more clear when he delivered his inaugural address. The commissioners were charged with resolving several major issues.

The first was disposition of the Federal property located in the seceded states, especially the forts. This was not only a practical problem for the people of the South, but had great symbolic value. The customs houses were critical to both sides because in those days virtually the only source of Federal revenue was customs duties. The military facilities were mostly in Southern hands after January, but U. S. troops still occupied Fort Sumter and three other forts in Florida.

The second was the right of unrestricted navigation on the Mississippi River. For the people of the Northwest this was not only symbolic, but of great practical significance. It was a matter on which the Confederate government could act independently. This was the easier of the three issues to deal with, especially since the Mississippi state secession convention, sensitive to the well-understood and absolute condition that the United States would go to war if any nation sought to block its use of the river, passed a resolution "That we, the people of Louisiana, recognize the right of free navigation of the Mississippi River and its tributaries by all friendly States bordering thereon; and we also recognize the right of egress and ingress of the mouths of the Mississippi by all friendly States and Powers." Davis's government acted on February 25, when the Provisional Congress passed *An Act to Declare and Establish the Free Navigation of the Mississippi River*. It was followed the next day by *An Act to Modify the Navigation Laws and Repeal All Discriminating Duties on Ships or Vessels*.

The third, and ultimately the most crucial, was recognition of the Confederate States by the United States. Although Davis and his supporters hoped, even believed, that Lincoln might chose to accept secession as a fait accompli, that was not to be the case. Lincoln would not even agree to receive the commissioners, since that could be seen as de facto recognition. The commissioners slowly realized that recognition was not possible. In fact, the United States never considered the Confederacy to be a legitimate government.

With the help of two justices of the Supreme Court who acted as intermediaries, they presented their case to Secretary of State Seward, who was by nature a dissembler, but in this case believed what he said when he told them Fort Sumter would be evacuated by March 17. Lincoln, however, had made no decision to do that. His policy was to avoid a crisis by refraining from overt action. Despite his pledge to "hold, occupy and possess the property and places belonging to the government," he did not attempt to recover the forts and arsenals seized by the seceded states during January and February, and took no steps toward mobilizing for war. Unionist politicians, North and South, hoped that the seceded states, after a period of reflection on the enormity of what they were doing, would voluntarily revoke their acts of separation. An aggressive minority in the South wanted to end the stalemate by attacking the forts and thereby uniting the people in a war to establish the Southern Nation. Power, however, was still in the hands of men who desired peaceful separation followed by friendly relations, but who were committed to absolute independence.

The Problem of the Forts

Four U. S. forts in the seceded states remained in Federal hands after scores of military posts and civil facilities had been seized by the Southerners. The Confederates regarded two of these, Fort Pickens and Fort Sumter, as particularly insulting, and felt they must be removed. The attention of the public, and that of the new president, was focused on Fort Sumter. It was, after all, astride the harbor of the city where secession began. When Lincoln went to his office on the morning of March 5, he found a letter from Holt, who was still acting as secretary of war, with important news from Fort Sumter. This was Anderson's report No. 58 of February 28. No copy has been found, but Nicolay described its contents:

> Fort Sumter must, in the lapse of a few weeks at most, be strongly re-enforced or summarily abandoned. Major Anderson had in the previous week made an examination of his provision. There was bread for twenty-eight days; pork for a somewhat longer time; beans, rice, coffee, and sugar for different periods from eight to forty days. He had at the same time consulted his officers on the prospects and possibilities of relief and reenforcement. They unanimously reported that before Sumter could be permanently or effectively succored, a combined land and naval force must attack and carry the besieging forts and batteries, and hold the secession militia at bay.... "I confess," wrote Anderson ... "that I would not be willing to risk my reputation on an attempt to throw reenforcement into this harbor within the time for our relief rendered necessary by the limited supply of our provisions ... with a force of less than twenty thousand good and well-disciplined men."

Holt said that this report had taken the War Department by surprise. Scott's comment was that "Evacuation seems almost inevitable." Lincoln had hoped that he would have some time to deal with the situation. Instead, he faced an emergency.

Simultaneously, the White House was besieged by men seeking office in the new Republican administration that was succeeding the Democrats.

On March 9, Lincoln (who usually spelled Sumter with a "p") asked Scott to give him answers, in writing, to three questions:

> 1st. To what point of time can Major Anderson maintain his position at Fort Sumpter, without fresh supplies or reinforcement?
>
> 2d. Can you, with all the means now in your control, supply or re-inforce Fort Sumpter within that time?
>
> 3d. If not, what amount of means and of what description, in addition to that already at your control, would enable you to supply and reinforce that fortress within the time?

Scott replied that Anderson could hold out for perhaps forty days, but that the fort could be taken by assault at any time. Four months, he believed, was the shortest time in which the required warships and transports could be assembled. To enlist 5,000 regulars and 20,000 volunteers for land operations would require six months. Scott's advice, therefore, was "that Major Anderson be instructed to evacuate the fort . . . and embark with his command for New York."

On March 13, as Lincoln considered his alternatives with regard to the forts, Gustavus V. Fox was brought to the White House by his brother-in-law, Postmaster-General Blair. Fox was a thirty-nine-year-old graduate of the Naval Academy at Annapolis who would later become assistant secretary of the navy. He presented to Lincoln the plan he had prepared on February 6 at the St. Germain Hotel in New York, and submitted to Scott. Despite the general-in-chief's approval, it had been rejected by Buchanan. Fox believed that, because the bar of Charleston harbor was four miles long, it could not be obstructed everywhere, and "at high water and smooth sea the harbor is perfectly accessible to vessels drawing, say, seven feet of water." Since the South Carolinians knew that the U. S. Navy had no such vessels, they would conclude that any attempt at re-supply would be made only by shallow-draft vessels at high tide. He thought that trying to elude their vigilance was "too liable to failure," but he had a plan he was confident would succeed:

> I propose to put the troops on board of a large, comfortable sea steamer, and hire two powerful light-draught New York tug-boats, having the necessary stores on board; these to be convoyed by the U. S. steamer *Pawnee*, now at Philadelphia, and the revenue cutter *Harriet Lane*. . . . Arriving off the bar I propose to examine by day the naval preparations and obstructions. If their vessels determine to oppose our entrance . . . the armed ships must approach the bar and destroy or drive them on shore. Major Anderson would do the same upon any vessels within the range of his guns, and would also prevent any naval succor being sent down from the city. Having dispersed this force the only obstacles are the forts on Cummings Point and Fort Moultrie. . . . At night, two hours before high water, with half the force on board of each tug within relieving distance of each other, I should run in to Fort Sumter.

Lincoln was interested in the plan, and suggested that Fox go to Charleston to reconnoiter. He left on March 19, and arrived there two days later.

On March 15, Lincoln sent a brief note to Secretary of War Cameron: "Assuming it to be possible to now provision Fort Sumter, under all the circumstances is it wise to attempt it? Please give me your opinion in writing on this question." Two days later Cameron answered with a great deal of writing -- his own and that of others, but he quickly came to the point: ". . . my mind has been most reluctantly forced to the conclusion that it would be unwise now to make such an attempt." He reasoned that it would not be possible to do it without capturing "all the opposing batteries," which would require a large landing force and many ships. He explained the basis for his conclusion in detail, then attached eight reports, by army and navy officers, that proposed various plans for the relief of the fort, and stated the risks and difficulties associated with each. Four of these were written by Fox.

Three days later Lincoln prepared for himself a list of "Some considerations in favor of withdrawing the Troops from Fort Sumpter." It stated eight reasons:

> The Fort cannot be permanently held without reinforcement. . . . The Fort cannot now be re-inforced without a large armament, involving of course a bloody conflict and great exasperation on both sides. . . . The Fort in the present condition of affairs is of inconsiderable military value. . . . The abandonment of the Post would remove a source of irritation to the Southern people and deprive the secession movement of one of its most powerful stimulants. . . . It would indicate both an independent and a conservative position on [the] part of the new administration. . . . It would tend to confound and embarrass those enemies of the Union both at the North and South who have relied on the cry of "Coercion.". . . If the garrison should . . . be successfully attacked, or from want of proper supplies should be cut off by disuse the administration would be held responsible. . . . The moral advantage to the Secessionists of a successful attack would be very great.

The memorandum ended with two "Objections:"

> 1st. The danger of demoralizing the Republican Party by a measure which might seem to many to indicate timidity or in common parlance, 'want of pluck.' That this may be the first impression is probable but if the measure is justified upon the double ground of the small importance of the post in a military point of view and the desire to conciliate wherever this can be safely done[,] a second thought will discover the wisdom of the course, and increase rather than diminish the confidence of the party in its leaders. 2d. The danger of the movement being construed by the Secessionists as a yielding from necessity, and in so far a victory on their part.

On the same day Lincoln wrote to Secretary of the Treasury Chase, asking "whether any goods, wares and merchandize, subject by law to the payment of duties, are now being imported into the United States without such duties being paid, . . . And if yea . . . for what cause do such duties remain unpaid? . . . I will also thank you for your opinion whether, as a matter of fact, vessels off shore could be effectively used to prevent such importation, or to enforce the payment or securing of the duties." Collection of customs duties was a matter of double importance to the government. On one hand, it was a principal means of asserting the authority of the United States in the states that claimed to have seceded. It was also, in those pre-income tax days, the primary source of public funds. Total Federal revenues in 1860 amounted to $56,065,000. The preponderance, 95 percent, came from import duties, while 3 percent came from public lands sales and 2 percent from all other sources.

Also on March 18, Lincoln, concerned about the poor state of the nation's military establishment, considered means for increasing the readiness of the state militias. He asked the attorney general, Bates, for his opinion on the legality of establishing, without action by Congress (which was not in session) a Militia Bureau. The draft of the letter he proposed to send to the secretary of war would have appointed a regular officer to be:

> Adjutant and Inspector General of Militia of the United States, and in so far as existing laws will admit, charge him with the transaction . . . of all business pertaining to the Militia, to be conducted by a separate bureau . . . with instructions to take measures for promoting a uniform system of organization, drill, equipment, &c. &c. of the U. S. Militia, and to prepare a system of drill for Light troops, adapted for self-instruction, for distribution to the Militia of the several States. . . .

Because the opinion of Bates was unfavorable, Lincoln never sent the letter. However, establishment of the bureau would have had little effect: war was only weeks away.

Lincoln, like Buchanan, had done his best to avoid provoking the secessionists. He had been conciliatory in his inaugural speech, and had subsequently refrained from inflammatory statements. He had not ordered mobilization - not that there was much he could have done had he chosen to do so. He made no attempt to take back the forts and arsenals, which had been seized by the Southern states. The pressure to make a decision, especially about Fort Sumter, mounted. Lincoln sent Fox to Charleston, where he met with Anderson. Fox learned that the fort's food supply would last no longer than April 15.

Some Talk of Surrender

On March 24, Lincoln's close friend, Ward Lamon, also visited Charleston. While there he made careless and unauthorized remarks to the governor. His statements, together with newspaper reports, some exaggerated, others completely untrue, plus rumors that Anderson might blow up the fort upon leaving it, caused considerable excitement in the city. Beauregard heard from Pickens (based on what Lamon had said) that Anderson's command "would be transferred to another post in a few days." He wrote to Anderson, his former instructor, on March 26 to clarify the basis on which this could occur:

> Understanding that you are under the impression I intended under all circumstances to require of you a formal surrender or capitulation, I hasten to disabuse you, and to inform you that our countries not being at war, and wishing as far as possible to avoid the latter calamity, no such condition will be exacted of you, unless brought about as the natural result of hostilities. . . . we will be happy to see that you are provided with proper means of transportation out of this harbor for yourself and command, including baggage, private and

company property. All that will be required of you on account of the public rumors that have reached us will be your word of honor as an officer and a gentleman, that the fort, all public property therein, its armament, &c., shall remain in their proper condition, without any arrangements or preparations for their destruction or injury after you shall have left the fort. On our part no objection will be raised to your retiring with your side and company arms, and to your saluting your flag on lowering it. Hoping to have the pleasure of meeting you soon under more favorable circumstances, I remain, dear major, yours, very truly.

Anderson sent his reply that day, assuring Beauregard that he had not credited the rumors that the Confederate commander would insist on formal surrender, or that he planned to try to mine the fort upon leaving. He was, in fact, incensed at the latter implication. He wrote, with unreserved feeling,

You must pardon me for saying that I feel deeply hurt at the intimation in your letter about the conditions which will be exacted of me, and I must state most distinctly that if I can only be permitted to leave on the pledge you mention I shall never, so help me God, leave this fort alive.

Beauregard quickly replied to this on the same day, and brought the exchange to an amicable conclusion. He said he had no intention of "wounding, in any manner whatsoever, the feelings of so gallant an officer." He had only alluded to the pledge "on account of the high source from which the rumors spoken of appeared to come," and he regretted having referred to the subject. Anderson's response:

I hasten, in reply to your kind and satisfactory note of yesterday afternoon, just received, to express my gratification at its tenor. I only regret that rumors from any source made you, for one moment, have the slightest doubt as to the straight path of honor and duty, in which I trust, by the blessing of God, ever to be found. I am, dear general, yours sincerely.

During the final week of March, Foster continued to report on the situation from the engineering point of view. Here are several examples: "In this fort the closing of the exterior openings in the first tier of the gorge is completed. . . . The sixth and last temporary building on the parade is being demolished for fuel. Some lumber and one condemned gun carriage have already been burned." "The only work being done this morning in the surrounding batteries is on Cummings Point. . . . They appear to be repairing the damages caused by the wind and rain of yesterday and last night. More guns were landed." "The floating battery was moved from her moorings last night. . . . Upon the whole, appearances are very pacific in this harbor at present, and no hostile demonstrations are made, or great activity in preparation exhibited."

THE U. S. ARMY AND NAVY

Lincoln's complex political problem might well culminate in war: "the continuation of politics by other means." For that, the nation was ill prepared. Large standing armies were traditionally regarded in the United States as a threat to liberty. This was so despite the admonition of President George Washington to Congress that "Among the many interesting objects which will engage your attention, that of providing for the common defense will merit particular regard. To be prepared for war is one of the most effective means of preserving peace." President Thomas Jefferson saw the matter differently. He believed that a "well-disciplined militia" was all that the country needed. When the War of 1812 broke out, the U. S. Army consisted of 6,700 men. The Mexican War was declared in 1846 even though, after years of anticipation, the regular army had less than 7,900 men.

The country relied on the militia and on volunteers, with results that were not very satisfactory. In 1855, General Scott asked Congress to authorize additional forces, to consist of two cavalry and two infantry regiments, to deal with the increasingly warlike situation on the Plains. No action was taken. In 1858, a regiment of Texas mounted volunteers was accepted for the protection of immigrant and supply trains and for suppression of Indian hostilities. Then Congress voted to accept two regiments of volunteers, whose service was limited to eighteen months, to deal with disturbances involving the Mormons in Utah.

At the beginning of 1861, to protect the thirty-one million people living in three million square miles of territory, the United States had 16,367 soldiers, of whom 14,663 were present for duty. They were assigned to 198 companies, 183 of which were located on the western frontier. The rest garrisoned the forts and arsenals. The men of the Corps of Engineers were engaged in surveying railroad routes, constructing military roads, and maintaining coastal defenses. This meager force had been diminished, as we have seen, by the surrender of several regiments in Texas three weeks before the inauguration. Buchanan's policy of appeasement had been abetted by the Southerners in Congress, who actively endeavored to prevent the strengthening of the army.

In December of 1860, the U. S. Congress, where the chairman of the Senate Committee on Military Affairs was Jefferson Davis of Mississippi, had responded to the threat of secession by inquiring whether the U. S. Army could reduce its spending! The War Department consisted of eight bureaus: Ordnance, Quartermaster, Subsistence, Paymaster, Medical, Engineers, Topographical Engineers, and Adjutant General. These bureaus were asked by the secretary of war to examine their expenditures. Six simply said that they were already operating on minimum funds. Two departments, however, responded with specific ideas. On behalf of the Ordnance Corps, Captain William Maynadier told Congress what might be done:

I have no doubt that a change in the present organization of its personnel, and in the character and use of its arsenals, can be made which will attain the object of the committee's inquiry. There is a bill before the Senate, reported from its Military Committee, for the better organization of the general staff and the Engineer and Ordnance departments. . . we have too many arsenals used as places of construction. This has resulted, in a measure at least, from legislation seeking to distribute public expenditures instead of concentrating them at a few points, where they can be most effectively and economically applied. . . .

Maynadier proposed to have only four arsenals — one North, one South, one West and one on the Pacific Coast - for the "construction and preparation of ordnance supplies [and] to improve their quality." Several existing arsenals, he thought, "are no longer useful for military purposes." He told Senator Davis, through Secretary of War Floyd, "these are measures the execution of which, in their details, must be left to executive discretion." He went on to say, "A great source of our military expense lies in the vast number of posts or stations among which our troops are scattered. These posts should be as few as possible." He did not claim these ideas as original, but thought they were "a proper and legitimate answer to a call for views and opinions on a reduction of expenses . . . even if it tends only to show that legislation is not necessary for all reformation in this respect, and that much may be affected by, if left to, executive management."

The second response was from the adjutant-general, Colonel Cooper. What he wrote is instructive because it provides insight into what this senior officer, who became a Confederate general three months later, had on his mind in the weeks following South Carolina's secession. He pointed out that the amount of money disbursed annually by his office averaged $60,000, mostly for the recruiting service. "Any very great retrenchment, therefore, on so small an amount, is manifestly impracticable." Nevertheless, he suggested that the bounty of three months extra pay to soldiers who re-enlisted should be eliminated, because many pocketed the money and then deserted. Under an 1838 law, he explained, $1 was withheld from each soldier's monthly pay, to be returned when he was discharged. To further discourage desertion, he proposed to increase this to $2, perhaps even $3.

Cooper urged that the punishment of flogging be abolished, since it discouraged deserters from returning to duty. Instead, he suggested that they be disenfranchised "wherever Congress has the power of doing so." He pointed out that most new soldiers, who were mainly immigrants, were recruited in the Atlantic cities, and that it was costly to transport them west to the Indian country where most served. He did not indicate how many deserted, but said, "everything that may tend to suppress desertion will also tend to reduce the expenditures of the Army." Cooper also recommended the establishment of an Army savings institution. He did not, however, mention the subject of preparations for war.

Militias and Volunteers

While the U. S. War Department, in keeping with Buchanan's and later Lincoln's policies of avoiding provocation, did nothing, the governors of the Northern states were aware of the preparations being made in the South, and realized that if war came they would be called upon to furnish troops. The source of these troops would be the state militias and volunteer organizations. There were nominally 2,471,377 men on the militia rolls in the North - and 692,334 in the South. These figures, however, were based on records that had not been updated for years. The actual numbers were not known, but in all likelihood were much, much lower. Moreover, numbers are no indication of the quality of the forces, which was extremely poor.

An 1864 study of the condition of the Northern militia at the start of the war concluded that its numerous defects included: a lack of uniformity in arms and tactics, inadequate and obsolete equipment, little or no training, and incompetent officers. Most units seldom, if ever, engaged in target practice or conducted long marches. The occasional drills were more social than military in nature. In short, the militias of 1860 were not even close to being a fighting force. There were numerous volunteer companies. These, too, had a social component, in that they were very much like clubs. They typically met more often than the militias, but for holiday parades rather than for drill. Each company had a name, such as the Conshohocken Rifles or the Auburn Light Artillery, and a fancy uniform replete with gaudy colors and plumes, meant for show rather than for fighting.

In Massachusetts, a new governor took office on January 5 - one week after South Carolina occupied the Charleston forts and arsenal. In his inaugural address, John A. Andrew publicly stated his belief that war was imminent. On the same day, he secretly sent messengers to the other five New England governors, urging them to make preparations. There were 155,389 names on the rolls of the state militia, though only 5,593 were carried as active (and even these were slightly more that 5,000 men to which the active militia was limited by law). In the arsenal at Cambridge were seventy-one field pieces and about 10,000 muskets, 2,500 of which were Springfield rifles. The General Assembly, after debating revisions to the militia act, appropriated $100,000 for an emergency fund and $25,000 to equip 2,000 men. It also amended the law to permit the governor to raise as many companies and regiments as he thought the situation required.

The governor, in addition to corresponding with the state's Congressional delegation and the other New England governors, acted promptly to increase the strength, quality and readiness of the militia. On January 16, the state adjutant-general issued General Order No. 4:

> Events which have recently occurred . . . require that Massachusetts should be at all times ready to furnish her quota upon any requisition of the President of the United

States, to aid in the maintenance of the laws and the peace of the Union. His Excellency the Commander-in-Chief therefore orders — That the commanding officer of each company of volunteer militia . . . make strict inquiry, whether there are men in their commands, who from age, physical defect, business, or family causes, may be unable or indisposed to respond at once . . . that they be forthwith discharged; so that their places may be filled by men ready for any public exigency . . . no discharge, either of officer or private, shall be granted, unless for cause satisfactory to the Commander-in-Chief. If any companies have not the number of men allowed by law, the commanders of the same shall make proper exertions to have the vacancies filled, and the men properly drilled and uniformed . . .

The governor was also concerned about the defenses of Boston harbor. Fort Warren mounted one gun, Fort Winthrop none. In Fort Independence there were twenty guns, but they were mostly trained landward. If seized by an enemy, the fort would menace the city. Inside, the forts were a shambles. The whole coast of Massachusetts was open to attack from the sea. Existing guns had to be put in working order, more guns found, and the forts garrisoned by the militia.

In Michigan, by contrast, as a result of years of domestic tranquility, the militia was neglected and feeble, and was to remain so. At the beginning of 1861 it consisted of 238 companies enrolling a minimal 1,241 officers and men, on which the state spent $3,000 a year. The out-going governor, Moses Wismer, said in his final address that "This is no time of timid and vacillating councils, when the cry of treason and rebellion is ringing in our ears. . . . Michigan cannot recognize the right of a state to secede from the Union." The new governor, Austin Blair, added his views: "The Union must be preserved, and the laws must be enforced in all parts of it at whatever cost. . . . It is a question of war that the seceding states have to look in the face. . . . let us abide in the faith of our fathers — 'Liberty and Union, one and inseparable, now and forever.'"

Rhetoric notwithstanding, the state took no action to prepare for war. The legislature did voice its support for the Union by passing, on February 2, a joint resolution saying it would adhere to the Government of the United States, and pledging the support of the state's military manpower and natural resources. When the call came in April, however, Michigan supplied more than its quota with enthusiastic, albeit untrained and poorly equipped, citizen volunteers.

THE STATUS QUO AT FORT PICKENS

While the administration pondered what to do about Fort Sumter, Federal forces continued to hold Fort Pickens. Lieutenant Slemmer and his men remained in the fort, purchasing food and other supplies from sources on the mainland and remaining in touch with the Confederates, whose forces were slowly growing. On board the sailing frigate *U. S. S. Sabine* (1,726 tons), Captain H. A. Adams commanded the naval vessels anchored off shore, with the powerful screw-propelled *U. S. S. Brooklyn* (2,070 tons) as his main firepower.

On March 11, General Braxton Bragg took command of Confederate forces in Florida. An 1837 graduate of West Point, he had fought in the Seminole Wars and the Mexican War, distinguishing himself in the latter by his skillful handling of horse artillery. Bragg was known as a disciplinarian and strict observer of the army regulations. He promptly ordered work resumed on the batteries to which Slemmer had objected in February.

On March 12, Scott reversed the January instructions at Pensacola and sent orders to Captain Israel Vodges who was on board the *Brooklyn* with his men. "At the first favorable moment you will land your company, re-enforce Fort Pickens, and hold the same till further orders." On March 18, Vodges (who had not yet received Scott's orders) wrote to army headquarters, pointing out that the January decision not to land his company had effectively deprived him of the right of command. He said, "In the present critical state of affairs it is [important] to have a perfect unity of command." He had made arrangements with Captain Adams "to land a force of marines and sailors, which, with my company and the troops now in the fort, will raise the command to five hundred men." He noted the "great deficiency both of ammunition and supplies for so large a command," and pointed out that there was no place for all these men to sleep. He asked that requisitions be made for lumber, bunks, clothing and medicines, and that money be sent to buy supplies, but it was most important, he said, "all ambiguity as to my right to command should be at once removed."

On March 19, the day after Vodges's letter was sent to Washington, Slemmer dispatched his monthly report. He said that nothing had disturbed "the peaceable relations existing between the United States forces and those opposing us." But, he complained, "The contractor has refused to furnish fresh beef, alleging that he is without funds for purchasing cattle. The United States is indebted to him for three months' supply." If the War Department intended to land reenforcements, he said, subsistence stores should be sent. He also recounted a non-military event:

> On the morning of the 12th instant four negroes (runaways) came to the fort, entertaining the idea that we were placed here to protect them and grant them their freedom. I did what I could to teach them the contrary. In the afternoon I took them to Pensacola and delivered them to the city marshal, to be returned to their owners. The same night four more made their appearance. They were also turned over to the authorities next morning.

Slemmer then described an exchange of notes with General Bragg, who had written to him on March 13 saying that he was sending a Confederate officer "with the purpose of obtaining information necessary to enable me to understand our relative positions." Slemmer replied by sending him "a copy of the agreement entered into by Colonel Chase, Senator Mallory, and the War and Navy Departments." He added an important query: "Please let me know as soon as convenient whether you will consider the agreement binding on your part or not." Bragg answered the same day:

> In announcing to you my intention to conform strictly to the spirit of the agreement . . . I beg to suggest to you that the erection of a battery on Santa Rosa Island bearing directly on our navy-yard is, in my view, directly in conflict with the spirit of the agreement. The erection of the works on this side bearing on the channel cannot, I conceive, be taken as a menace against Fort Pickens, and the act seems to me fully justified as a means of defense, and especially so under the threats of the new administration.

Two days later Slemmer sent a note saying he had consulted with the commander of the naval squadron and that the assurances were perfectly satisfactory, but added: "Of the erection of the batteries on either side, I have only to say that our views on that point are directly opposite." He closed his report to army headquarters by saying that "there is mention of a notification being given as to the termination of the agreement on either side."

During this exchange Slemmer was unaware that on March 18 Bragg had issued General Orders No. 6:

> The commanding general learns with surprise and regret that some of our citizens are engaged in the business of furnishing supplies of fuel, water, and provisions to the armed vessels of the United States, now occupying a threatening position off the harbor. That no misunderstanding may exist on this subject, it is announced to all concerned that this traffic is strictly forbidden and that all such supplies which may be captured in transit to said vessels or to Fort Pickens will be confiscated.

On March 22, Adams wrote to Welles to report the difficulty he was having in procuring water, the distillation units on his ships being inadequate to the task. Bragg's order, he said, "besides other inconveniences, cuts off a daily supply of fresh bread. . . . Under these circumstances I have felt compelled to order the *Brooklyn* to Key West or Havana if necessary to procure suppliers." Sending the *Brooklyn* away was worrisome because it left him without his heaviest guns in case hostilities should break out. (The ship returned on March 31). On March 27, Welles ordered the bark *Release* to sail to Pensacola with supplies for the ships at the anchorage there. Adams had also been sending a supply ship to Mobile for provisions, but the Confederates now put a stop to that.

Slemmer reported on March 28: "Troops are being quietly concentrated and preparations made for an immediate movement should the present amicable agreement be interrupted." He thought the Confederates had about a thousand men, "and five thousand expected." Two batteries, each with four eight-inch columbiads, were aimed at the fort. If guns were placed on the island, he said, "Fort Pickens would be in almost as bad a position as Fort Sumter."

The really bad news he had to report was that, because of Bragg's order, "Fresh provisions are now denied us. If it is the intention of the Government to hold this fort . . . the stores and supplies necessary for the effective defense of the work [should] be forwarded immediately, [and] landed." The U. S. postal service was still in operation, as Lincoln had promised in his inaugural address that it would be. The mail of the army and navy had been moving freely, but Bragg decided on April 12 to tighten controls a bit. He told Adams, "As an act of prudence I deem it best to prevent any mail boat from Fort Pickens landing on this side. [We] will send all mail matter for your fleet and Fort Pickens daily."

Chapter 5

Fort Sumter Surrenders
April 1861

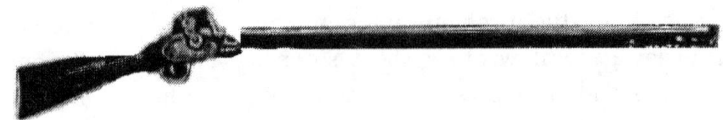

The Decision: Relieve Both Forts

Several things happened on March 28 that caused it to be a critical day in Lincoln's decision making. A Republican senator proposed a resolution that "in the opinion of the Senate, the true way to preserve the Union is to enforce the laws of the Union; that resistance to their enforcement, whether under the name of anti-coercion or any other name, is encouragement to disunion; and that it is the duty of the President of the United States to use all the means in his power to hold and protect the public property . . ." Lincoln held his first state dinner that evening, and took the cabinet members aside briefly to tell them the astonishing news that Scott was now advising the evacuation of both forts. The general had written to the president that:

> It is doubtful . . . whether the voluntary evacuation of Fort Sumter alone would have a decisive effect upon the States now wavering between adherence to the Union and secession. It is known, indeed, that it would be charged to necessity, and the holding of Fort Pickens would be adduced in support of that view. Our Southern friends, however, are clear that the evacuation of both the forts would instantly soothe and give confidence to the eight remaining slave-holding States, and render their cordial adherence to the Union perpetual . . . .

This view was inconsistent with Scott's orders of sixteen days earlier to Vodges, to land his company to reinforce the fort, which was understood to be safe from Confederate seizure. Moreover, since this opinion was not based on military considerations, but was rather a political judgment consonant with Seward's policy, the other cabinet members saw in it the hand of the secretary of state. Besides, it conflicted with the strong opposition of most Republican senators to evacuation.

The cabinet met at noon on March 29 to discuss the forts. The elements of the problem were by now well understood. The attorney general wrote a short summary of his conclusions and read it aloud. The president then asked the other members to do the same. What each said:

> Seward: The dispatch of an expedition to supply or reenforce Sumter would provoke an attack . . . I do not think it wise to provoke a civil war beginning at Charleston and in rescue of an untenable position. . . . I would at once, and at every cost, prepare for a war at Pensacola and Texas . . .
>
> Chase: If war is to be the consequence of an attempt to provision Fort Sumter, war will just as certainly result from the attempt to maintain possession of Fort Pickens. I am clearly in favor of maintaining Fort Pickens, and just as clearly in favor of provisioning Fort Sumter. . . .
>
> Welles: I concur in the proposition to send an armed force off Charleston, with supplies of provisions and reenforcements for the garrison at Fort Sumter . . . Fort Pickens and other places retained should be strengthened . . . the time has arrived when it is the duty of the Government to assert and maintain its authority.
>
> Smith: Believing that Fort Sumter cannot be successfully defended, I regard its evacuation as a necessity, and I advise that Major Anderson's command shall be unconditionally withdrawn. At the same time I would adopt the most vigorous measures for the defense of the other forts, and . . . blockade the Southern ports . . .

Blair: As regards General Scott, I have no confidence in his judgment . . . It is acknowledged to be possible to relieve Fort Sumter. It ought to be relieved without reference to Pickens or any other possession. . . .

Bates: . . . Fort Pickens and Key West ought to be reenforced and supplied . . . [and] a naval force kept upon the Southern coast sufficient to command it . . . As to Fort Sumter – I think the time is come either to evacuate or relieve it.

Two weeks previously the opinion of the cabinet had been against trying to provision Fort Sumter. Now the majority favored it, though not Seward, who nevertheless, contrary to Scott's view, advocated reinforcement of Fort Pickens. This was probably because, if that place were held, it would help limit the political and morale damage from the likely loss of Fort Sumter. In the South, the powers-that-be were adamantly committed to secession. In the North, the peace party was growing in strength even as the Republican leadership insisted on resolute action. The time for decision had indeed arrived, and the possible outcomes were clear. If an attempt were made to relieve Fort Sumter, the Confederates would start a civil war. If Fort Sumter were to be evacuated, the United States would have to recognize the Confederacy or start a civil war. It is not clear whether Lincoln now decided to make that attempt. On March 30, he sent notes to the secretaries of war and navy that "I desire that an expedition, to move by sea, be got ready to sail as early as the 6th of April . . ." Despite his use of the singular word "expedition," he apparently wanted to be prepared to send expeditions to both forts. The two efforts were, in fact, organized concurrently but secretly.

The next day Seward, in need of a new military adviser since Scott was out of favor, brought to the White House his friend, Captain Montgomery C. Meigs, a forty-four-year-old engineer officer who had recently returned from Fort Jefferson, Florida and was assigned to construction of the new dome of the Capitol. He told the president that Meigs was just the man to conduct the Fort Pickens expedition, and Lincoln agreed. Seward then went to see Scott and told him of the president's decision, the general's advice notwithstanding, to reinforce Fort Pickens. After Seward left,

Scott's assistant, Lieutenant Colonel Erasmus D. Keyes, showed maps of the Pensacola area to the general and told him that it would be nearly impossible to get heavy guns across the beach to the fort. [More than enough guns were already mounted in the fort].

Scott sent Keyes to describe the problem to Seward, who told Keyes to find Meigs, devise a plan, and bring it to the White House at 3:00 P.M. that day, Easter Sunday, March 31. Meigs and Keyes hastily prepared a plan and presented it to the president and the secretary. Meigs insisted that absolute secrecy was necessary because the Confederates would attack Fort Pickens if they knew reinforcements were coming. This meant not telling the war and navy departments, where there were still many Southern sympathizers (though that fact hardly explains why the department secretaries, Cameron and Welles, were not told). Lincoln agreed to this arrangement and authorized, as part of the secrecy, $10,000 for Meigs from the "secret service" fund. He delegated the whole Fort Pickens operation to Seward, an inappropriate duty for the secretary of state, aside from the confusion that resulted from this unsound division of responsibility.

Seward in turn relied on Meigs and Keyes, and Meigs chose his friend, Lieutenant David D. Porter, as naval commander, without the knowledge of the secretary of the navy. Welles, meanwhile, unaware of the Pensacola mission, was organizing a squadron for Charleston, which he assumed was where the expedition was to go. This awkward, uncoordinated arrangement may have resulted from Lincoln's lack of executive experience, or from the excruciating pressure of dealing with the secession crisis, or from the strain placed on him by a legion of office seekers. In any case, his endeavors to keep this movement absolutely secret proved to be a serious mistake. The Pickens and Sumter groups, neither knowing about the other's assignment, competed to collect the necessary ships, men, weapons and supplies from the scarce resources available.

There were only three warships on the Atlantic coast: two screw-propelled steamers, the *U. S. S. Pawnee* (1,289 tons) and the

U. S. S. *Pocahontas* (694 tons), at Washington and Norfolk, and the eleven-gun side-wheeler *U. S. S. Powhatan* (2,415 tons) in New York, her engines torn down for repairs. In preparation for the Fort Pickens effort, Lincoln issued a number of orders on April 1. To Captain Andrew H. Foote, Commandant of the Brooklyn Navy Yard, he wrote a note: "You will fit out the Powhatan without delay. Lieutenant Porter will relieve Captain Mercer in command of her. She is bound on secret service, and you will under no circumstances communicate to the Navy Department the fact that she is fitting out." Foote was dumb-founded: Welles had just ordered him to prepare the *Powhatan* for use by Fox's expedition. Lincoln also wrote to Lieutenant Porter: "You will proceed to New York, and with the least possible delay assume command of any naval steamer available. Proceed to Pensacola Harbor, and at any cost or risk prevent any expedition from the mainland reaching Fort Pickens or Santa Rosa [Island]. . . . This order, its object, and your destination will be communicated to no person whatever until you reach the harbor of Pensacola."

The confusion was compounded when Welles wrote to Captain Samuel Mercer, commanding the *Powhatan*, on April 5, saying that

> Powhatan, Pawnee, Pocahontas and Harriet Lane will compose a naval force under your command . . . The primary object of the expedition is to provision Fort Sumter . . . Should the authorities at Charleston, however, refuse to permit or attempt to prevent the vessel or vessels having supplies on board from entering the harbor . . . you will protect the transports or boats of the expedition in the object of their mission . . . The expedition has been intrusted to Capt. G. V. Fox, with whom you will put yourself in communication, and co-operate with him . . . You will leave New York with the Powhatan in time to be off Charleston Bar, ten miles distant from and due east of the light-house, on the morning of the 11th . . .

In New York, Captain Foote faced conflicting orders: from Lincoln to give the Powhatan to Porter (and Meigs) and from Welles to give it to Fox (and Mercer). After a heated discussion between Foote and Porter, a telegram was sent to Seward who, reluctantly, informed the president of the problem. Lincoln told Seward to order Porter to turn the ship over to Fox for the Fort Sumter task force. Seward sent the order, but signed his name rather than Lincoln's. Since Porter's original order was from the president, with instructions to communicate "to no person whatever," he refused to obey the order from Seward and the Powhatan steamed on to Pensacola - where, as it turned out, it was not needed.

With the rising tempo of military activity, Lincoln felt the need to be regularly informed, and wrote to Scott in his usual polite but explicit way: "Would it impose too much labor on General Scott to make short, comprehensive daily reports to me of what occurs in his Department, including movements by himself, and under his orders, and the receipt of intelligence? If not I will thank him to do so. Your Obedient Servant." Lincoln certainly needed to improve his command arrangements.

At this crucial moment Seward came to the White House, and calmly presented a memorandum suggesting that Lincoln delegate his presidential authority to the secretary of state, who would then conduct the government on the president's behalf. Seward complained that the country had neither a domestic nor a foreign policy, and again opposed the re-supply of Fort Sumter. Then he proposed a far-fetched scheme: to bring the cotton states back into the Union by precipitating a foreign war and invoking their patriotism (and possibly their fear of having the Union, in a war with Spain, seize Cuba and free the slaves there). He wrote:

> I would demand explanations from Spain and France, categorically, at once. I would seek explanations from Great Britain and Russia, and send agents into Canada, Mexico, and Central America, to rouse a vigorous continental spirit of independence . . . against European intervention. And if satisfactory explanations are not received from Spain and France, would convene Congress and declare war against them.

Lincoln wrote a short, tactful note in which he clearly stated the administration's policies, citing his inaugural address and the instructions that he and Seward had agreed to send to the ambassadors. Though Lincoln never sent this note, he probably discussed its contents with Seward. In any case, from then on it was evident to Seward that not he, but Lincoln, was leading the nation. The extent to which Seward's policy of appeasement toward the South was unsuccessful would become clear in less than two weeks.

The Fort Pickens Operation

As part of the relief of Fort Pickens, an order from Scott, dated April 1 and approved by Lincoln the next day, directed Colonel Harvey Brown of the Second U. S. Artillery, a sixty-five-year-old graduate of West Point in 1818, to lead the army effort:

> You have been designated to take command of an expedition to re-enforce and hold Fort Pickens, in the harbor of Pensacola [and] assume command of all the land forces of the United States within . . . Florida. You will proceed to New York, where steam transportation for four companies will be engaged . . . Captain Meigs will accompany you as engineer . . . The object and destination of this expedition will be communicated to no one to whom it is not already known. . . . Should a shot be fired at you, you will defend yourself and your expedition at whatever hazard, and, if needful for such defense, inflict upon the assailants all the damage in your power within the range of your guns. . . . other steamers will follow that on which you embark, to carry re-enforcements, supplies, and provisions for the garrison of Fort Pickens for six months. . . You will make Fort Jefferson your main depot and base of operations.

The transport *Atlantic*, a steamship built under contract to be available for service in case of war, was chartered by Meigs for $2,000 a day. Newspaper reporters observed the activity on the docks, but were unable to find out what was happening or where the ships might be going. When 300 horses were put aboard, they concluded that the destination was neither Fort Sumter nor Fort Pickens, since horses would be of no use at either place: perhaps Texas, they thought. The *Atlantic* left New York with 600 troops at 3:30 A.M. on April 7, fourteen hours after the *Powhatan* sailed. It was followed on April 8 by the *Illinois*, carrying supplies.

Meigs, addressing the man who was driving the Pensacola operation, but the wrong man for his purposes, told Seward that "This is the beginning of the war which every statesman and soldier has foreseen since the passage of the South Carolina ordinance of secession. You will find the Army and the Navy clogged at the head with men, excellent patriotic men, men who were soldiers and sailors forty years ago, but who now merely keep active men out of the places in which they could serve the country. . . . Let us be supported; we go to serve our country, and our country should not neglect us or leave us to be strangled in tape, however red."

The *Atlantic* arrived at the tip of Florida on April 12, and Brown advised the general-in-chief: "We go into Key West for two or three hours on important duty . . . and from thence to Fort Jefferson for some indispensable articles, where we shall be delayed only a short time." From his headquarters on board the ship he asked Captain Hunt at Fort Taylor to survey the island of Key West with a view to erecting field works to prevent a hostile landing. To Major Arnold, commanding at Fort Jefferson, he sent instructions to construct earthen batteries to protect the six adjacent keys and to defend the Dry Tortugas harbor. Brown, apparently lacking any sense of urgency, remained at Key West for three days, then went to Fort Jefferson.

Meanwhile, on April 1, Vodges asked Adams to make boats available to him to land his company. He declined. Adams was reluctant to violate the agreement with the Confederates and unwilling to recognize the general-in-chief as "proper authority." Instead he wrote to Welles saying:

> The instructions from General Scott to Captain Vodges are of an old date (March 12) and may have been given without a full knowledge of the condition of affairs here. Such a step is too important to be taken without the clearest orders from proper authority. It would most certainly be viewed as a hostile act, and would be resisted to the utmost. . . . while I cannot take on myself on such insufficient authority as

General Scott's order the fearful responsibility of an act which seems to render civil war inevitable, I am ready at all times to carry out whatever orders I may receive from the honorable Secretary of the Navy. . . . please send me instructions as soon as possible, that I may be relieved from a painful embarrassment.

Exasperated by this message from Adams, Welles replied with instructions on April 6, sending naval Captain John L. Worden to carry them to Pensacola. Worden traveled by way of Richmond and the Southern railroads. Approaching Atlanta on a train full of Southern soldiers, he decided to destroy the copy he was carrying. He arrived at Pensacola late on April 10, but was unable to get out to the Sabine because of strong winds and because he had to get a pass from Bragg. On April 12, he delivered an oral version of the instructions to Adams. (Worden then started back to Washington, but was arrested by the Confederate authorities in Montgomery, and held as a prisoner of war). The original message from Welles to Adams read:

> The [Navy] Department regrets that you did not comply with the request of Captain Vodges to carry into effect the orders of General Scott sent out by the Crusader under the orders of the Department. You will immediately on the first favorable opportunity after receipt of this order afford every facility to Captain Vodges by boats and other means to land the troops under his command. . . .

On April 14, Adams reported to Welles who, in view of the disaster at Fort Sumter, must have been delighted when he received the good news:

> I have the honor to inform you that immediately on the receipt of your order by Lieutenant Worden, on the 12th instant, I prepared to re-enforce Fort Pickens. It was successfully performed, on the same night, by landing the troops under Captain Vodges, and the marines of the squadron under Lieutenant [John C.] Cash. No opposition was made, nor do I believe the movement was known on shore until it was accomplished. . . . The *Brooklyn* . . . and the

Wyandotte . . . were very skillfully managed. They carried the landing party to the designated spot with accuracy in spite of the darkness of the night, and not having the light-house to guide them.

Thus at dawn on April 13, a few hours before Fort Sumter was surrendered, Vodges reported to Adams that "Here we are all safe. The enemy evidently did not deem it prudent to attack us." In addition to Vodges's 200 soldiers, Adams sent ashore 250 marines and sailors. Vodges asked Adams to send him "four barrels of whisky, three pieces of flannel, as many axes and shovels as you can spare, and some canvas." Brown, after lingering at Key West and the Dry Tortugas, arrived at Pensacola on April 17 and landed his 600 troops. Just as the soldiers had done, supplies, adequate for six months, went ashore through the surf. Including the men who had occupied the fort in January, there were now more than 1,100 men inside Fort Pickens, though the marines and sailors were soon returned to the fleet. Brown sent Vodges to see Bragg, who said that Brown's reinforcement of Fort Pickens had broken the truce. Sentiment in the South favored seizing the fort but Bragg, fearing the high cost of an attack, did not attempt to take it. It remained in Union hands throughout the war, denying to the Confederacy the use of Pensacola harbor.

THE FORT SUMTER OPERATION

Lincoln learned through Welles on April 6 that the order for Vodges to land troops at Fort Pickens had not been carried out. Possession of that fort could not be counted on to balance the probable loss of Fort Sumter. Sumter was of no military importance, so what happened there would be of political significance only. Fifteen months later Lincoln stated the predicament as he then remembered it:

> To now reinforce Fort Pickens before a crisis would be reached at Fort Sumter was impossible — rendered so by the near exhaustion of provisions in the latter-named fort. In precaution against such a conjuncture, the government had, a few days before, commenced preparing an expedition as well

adapted as might be to relieve Fort Sumter, which expedition was intended to be ultimately used, or not, according to the circumstances. The strongest anticipated case for using it was now presented, and it was resolved to send it forward.

The surrender of Fort Sumter, whether from starvation or from attack, must now have appeared inevitable to Lincoln. It was at the very last minute - too late, as events demonstrated - that he resolved on re-supplying the garrison in Charleston harbor. It is unclear what could be gained by that other than further delay in finally resolving the dispute. More likely Lincoln was simply allowing the Confederates to initiate war by provoking them into attacking the fort. It was certainly unrealistic to think that if the Confederates did not try to prevent the re-supply, the expedition would land only food and supplies while, if they did interfere, it would also land troops and ammunition. Fox would presumably have to make this decision while he was trying to unload the ship's cargo under fire, in darkness! Surely the Confederates would interfere: if they had wished to allow the men in the fort to have food, they would have continued to permit Anderson to purchase it locally. They did not do that, and they were not going to stand idly by and watch the Federals re-supply the fort. One can only believe, given the well-stated position of Davis that the Union was broken insofar as the seven seceded states were concerned, and the military readiness of the Confederates, that Lincoln expected them to fight.

In New York, Fox collected what resources he could to put his plan into effect. The five-gun revenue cutter *Harriet Lane* and the transport steamer *Baltic* were there. So was (as he thought) the *Powhatan*, and the three steam tugs that he had been able, with great difficulty, to charter: the *Freeborn*, the *Yankee* and the *Uncle Ben*. Of the other two warships, the *Pocahontas* was at Norfolk and the *Pawnee* at Washington. The flotilla sailed from its ports between April 8 and 10. The *Baltic* was carrying 200 recruits and enough provisions for a year, and Fox was counting on *Powhatan*'s boats to carry the supplies to the Fort Sumter dock. He did not learn that the warship had been taken from him until well after he arrived off Charleston. Eleven vessels were now on their way: three to Fort Pickens and eight to Fort Sumter. The *Brooklyn* was ordered, again at the last minute, to follow and support Fox's fleet.

Just before the ships sailed, a state department clerk, Robert S. Chew, carrying out instructions given to him by Lincoln on April 6, headed for Charleston to inform Pickens that provisions, but not reinforcements, were being sent. Lincoln reasoned, it would seem, that an attack on food for hungry men would make the Southerners appear to be in the wrong, and in any event it would be they who were the aggressors, a point he had made in his inaugural address. Chew read the message to Pickens on the evening of April 8:

> I am directed by the President of the United States to notify you to expect an attempt will be made to supply Fort Sumter with provisions only; and that, if such attempt be not resisted, no effort to throw in men, arms, or ammunition will be made, without further notice, or in case of an attack upon the fort.

Chew immediately telegraphed the president to tell him that he gave a copy to Pickens, who submitted it to Beauregard as the officer in charge of military operations in Charleston.

On the same day in Washington, Seward informed the three commissioners that Fort Sumter would not, after all, be abandoned, and that the United States would not recognize the Confederate government. The point had now been reached at which any practical or moral consideration would prevent the secessionists from acting. They knew from Seward, from the president's notice to Pickens, and from newspaper accounts, that an attempt to reinforce Fort Sumter was about to be made. The continued presence of the flag of the United States over the fort offended the sovereignty of the Confederate States, and their only solution was to take it down.

Inside Fort Sumter, Anderson was both anxious and annoyed. Incredibly, he had not heard anything from Washington since February 23, and nothing at all from Secretary of War Cameron. Food supplies were running low for the 114 men still in the fort: ten officers, sixty-eight soldiers and thirty-six laborers. Anderson tried to send the workmen away, but his repeated attempts to get permission to do so from the Confederates were unsuccessful:

Beauregard's orders were to allow no one to leave unless everyone left.

About 3:00 P.M. on April 3, a battery on Morris Island suddenly opened fire on a small schooner flying the American flag that appeared out of the fog in the Main Ship Channel. Anderson, angry that the flag was again being fired upon, doubted that this little vessel could have been sent with supplies for the fort. Since his guns were unable to reach the Confederate battery that was firing, he agonized over whether to fire on Fort Moultrie instead. His officers were sharply divided, five for retaliating, three for going to Morris Island for an explanation. He decided not to fire, and two of his officers rowed across to Morris Island. There the Confederate officer in charge, Lieutenant Colonel DeSaussure, said he was simply obeying orders to prevent any vessel under the U. S. flag from entering the harbor.

The Union officers rowed out to the vessel, which proved to be the 180-ton schooner *Rhoda H. Shannon.* It had gotten lost in fog while carrying a cargo of ice from Boston to Savannah. The captain, Joseph Marts, whose knowledge of navigation was limited, thought he had seen Tybee lighthouse and that he was off Savannah. He had shown the flag as a signal for a pilot, but when none came he took it down and tried to enter the harbor on his own. As he passed Morris Island, shots were fired across his bow. Thinking they wanted him to show his colors, he raised the U. S. flag to the peak. After a shot went through his main sail, he headed seaward and anchored in the Swash Channel.

The officers returned to Cummings Point, where DeSaussure told them that the schooner would not be molested if it entered the harbor, but Marts weighed anchor and took his cargo to sea. Anderson sent a protest to Pickens: "I regret very much that there were no boats to warn her, or to give her instructions." Pickens apologized, saying that there had in fact been a guard boat for that purpose, but that its captain had left the station and would be dismissed. If Anderson had replied to the Confederate fire on the schooner, civil war might have begun over a load of ice.

BEAUREGARD STOPS ALL SUPPLIES

Before this incident, on April 1, Anderson wrote to Colonel Lorenzo Thomas, who had replaced Cooper as adjutant general. He said:

> Everything is still and quiet, as far as we can see, around us. The South Carolina Secretary of State has not sent the authority, asked for yesterday, to enable me to send off the discharged laborers. Having been in daily expectation, since the return of Colonel Lamon to Washington, of receiving orders to vacate this post, I have kept these men here as long as I could; but now . . . I am compelled, in consequence of the small supply of provisions on hand, to discharge them. . . . the supply of provisions . . . would, had the issues been limited to my command, have lasted for a longer period . . . I told Mr. Fox that if I placed the command on short allowance I could make the provisions last until after the 10th of this month; but as I have received no instructions from the Department that it was desirable I should do so, it has not been done. If the government permits me to send off the laborers we will have rations enough to last us about one week longer.

Incredible as it may seem, the first word received by Anderson from the Lincoln administration was in a letter from Secretary of War Cameron dated April 4, a month after the inauguration. Motivated by Anderson's news, he told him, in a singular understatement, that his letter "occasions some anxiety to the President." He continued:

> [The president] had supposed you could hold out until the 15th instant without any great inconvenience; and had prepared an expedition to relieve you before that period. Hoping still that you will be able to sustain yourself till the 11th or 12th instant, the expedition will go forward; and, finding your flag flying, will attempt to provision you, and, in case the effort is resisted, will endeavor also to reinforce you. You will therefore hold out, if possible, till the arrival of the expedition. It is not, however, the intention of the President to subject your command to any danger or hardship beyond

what, in your judgment, would be usual in military life. . . . Whenever, if at all, in your judgment, to save yourself and command, a capitulation becomes necessary, you are authorized to make it.

Anderson was as stunned by this as Lincoln had been by his statement about how long his provisions would last. Like Pickens, he had received the impression from Lamon that Lincoln intended to evacuate the fort. He desperately replied to Cameron that the scheme would fail:

> . . . a movement made now, when the South has been erroneously informed that none such will be attempted, would produce most disastrous results throughout our country. It is, of course, now too late for me to give any advice in reference to the proposed scheme of Captain Fox. I fear that its results cannot fail to be disastrous to all concerned. Even with his boat at our walls the loss of life . . . in unloading her will more than pay for the good to be accomplished by the expedition . . . We have not oil enough to keep a light in the lantern for one night. The boats will have, therefore, to rely at night entirely upon other marks. I ought to have been informed that this expedition was to come. . . .

Cameron never received this letter. The situation had begun to deteriorate rapidly on April 7, when Beauregard notified Anderson that:

> In compliance with orders from the Confederate Government at Montgomery, I have the honor to inform you that, in consequence of the delays and apparent vacillations of the United States Government at Washington relative to the evacuation of Fort Sumter, no further communications for the purposes of supply with this city from the fort and with the fort from this city will be permitted. . . . The mails, however, will continue to be transmitted. . .

The next day Beauregard changed that when he notified Anderson "that from and after this day no mails will be allowed to go to or come from Fort Sumter." The day after that Anderson was told that, because the Confederates suspected Fox of having discussed more with Anderson during his visit than they were willing to allow,

> [recent public letters] were sent to the Confederate Government at Montgomery, in return for the treachery of Mr. Fox, who has been reported to have violated his word given to Governor Pickens before visiting Fort Sumter.

Anderson now knew that his official dispatches had been read (by Pickens and Beauregard, in fact, as well was by officials in Montgomery). Communication with the U. S. Government was now cut off, but Anderson continued to prepare his daily reports. On April 11, on the eve of the bombardment, he wrote No. 100 to Thomas:

> These people are expecting the arrival of a hostile force, and they are making most judicious arrangements to prevent the landing of any supplies at this fort. . . . the guard boats, consisting, as far as we could observe, of seven steamers and four schooners . . . We see the iron floating battery this morning at the west end of Sullivan's Island, admirably placed for pouring a murderous fire upon any vessel attempting to lay alongside of our left flank . . . had they been in possession of the information contained in your letter of the 4th instant, they could not have made better arrangements . . . The least dangerous course would be for . . . the supply vessel, after passing Cummings Point, to run to our wharf and round to, alongside the west face of it. . . . It would be hot work unloading her, but not so bad as the other place. . . . The officers and men, thank God, are in pretty good health; and, although feeling aware of the danger of their position, have greater anxiety about the fate of those whom they expect to come to their succor than they entertain for themselves.

THE CONFEDERATES OPEN FIRE

This anxiety for the relief force stemmed from new artillery emplacements by the Confederates. The floating battery, with its four heavy guns, was well protected by a stone breakwater. Next to it was a potent nine-inch Dalgren gun. A Blakely rifled cannon, a gift from Charles K. Prioleau of the Fraser company's branch in Liverpool, which arrived from England on April 8, was mounted on Cummings Point. This highly accurate weapon greatly increased the firepower against the southwest side of the fort, where the landing place was located. The men of the garrison had no way to warn the coming ships of the danger. The Confederates, who by now had assembled some 6,000 troops in the Charleston area, had a total of thirty guns and eighteen mortars bearing on the fort or the channels. The mortars were to be especially effective because they would be firing against a fixed target at a known range, and their shells would drop inside the fort. Beauregard was prepared to begin the attack as soon as he received a shipment of gunpowder, which was due to arrive from Augusta late on April 11. On April 10, after a debate in the Confederate cabinet over whether to attack the fort now or wait for the supply ships to arrive, Secretary of War Walker told Beauregard to be ready to bombard the fort if Anderson refused to surrender immediately.

At 3:30 P.M. on April 11 a small boat arrived at the fort carrying three of Beauregard's aides-de-camp, Colonel James Chesnut, Jr., Captain Stephen D. Lee, and Lieutenant Colonel A. R. Chisolm. They bore a letter from the general saying that the Confederacy could wait no longer for "actual possession of a fortification commanding the entrance to one of our harbors." It continued:

> I am ordered by the Government of the Confederate States to demand the evacuation of Fort Sumter. . . . All proper facilities for the removal of yourself and your command, together with company arms and property, to any post in the United States which you may select. The flag which you have upheld for so long and with so much fortitude, under the most trying circumstances, may be saluted by you on taking it down. Colonel Chesnut and Captain Lee will, for a reasonable time, await your answer.

Anderson met in council with his officers, who unanimously rejected this generous offer. The major then wrote out his reply and handed it to one of Beauregard's aides:

> General: I have the honor to acknowledge the receipt of your communication demanding the evacuation of this fort, and to say, in reply thereto, that it is a demand with which I regret that my sense of honor, and of my obligation to my Government, prevent my compliance. Thanking you for the fair, manly, and courteous terms proposed, and for the high compliment paid me, I am, general, very respectfully, your obedient servant,
>
> Robert Anderson
> Major, First Artillery, Commanding

One of the Confederates later recorded that, as they left, Anderson said: "I will await the first shot, and if you do not batter us to pieces, we shall be starved out in a few days." The delegation returned to Beauregard, who telegraphed to the secretary of war for final instructions. Walker replied that, unless Anderson would state the time when he would evacuate, Beauregard should "reduce the fort as your judgment decides to be most practicable."

At 12:45 A.M. on the fateful April 12, the three officers, accompanied by a fourth man, Roger A. Pryor of Virginia, returned to the fort. They presented another letter from Beauregard:

> If you will state the time at which you will evacuate Fort Sumter, and agree that in the mean time you will not use your guns against us unless ours shall be employed against Fort Sumter, we will abstain from opening fire upon you. Colonel Chesnut and Captain Lee are authorized by me to enter into such an agreement with you.

Anderson, knowing he had food for only two more days, again discussed the matter with his officers. He replied that "I will, if provided with the proper and necessary means of transportation, evacuate Fort Sumter by noon on the 15th instant . . . should I not receive prior to that time controlling instructions from my Government or additional supplies." Dismayed by Anderson's conditional answer, the Confederate officers discussed the situation privately, then handed him a penciled note at 3:20 A.M. It said: "By authority of Brigadier-General Beauregard, commanding the provisional forces of the Confederate States, we have the honor to notify you that he will open the fire of his batteries on Fort Sumter in one hour from this time." Anderson was warned. There was little he could do except awaken the men.

The four officers were rowed to Fort Johnson. There, Captain George S. James offered the honor of firing the opening shot to Pryor. He declined, saying "I could not fire the first gun of the war." The officers then left, headed for Fort Moultrie. While they were on the water, at 4:30 A.M., James had his men fire a ten-inch mortar as a signal shot. Shortly thereafter the first directed shot was fired from Morris Island by Edmund Ruffin, a Virginian and an ardent, long-time advocate of secession, starting a sustained bombardment by the forty-eight guns of the shore batteries. Some of Fort Sumter's fifty-nine guns began to return the fire at 7:00 A.M., but even with the help of the workmen still inside the fort there were not nearly enough men to serve them.

Fox's squadron, meanwhile, each ship sailing independently, was slowed by a gale on the way south. The *Harriet Lane* was already at the rendezvous ten miles east of Charleston lighthouse when the *Baltic*, carrying the supplies, arrived at 3:00 A. M., just before the firing began, followed by the *Pawnee* at 6:00 A.M. The *Powhatan*, of course, which Fox still mistakenly thought was part of his fleet, was on its way to Pensacola. Nor were the tugboats there, and none of them ever arrived. One was driven by the storm into Wilmington and another into Savannah. The third never left New York. (The *Pocahontas*, which had been the last to sail, did not reach the area until 2:00 P.M. on April 13). The *Baltic* and the *Harriet Lane* could do nothing but wait in the rain and heavy seas, out of range of the shore guns.

Fox went aboard the *Pawnee* and asked the captain to approach the bar along with the *Baltic*, but the officer refused. His orders, he said, were to wait for instructions from the captain of the *Powhatan* when it arrived. He, like Fox, did not know that that ship was on its way to Pensacola. In his planning, the optimistic Fox seems not to have allowed for the difficulty ships would have in approaching the fort as a result of the Confederates having removed the buoys marking the channels and the bar. Now the problem was compounded by bad weather, and a warship's captain who was unwilling to take the initiative in starting a war.

The *Baltic* and the *Harriet Lane* then approached the bar, heard the firing, and saw the clouds of smoke drifting across the harbor entrance. Since it was obvious that an effort to re-supply peaceably was not possible, Fox's alternative orders were to run the batteries and reinforce as well as re-supply the fort. The captain of the *Pawnee*, seeing that war had begun, offered to go to the rescue of the garrison. Now it was Fox who decided not to take the risk, but to wait instead for the *Powhatan* and the tugs. With these he would attempt to land men and supplies after dark. But the ships he expected never came.

As the bombardment continued, the Confederates were concerned that the Federals would land a force on Morris Island. Colonel Louis T. Wigfall sent a message to Beauregard:

> . . . we greatly need infantry, to defend the batteries from assault. Four large steamers are plainly in view, and standing off the bar all day. Unanimous opinion [of officers] that a landing will be attempted, and fears that some of the batteries will be taken, unless supported. . . . Should you not be here personally to direct?

Landing troops other than at Fort Sumter was not part of the U. S. Army's plan, and Beauregard's responsibilities were too great to allow him to go to Morris Island. His concern was that, since there was no way to know how long the bombardment would have to continue, his guns might run out of ammunition. He ordered DeSaussure, starting at noon, to "double the interval between the firing of the shells; that is, four minutes instead of two during the day, and twenty minutes instead of ten during the night. The action of your mortar batteries in that respect will guide the others elsewhere."

Foster described the events inside the fort that Friday, April 12:

> All the officers and soldiers of Major Anderson's command were divided into three reliefs, of two hours each, for the

> service of the guns. . . . Of the forty-three workmen constituting the Engineer force in the fort nearly all volunteered to serve as cannoneers, or to carry shot and cartridge to the guns. . . . At 1 o'clock two United States men-of-war were seen off the bar, and soon after a third appeared. The fire of the batteries continued steadily until dark. The effect of the fire was not very good, owing to the insufficient caliber of the guns for the long range. . . . One or two shots were thrown at the hulk which had been anchored in the channel . . . to be [set afire] at night if our fleet should attempt to come in.

The barracks caught fire three times during the day, but each time the flames were put out by water from a pump. "Three of the iron cisterns over the hallways were destroyed by shots during the day, and the quarters below deluged by their contents of water, aiding in preventing the extension of the fire." For several hours after the beginning of the bombardment "a large proportion of their shot missed the fort," and Confederate direct fire never penetrated the walls. Foster, however, was impressed by the effect of the vertical fire:

> This was so well directed and so well sustained, that from the seventeen mortars engaged in firing 10-inch shells, one-half of the shells came within or exploded above the parapet of the fort, and only about ten buried themselves in the soft earth of the parade without exploding. In consequence of this precision of vertical fire, Major Anderson decided not to man the upper tier of guns, as by doing so the loss of men . . . must have been great. . . .The vertical fire . . . prevented the working of the upper tier of guns, which were the only really effective guns in the fort.

ANDERSON AGREES TO EVACUATE

The night was stormy, with high wind and tide. The firing slackened after dark to every ten or fifteen minutes. Anderson's men went to work, using the six needles they had, sewing cartridge bags out of extra clothing, sheets and coarse paper. When the second day of the bombardment dawned on April 13, the soldiers gazed at the ships still off the bar and wondered why they were there. (Several merchant ships had arrived, giving the appearance to those on shore of a large fleet). The last of the rice was cooked and served with pork, of which there was still a small supply. With daylight the fire of the Confederates became more rapid, their aim was better than on the first day, and many of their rounds were hot shot. After a rainstorm, the officers' quarters caught fire, and it was impossible to extinguish the flames. The fire spread quickly toward the nearby magazine, which held 275 barrels of powder. About fifty barrels were taken to the casements (and were later thrown into the harbor) before the fire became too dangerous to continue removing the powder. The copper door of the magazine was closed and dirt piled over it.

By noon the barracks were again in flames. The heat and smoke were stifling. When the fire reached the grenades that were stored in the stair towers, they exploded. The Confederates, seeing that the whole place seemed to be ablaze, began cheering for the men in the fort, expecting a white flag at any minute. Bits of brick, wood and other debris were flying everywhere, causing some wounds. Anderson kept his crews at the guns, but restricted firing to every ten minutes because of the shortage of cartridges. Then a Confederate shot cut the flag staff, the flag falling into material burning on the parade, from which a lieutenant saved it. Before it could be raised again on a spar rigged to the parapet, former Texas senator and now Colonel Wigfall came to the fort in a small boat from Morris Island. He asked a lieutenant if this meant that they desired to stop fighting. No, said the officer, the flag was flying, and pointed to where it had been put up again.

Anderson arrived and talked with Wigfall, who had come on his own, without authority. Anderson, not knowing this, told him he would evacuate the fort now, instead of on April 15, on the same terms that Beauregard had proposed two days ago. About 1:30 P.M. the flag was taken down and replaced by a sheet. Observing that the fort was being consumed by flames and that the flag was down, and unaware of Wigfall's visit, Chesnut, Lee, Pryor, and Colonel William P. Miles came to ask Anderson if he wanted assistance. Anderson said he did not, but told them that Wigfall had just left and that he had agreed to surrender. Astounded, they explained that Wigfall represented no one but himself. In that case, Anderson said, the action would continue.

The four Southerners went into the infirmary to discuss the situation. Pryor, in need of a stiff drink, picked up a bottle of what he thought was whiskey and took a swig. It proved to be potassium iodide. Surgeon Samuel W. Crawford, realizing that Pryor had poisoned himself, took him out on the parade ground and used a stomach pump on him. Desperate as was the fort's situation, some of the U. S. officers saw humor in Pryor's plight and informed the doctor that they did not think it was his duty to interfere with a Confederate officer who wished to poison himself. The doctor replied that the medicine was U. S. property for which he was responsible, and he could not permit it to be carried away. Meanwhile, the other three Confederates had resumed the parley with Anderson and persuaded him not to continue the battle. At 2:20 P.M. Anderson wrote to Beauregard:

> I thank you for your kindness in having sent your aide to me with an offer of assistance upon your having observed that our flag was down. . . . I will now state that I am willing to evacuate this fort upon the terms and conditions offered by yourself on the 11th instant, at any hour you may name tomorrow, or as soon as we can arrange means of transportation. I will not replace my flag until the return of your messenger.

All firing ceased while this was being delivered. The Confederate commander replied at 5:55 P.M., offering the following terms:

> All proper facilities for the removal of yourself and your command, together with company arms and private property, to any point within the United States you may select. Apprised that you desire the privilege of saluting your flag on retiring, I cheerfully concede it, in consideration of the gallantry with which you have defended the place under your charge. The Catawba steamer will be at the landing of

Sumter to-morrow morning at any hour you may designate for the purpose of transporting you whither you may desire.

In the ferocious exchange of shot and shell that lasted thirty-four hours, the Confederates fired 3,341 rounds. They scored about 600 direct hits on the fort, filling it with smoke from burning barracks and other structures. This did not prevent the Federals from firing about a thousand rounds, which succeeded only in destroying the Fort Moultrie barracks. The sole casualty was a horse, killed on Morris Island. Thus, without loss of human life on either side, Federal possession of Fort Sumter was brought to an end. The next day Anderson and his men were permitted to fire a farewell salute to the Stars and Stripes, during which one of the guns exploded. Private Daniel Hough, the first soldier to die in the war that was to cost 620,000 lives, was buried in the parade ground by the Confederates. Five other men were wounded, one of them mortally. They and the men wounded during the bombardment were taken to the state hospital. The rest of the garrison, eighty soldiers and forty workmen, sailed north on the *Baltic*. When the vessel arrived off Sandy Hook, Anderson sent this message to Secretary of War Cameron:

> Having defended Fort Sumter for thirty-four hours, until the quarters were entirely burned, the main gates destroyed by fire, the gorge walls seriously injured, the magazine surrounded by flames, and its door closed from the effects of heat, four barrels and three cartridges only of powder being available, and no provisions remaining but pork, I accepted terms of evacuation offered by General Beauregard . . . and marched out of the fort Sunday afternoon, the 14th instant, with colors flying and drums beating, bringing away company and private property, and saluting my flag with fifty guns.

Two days later Cameron replied:

> I am directed by the President of the United States to communicate to you, and through you to the officers and men under your command, at Forts Moultrie and Sumter, the approbation of the Government for your and their judicious

and gallant conduct there, and to tender to you and them the thanks of the Government for the same.

Lincoln Calls Forth the Militia

A letter sent to Lincoln from William M. Thomas of Augusta, Georgia on April 12 serves as a measure of the military confidence felt in the South. It said:

> President of U. S. –
>
> Sir. I propose to bet you or any other Black Republican five hundred dollars that you nor your government will fight the Southern Confederacy. I also propose to bet you or any other Black Republican that if you do fight us we will take your scalp in 12 months after the war commences.

The people of the Southern states were energized by the bombardment and capture of Fort Sumter. They had anticipated a fight for independence, and welcomed it now that it had come. They were confident that they could win the fight in a short time. The loss of Sumter also galvanized the people of the North. The Stars and Stripes had been fired upon, an act that had to be forcefully avenged. State governors telegraphed Washington with offers of troops for the defense of the Union.

On Monday, April 15, Lincoln issued a proclamation:

> Whereas the laws of the United States have been for some time in the past, and now are opposed, and the execution thereof obstructed, in the States of South Carolina, Georgia, Alabama, Florida, Mississippi, Louisiana and Texas, by combinations too powerful to be suppressed by the ordinary course of judicial proceedings, or by the powers vested in the Marshals by law, Now, therefore, I, Abraham Lincoln, President of the United States . . . hereby do call forth, the militia of the several States of the Union, to the aggregate number of seventy-five thousand, in order to suppress said combinations, and to cause the laws to be duly executed. . . . I appeal to all loyal citizens to favor, facilitate, and aid this effort to maintain the honor, the integrity, and the existence of our National Union, and the perpetuity of popular

government; and to redress wrongs already long enough endured.... And I hereby command the persons composing the combinations aforesaid to disperse, and retire peaceably to their respective abodes within twenty days from date.... Deeming that the present condition of public affairs presents an extraordinary occasion, I do hereby, in virtue of the power in me vested by the Constitution, convene both Houses of Congress ... to assemble ... on Thursday, the fourth of July next, then and there to consider and determine, such measures, as, in their wisdom, the public safety, and interest may seem to demand.

Lincoln carefully observed the requirements of the law by declaring the situation too powerful to be handled by the courts and the marshals and by commanding the offenders to disperse in a specified time. In calling for a special session he set the date for seven weeks later, allowing him time to act before Congress met. Buchanan's lawyerly reasoning had been that the Constitution empowered the president only to enforce the laws against individual persons, not against states. Lincoln's lawyerly reasoning now was that the states themselves had not seceded, but that "a combination of persons" in them had rebelled, and he was prepared to enforce the laws against those persons - every last one of them.

As already noted, the regular army was small, and to fight the war it was enlarged by only two regiments. Throughout the four years it consisted of nineteen regiments of infantry, six of cavalry, and five of artillery. (One regiment of cavalry and one of infantry remained in the West and did not participate in the fighting with the South). Of the 1,080 regular officers at the beginning of 1861, 620 were from Northern states, and all but sixteen of them (who had married Southern women) remained loyal. The other 460 were from Southern states, and of these 163 stayed on duty. In total, 767 of the officers, 71 percent, stayed while 29 percent resigned to serve the Confederacy. As a matter of War Department policy, a great many of the West Pointers who stayed were assigned to, and remained with, the thirty regular regiments. This greatly reduced their opportunities for promotion, and few of them rose above the rank of major. To some extent at least, Confederate battle successes can be attributed to their better use of professionals as senior commanders. The North did not take full advantage of its West Point trained officers and was burdened with too many amateur political generals.

On April 16, to assist the governors in their task of assembling the troops (the actual number of militiamen called was 73,391), the adjutant general issued a table of organization for the state forces:

- A company of infantry - 1 captain, 1 first lieutenant, 1 ensign, 4 sergeants, 4 corporals, 1 drummer and 1 fifer, 64 privates.
- A regiment of infantry or foot riflemen, to consist of ten companies — 1 colonel, 1 lieutenant-colonel, 1 major, 1 adjutant, 1 regimental quartermaster, 1 surgeon, 1 assistant surgeon, 1 sergeant-major, 1 quartermaster-sergeant, 1 drum-major, 1 fife-major.
- A brigade, to consist of four or more regiments - 1 brigadier-general, 1 aide-de-camp, 1 brigade inspector.
- A division, to consist of two or more brigades - 1 major-general, 2 aides-de-camp, 1 division inspector.
- Some of the companies composing a regiment may be of infantry and the others rifle, if desired.

The response was immediate. In Pennsylvania, the first volunteers to head for Washington included a company from Pottsville, the National Light Infantry, formed in 1831. At a meeting on April 11, the day before the bombardment of Fort Sumter began, the members had resolved, "that the services of this company be tendered to the Secretary of War and the Governor of Pennsylvania in defense of the Union, and that the company be ready to march at six hours' notice." The 106 men left by train at 2:15 P.M. on April 17 for the state capital, Harrisburg, accompanied by another Pottsville unit, the 130 men of the Washington Artillerists.

In Reading, the Ringgold Light Artillery, under Captain James McKnight, had been drilling almost daily since January, and was at drill when the news arrived of the attack on Fort Sumter. A telegram from McKnight to Governor Andrew Curtin informed him that the Ringgolds "are on parade. Every one of them expects to be ordered on duty for the U. S. service before they leave their guns." Marching orders were received from the governor on April 16, and the 132 men of the company left the next day for Harrisburg, where they arrived at 8:00 P.M. There they joined with the two companies from Pottsville, and with the Logan Guards (ninety-two men) of Lewistown and Allentown's Allen Infantry (seventy-eight men). All 538 officers and men were quartered that night in halls and public buildings.

The five companies assembled at the railroad station at 6:00 A.M. on April 18, and were mustered into the service of the United States by Captain Seneca G. Simmons of the Seventh U. S. Infantry. They were joined by a detachment of Company H, Fourth U. S. Artillery that had just arrived by train from the west on its way to Fort McHenry. (These men were commanded by a Pennsylvanian, Captain John C. Pemberton, who resigned to join the Confederacy, and was fated to surrender Vicksburg two years later.) The troops traveled by train to Baltimore, where they arrived at noon and marched more than a mile from one station to another.

Secessionist sympathizers insulted and harassed them, but since few of the troops were armed, and those who were had no ammunition, they ignored the taunts as best they could. As they boarded the train, bricks, stones and clubs were hurled at them. Luckily, none were seriously injured. The men of the Pennsylvania battalion, the first responders to Lincoln's call, arrived in Washington at 6:00 P.M. Three hours later, in the basement of the Capitol, they were issued new Springfield rifles in the presence of Secretary of War Cameron. The next day, when the Sixth Massachusetts Volunteer Infantry passed through Baltimore, three soldiers were killed by the secessionist crowd.

Four days after calling up the militia Lincoln, as a further step, proclaimed a naval blockade:

> Whereas an insurrection against the Government of the United States has broken out in the States of South Carolina, Georgia, Alabama, Florida, Mississippi, Louisiana and Texas, and the laws of the United States for the collection of the

revenue cannot be effectually executed therein . . . And whereas a combination of persons engaged in such insurrection have threatened to grant pretended letters of marque authorizing the bearers thereof to commit assaults on the lives, vessels, and properties of [citizens] lawfully engaged in commerce on the high seas and in the waters of the United States . . . I, Abraham Lincoln . . . have . . . set on foot a blockade of the ports within the States aforesaid. . . For this purpose a competent force will be posted so as to prevent entrance and exit of vessels from the ports. . . . if any person . . . shall molest a vessel of the United States, or the persons or cargo on board of her, such person shall be held amenable to the laws of the United States for the prevention and punishment of piracy.

Stating the matter in modern terms, Lincoln declared that the United States was prepared to play hardball. On May 6, the Confederate Congress passed, and Davis signed, a bill declaring a state of war between the Confederate States of America and the United States of America.

The Final Four States Secede

Formation of the Confederacy was completed when four more states seceded. In Virginia, a state convention on April 4 had voted 89 to 45 against secession. However, the attack on Fort Sumter, followed by Lincoln's proclamation of April 15 calling on Virginia for 2,340 troops, caused reconsideration of the issue. On April 16, ex-governor Henry Wise arranged for Virginia militia to seize the U. S. arsenal at Harpers Ferry, clearly an act of rebellion. The following day the Virginia convention voted 88 to 55 to leave the Union:

The people of Virginia in their ratification of the Constitution . . . having declared that the powers granted under said Constitution were derived from the people of the United States and might be resumed whensoever the same should be perverted to their injury and oppression . . . we, the people of Virginia, do declare . . . that the State of Virginia is in the full possession and exercise of all the rights of sovereignty which belong and appertain to a free and independent State. And they do further declare, That said Constitution . . . is no longer binding on any of the citizens of this State. This ordinance shall take effect . . . when ratified by a majority of the votes of the people . . . at a poll [on May 23].

Virginia, whose secession was ratified by the vote of the people, entered into what amounted to a treaty with the Confederacy, and soon formally joined. The Confederate capital was transferred to Richmond on June 21. Unionists in the western two-fifths of Virginia formed a separate state. It was admitted to the Union as the state of West Virginia in June of 1863, with a constitution that provided for the gradual abolition of slavery. Thus Virginia, on whose soil more battles were fought than in any other state, was the only state that lost territory as a result of the war.

The government of Arkansas, which was asked for 780 men, also refused to respond to the president's call. North Carolina and Tennessee, both asked for 1,560 men, also did not respond to the calling out of the militia. Public sentiment in these states had favored some sort of compromise, and there was strong support for the Union in western North Carolina and eastern Tennessee, but majorities now favored secession, though no referendums were taken. On May 6, Arkansas seceded by a vote of 69 to 1, and on the same day Tennessee by 66 to 25 -- subject to confirmation by a popular vote on June 6. On May 20 North Carolina, by unanimous vote, become the eleventh of the states that comprised the Confederacy.

Secession of the final four states added 213,000 square miles to Confederate territory. More importantly, it added 4,134,191 people, thereby increasing the population of the Confederacy by 83 percent. Of these, 2,829,484 were white, 1,208,758 slaves and 95,949 free Negroes (92 percent of them in Virginia and North Carolina). Perhaps more importantly, it strengthened the Confederate industrial capacity, especially in the Richmond area, and provided a more diversified agricultural and mineral base. The North Carolina seaports of Wilmington and New Bern, both with railroads to the interior, and the port of Norfolk, with its large shipyards, greatly increased the Confederacy's capacity to import and export goods, and to build naval vessels. Four slave states remained in the Union: Delaware, Kentucky, Maryland and Missouri. Numerous secessionists in Kentucky and Missouri provided regiments to the Confederate army, and in December of 1861, they sent representatives to the C. S. Congress in Richmond.

Five months after the November election, the military strength of the two sides was unbalanced. The officials of the nascent Confederacy, convinced that conflict was inevitable, had prepared for war. They had enacted legislation providing for the enlistment of 100,000 men, thus creating an army several times the size of the army mustered by the United States. They had supplemented the arms obtained by the seizure of the Federal arsenals, and those which already belonged to the Confederate states, by purchasing munitions from manufacturers in the North and by contracting for weapons from sources in Europe. As a result, the Confederate States were, temporarily at least, better prepared militarily than the United States. This degree of preparedness helped to suppress whatever inhibitions against war there might have been in the South.

The U. S. Army, on the other hand, had been weakened by losses of munitions as the seceding states seized arsenals and forts. It suffered reductions in manpower as officers resigned to serve in their home states, or went South for personal or political reasons, and as troops were surrendered in Texas. Buchanan, who believed the Federal government had no right to oppose secession, saw no need to build up the military for that purpose, and took no action that would provoke hostilities. Similarly, in the five weeks of the Lincoln administration that preceded war, the new president was careful to avoid the appearance of any wartime preparations that might instigate further conflict with the South.

The situation quickly changed after Fort Sumter. The soldiers called for by Lincoln from Virginia, North Carolina, Tennessee and Arkansas were more than made up for by troops contributed by the twenty-three loyal states. Their governors, whose quotas totaled 67,111 men, quickly answered Lincoln's call by sending 93,000 men, followed within a few weeks by 100,000 more. The disparity in population between the North and the South was particularly ominous for the Confederacy. The North had two and a half times as many people, four times as many whites, and steady population growth from immigration. The Union army fast became a formidable fighting force, reaching a maximum strength of 980,000 men in 1864.

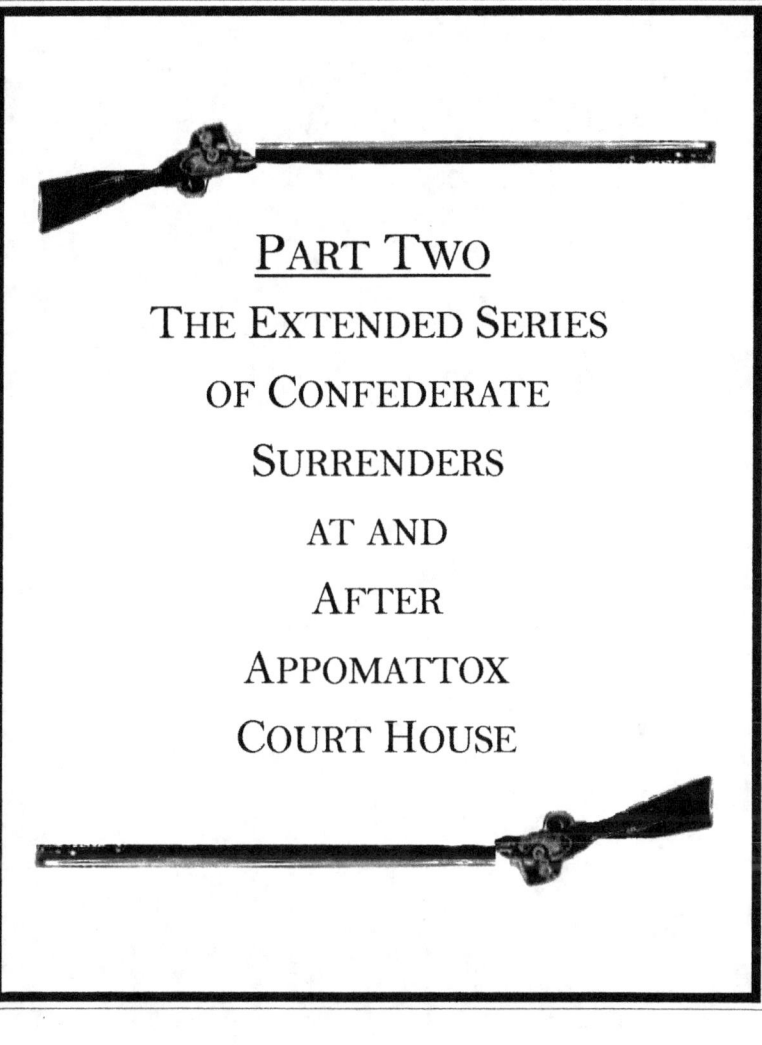

Part Two
The Extended Series of Confederate Surrenders at and After Appomattox Court House

INTERVAL:

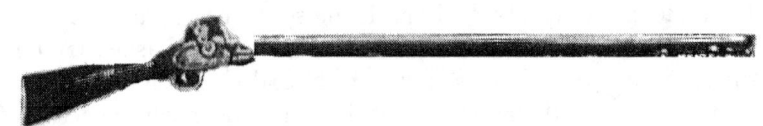

FOUR YEARS OF WAR

Following the surrender of Fort Sumter, the war between the Confederate States and the United States gradually intensified. The South began to experience territorial losses, including some of strategic significance, at the very beginning of the war. These losses continued, more or less unabated, for four years. Readers interested in the details may wish to peruse the following year-by-year summary before continuing with Part Two in March of 1865.

1861

Across the Potomac River from Washington, in northeastern Virginia, Alexandria and Arlington Heights (where Lee's house was located) were occupied by Federal troops on May 24. Hampton was taken the following day, and Newport News on May 29. Soon large areas of western Virginia were in Federal hands: Grafton on May 30, Philippi on June 3, Romney and Harpers Ferry on June 13 and 14, Martinsburg on July 3, Beverly on July 12 and Charleston on July 24. The first of the coastal places was lost on August 29, when an amphibious force captured Fort Hatteras and Fort Clark, two small bastions in North Carolina that guarded the back door to Norfolk. The Confederate commander asked for terms and was told that he would have to surrender unconditionally, which he did with 700 men. On November 7, a Union force attacked Port Royal Sound, South Carolina. Four days later, the Confederates surrendered Fort Beauregard on St. Philip's Island and Fort Walker on Hilton Head Island. Beaufort was occupied and a base established on Hilton Head. Ship Island, Mississippi was evacuated by the Confederates on September 16 and occupied on December 3 by the Federals, who developed it as a fueling station for ships blockading Mobile and New Orleans.

1862

On February 8, the Confederates yielded another foothold on the east coast: Roanoke Island, North Carolina. More than 2,000 men, having no means of escape, were surrendered. Far inland, in western Tennessee, Federal forces took Fort Heiman and Fort Henry, outposts of Fort Donelson, on February 5 and 6. When the general in command at Fort Donelson asked for terms on February 16, the answer was brief and clear: "No terms other than an unconditional and immediate surrender can be accepted." The terms were accepted, with the result that much of Tennessee was lost. Clarksville and Fort Defiance fell on February 19. Nashville, the state capital, with a population of 16,988, was evacuated on February 23, and Pittsburg Landing was lost on March 14. West of the Mississippi River, Fayetteville, Arkansas was occupied on February 23.

In the east, a Union effort along the Potomac River resulted in the capture of Harpers Ferry (again) on February 24, Charles Town on the 28th, Martinsburg on March 3, Manassas on the 7th, Leesburg on the 8th, and Winchester on the 11th. Up the Shenandoah Valley, Harrisonburg and Luray were occupied on April 22. Closer to the Confederate capital, Fredericksburg and Falmouth were lost on April 17 and 18, Yorktown was evacuated the day before Federal troops moved in on May 4, Williamsburg the next day, and Norfolk and Portsmouth on May 10. A number of additional places farther south on the Atlantic coast were lost. New Bern, North Carolina was taken on March 14 and Fort Macon on April 26. Amelia Island, Florida was evacuated on March 3, Jacksonville on March 12, and Edisto Island, South Carolina on April 5. Fort Pulaski, Georgia was captured on April 11, after a thirty-hour bombardment, closing the port of Savannah. In western Florida, Apalachicola was lost on April 3, followed by Pensacola, with its important naval yard, on May 9.

In the Mississippi River valley, the Confederates were forced to give up strategic Island Number Ten and 7,000 soldiers on April 7. In Alabama, Huntsville and Decatur fell on April 11 and 13. The reverses continued with the loss of New Orleans, the Confederacy's largest economic center and port. With its population of 168,675, it was more than twice the combined sizes of Charleston and Richmond. On April 25, a Union fleet forced the 3,000 defenders to evacuate, abandoning four small forts and 172 guns. Fort Jackson and Fort St. Philip, below the city, were abandoned on April 28. The city was officially surrendered by civilians on the 29th and occupied by Union troops on May 1. Baton Rouge, the capital of Louisiana, was occupied on May 8, followed closely by Natchez and Corinth, Mississippi on May 12 and 30. Fort Pillow, Tennessee surrendered on June 3, Memphis, population 22,623, on June 6, and Jackson on June 7. The pace of losses then slackened: besides some small towns in Virginia, Tennessee, Mississippi and Louisiana, the only important places occupied by Union forces in the last half of the year were Galveston, Texas on October 5 and Fredericksburg, Virginia on December 11.

1863

The new year began with Union occupation of Murfreesboro, Tennessee on January 5 and of Franklin on February 1. In Mississippi, Yazoo City and Meridian were lost on February 9 and 14. Haynes Bluff was taken on May 18, following the evacuation of Jackson on May 14. Five days later the siege of Vicksburg began. That city, with its 3,158 white inhabitants and 1,402 slaves, was surrendered on July 4. To a request for terms, the initial response was "unconditional surrender," but 30,000 men of the garrison were paroled rather than taking them prisoner. Four days later the 6,500 defenders of Port Hudson, out of food and ammunition, also surrendered. That was the last place held by the Confederacy on the Mississippi, and put the Union in control of the entire river. Arkansas, Louisiana and Texas were effectively severed from the eight states to the east. Near Charleston, on September 6, Battery Wagner, on Morris Island a mile and a half south of Fort Sumter, was abandoned by the Confederates after a two-month siege and three bloody attacks. Fort Smith, Arkansas was lost on September 1, followed by Little Rock on September 10. In eastern Tennessee, Knoxville was evacuated on September 2 and Chattanooga one week later. In November, the Confederates abandoned three places in Texas: Brazos Island on the 2nd, Corpus Christi on the 16th, and Fort Esperanza on the 30th.

1864

In the first half of the year only Alexandria, Louisiana was lost, on March 16. Then, on August 5, at the entrance to Mobile Bay, Fort Powell was captured, and Fort Gaines fell three days later.

This resulted in the surrender of Fort Morgan on August 23, denying use of the port of Mobile to the Confederacy without the need of a Union blockade. Little Rock, the capital of Arkansas, was captured on September 10. Atlanta, population 9,554, was evacuated by the Confederates on September 1. After an eleven-week occupation, the Union forces left the city on November 15, marched southeast, and on November 23, entered and briefly occupied Milledgeville, the Georgia capital. On December 11, they laid siege to Savannah, population 22,292. One week later, the 10,000 Confederate soldiers in and around the city escaped, abandoning 250 heavy guns. Possession of the port allowed the Union army to be supplied by sea for the planned campaign into the Carolinas.

1865

On January 15, in North Carolina, the Confederates were driven from Fort Fisher, effectively closing Wilmington, their last port on the Atlantic coast. During the late winter and spring, more than a dozen Confederate cities were surrendered. Columbia was evacuated on February 16 and Federal forces entered on the 17th, the same day that Charleston was abandoned. Union troops took the city of Wilmington unopposed on February 22 and Camden, South Carolina on the 25th. Fayetteville was occupied on March 11 and Goldsboro on March 23, in both instances without resistance. In Alabama, Selma was taken by storm on April 2 and Spanish Fort captured on April 9. In Virginia, Petersburg was evacuated on April 2 and Richmond the following day. All of these places fell before the first Confederate field army surrendered on April 9. On April 12, following that event, Montgomery and Mobile, Alabama, and Raleigh and Salisbury, North Carolina were occupied by Federal troops. In Georgia, the Union gained control of West Point and Columbus on April 16, Macon on April 20, and Augusta on April 24. Finally, the Union occupied Tallahassee, Florida on May 10.

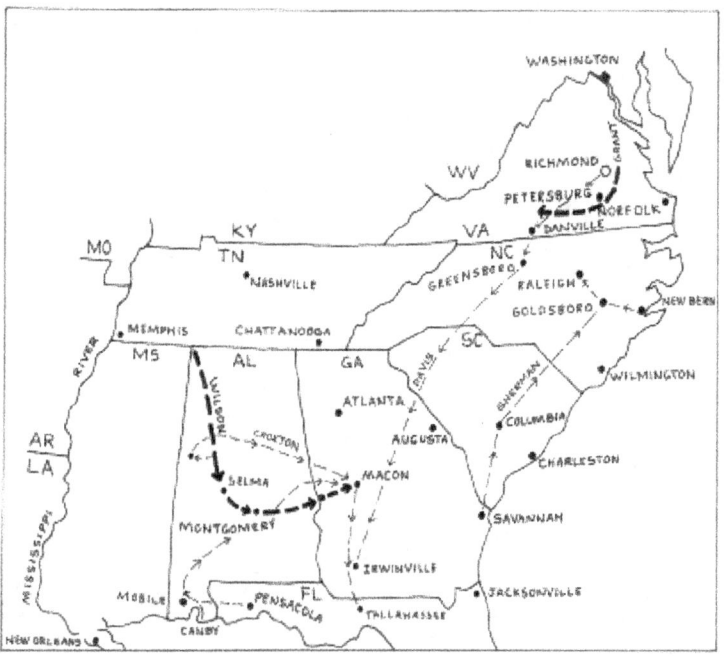

The Spring Campaigns 1865

Chapter 6

Lee Surrenders in Virginia
April 9, 1865

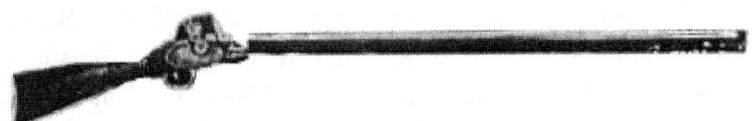

The Final Campaigns Begin

Commanders on both sides expected that the war would end with a decisive battle. That did not happen. There were, however, several engagements in the final campaigns of the war that were in a sense decisive. Except for the Tennessee offensive of General John B. Hood, which ended in his defeat by General George H. Thomas at the Battle of Nashville on December 15-16, military activity was limited during the winter months. Campaigning was not practicable until the roads became firm enough to permit movement by large forces. Widespread severe weather in the late winter of 1865 meant that the planned advances were delayed. Once under way, they were hampered by the need to corduroy roads, build bridges, detour around unusable fords and repair vehicles damaged by rough usage. Troops struggled to advance artillery and supply wagons through deep mud, often double-teaming to move some of the wagons and caissons while others waited their turn.

General-in-Chief Ulysses S. Grant ordered Union armies to advance on four fronts. (1) In Virginia, General George G. Meade's Army of the Potomac and General Edward O. C. Ord's Army of the James were to intensify their efforts to penetrate the defenses of Richmond and Petersburg and to defeat General Robert E. Lee's

Army of Northern Virginia. General Philip H. Sheridan's cavalry was to poke aggressively at Lee's right flank and to sever the rail lines southwest to Danville and west to Lynchburg. (2) In Alabama, General E. R. S. Canby's army, based on New Orleans and Pensacola, was to attack the city of Mobile and advance north to defeat General Richard Taylor's army. General James H. Wilson's Cavalry Corps was to sweep south and east, supporting Canby's offensive and destroying industrial facilities in Alabama and Georgia. (3) In North Carolina, General William T. Sherman was to interrupt the lines of supply to Lee's army, pursue and defeat Confederate forces under General Joseph E. Johnston, and then link up with the Union army in Virginia to defeat Lee. General George Stoneman's cavalry from Tennessee was to raid western Virginia and North Carolina, destroying supplies and rail lines to impede withdrawal by Lee to the west. (4) West of the Mississippi, which was least vital to his spring strategy, Grant asked General John Pope to devise a plan for attacking General Edmund Kirby-Smith and his Army of the Trans-Mississippi, and to deal with guerilla bands.

When Sherman left Atlanta in November 1864 on his famous "march to the sea," his destination was actually Goldsboro, North Carolina. There he could receive provisions and reinforcements by the railroads from New Bern and Wilmington. After resting and re-supplying in Savannah, he began moving his divisions northward during January by way of Columbia and Fayetteville. At Goldsboro he was to be joined by two corps under General John M. Schofield, one of which Grant had ordered east from the Army of Tennessee as a result of Thomas's defeat of Hood at Nashville.

The condition of the Confederate army continued to deteriorate during the winter. Around the beginning of 1865 there were 160,198 men present for duty. This was only 45 percent of the total of 358,692 carried on the rolls. Returns are not available for all armies for the same date, but these figures are based on the following reports:

Army of Northern Virginia (Lee)	February 20	73,349
Department of Richmond (Ewell)	March 20	5,175
Army of Tennessee (Johnston)	April 17	20,829
Alabama, Mississippi, and East Louisiana Department (Taylor)	March 10	12,040
Trans-Mississippi Department (Kirby-Smith)	December 31	43,054
Western Virginia, East Tennessee and Western North Carolina	February 28 and March 10	5,751

Half of the army, about 78,500 men, was in the Richmond-Petersburg area, and more than a quarter was west of the Mississippi River.

In Richmond, a high-level meeting and several appointments influenced the course of events. On February 3, at Hampton Roads, Confederate Vice-president Alexander H. Stephens and two others met for four hours with President Lincoln and Secretary of State Seward. The purpose was to explore the possibility of negotiating peace. Lincoln firmly insisted that the only acceptable resolution of the conflict required two things: return of the eleven seceded states to the Union and emancipation of the slaves. On February 6, President Davis informed his Congress that Lincoln:

> refused to enter into negotiations with the Confederate States, or any of them separately, or to give to our people any

other terms or guarantee that those which the conqueror may grant, or permit us to have peace on any other basis than our unconditional submission to their rule.

Important changes were made in the Confederate command structure. On February 9, Secretary of War James A. Seddon, who had submitted his resignation several weeks earlier, was replaced by General John C. Breckinridge, the presidential candidate of the Southern Democrats in 1860. Two weeks earlier, on January 23, Congress enacted that there be "an officer . . . as General in Chief, who shall be ranking officer of the Army, and as such shall have command of the military forces of the Confederate States." By General Orders No. 3 on February 9, it was announced that "General Robert E. Lee . . . will assume the duties thereof, and will be obeyed and respected accordingly." Davis promoted Lee with the understanding that he would remain commander of the Army of Northern Virginia. From his headquarters in Petersburg, Lee thanked Jefferson for appointing him, but expressed concern about the rate at which the size of the army was being reduced. The Bureau of Conscription had estimated that there were as many as 100,000 deserters dispersed throughout the South. Lee wrote:

> As it is necessary to bring every man back to the ranks that we can, I [propose] . . . to proclaim by your authority a pardon to all deserters and absentees who will return to their regiments or companies within thirty days . . . with the assurance that this will be the last act of amnesty extended for such offenses. . . . It is the only method that I can propose to cause the return of our absentees, and perhaps if done at this time, when we may expect a reaction of public sentiment, the people at home may force them out.

Two weeks later Lee appointed General Joseph E. Johnston, inactive since he had been relieved in Georgia by Davis seven months earlier, to replace General P. G. T. Beauregard in command of the Confederates in North and South Carolina, Georgia and Florida. Lee told Johnston to "concentrate all available forces and drive Sherman back." The Confederates, however, could barely muster 20,000 poorly equipped and ill-fed men, patched together from remnants of the Army of Tennessee, the Charleston and Savannah garrisons, and various smaller units. This force was utterly inadequate to oppose Sherman as he continued northeastward from Columbia in two columns totaling 60,000 men. Johnston replied, "It is too late to expect me to concentrate troops capable of driving back Sherman. The remnant of the Army of Tennessee is much divided. So are other troops."

THE CONFEDERATE CONGRESS ADJOURNS

With the Confederacy verging on collapse, its army short of men as well as of arms, food, clothing and fuel for those present for duty, Congress continued to deal with trivialities, and to pass detailed legislation that could not, under the circumstances, be made effective. On March 6, it was resolved that:

> the President be respectfully requested to inform the Senate why he gives to aides-de-camp to general officers above the grade of brigadier general only the rank of first lieutenant in his nominations made to the Senate.

Incredible as it seems, the Constitution provided that regular officers were to be appointed by the president only with the advice and consent of the Senate. Davis could not fill even the most inferior of positions without confirmation by that body. Despite the critical situation, he took the time to reply with a long, legalistic explanation.

Congress also addressed more substantial military matters. On February 23, it passed *An Act to Authorize the Consolidation of Companies, Battalions, and Regiments.* This was necessary because the number of men in many units had been reduced, by casualties, desertions and illness, to mere fractions of authorized strength. The law provided that:

> whenever any companies which are now in the service shall be so reduced as to number less than thirty-two men . . . present and fit for duty, and when . . . they cannot be recruited to that number within a reasonable time, the general commanding . . . may, under general regulations to be issued by the Secretary of War, consolidate such companies. . . . New companies may be organized from . . . the companies thus consolidated, if [the men] are from the same State, having a number, rank and file, not less than sixty-four nor more than one hundred and twenty-five.

This reorganization would result in a need for fewer officers. Congress dealt with this problem in the most awkward way imaginable, by providing that "Officers . . . not selected" would be notified and "dropped from the rolls," but could, if they wished, within sixty days:

> organize themselves in numbers sufficient to form companies, battalions, or regiments, and shall be officered from among themselves, by appointment of the President, by and with the advice and consent of the Senate.

To prevent them from flocking to join Kirby-Smith's army, Congress further provided:

> That no officer shall be permitted to select a company on the opposite side of the Mississippi River from where he is now on duty, unless he reside beyond said river.

During these early months of 1865, the Confederacy considered two radical changes in its position on slavery as a means of influencing the outcome of the war. In January, Davis sent representatives to Europe to propose emancipation in exchange for recognition of the Confederate government. They proposed the idea to the British foreign secretary on March 14. By then all of the South's Atlantic ports were in Federal hands and Sherman was advancing almost unopposed in the Carolinas. In British eyes, the prospects for Southern independence had vanished. Besides, it was an impotent offer: slavery was guaranteed by the Confederate Constitution, and the representatives were unable to guarantee that the eleven sovereign states would abolish it, as indeed, they surely would not have done.

The other change was an exceedingly controversial piece of legislation called *An Act to Increase the Military Forces of the Confederate States.* It authorized the use of Negro slaves as soldiers - a drastic response that revealed the desperate need to raise more manpower. The idea had first been advanced three years earlier, and had the support of Lee. One of the arguments in its favor was the knowledge that the Federal army had nearly 200,000 Negroes, most of them former slaves, serving in more than a hundred regiments, styled U. S. Colored Troops. If they could fight for the North, why not for the South? The principal argument against it was that, if Negroes were capable of being soldiers, the basic notions on which slavery rested were wrong, and secession had therefore been a mistake. Immediately following Virginia's decision to enlist Negroes in state regiments, the Confederate Congress, after lengthy and acrimonious debate, enacted the law -- by a vote of 40 to 37 in the House and by a minimal 9 to 8 in the Senate. The act said:

> In order to provide additional forces to repel invasion, maintain the rightful possession of the Confederate States, secure their independence, and preserve their institutions, the President be . . . authorized to ask for and accept from the owners of slaves, the services of such number of able-bodied negro men as he may deem expedient, for and during the war, to perform military service in whatever capacity he may direct.

Congress authorized the general-in-chief "to organize the said slaves into companies, battalions, regiments, and brigades." They were to "receive the same rations, clothing, and compensation as are allowed to other troops in the same branch of the service." However, if by enrolling slaves,

> The President shall not be able to raise a sufficient number of troops to prosecute the war successfully and maintain the sovereignty of the States and the independence of the Confederate States, then he is hereby authorized to call on each State . . . for her quota of 300,000 troops, in addition to those subject to military service under existing law . . . from such classes of the population, irrespective of color, in each State, as the proper authorities thereof may determine: Provided, That not more than twenty-five per cent of the male slaves between the ages of eighteen and forty-five, in any State, shall be called.

Admitting that slaves could be soldiers was a surrender of principle. To allay the fears of the strongest opponents, especially among the planter class, and to reaffirm state rights, Congress concluded with a provision:

> Nothing in this act shall be construed to authorize a change in the relationship which the said slaves shall bear toward their owners, except by consent of the owners and of the States in which they may reside, and in pursuance of the laws thereof.

Five days later, on March 18, the Confederate Congress adjourned for the last time.

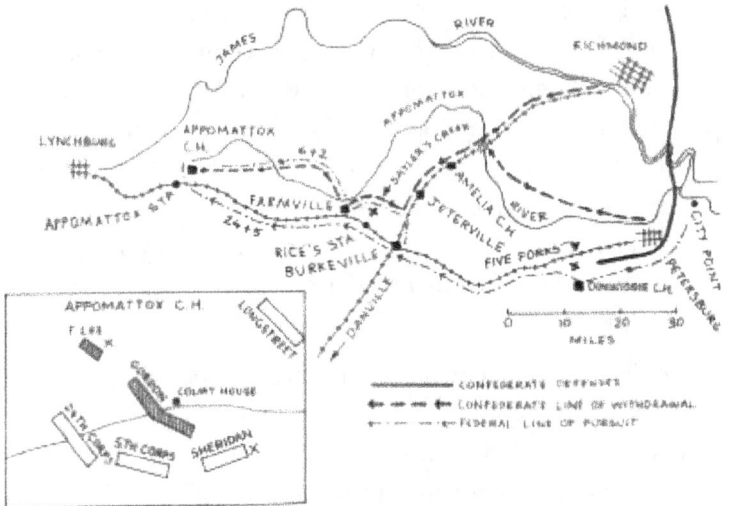

The Appomattox Campaign
March 27 – April 9

PETERSBURG AND RICHMOND

When Sherman and Schofield united at Goldsboro on March 23, the Union force of 90,000 men was only 120 miles south of Petersburg. Sherman was in position to attack and defeat Johnston, and then move quickly north to reinforce Grant. Lee notified Davis on March 26:

> I fear now it will be impossible to prevent a junction between Grant and Sherman, nor do I deem it prudent that the army should maintain its position until the latter shall approach too near. Genl Johnston reports that the returns of his force of the 24th instant gave his effective infantry thirteen thousand five hundred. . . . This could hardly have resulted from the casualties of battle, and I fear must be the effect of desertion.

To deal with this severe problem, General Orders No. 8 were issued on March 27:

It having been reported that the evil habit prevails with some in this army of proposing to their comrades in jest to desert and go home, the commanding general earnestly warns those guilty of this practice against the danger they incur. The penalty for advising or persuading a soldier to desert is death. . . . This order and the 23d Article of War will be forthwith read to each company in the army once a day for three days, and to every regiment at dress parade once a week for a month . . .

Confederate strategy had envisioned two options. One was that while part of Lee's army held Richmond, the rest would join Johnston in North Carolina to defeat Sherman. The combined forces would then march to Virginia and, together with the holding force there, defeat Grant. The alternative was that Johnston would defeat Sherman, then come to Lee's assistance. Since it was clear that neither of these options was possible, a third would be tried: the entire Army of Northern Virginia would march to North Carolina and join Johnston. Grant would then undoubtedly join Sherman. The combined Confederate forces of perhaps 75,000 men would face the combined Union armies of 215,000 men. "The idea was pure fantasy," Grant said later. It was certainly an unrealistic concept, a desperate gamble by desperate men, but it was the only option that remained.

The Confederate defenses in Virginia, which now must be abandoned, stretched for thirty miles, from just north of Richmond to west of Petersburg at Hatcher's Run. The limited provisions the army had been receiving came mostly by way of the rail lines from southwestern Virginia and North Carolina. The two lines, the Richmond and Danville Railroad and the Southside Railroad (from Petersburg to Lynchburg) crossed at Burkeville. Lee and Grant both recognized that it was essential to Lee to keep these lines open so that his army could withdraw to unite with Johnston. To prevent this from happening, Grant intended to move a large part of his army around the Confederate right, blocking the roads and rail lines west of Petersburg. General John B. Gordon, in an attempt to disrupt the Federal move, launched a night attack on Fort Stedman on March 25. It was repulsed with the loss of nearly 5,000 Confederate soldiers.

General Sheridan, after defeating the small force under General Jubal A. Early near Waynesboro in the Shenandoah Valley on March 2, brought his cavalry corps across the Blue Ridge at Rockfish Gap. He destroyed the railroad out of Charlottesville, locks and culverts on the James River canal, and mills, factories and stables on his line of march. He reached White House on the Pamaukey River on March 19. Five days later he and his 10,000 troopers were at City Point, where he rested the horses, re-equipped the men and prepared for the movement around Lee's right flank. Because of severe spring storms, Grant was unable to begin the movement to the Union left until March 29, after several rain-free days. Aware of how critical the roads were to Lee, Grant feared that he might begin to evacuate before the Federal troops had shifted into position. Grant therefore had General Ord start the move of 2nd and 5th Corps on the night of March 27. Two days later Sheridan crossed the James River and headed west below Petersburg, with orders to occupy the road junction at Five Forks. In a letter to Sherman on March 22, Grant explained the mission:

> [Sheridan] will proceed directly to the Southside and Danville [rail]roads. His instructions will be to strike the Southside road as near Petersburg as he can, and destroy it so that it cannot be repaired for three or four days, and push on to the Danville road, as near to the Appomattox [River] as he can get. Then I want him to destroy the road toward Burkesville as far as he can; then push on to the Southside road, west of Burkesville, and destroy it effectually. From that point I shall probably leave it to his discretion either to return to this army, crossing the Danville road south of Burkesville, or go and join you, passing between Danville and Greensboro. . . . It is most difficult to understand what the

rebels intend to do. . . . Lee's army is much demoralized, and great numbers are deserting.

Sheridan's cavalry moved parallel to the Southside Railroad toward Burkeville. The rains resumed, making the roads impassable for artillery and wagons, so the army had to corduroy them. After three days of skirmishing, Sheridan was engaged by General George E. Pickett, who had been assigned the task of protecting the Confederate Army's right flank. With a mixed force of cavalry and infantry, Pickett marched to within half a mile of Dinwiddie Court House on March 31. There he discovered elements of 5th Corps on his left and in his rear, and the Union cavalry in strength in his front. After hitting the cavalry hard enough to cause it to fall back, he was compelled by the situation to withdraw. Three miles to the north was Five Forks, where several country roads intersected. It was two miles south of the railroad and three miles west of the end of the Confederate trenches.

The Battle of Five Forks

Sheridan's task was to seize Five Forks, while Lee's orders to Pickett were to "Hold Five Forks at all hazards. Protect road to Ford's Depot and prevent Union forces from striking the Southside Railroad. Regret exceedingly your forced withdrawal, and your inability to hold the advantage you had gained." On April 1, Pickett formed a defensive line along the south side of White Oak Road. His division consisted of five brigades of infantry, numbering about 7,000 men, supported by 2,000 cavalrymen under General Fitzhugh Lee (R. E. Lee's nephew). One division of cavalry, commanded by General W. H. F. Lee (R. E. Lee's son) took position on the right of the line. The other cavalry division, under General Thomas L. Rosser, was placed in reserve more than a mile in the rear of the line, along Hatcher's Run. On his extreme left Pickett angled his line rearward for about 150 yards to guard against attack from the east. Perhaps because of overconfidence, or

The Beginning and the End.

failure to understand the size of the infantry force opposing him, Pickett had the men dig only light fortifications. The artillery consisted of two batteries, each of three guns.

Sheridan's force, facing north, numbered almost 30,000. General Thomas C. Devin's First Cavalry Division was in the center and General George A. Custer's Third Cavalry Division on the left. The three infantry divisions of General Gouverneur K. Warren's 5th Corps, a total of 17,000 men, were slowly taking position on the Union right. Although the cavalry kept up a steady fire, the afternoon was largely quiet. Shad were running in the river and Rosser, who had caught quite a few, invited Pickett and Fitzhugh Lee to come back to his camp for a shad bake. Carelessly, the two senior generals left the field without informing the brigade commanders of their whereabouts.

About 4:00 P.M. the Federal attack opened. Sheridan's scouts had noted the angle on the Confederate left, but had mistakenly reported it to be about two-thirds of a mile east of its actual position. As a result, the Union infantry was extended beyond the east end of Pickett's line. The situation became clear as the infantry advanced and Warren swung one of his divisions to the northwest, hitting the angle with three brigades and overwhelming the defenders. While the Union cavalry attacked directly to the front, the infantry rolled up the Confederate line from east to west.

The Confederates had seen the Federals moving into position in the afternoon, but no dispositions had been made to meet them except at the brigade level. The defense was seriously hampered by the absence of the generals. Belatedly trying to return to the front, Pickett rode rapidly down the road as Federal infantry fired at him. He barely got through, but Fitzhugh Lee was unable to reach the fight. The battle ended in complete victory for the Union, with more than 5,000 Confederates taken prisoners: 3,244 by the infantry and an estimated 2,000 by the cavalry. The rest of Pickett's division was driven from the field in disarray, though the cavalry escaped in good order. The Federals suffered 634 casualties. Sheridan, perhaps in order to avoid sharing credit for the victory, relieved Warren of command, saying he had not moved as quickly as he should have.

The battle was tactically decisive: the way to the Southside Railroad was open to the Federals, and the right of the Confederate line was exposed. As soon as news of Pickett's defeat reached Grant, he ordered "a general assault along the lines." An artillery barrage began at 10:00 P.M. and lasted four hours. At first light on April 2, 4:30 A. M., the Army of the Potomac attacked. On the east side of Petersburg, General John G. Parke's 9th Corps struggled fiercely for hours and suffered great losses, but was unable to break the Confederate lines. On the south side of town, 14,000 men of 6th Corps under General Horatio G. Wright quietly moved into position between the lines of the armies in the pre-dawn darkness. A signal gun was fired at 4:40. The men surged forward under heavy fire, breached the line, scattered the defending troops and killed Confederate Third Corps commander General A. P. Hill.

The Confederates desperately rushed a brigade that had just arrived from the Richmond area into two inner redoubts, Forts Gregg and Whitworth. These were assaulted by the men of General Andrew A. Humphrey's 2nd Corps and General John Gibbon's 24th Corps. The latter captured one of the forts and forced the defenders out of the other by late afternoon. For all practical purposes, resistance was now over. The siege of Petersburg was ended. Confederate soldiers hurried across to the north side of the river and began marching westward. Lee sent a late afternoon message to Secretary of War Breckinridge in Richmond:

> It is absolutely necessary that we should abandon our position tonight, or run the risk of being cut off in the morning. I have . . . taken every precaution that I can to make the movement successful. It will be a difficult operation, but I hope not impracticable. . . . The troops will all be directed to Amelia Court-House [forty miles to the west].

Late on the morning of April 2, fifteen miles west of Petersburg, the Confederate survivors of the Battle of Five Forks formed a defensive line at Sutherland's Station. General Nelson A. Miles's division of 2nd Corps attacked. His first and second assaults were repulsed, but a third, advancing quickly, turned the defender's left flank, capturing 600 prisoners and two guns. Lee's army was dwindling as it moved westward, hampered by lack of food and by weakened horses and mules. The Confederates stayed mostly on the roads, however inadequate. The Union troops, as they tried to get ahead of them, were forced to move across rough country, with forests, dense undergrowth and swamps interspersed with cultivated fields.

THE CONFEDERATES ABANDON THEIR CAPITAL

The chaos and destruction inflicted on Richmond by the Confederates as they left the city exceeded anything done elsewhere in the South by the Union army. Tragically, the Confederate government fled its capital in haste and disarray, without making any provisions for the safety of the citizens or their property. No negotiation was entered into with the Union forces, nor was any notice of evacuation given, either to the people of the city or to Grant. The state government also completely failed to act. The city was simply abandoned, with devastating results.

On Sunday morning, April 2, Davis learned that Lee was evacuating Petersburg and Richmond. During the afternoon the government made preparations to flee. The president, the cabinet, and dozens of clerks departed by train before midnight. On a separate train was the Confederate treasury, consisting of some $500,000 worth of U. S. gold coins, Mexican silver dollars, and assorted gold and silver ingots. It was packed in boxes and barrels and guarded by sixty midshipmen from the naval school, commanded by Captain William H. Parker. Because of the poor condition of both the railways and the trains in the South, it took the president's party eighteen hours to cover the 140 miles to Danville.

The mayor of Richmond, Joseph Mayo, convened the city council on Sunday evening. They decided to try to destroy as much of the city's supply of alcoholic beverages as possible, and appointed a person in each ward to carry out their order. As a result, hundreds of barrels and thousands of bottles of liquor were smashed. Retreating soldiers and marauding civilians were still able to get hold of plenty to drink. Disorder was augmented when the penitentiary guards abandoned their posts, allowing prisoners to escape and roam the streets.

Many of the regiments that had been defending Richmond passed through the city and crossed to the south side of the James River on the several bridges spanning the river and the canal, setting them afire after they passed over, sometimes leaving their own troops to find a way across. The Confederate command ordered the destruction of the iron-clad naval vessels in the James River, as well as ammunition that could not be removed. About 1:30 A.M. the magazine of the *C. S. S. Virginia* exploded, creating a tremendous roar and shaking the earth for miles around. The army also set afire the Tredegar Iron Works, and artillery shells stored there continually burst, endangering people over a wide area. Most serious in its consequences was the decision by the Confederate military to implement the law requiring that stores of cotton and tobacco be burned. When the four great tobacco warehouses were set afire, the flames quickly spread to other buildings and eventually destroyed the whole commercial section of the city as well as many private homes.

The army's commissary warehouses were, reasonably enough, thrown open to the public, but without arrangements for orderly distribution. Mobs carried off whatever quantities of flour, sugar and other food they could get their hands on. This conduct soon spread, and the mob broke into private shops and stores, stealing goods of every kind: jewelry, clothing, hardware, furniture, books, etc. The mayhem was augmented by the availability of whiskey, despite efforts to pour it into the sewers. The noise and flashes from the explosions and fires served to aggravate the riotous behavior of the people, compounded by the conduct of now-free slaves who joined the whites in pillaging. Householders urgently tried to hide their most valuable possessions, and stood guard to protect their homes from being set afire by flying sparks and embers. The fires provided the only light, since the city gas supply had been, fortunately, shut off at the works. Law and order ceased to exist.

Mayor Mayo was authorized by the council to meet with the Federal authorities and arrange for the city's surrender in a way that would protect the interests of the citizens. About 2:30 A. M. on Monday, April 3, accompanied by three judges and two other men, he started toward the Union lines in a carriage flying a white flag. About two miles from the Capitol and a mile from Rocketts Landing they met a Union provost marshal, Major Atherton Stevens, to whom the mayor handed a letter. No copy survives, but it proposed the surrender of the city. General Godfrey Weitzel, commanding the mainly Negro 25th Corps, soon arrived on the scene and the surrender party accompanied him to the Capitol. Weitzel reported the scene there:

> When we entered Richmond we found ourselves in a perfect pandemonium. Fires and explosions in all directions; whites and blacks, either drunk or in the highest state of excitement, running to and fro on the streets, apparently engaged in pillage or in saving some of the scanty effects from the fires; it was a yelling, howling mob. . . . A sad sight met us on reaching Capitol Square. It was covered with women and children who had fled here to escape the fire. . . . Most had only a few articles of bedding, such as a quilt, blanket, or pillow, and were lying upon them. Their poor faces were perfect pictures of utter despair.

Weitzel arrived at City Hall at 8:15 and accepted Mayo's surrender, which was unwritten and unconditional. The general then issued an order announcing

> the occupation of the city of Richmond by the Armies of the United States, under command of Lieutenant General Grant. The people of Richmond are assured that we come to restore to them the blessings of peace, prosperity, and freedom, under the flag of the Union. The citizens of Richmond are requested to remain, for the present, quietly within their houses, and to avoid all public assemblages or meetings in the public streets. An efficient provost guard will immediately re-establish order and tranquillity within the city. Martial law is, for the present, proclaimed. Brigadier General George F. Shepley, United States Volunteers, is hereby appointed military governor of Richmond.

Union troops entered the city in the face of roaring flames and dense clouds of black smoke. Little was being done about the fires; only four engines were in operation. These were quickly manned by the troops, who set to work fighting the fires. Other troops turned to the task of restoring order by performing normal police functions. They arrested deserters, stragglers and thieves. Sentries were posted in every street, as well as at some residences (including Robert E. Lee's) at the owners' requests. Temporary rules for governing the city were printed and distributed. No Union troops except those on duty were allowed into the city. Order was so well restored that President Lincoln was able to visit Richmond the next day.

Throughout the loyal states, news of the fall of the Confederate capital was joyously received. After the long siege, it was now easily possible to anticipate the end of the war. Celebrations were held everywhere. Typical of the military response was the Special Order at a small Federal post in Missouri:

> At 8:15 o'clock on the morning of Monday, April 3rd, A. D. 1865, the army of General Grant occupied the city of

Richmond, late capital of the so-called Southern Confederacy. ... The troops at this post will this day celebrate the glorious victory. Military offices, including district headquarters, will be closed at noon, at which hour a national salute will be fired from Fuchs' battery, Second Missouri Artillery. All the troops at this post will be paraded under arms at 3 p.m.

Before the campaign began, Grant had received, from a group of patriotic citizens, $460 to be awarded to the soldier who should first raise the flag of the United States over Richmond. Since the city was not taken by assault, Grant decided to have each of three corps commanders select a man who was conspicuous for gallantry in the final attack on Petersburg. Two sergeants and a corporal were chosen, each receiving $153.33.

Toward Danville, Then Toward Lynchburg

Lee's army was in critical condition as it withdrew westward on April 3, the men hungry and disheartened, the horses starving. Decisions by the generals and other officers were impaired by fatigue and confusion, and the army was moving uncertainly through unknown terrain. This latter reflects negatively on Lee's staff work, since accurate maps should have been prepared for territory through which it had been known for months that the army might have to withdraw. Divisions moved independently, with orders to concentrate at Amelia Court House, on the Richmond and Danville Railroad about forty miles from Richmond and Petersburg.

The next day the army crossed to the south side of the Appomattox River, following the railroad toward Danville and, eventually, to a link-up with Johnston's army. In doing so they no longer had the river to screen them from the Union army. When they arrived at Amelia Court House, the food that was expected to have been shipped by train from Richmond was not there. It never left the city, again because of faulty staff work. Lee therefore decided to pause for a day while the men foraged in the countryside. This decision proved to be a mistake: they were able to find little in the way of food, but the delay allowed Sheridan's horsemen to get ahead of them.

In the late morning of April 5, Lee reduced the number of guns going with the army to two battalions and had the reserve artillery ammunition blown up. He then began marching toward Jetersville, but his advance soon ran into Sheridan's entrenched dismounted cavalry, supported by 5th Corps infantry, blocking the road. When Lee observed the Union battle line he decided that it was too strong to attack. Forced to abandon his plan to go to Danville, he headed instead for Lynchburg. He ordered the army to march by way of Deatonville to the Southside Railroad at Farmville, twenty three miles to the west, where he could get supplies by train. As he changed direction to the northeast, Union troops of 2nd and 6th Corps streamed into Jetersville.

Other Union infantry, moving northeast to attack Lee at Amelia Court House, discovered that he was not there. They therefore changed direction too, heading west to what became the last big battle, at Sayler's Creek. General James Longstreet's First Corps, in the lead, reached and stopped at Rice's Station on the Southside Railroad. He was followed, in order, by the unnumbered, division-sized corps of General Richard H. Anderson and the Third Corps under General Richard S. Ewell (who has replaced Hill). General Gordon's Second Corps, bringing up the rear, was pressed hard by 2nd Corps from the time contact was made sometime after 9:00 A.M. Ewell, in order to keep the only road to Rice's Station open for the infantry, ordered the wagon train to take a road that went to Farmville by way of a loop to the northwest. Gordon mistakenly followed this road, rather than the one used by the other corps, thereby uncovering the rear of Third Corps.

In the early afternoon, Anderson found that Custer's cavalry division was blocking the road to Rice's Station. He formed a battle line facing southwest and launched an attack, which collapsed in five minutes. Ewell was attacked in the rear at the same time by two divisions of 6th Corps, and formed a line facing northeast. The two Confederate corps were then roughly back to back, about a mile apart. Ewell had no artillery, but was able to hold off the Federals until they brought twenty guns into action at a range of 800 yards to support their attacks. The Federals turned Ewell's left-flank brigade, commanded by General Custis Lee (also R. E. Lee's son), capturing it entire. Most of the men of Ewell's division were surrounded, and he and his staff surrendered. The division next in line, General Joseph B. Kershaw's, then also collapsed. At the same time Anderson's bid to open the road failed; he was defeated by the Federal cavalry and two-fifths of his men were taken prisoner.

Sayler's Creek was a disaster for the Army of Northern Virginia. Nearly 8,000 Confederates were killed or captured, including six generals. Ewell's corps was essentially wiped out, losing 2,800 prisoners out of 6,000 men engaged. Anderson lost 2,600 men out of 6,300. Gordon's losses were 300 killed and nearly 1,700 taken prisoner. Lee's army now comprised less than 15,000 men. Longstreet's and Gordon's corps, though reduced in strength, were still functioning. There were six nominal divisions, but four of them were wrecked. The army was literally falling apart. The roads were littered with the detritus of war: rifles, bayonets, cartridge boxes, revolvers, sabers, mortars, cannons, caissons, limbers, wagons, forges, artillery shells, bottles, tin cups, plates, frying pans, knives, spoons, canteens, tents, blanket rolls, oilcloths, knapsacks, saddles, harness, baggage, hats, belts, exhausted horses and mules, and dead animals. The battle's human forfeiture was stragglers, deserters, prisoners, casualties and corpses.

At Farmville, supply trains from Lynchburg were waiting with 80,000 rations of bacon and cornmeal. The Confederates burned four spans of the railroad trestle at High Bridge, but failed to destroy the adjacent covered bridge that carried wagon traffic. As a result, a brigade of 2nd Corps was able to cross the Appomattox

River and press the Confederates as they were preparing to eat. There was not enough time to distribute rations to all the men before the trains had to be moved away from the battle area, so many soldiers continued to go hungry. Lee had no choice but to move northward before turning west toward Appomattox Station, where he hoped to be able to again receive supplies by train. He would then march on to Lynchburg, and from there head south toward Danville.

The race of the armies continued. Gordon's corps was now leading the remnants of the Army of Northern Virginia, followed by Longstreet's corps. Meade was close behind with 2nd Corps (Humphreys) and 6th Corps (Wright). South of the Appomattox River, moving along the stage road through Cumberland Court House, Ord with 24th Corps (Gibbon) and 5th Corps (Griffen) struggled to get ahead.

The Union forces halted at midnight and the men were exhausted and famished. Their orders were to resume pursuit at 6:00 A.M. In preparation, division commanders were told to issue five days rations. That was roughly twelve pounds of food for each man, since one ration was three-quarters of a pound of hard bread and a pound and a half of fresh meat. They were also to issue a half ration of whiskey if it was available in their supply train, and if they desired to do so.

Grant Initiates Negotiations

On April 7, Grant's headquarters was at Burkeville. One of the captured Confederate officers being held there told him (as related in Grant's *Memoirs*) that Ewell had said:

> When [the Union forces] had got across the James River he knew their cause was lost, and it was the duty of their

authorities to make the best terms they could while they still had a right to claim concessions. The authorities thought differently, however. Now the cause was lost and they had no right to claim anything. He said further, that for every man that was killed after this in the war somebody is responsible, and it would be but very little better than murder. He was not sure that Lee would consent to surrender his army without being able to consult with the President, but he hoped he would.

This information, together with the news that Sheridan, by a forced march, had gotten possession of Appomattox Station and several trains of provisions and forage, gave Grant the idea of initiating correspondence regarding the surrender of Lee's army. At 5:00 P.M. he wrote to Lee:

> The results of the last week must convince you of the hopelessness of further resistance on the part of the Army of Northern Virginia in this struggle. I feel that it is so, and regard it as my duty to shift from myself the responsibility of any further effusion of blood, by asking of you the surrender of that portion of the Confederate States army known as the Army of Northern Virginia.

Lee received the letter under a flag of truce shortly after 9:00 P.M. near Farmville. He replied that evening, though Grant did not receive his note until the next morning. It said:

> I have received your note of this date. Though not entertaining the opinion you express on the hopelessness of further resistance on the part of the Army of Northern Virginia, I reciprocate your desire to avoid useless effusion of blood, and therefore before considering your proposition, ask the terms you will offer on condition of its surrender.

While Grant did not consider this satisfactory, he regarded it as deserving another letter, and wrote again on April 8:

THE BEGINNING AND THE END.

> Your note of last evening in reply to mine of same date, asking the condition on which I will accept the surrender of the Army of Northern Virginia, is just received. In reply I would say that, peace being my great desire, there is but one condition that I insist upon, namely: that the men and officers surrendered shall be disqualified for taking up arms again against the Government of the United States until properly exchanged. I will meet you, or will designate officers to meet any officers you may name for the same purpose, at any point agreeable to you, for the purpose of arranging definitely the terms upon which the surrender of the Army of Northern Virginia will be received.

On April 7, several of the Confederate generals had discussed the situation. One alternative was to disperse the army and try to reorganize it later. This was unsatisfactory because it would expose the population of the countryside to devastation from foraging and marauding, and the army to defeat in detail by the Union forces. Another was to abandon the guns and wagon train and try to fight their way out, but in that case they would soon run out of ammunition. They concluded that surrender was inevitable. They thought that if they suggested to Lee the necessity of surrender - that further bloodshed would serve no purpose - the blame or odium might be laid on them instead of on him. It was agreed that General William N. Pendleton, chief of artillery, would talk to Lee, but only after discussing the matter with Longstreet. When Pendleton did this the next day, Longstreet reminded him that the penalty for proposing surrender was death. This was not correct. The *Articles of War* provided that:

> If any commander of any garrison, fortress, or post shall be compelled by the officers and soldiers under his command, to give up to the enemy, or to abandon it, the commissioned officers, non-commissioned officers, and soldiers who shall be convicted of having so offended, shall suffer death, or such

other punishment as may be inflicted upon them by the sentence of a court-martial.

Death was only a possible punishment, Lee was not a garrison commander, and there was no question of trying to compel him: only to suggest it as an option. Longstreet also reminded Pendleton that Lee did not need to be told when it was time to surrender. Nevertheless, Pendleton went to Lee and stated the case. Lee told him that it was not yet the time to consider it, because there were too many men with arms in their hands to think of laying them down. Lee, however, unknown to his officers, had already responded to Grant's initiative.

Lee and His Horse Traveler
Leaving Appomattox

LEE DECIDES TO SURRENDER

The alternative to surrender was guerilla warfare, and there were many officers who advocated it, though perhaps more out of desperation than a realistic understanding of what it would mean. Davis, as Lee well knew, favored that course, but Lee

The Beginning and the End.

believed that the South could only achieve its independence through decisive, conventional battles. As the army retreated, General Porter Alexander told Lee that he thought they should "scatter like rabbits." Lee said he was afraid of the consequences for the Southern people (and perhaps realized that the struggle would have to be based in the mountains and back country, where support for the guerillas would be weak because the people tended to be pro-Union). His reply to Alexander states his reasons for opposing the guerilla option:

> Suppose I should take your suggestion & order the army to disperse & make their way to their homes. The men would have no rations & they would be under no discipline. They are already demoralized by four years of war. They would have to plunder & rob to procure subsistence. The country would be full of lawless bands in every part, & a state of society would ensue from which it would take the country years to recover. Then the enemy's cavalry would pursue in the hopes of catching the principal officers, & wherever they went there would be fresh rapine & destruction. And as for myself, while you young men can afford to go bushwacking, the only proper & dignified course for me would be to surrender myself & take the consequences of my actions.

It is impossible to know what was now in Lee's mind, but it is reasonable to imagine that, while grappling with the inevitable, he was unwilling to admit to himself the reality he faced. Since he knew of the position stated by Lincoln in his meeting with Stephens at the Hampton Roads meeting two months earlier, he can hardly have believed that Grant could discuss a political settlement. Moreover, as the general-in-chief of a government founded on state rights and limited national power, with whose president he could not communicate, he cannot have believed that he had the authority to act for the Confederate government. In his ambiguous reply to Grant on April 8, he said that he did not intend, in his note of the day before

> to propose the surrender of the Army of Northern Virginia, but to ask the terms of your proposition. To be frank, I do not think the emergency has arisen to call for the surrender of this army, but as the restoration of peace should be the sole object of all, I desire to know whether your proposals would lead to that end. I cannot, therefore, meet you with a view to surrender the Army of Northern Virginia; but as far as your proposition may affect the C. S. forces under my command, and tend to the restoration of peace, I shall be pleased to meet you at 10 A.M. tomorrow, on the old stage road to Richmond, between the picket-lines of the two armies.

Grant now had a clear appreciation of what was about to happen, both from the tactical situation of the armies and from the mind-set of the Confederate commander, who had written that it was not time "for the surrender of this army." Despite this, since Lee was Confederate general-in-chief, Grant must have wondered whether "the C. S. forces under my command" referred to all of the Confederate armies. More importantly, exactly what did the phrase "restoration of peace" mean?

Back on February 21, Longstreet and Ord, friends in the Old Army, had met under a flag of truce and exchanged views about arranging terms for ending hostilities. Longstreet then suggested to Lee that he write to Grant, which he did on March 2:

> . . . General Ord stated that if I desired to have an interview with you on the subject [of a military convention] you would not decline, provided I had authority to act. Sincerely desiring to leave nothing untried which may put an end to the calamities of war, I propose to meet you at such convenient time and place as you may designate, with the hope that upon an interchange of views it may be found practicable to submit the subjects of controversy between the belligerents to a convention of the kind mentioned.

Grant notified Secretary of War Stanton, who telegraphed this response:

> The President directs me to say to you that he wishes you to have no conference with General Lee unless it be for the capitulation of Gen. Lee's army, or on some minor and purely military matter. He instructs me to say that you are not to decide, discuss or confer upon any political question. Such questions the President holds in his own hand; and will submit them to no military conferences or conventions. Meanwhile you are to press to the utmost your military advantage.

THE TWO GENERALS MEET

With these unequivocal instructions, and his knowledge of the February meeting at Hampton Roads, Grant sent another letter to Lee early on April 9:

> Your note of yesterday is received. As I have no authority to treat on the subject of peace the meeting proposed for 10 A.M. to-day could lead to no good. I will state, however, general, that I am equally anxious for peace with yourself, and the whole North entertain the same feeling. The terms upon which peace can be had are well understood. By the South laying down their arms they will hasten that most desirable event, save thousands of human lives, and hundreds of millions of property not yet destroyed.

Meanwhile, the situation of Lee's army had seriously deteriorated. Longstreet's First Corps began arriving at Appomattox Court House in the late afternoon of April 8. They learned that Union cavalry, in possession of Appomattox Station, four miles to the southwest, had captured four trains, with their engines, and had sent them toward Farmville for safety. Gordon's Second Corps then arrived and passed through to the front. After sunset the sky was aglow with the reflection of Union campfires to the east, south and west. The sky was dark only to the north, and in that direction the Confederates did not want to go. Lee, Longstreet and Gordon decided that in the morning Second Corps would try to break out to the west, on the Lynchburg road. Fitzhugh Lee, whose cavalry force of 2,000 men was to be posted on Gordon's right, asked that he be notified in case Lee surrendered. He and his men would then leave the field of battle, so as not to be included in the surrender, and would ride south to join Johnston's army.

At dawn on April 9, Gordon's men attacked a line of dismounted Union cavalry on the Lynchburg road, drove them off and captured two guns. Soon an infantry brigade of 24th Corps appeared and blocked the road. Reinforcements steadily poured in. Then 5th Corps troops also began to arrive. The Confederates, surrounded except on the north, were now outnumbered at least five to one. Moreover, while the men still had an average of seventy-five rounds of ammunition, they had no food, and no hope of getting any. Intense rifle and cannon fire continued for several hours. While this action was taking place, Lee had gone to the picket line for the proposed meeting. He received Grant's note there. It was clear that the time had finally come. He replied, "I now request an interview in accordance with the offer contained in your letter of yesterday for that purpose." In a separate note somewhat later, Lee asked for "a suspension of hostilities pending the adjustment of terms of the surrender of this army."

When Gordon received word of this truce, he sent an officer to notify Sheridan and Ord. He also signaled to Fitzhugh Lee, who rode off to the northwest with his command. A few days later, convinced of the impracticality of what he was trying to do, he rode into the Federal lines and accepted the terms offered to officers. His men were later paroled in their home counties.

Lee waited under an apple tree for the response from Grant who, anxious for the matter to be resolved, promptly wrote:

Your note of this date is but this moment (11.50 A.M.) received. In consequence of my having passed from the Richmond and Lynchburg road to the Farmville and Richmond road I am at this writing about four miles west of Walter's Church, and will push forward to the front for the purpose of meeting you. Notice sent to me on this road where you wish the interview to take place will meet me.

McLean's House at Appomattox Court House

The two generals-in-chief met at the house of Wilmer McLean in the village of Appomattox Court House on the afternoon of April 9. Lee and an aide arrived about 1:30; Grant came about 2:00, accompanied by a dozen generals. They all crowded into the living room. After a brief exchange of pleasantries, mostly about their mutual experiences in the Mexican War, Grant wrote out his terms:

> General: In accordance with the substance of my letter to you of the 8th instant, I propose to receive the surrender of the Army of Northern Virginia on the following terms, to wit: Rolls of all the officers and men to be made in duplicate —

one copy to be given to an officer to be designated by me, the other to be retained by such officer or officers as you may designate; the officers to give their individual paroles not to take up arms against the government of the United States until properly exchanged, and each company or regimental commander sign a like parole for the men of their commands. The arms, artillery, and public property to be parked and stacked, and turned over to the officers appointed by me to receive them. This will not embrace the side-arms of the officers, nor their private horses or baggage. This done, each officer and man will be allowed to return to their homes, not to be disturbed by United States authority so long as they observe their parole and the laws in force where they may reside.

Lee said that the provision regarding horses would have a happy effect, but pointed out that in his army the enlisted men of the cavalry and artillery furnished their own horses, and asked whether it would apply to them. Grant said that it would not. He realized, however, that the men were mostly small farmers who would need the animals to help them put in a crop, and that the U. S. Army would have no use for them. He would not change the terms, Grant said, but he would instruct his parole officers that any soldier who claimed to own a horse or mule be allowed to take it. Lee then explained that his army was without food or forage. Grant said that he would authorize Lee's commissary officers to go to Appomattox Station and obtain the food on the captured Confederate trains. As to forage, he said that his army too was without any supply. Lee then formally acknowledged receipt of the terms of surrender: "As they are substantially the same as those expressed in your letter of the 8th instant, they are accepted. I will proceed to designate the proper officers to carry the stipulations into effect."

Conditions Are Agreed To

The six officers assigned to arrange the conditions of surrender were Gibbon, Griffin and Merritt for the United States and Longstreet, Gordon and Pendleton for the Confederate States. On April 10, they issued this agreement:

- 1st. The troops shall march by brigades and detachments to a designated point, stack their arms, deposit their flags, sabers, pistols, &c., and from thence march to their homes under charge of their officers, superintended by their respective division and corps commanders, officers retaining their side arms, and the authorized number of private horses.

- 2nd. All public horses and public property of all kinds to be turned over to staff officers designated by the United States authorities.

- 3rd. Such transportation as may be agreed upon as necessary for the transportation of the private baggage of officers will be allowed to accompany the officers, to be turned over at the end of the trip to the nearest U. S. quartermasters, receipts being taken for the same.

- 4th. Couriers and mounted men of the artillery and cavalry, whose horses are their own private property, will be allowed to retain them.

- 5th. The surrender of the Army of Northern Virginia shall be considered to include all the forces operating with that army on the 8th instant, the date of commencement of negotiations for surrender, except such bodies of cavalry as actually made their escape previous to the surrender, and except such pieces of artillery as were more than twenty miles from Appomattox Court-House at the time of surrender on the 9th instant.

Grant, who was returning to Washington on April 10 to stop purchases of supplies and "other useless" outlays, first rode over to Lee's headquarters, preceded by a bugler and an officer carrying a white flag. The two men met on horseback for half an hour. Lee left no records, but according to Grant's *Memoirs*, he said

> that the South was a big country and that we might have to march over it three or four times before the war entirely ended, but that we would now be able to do it as they could no longer resist us. . . . I then suggested to General Lee that there was not a man in the Confederacy whose influence with the soldiery and the whole people was as great as his, and that if we would but advise the surrender of all the armies I had no doubt that his advice would be followed with alacrity. But Lee said that he could not do that without consulting the President first.

Lee declined the opportunity to use his powers as general-in-chief to end the war by surrendering all of the Confederate armies because he could not confer with Davis. He had already surrendered the Army of Northern Virginia without consulting the president, although this was because he was forced to do so after being surrounded. His personal surrender, and that of six of his staff officers, was effected by a parole signed on April 9:

> We, the undersigned prisoners of war belonging to the Army of Northern Virginia, having been this day surrendered by General Robert E. Lee, C. S. A., commanding said army, to Lieut Genl U. S. Grant, commanding Armies of the United States, do hereby give our solemn parole of honor that we will not hereafter serve in the armies of the Confederate States, or in any military capacity whatever, against the United States of America, or render aid to the enemies of the latter, until properly exchanged, in such manner as may be mutually approved by the respective authorities.

Lee asked that each of the men he surrendered have a paper to protect them from arrest or annoyance as they went home. Grant assigned the assistant provost marshal, General George H. Sharpe, to have parole passes printed. They looked like this:

Appomattox Court House, Virginia

April 10th, 1865

THE BEARER _____ of Co. _____ Regt. of _____, a Paroled Prisoner of the Army of Northern Virginia, has permission to go to his home, and there remain undisturbed.

General Gibbon's headquarters had a hand-cranked printing press, which was set up in the Clover Hill Tavern a hundred yards from the McLean House. Starting on the afternoon of April 10, about 30,000 passes were printed over five days. Each man's pass was signed by his commanding officer, rather than by the U. S. provost marshal, a concession that was much appreciated by the Confederates. The number of men present and armed on April 9 was 7,892, but thousands of stragglers and deserters soon came in to claim the benefit of surrender. The final total on the lists was 28,231 (2,781 officers and 25,450 enlisted men). There were thirty-one Negroes: eight were bandsmen, the others cooks and servants. By Special Orders No. 73, Grant generously directed that "All officers and men . . . paroled at Appomattox . . . who, to reach their homes, are compelled to pass through the lines of the Union armies, will be allowed to do so, and to pass free on all Government transports and military railroads."

While Lee would have preferred to avoid it, Grant insisted on an actual surrender of arms. This took place on April 11 and 12. The artillery was surrendered on the first of these days because of the poor condition of the horses. General Joshua L. Chamberlain, who had commanded the 20th Maine Infantry during its famous stand on the extreme left of the Union line at Gettysburg, was designated to receive the surrender for the United States. No bands played and there was no sign of jubilation or triumph. Grant, Meade and Sheridan were deliberately absent. Two brigades of the 5th Corps lined the road as the Confederate infantry, led by Gordon, marched up. When they approached Chamberlain he gave the order for the blue-clad troops to "Carry Arms," the marching salute. Taken by surprise, Gordon and his men quickly returned the salute, then stacked their muskets, cartridge boxes and flags.

On April 12, Lee wrote to Davis, giving the president official word of what had happened:

> It is with pain that I announce to Your Excellency the surrender of the Army of Northern Virginia. . . . Learning of the condition of affairs on the lines, where I had gone . . . to learn definitely the terms [Grant] proposed . . . in the event of the surrender of the army, I requested a suspension of hostilities until these terms could be arranged. . . . terms having been agreed on, I surrendered that portion of the Army of Northern Virginia which was on the field, with its arms, artillery, and wagon trains; the officers and men to be paroled, retaining their side arms and private effects. I deemed this course the best under all the circumstances by which we were surrounded. . . . If we could have forced our way one day longer it would have been at a great sacrifice of life; at its end, I do not see how a surrender could have been avoided. . . .

Then he rode home to his wife in Richmond, taking the captured U. S. Army ambulance that he had been using as his headquarters wagon. He carried a pass signed by Grant:

> All officers commanding posts, pickets, or detachments will pass General R. E. Lee through their lines north or south on presentation of this pass. General Lee will be permitted to visit Richmond at any time unless otherwise ordered by

competent authority, and every facility for his doing so will be given by officers of the U. S. Army to whom this may be presented.

The Army of Northern Virginia was only the first of the Confederate armies to lay down its arms. The Army of Tennessee under General Johnston, the Army of Alabama-Mississippi-Louisiana under General Taylor, and the Army of Trans-Mississippi under General Kirby-Smith, as well as numerous smaller forces, remained in the field. The terms afforded to Lee, however, were essentially those that were later accepted by the other surrendering Confederate forces. In North Carolina, Sherman was about to advance against Johnston. Grant ordered two corps to encamp around Burkeville, to be in position to move southwest along the railroad to attack Johnston's flank or rear in case he did not surrender.

The Government Moves to Danville

Davis and other government officials arrived in Danville late on April 3 and remained until April 10. Major William Sutherlin offered Davis the use of his home. A boxcar and a passenger car served as the Confederate capitol. On April 5, Davis issued a proclamation, which, because of the poor state of communications, was printed in only a few Southern newspapers, but powerfully expresses his determination to carry on:

> It would be unwise to conceal the moral and material injury to our cause resulting from the occupation of our capital by the enemy. It is equally unwise and unworthy of us to allow our own energies to falter, and our efforts to become relaxed under reverses, however calamitous they may be. . . . We have now entered a new phase of the struggle. Relieved from the necessity of guarding particular points, our army will be free to move from point to point, to strike the enemy in detail far from his base. Let us but will it, and we are free. . . . If by

the stress of numbers we should ever be compelled to a temporary withdrawal from [Virginia's] limits, or those of any other border State, we will return until the baffled and exhausted enemy shall abandon in despair his endless and impossible task of making slaves of a people resolved to be free.

While at dinner on the night of April 9, before word arrived of the event at Appomattox, Davis was asked by his hostess whether the war would be over in case of Lee's surrender. He replied: "By no means. We will fight it out to the Mississippi River." His plan was to cross Georgia to join Taylor in Alabama, or to escape via Florida to Havana, and by either route to reach Texas, where General Kirby-Smith had an army of 40,000 men. They were without much combat experience, but had suffered neither defeat nor deprivation. They would form the nucleus for carrying on the war, and would be joined by Confederate units and individual soldiers who would find their way across the river from the east.

Lee had declined to surrender all Confederate forces without referring the matter to Davis. Was Davis inclined or able to discharge this responsibility? Indeed, whose responsibility was it? The wording in the C. S. Constitution was identical to that in the U. S. Constitution: "Congress shall have power . . . to declare war." In neither document was a means specified for ending a war once declared. Both provided that "The President . . . shall have power, by and with the advice of the Senate, to make Treaties," and the two American wars of the first half of the 19th Century had been ended by treaties: the War of 1812 by the Treaty of Ghent and the Mexican War by the Treaty of Guadalupe Hidalgo. Jefferson Davis, a "strict constructionist," held that the Constitution was to be interpreted literally and narrowly. How, therefore, might the hostilities that the C. S. A. had declared against the U. S. A. on May 6, 1861 be legally concluded?

Davis might make peace on whatever terms he could obtain by exercising his political powers as president and his military powers as commander-in-chief. However, this was inconsistent with the doctrine of strict construction. A clearly constitutional method would be for the president to conclude a treaty with the United States and have it approved by the Confederate Senate. Unfortunately, he was in no position to negotiate such a treaty, and the Senate was irretrievably dispersed. Alternatively, one could conceive that the power to end war rested not with the Confederate government (though it was the Confederate government that had declared war), but with each of the eleven states of which it was composed. This was, after all, a "war between the states," and each state was "sovereign." In any event, the issue was moot. No treaty of peace was ever entered into: the Confederate government simply disintegrated and ceased to exist.

On April 10, fugitives streamed into Danville with news of the surrender. Only after 4:00 P.M. did Davis receive official word. Since Lee was now a paroled prisoner of war, Confederate forces no longer had a general-in-chief. Responsibility for overall command reverted to Davis, but because he was not in communication with the remaining Confederate forces, he was unable to exercise any command function. The government immediately prepared to leave by train for Greensboro, North Carolina. Considerable amounts of food and ammunition had been stockpiled in Danville in anticipation of the arrival of Lee's army, and two infantry companies were assigned to protect them. Local people, frightened and hungry, attacked the guards and helped themselves to the food. As this was happening the ammunition exploded, killing fifty soldiers and civilians.

Greensboro, a county seat of 2,000 people, did not welcome the arrival of Davis and his five cabinet members. The area had not been pro-Confederate from the beginning, and had petitioned the state government to make peace. Moreover, the people knew what had happened to Atlanta and Columbia and were fearful of reprisals. With difficulty, a room was found for Davis in a boarding house. For the four days the government remained there, the cabinet members lived uncomfortably on the train, sleeping in the shabby coaches and boxcars and eating meager meals on tin plates.

THE GUERILLA CHIEF MOSBY

Following the surrender at Appomattox, Federal commanders in the Shenandoah Valley wondered whether the Confederate forces there were included. Since they were not "forces operating with" the Army of Northern Virginia, they were not. This was soon understood, and on April 10, General Winfield S. Hancock, who commanded the Middle Military Division headquartered at Winchester, published a circular informing the civilian population of Lee's surrender. Explaining what had happened, it said:

> The arms, artillery, and baggage were delivered up, the Confederate officers being allowed to retain their sidearm and personal property. Officers and men were all paroled. . . . All detachments and stragglers from the Army of Northern Virginia will, upon complying with the above conditions, be paroled and allowed to go to their homes. Those who do not so surrender will be brought in as prisoners of war. The guerilla chief Mosby is not included in the parole. . . . It is for you to determine the amount of freedom you are to enjoy. The marauding bands which have so long infested this section, subsisting on the plunder of the defenseless, affecting no great military purpose, and bringing upon you the devastation of your homes, must no longer find shelter and concealment among you. Every outrage committed by them will be followed by the severest infliction, and it is the purpose of the Major General Commanding to destroy utterly the haunts of these bands if their depredations are continued.

The "guerilla chief" referred to was Colonel John S. Mosby of the 43rd Virginia Cavalry Battalion of irregular rangers, or partisans. On April 11, General C. H. Morgan, Hitchcock's chief of staff, wrote a letter to Mosby, offering to receive the surrender of his command on the same terms as those given to Lee, and to have an officer meet with him to arrange details. He entrusted the letter to J. H. Clarke, a merchant and hotel owner in Millwood who said he could get in touch with Mosby, and who delivered it the next day. On April 12, Hancock wrote to the U. S. Army chief-of-staff, General Henry W. Halleck, telling him that he had sent the letter to Mosby, but had not yet received an answer. He went on to give his opinion:

> It is quite as likely that Mosby will disband as that he will formally surrender, as all his men have fine animals and are generally armed with two pistols only. They will not give up these things, I presume, as long as they can escape. I will employ the cavalry here in hunting them down.

Mosby answered Hancock on the day of Lincoln's death, April 15. His reply was delivered by Lieutenant Colonel William H. Chapman and three other partisan officers who came to Carter Hall, a brick mansion on the edge of Millwood, under a flag of truce. Hancock expressed sympathy for their misfortune, which surprised the Confederates, who had expected a harsh reception. Mosby's message said:

> As yet I have no notice, through any other source, of the facts concerning the surrender of the Army of Northern Virginia; nor, in my opinion, has the emergency yet arisen which would justify the surrender of my command.... [however] I am ready to agree to a suspension of hostilities for a short time, in order to enable me to communicate with my authorities, or until I can obtain sufficient intelligence to determine my future action. . . . I am ready to meet any person you may designate to arrange the terms of an armistice.

Col. John S. Mosby

No agreement was reached at the conference, but on Easter Sunday, April 16, Morgan responded to Mosby on behalf of Hancock:

The General is very willing to allow a reasonable time for you to acquire the information you desire. It is not practicable for you to communicate with General Lee, as he is no longer in authority. . . . the General will not operate against your command until Tuesday [April 18] at 12 M[eridian], provided there are no hostilities from your command. . . . It is possible some difficulties may arise from the operation of guerilla parties not under your command, but the General hopes you can control the whole matter. On Tuesday at noon, the General will send an officer of equal rank with yourself to Millwood. . . . If you consent to the above arrangement, please notify Brigadier General Chapman, at Berryville, as soon as possible.

On April 17, the 43rd Battalion, summoned by Mosby, assembled at Salem (now Marshall). There were 700 men on the battalion roster, about 100 of whom were prisoners of war. The men had learned about Appomattox through Hancock's circular, but had also heard a rumor that Johnston had defeated Sherman. Now told that there was a truce, they discussed the possibility of riding south to join Johnston's army, or of going to Mexico to enlist in Maximilian's army, which was seeking recruits to prepare against invasion by the United States. One of the officers had just returned from Richmond, where he had sought the counsel of Lee. The former general had said that he could not give advice because he was on parole, but when pressed he suggested that the men go home and help to rebuild Virginia.

Mosby, arriving with an escort of fifteen men, met with General George H. Chapman at Clarke's hotel in Millwood on the morning of April 18. Mosby told Chapman that he would not surrender the battalion, but would disband it. Each ranger could then decide for himself whether or not to surrender on his own. He, Mosby, did not intend to do so. He asked that the cessation of hostilities continue for two more days, until noon on April 20, to which Chapman agreed. For his part, Mosby agreed "to use his influence and authority in the mean time to prevent any acts of hostility by bands or organizations of Confederate soldiers operating from Loudoun or Fauquier counties." Chapman and Mosby also drafted a proposed agreement, subject to Hancock's approval, that would have extended the cease-fire until April 30. Hancock, however, did not approve the proposal, and Mosby was so informed on April 19, with the added information that "After the expiration of this truce, General Hancock is commanded not to offer you or your men terms again."

When Mosby returned to Millwood on April 20, he was shown a copy of a telegraph message to Hancock from Grant, dated April 19:

> You may receive all rebel officers or soldiers who surrender to you on exactly the same terms that were given to General Lee, except have it distinctly understood that all who claim homes in states that never passed Ordinances of Secession have forfeited them, and can only return on compliance with the amnesty proclamation. Maryland, Kentucky, Delaware and Missouri are such states. They may return to West Virginia on their parole.

Mosby sent orders for the active members of his command to rendezvous again on Friday, April 21 at Salem. On that rainy morning about 200 men (the roll was not called) lined up in eight companies, in the chronological order in which the companies had been formed. Wearing their gray uniforms with black plumes on their hats, each man was armed with two revolvers and rode his best mount. The company commanders read Mosby's farewell message to their men:

> Soldiers — I have summoned you together for the last time. The vision we cherished of a free and independent country has vanished, and that country is now the spoil of a conqueror. I disband your organization in preference to surrendering to our enemies. I am no longer your commander....

Colonel Chapman announced that he was going to Winchester the next day to offer his parole and invited anyone who wanted to go with him to meet at Paris. About 200 men rode together along the Blue Ridge, many on blind or lame horses, assuming that the animals would be taken from them. They waited at a Federal camp a mile outside of town until a provost marshal officer arrived with parole forms for them to sign. They found that the U. S. Army was not interested in their horses, and left for their homes. The next day a Federal officer came to Millwood, where additional rangers signed paroles. In the following month, some 400 other members of the battalion, from scattered locations in the valley and the mountains, also signed.

Mosby himself did not at that time sign a parole, as he had said he would not. He and several other officers rode to within thirteen miles of Richmond, to find out what they could about the situation. They learned, from a newspaper obtained from Federal officers on a passing boat on the James River canal, that Johnston's army no longer existed. Mosby held out for two months, despite a $5,000 reward for his capture, but decided to accept parole on June 13. He came into town in uniform, armed with two revolvers. Told by Federal officers that they had an order for his arrest, he angrily left. Three days later his parole was accepted on instructions from Grant. By September, Mosby was again practicing law in Fauquier County.

THE ARMY'S WORK IS NOT FINISHED

There were jobs for the army, especially the cavalry, to do as the war wound down. In the Shenandoah Valley and in the mountains, Federal troops looked for deserters and soldiers who had not given their paroles and did not know that they could or should do so. Typical of this activity was a scout through Randolph and Pocahontas Counties by the Eighth Ohio Cavalry. Captain Joseph Badger left Philippi, West Virginia on April 15 with 150 men. Forty were armed with Spencer carbines and 110 with Burnside carbines. After fording Tygart River, Badger "heard that Joe Gay had a few bushwackers and horse thieves about Stony Creek" and that "Captain McNeill, a noted guerilla, was at his home near Huntersville." After dispatching small parties to pick them up, he heard stories of guerilla groups ranging in size from fifty to 400, but placed no reliance in the reports. On April 18, his advance was "suddenly and furiously attacked," but soon afterward "the enemy were running up the side of the mountain to get away." The patrol bivouacked near Warm Springs. Fifty men stayed on picket while the others slept, and the horses remained saddled and bridled.

The next day they "Picked up several rebels along the road to Crab Bottom and . . . captured Major Armesy, Thirty-Third Virginia [Cavalry], commander of reserves of three counties." On the 20th, they found good grazing at a ford on the Greenbrier River and stopped for two hours to feed the horses. When they moved on, the rear guard was ambushed by four or five men. Badger had his men "scatter about 2000 cartridges all over the face of the hill, which made it so warm that the bushwackers had to get out of their holes and leave on double-quick." He was now on the trail of a Captain Harding, who had three or four men with him. At the next village, Badger had two squads search every house and barn within three miles, but found no trace of them. On April 21, after gathering enough grain to feed his command, he moved on to Beverly where the quartermaster had sent forage, and he was able to rest his men and horses. The appraisal that Badger made in the report of his nine-day patrol serves as a useful summary of the situation in the mountains as the war came to an end:

> I found the people all through my route completely conquered; Lee's surrender has finished them. They see no hope in further resistance and are willing to submit on our terms. They seemed gratified when they heard the terms. There are a great many stragglers and deserters all through

the country who have no idea of going back to the army, but being afraid of us they run and hide as much as possible. I believe when they understand our terms they will come in and give their parole. I met several paroled men of Lee's army. I judge from their talk that they will be an army of missionaries all through the South to preach to the people a doctrine of common sense and the folly of further resistance. . . . Their only desire seems to be to get back their sons, brothers, and husbands who have been in the army, and live in peace. Before I explained to them they supposed that all who had been in the rebel army would be confined in Northern prisons for life.

Elsewhere in Virginia, a cavalry patrol brought to an end a search that had held public attention for nearly two weeks. Ubiquitous public elation in the North over Lee's surrender on April 9 was followed by profound shock and sorrow over the death of Lincoln six days later. His body lay in state in Washington until April 21. It was then moved slowly by train toward burial in Illinois. Meanwhile Federal forces, military and civilian, were pursuing the murderer and his accomplices. On April 20, Secretary of War Stanton posted notice of $100,000 reward for information "that shall conduce to the arrest of the . . . criminals:" $50,000 for John Wilkes Booth, $25,000 each for John H. Surratt and David E. Herold. The notice said:

> The murderer of our late beloved President Abraham Lincoln is still at large. . . . All persons harboring or secreting the said persons . . . or aiding or assisting their concealment or escape, will be treated as accomplices in the murder of the President and the attempted assassination of the Secretary of State, and shall be subject to a trial before a military commission and the punishment of death. Let the stain of innocent blood be removed from the land by the arrest and punishment of the murderers.

Booth was killed and Herold captured at the farm of Richard Garrett, a Confederate sympathizer, near Port Royal, Virginia on April 26. One of the parties searching for them was a twenty-six-man detachment of the 16th New York Cavalry, led by Lieutenant Edward P. Doherty. Accompanied by two detectives, Colonel E. J. Conger and Lieutenant Luther B. Baker, they traveled on the steamer *John S. Ide* from Washington to Belle Plain on April 24, riding in a westerly direction until they reached the Rappahannock River. They made frequent inquiries and learned that the two men they were seeking had come across the river. For two days they followed the leads they were given. When they got to the Garrett farm in the middle of the night, one of the owner's sons admitted that Booth was in the barn. The troopers surrounded it, but were ordered not to shoot, for fear of hitting other soldiers in the dark.

Doherty and the detectives negotiated with Booth, who refused to surrender even after they threatened to set the barn on fire. He said, however, that there was a man with him who wanted to surrender, and Herold then appeared. As soon as he did so, Conger ignited hay in the rear of the barn, which soon filled with smoke. When Booth still did not come out, Sergeant Boston Corbett, despite orders, aimed his weapon through a crack in the wall and shot him in the back of the neck. Booth lived for several hours, lying on the porch of the house. Doherty had the body sewed up in a saddle blanket and the detachment took it in a wagon to the boat and then to Washington. The exhausted cavalrymen had been up for sixty hours, and had crossed the river twice. In his report, Doherty said that

> it has afforded my command and myself inexpressible pleasure to be the humble instruments of capturing the foul assassins who caused the death of our beloved President and plunged the nation in mourning.

Chapter 7

Johnston Surrenders in North Carolina
April 26, 1865

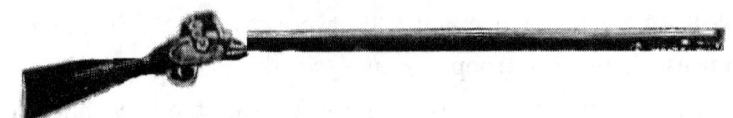

Sherman Advances to Goldsboro

After resting for a month in Savannah from the "march to the sea," Sherman's army started north in late January. The Confederates did not believe this large force could cross the swamps and rivers of the low country in winter, but it did, and rapidly. After feinting in the directions of Augusta and Charleston, Sherman reached Columbia on February 17, then continued toward Goldsboro. He had chosen that place as his destination because it was the junction of the railroads northward from Wilmington and westward from New Bern. At Bentonville, the Confederates attempted to block his advance on March 19-21. This was the last large-scale engagement fought by the army of General Joseph E. Johnston.

On March 23, Sherman's troops arrived in Goldsboro, where they united with 10th Corps and 23rd Corps, the latter having been transferred from Nashville. They had come by train from New Bern and by marching from Wilmington, which had finally been captured a month earlier, but the railroad had not yet been restored. Sherman designated these two corps the Army of Tennessee (Johnston's Confederate army had the same name), under the command of General John M. Schofield, and assigned it to the center of the enlarged Union formation. The Army of Georgia, under General Henry W. Slocum, consisting of 14th and 20th Corps, was assigned the left. The Army of Ohio, under General Oliver O. Howard, consisting of 15th and 17th Corps, was assigned the right. The Cavalry Corps was commanded by General H. Judson Kilpatrick. The troops now numbered 88,948, of which 2,448 were artillerymen and 5,650 were cavalry. Sherman decided to pause to rest the troops because two-thirds of his men had been campaigning for seven grueling weeks over the 425 miles from Savannah. During this time he distributed new uniforms, equipment and supplies.

On March 25, Sherman left for a conference with Grant, traveling by train to New Bern and then by steamship to Grant's headquarters at City Point, Virginia. Late on the 27th, and again at noon on the 28th, the two generals met with President Lincoln on the *River Queen* to discuss strategy for the conclusion of the war. The president indicated that he did not contemplate revenge or harsh measures toward the South, but suggested no specific surrender terms. Sherman returned by the same route and was back with the army on March 30.

After the battle of Bentonville, Johnston placed his army at Smithfield, midway between Raleigh and Goldsboro. At this time he had no clear idea from Lee as to the Confederate plan. He believed that Sherman might be marching to join Grant at Petersburg, in which case he too should move north, to support Lee. However, he was under the impression that Lee intended to come south with part of his army to join him in an effort to defeat Sherman. Neither of these options was realistic. While he waited for instructions, he formed his Army of Tennessee into three infantry corps, commanded by Generals William J. Hardee, A. P. Stewart and S. D. Lee, and a Cavalry Corps with about 5,000 poorly mounted men under General Wade Hampton.

There were reported to be 70,510 infantrymen and artillerymen, but only 18,578 were present for duty, and only 14,179, a meager 20 percent of those on the rolls, were effectives. These numbers clearly indicate the extent to which desertions, wounds and illness had reduced the fighting strength. Reorganization at lower levels was also necessary because many regiments consisted of only thirty or forty men, less than a full company. At least 1,300 infantrymen lacked weapons, some were without shoes, and the clothing of many was hardly more than rags. Johnston, whether anticipating the end of the war or being unwilling to further reduce his army, ordered that all executions be suspended.

On April 5, Sherman issued Special Field Orders No. 48 to the army and corps commanders. The army's next objective was to take position north of the Roanoke River, facing west, in communication with the Army of the Potomac and the Army of the James at Petersburg, and with Norfolk as a supply base. All preparations were to be complete by April 10 and the march was to begin on April 12. He closed the lengthy order by saying that he required a report "each night, whether any thing material has occurred or not, for often the absence of an enemy is a very important fact in military prognostication." The following day, however, news was received that Richmond had fallen and the Army of Northern Virginia was marching southwestward to join forces with the Johnston's army. The Union troops, thinking they would soon be able to go home, responded by building bonfires and firing rockets. Sherman changed his plan: the Federals would move directly against Johnston's army, which was believed to number 35,000 men.

On April 8, Sherman received a message, in cipher, from Grant dated April 5 (before the Sayler's Creek battle.) It said:

> All indications now are that Lee will attempt to reach Danville with the remnant of his force. Sheridan . . . reports all that is left with him — horse, foot, and dragoons — at twenty thousand, much demoralized. We hope to reduce this number one-half. I will push on to Burkesville, and, if a stand is made at Danville, will, in a few days, go there. If you can possibly do so, push on from where you are, and let us see if we can finish the job with Lee's and Johnston's armies. . . . Rebel armies are now the only strategic points to strike at.

Raleigh is Surrendered

On April 10, a lovely spring day with dogwoods and lilacs in blossom, the well-rested Union army resumed its advance. Morale was high and the soldiers looked splendid in their new uniforms. There was skirmishing the next day, and the troops passed houses that had been set afire by retreating soldiers and vengeful slaves. By afternoon on April 11, leading elements of 14th Corps reached Smithfield, where they heard the news of Lee's surrender. The men celebrated while bands played "John Brown's Body" and the recently composed "Marching Through Georgia."

Before dawn on April 12, as North Carolina Governor Zebulon B. Vance worked in his office in the Capitol, two former governors (and Union supporters) came to see him: William A. Graham, once U. S. Secretary of the Navy, and Davis L. Swain, president of the University of North Carolina. They wanted Vance to summon the legislature into session so the state could negotiate surrender terms. Johnston had advised him that the Army of Tennessee was unable to defend Raleigh and that he should try to negotiate. So Vance wrote a letter to Sherman:

> Understand that your army is advancing on this capital, I have to request, under proper safe-conduct, a private interview, at such time as may be agreeable to you, for the purpose of conferring upon the subject of a suspension of hostilities, with view to further communications with the authorities of the United States, touching the final termination of the existing war. If you concur in the propriety of such a proceeding I shall be obliged by an early reply.

He then appointed Graham and Swain as commissioners to deliver the letter and to open talks if possible. At 10:30 A.M., the two elderly men and three other officials, with safe conduct passes issued by General Hardee, boarded a one-car train flying a white flag. On the way to Smithfield, as it passed through the Confederate lines, the train was stopped by General Hampton, who objected to their mission. After reconsideration, he sent a message to Sherman asking him to receive them. Federal cavalrymen boarded the train and took the commissioners to the headquarters of General Kilpatrick, whose men had captured the railroad. After they were informed of Lee's surrender and robbed of their Confederate money, they were conducted to Sherman's headquarters. He met them at the train and told them that it looked to him like the fighting was over. The three men talked for hours over dinner, and the commissioners spent the night in the tents of Sherman and his staff.

Back in Raleigh, Governor Vance, who heard (erroneously) late on April 12 that Graham and Swain were being held prisoner, decided to head west. Before leaving he again wrote to Sherman, authorizing mayor William H. Harrison to surrender the city and asking that the Capitol, the museum and other public buildings not be destroyed. The last train departed at 9:00 P.M. carrying tens of thousands of blankets, abundant cloth for uniforms, enough leather for 20,000 shoes, and 40,000 bushels of corn. This was material that had been hoarded by Vance for the use of North Carolina troops and not shared with the hungry and poorly clothed men of Johnston's and Lee's armies. Vance left on horseback at midnight and rode eight miles west to the camp of North Carolina troops.

On the morning of April 13, the commissioners returned to Raleigh with a letter from Sherman saying that he hoped Vance would stay in Raleigh and continue as the state's executive, but doubted that hostilities between the armies could be suspended. When their train was a mile from the station, the commissioners saw clouds of smoke and learned that the depot had been set afire by the Confederate cavalrymen of General Joseph Wheeler, who had also plundered several stores as they left the capital. Hardee, who was in temporary command, had already left with the infantry. Johnston was absent in Greensboro with Davis, who had just arrived from Danville.

Raleigh, with its 8,000 inhabitants, became the seventh Confederate state capital abandoned or surrendered, with no terms agreed to. Before the commissioners got back to the city, the mayor and a delegation started east by carriage to meet Kilpatrick and implore him to save the city from destruction, to which the general assented after "some blustering." This agreed to, the first squadron entered the town and came upon a lone officer from Texas who had lingered to loot. He fired five revolver shots without hitting anyone. His horse fell as he rode hurriedly away and he was captured. Brought before Kilpatrick in Capitol Square, the general rendered summary judgment: the man was refused a few minutes to write a letter to his wife and was hanged from a tree in the yard of a house. Kilpatrick had the U. S. flag raised over the Capitol, then continued in pursuit of Wheeler, leaving a regiment as city guards. Sherman entered the city at 7:30 A.M. and established headquarters in the just-vacated governor's house.

JOHNSTON CONFERS WITH DAVIS

On April 10, Johnston, camped fourteen miles east of Raleigh on the Neuse River, received a telegram from Davis:

> A scout reports that General Lee surrendered the remnant of his army near to Appomattox Court-House yesterday. No official intelligence of the event, but there is little room for doubt as to result. . . . I will have need to see you to confer as to future action.

The president also told him that General H. H. Walker was ordered to join Johnston's forces at Greensboro. Davis sent a message to Vance, saying:

> I expected to visit you at Raleigh, but am accidentally prevented from executing that design, and would be very glad to see you here if you can come at once . . . We must redouble our efforts to meet present disaster. An army holding its position with determination to fight on, and manifest ability to maintain the struggle, will attract all the scattered soldiers and daily rapidly gather strength. Moral influence is wanting.

Johnston received a second telegram from Davis, rather long and in cipher, at 1:30 A. M. on the 11th. It was mostly unintelligible, so he had to ask that the whole thing be repeated. The second attempt produced this message:

> I will go to your headquarters immediately after the arrival of the Secretary of War, or you can come here. . . . I have no

official report from General Lee. . . . The important question first to be solved is, at what point shall concentration be made, in view of the present position of the two columns of the enemy and the routes which they may adopt to engage your forces before a prompt junction with General Walker and others. Your more intimate knowledge of the data for the solution of the problem deters me from making a specific suggestion at this point.

In a telegram at 3:30 P. M. Davis told Johnston:

> General Beauregard proposes, after General Walker shall join him, which will be ordered to commence forthwith, to unite with you at the Yadkin, in front of Salisbury. And this seems to me to be the most easy method, if pursued, of effecting the proposed junction.

This was followed an hour later by a telegram saying:

> Secretary of War has not arrived. To save time and have all the information it is probably better that you come here. In that event you will give the needful instructions to your second in command and, if circumstances warrant, suspend the movement suggested in dispatch of 3:30 P. M. for a time.

The vacillation and confusion in these messages suggests the chaotic state of Davis's mind, hardly surprising in view of the extremely stressful situation he was enduring. While the president and the general were communicating, Beauregard reported from Greensboro:

> Enemy cut road between this place and Salisbury at High Point and Jamestown; also cut road between this place and Danville, about twelve miles from here, this morning. Hope to repair the road at High Point and Jamestown in short time. Can hear nothing of pontoon train.

The Confederates were trying to clear the road west from Raleigh, in preparation for the movement of Johnston's army to the Greensboro area. There, according to the Confederate plan, it would combine with Lee's army when it arrived from Danville. Walker was coming north from Augusta with an assortment of troops, bringing along pontoons to make crossings for the army where the bridges were out. The purpose of the raid by Stoneman's Union cavalry in the western part of the state was to prevent Johnston and Lee from joining there, mainly by destroying bridges and railroads. Even though Lee had now surrendered, it was still important to open the road for Johnston's army.

Around midnight Johnston left Raleigh by train for his conference with Davis. He arrived at 8:00 A. M. on April 12 and again heard the news that Lee had surrendered. General Beauregard had also been called to Greensboro, and the two generals met with Davis in his private rail car at 10:00 A. M. Secretary of State Benjamin, Secretary of the Navy Mallory, and Postmaster-General Reagan were present. The news was bleak: Selma had been captured, and Montgomery, Columbus and Macon were threatened. Davis asked no questions about the condition of the army, or the tactical situation. Instead, he spoke of concentrating troops at Salisbury or Charlotte. He suggested to Johnston that he recall the thousands of soldiers who had deserted and that he draft men who had been exempted. When Johnston said he was certain that they would not come in the circumstances, Davis adjourned the meeting. They would reconvene, the president said, after the arrival of Secretary of War Breckinridge, who was expected late that afternoon with accurate information regarding the events in Virginia.

Breckinridge, a Kentuckian, was a lawyer. He served as an officer in the Mexican War, and was a member of the U. S. House of Representatives from 1851 to 1855. When Buchanan was elected president in 1857, Breckinridge became vice-president. He was a strong pro-slavery spokesman and was nominated for president by the Southern Democrats in 1860. In 1862, he was made a general in the Confederate army, and served as secretary of war during the War's final four months. When he arrived late in the day, Johnston and Beauregard went to see him, stated their views, and sought his help in convincing Davis.

A Suspension of Hostilities

At 8:00 P.M., in an upstairs bedroom of the home of Colonel John T. Wood, the cabinet meeting reconvened. After about two hours, Johnston and Beauregard were asked to join them. When Davis asked Johnston for his opinion of the situation, the general replied (as Mallory recalled years afterward):

> My views are, sir, that our people are tired of war, feel themselves whipped, and will not fight. . . . Our country is overrun, its military reserves greatly diminished. . . . My men are daily deserting in large numbers, and are stealing my artillery teams to aid their escape to their homes. Since Lee's defeat they regard the war as at an end. . . . My small force is melting away like snow before the sun.

When Davis asked Beauregard for his views, he concurred fully. The Army of Northern Virginia no longer existed, the main Confederate munition-making centers had been captured, and the Army of Tennessee was out-numbered by as much as ten to one. The situation was in fact hopeless and the only available course was to make peace. Breckinridge, Mallory and Reagan favored trying to come to terms, while Benjamin agreed with Davis that they should continue fighting.

The seven men met for the third time on the morning of April 13. Davis once more expressed optimism about the ability of the South to continue its struggle for independence. "The war had now shrunk into narrow proportions," he remembered years later, "but the important consideration remained to so conduct it that, if failing to secure our independence, we might obtain a treaty or quasi-treaty of peace which would secure to the Southern States their political rights, and to the people thereof immunity from the plunder of their private property." In short, he hoped that, in surrendering, the Confederacy could convince the United States to forget why the war had been fought!

Johnston then pointed out that the Confederacy was "without money, or credit, or arms, or ammunition, or means of procuring them." He again said that continuing the war was hopeless. His army consisted of about 20,000 infantry and artillery and 5,000 cavalry. He estimated that the Union army now consisted of 350,000 men. The Confederates, he said, should attempt to negotiate terms with Sherman. Davis reluctantly accepted Johnston's recommendation and, in a moment of reality, said he doubted that the Federal government would deal with him, since it did not recognize the Confederacy. Johnston observed that there was precedent for military commanders initiating peace talks. Confident that Sherman would treat with him, he asked permission to propose a meeting to arrange an armistice. Davis then dictated a letter for Johnston to sign and send through the lines:

> The results of the recent campaign in Virginia have changed the relative military condition of the belligerents. I am therefore induced to address you, in this form, the inquiry whether, to stop the further effusion of blood and the devastation of property, you are willing to make a temporary suspension of active operations . . . the object being to permit

the civil authorities to enter into the needful arrangements to terminate the existence of war.

On April 14, the letter was received by Sherman by way of Hampton and Kilpatrick. Sherman notified Grant and Stanton by telegraph, noting that he would "be careful not to complicate any points of civil policy" in his negotiations. He then sent Johnston a conciliatory letter, saying:

> I am fully empowered to arrange with you any terms for the suspension of further hostilities between the armies commanded by you and those commanded by myself, and will be willing to confer with you to that end. I will limit the advance of my main column, to-morrow, to Morrisville, and the cavalry to the university, and expect that you will also maintain the present position of your forces until each has notice of a failure to agree. That a basis of action may be had, I undertake to abide by the same terms and conditions as were made by Generals Grant and Lee at Appomattox Court-House, on the 9th instant, relative to our two armies; and, furthermore, to obtain from General Grant an order to suspend the movements of any troops from the direction of Virginia. General Stoneman is under my command, and my order will suspend any devastation or destruction contemplated by him. I will add that I really desire to save the people of North Carolina the damage they would sustain by the march of this army through the central or western parts of the State.

The letter was sent forward to Kilpatrick's headquarters at Durham Station, with instructions to have it delivered through the lines. But the cavalry general, whose view of the Confederates was disdainful, left the execution of this assignment to his staff. They did not hurry to move the message to Hampton's headquarters near Hillsboro, and it did not reach Johnston until April 16.

In the two intervening days, the Union forces advanced from Raleigh, skirmishing between there and Morrisville on April 13, with many men suffering sunstroke from the intense heat. The cavalry occupied Chapel Hill on April 14 and Sherman issued Special Field Orders No. 55, with instructions for the movement of the three armies. He concluded by saying:

> No further destruction of railroads, mills, cotton, and produce, will be made without the specific orders of an army commander, and the inhabitants will be dealt with kindly, looking to an early reconciliation. The troops will be permitted, however, to gather forage and provisions as heretofore; only more care should be taken not to strip the poorer classes too closely.

Meanwhile, on April 14 in Washington, Secretary of War Stanton ordered an end to the draft and began canceling orders for munitions and supplies. Before noon, the U. S. flag was raised at Fort Sumter by the man who had lowered in four years earlier, now General Robert Anderson. That evening, President Lincoln was shot. He died at 7:22 the next morning. At 10:00 A.M. at the Kirkwood Hotel, the presidential oath of office was administered to Vice-president Andrew Johnson of Tennessee by Chief Justice Salmon P. Chase.

THE BENNETT HOUSE MEETING

Davis left Greensboro for Charlotte on April 16, unaware of Lincoln's assassination, and without notifying Johnston that he had gone. The remaining remnant of the Confederate government was out of communication with its army and the nation. The railroad was not operating south of Greensboro, so Davis and several cabinet members rode horseback while others traveled in carriages. The party moved slowly because of the rain, the wagons heavily loaded with government archives and personal baggage.

The two armies were now several days march apart, the only contact being sporadic skirmishes between Kilpatrick's cavalry of the Union advance and Hampton's cavalry as it screened the Confederate rear. Hampton arranged for a meeting between Johnston and Sherman to take place midway between Hillsboro and Durham Station at noon on April 17. As Sherman boarded the train at Raleigh, the telegrapher told him that an important message was coming in. Sherman waited for half an hour while the telegram was decoded. It was from Secretary of War Stanton:

> President Lincoln was murdered about 10 o'clock last night in his private box at Ford's Theatre in this city, by an assassin who shot him through the head with a pistol ball. . . . I find evidence that an assassin is also on your track.

In addition, it said, Secretary of State Seward had been stabbed. Sherman did not disclose this information to the officers accompanying him on the twenty-five mile train ride to Durham Station. There Sherman was joined by an escort, the 13th Pennsylvania Cavalry. The Union party met the Confederates about five miles along the road to Hillsboro, between the picket lines of the armies. Seeking a place in which to talk, they asked permission to use the log farmhouse of James and Lucy Bennett. The Bennetts agreed, and Mrs. Bennett left with their four children.

Johnston was elegantly attired in his best gray uniform, his white mustache and beard neatly trimmed. In contrast, Sherman's appearance was disheveled, his beard was shaggy and, as usual, he wore no sword or boots. They were both West Pointers and had served at the same time in the U. S. Army, but had never met. Johnston, class of 1829, fought in the Seminole Wars and Mexican War. He was one of the most senior officers who resigned in 1861, and was the third-ranking Confederate general (after Lee and Cooper), but his relations with Davis were extremely poor. Sherman, an 1840 graduate, served as an artillery officer in the Mexican War, but resigned in 1853. In 1859, he became superintendent of the Louisiana Military Academy, and returned to active duty soon after the war began. After a rocky start, he became a close associate of Grant, who put him in charge of the western armies in the Atlanta campaign.

As soon as the two generals were alone inside the house, Sherman showed Johnston the telegram. As Sherman recalled the exchange years later in his *Memoirs*, Johnston

> Denounced the act as a disgrace to the age and hoped I did not charge it to the Confederate Government. I told him I could not believe that he or General Lee, or the officers of the Confederate army, could possibly be privy to acts of assassination, but I would not say as much for Jeff Davis.

They then discussed the surrender. Sherman offered the same terms given to Lee, without mentioning the reference to "civil authorities" in Johnston's letter. Johnston raised the matter and was told, as Davis had expected, that there could be no such negotiation because the United States did not recognize the Confederate States. Turning to the military situation, Johnston pointed out that, unlike Lee, his army was not surrounded. Moreover, Johnston and Sherman shared an apprehension about the possibility of guerilla warfare and its terrible consequences. They therefore explored the possibility of surrendering all Confederate forces, in exchange for which Johnston hoped for more generous terms. Johnston admitted that he lacked authority to do this, but he told Sherman he believed he could obtain it. There was also the issue of amnesty for Davis and the cabinet, which Sherman refused to grant. As it was late in the day and no agreement had been reached, they adjourned.

Sherman returned to Raleigh and telegraphed Grant about the meeting. He expressed concern that units of the Confederate army might break away and continue to fight as guerillas, a possibility that had concerned Grant at Appomattox. To prevent soldiers from trashing the city when he announced the news of Lincoln's death, Sherman strengthened the city garrison and had guards stationed on the roads between the city and the army camps. With these precautions taken he issued Special Field Orders No. 56, describing the attacks on Lincoln and Seward. He said he knew

> that the great mass of the Confederate army would scorn to sanction such acts. . . . We have met every phase which this war has assumed, and must now be prepared for it in its last and worse shape, that of assassins and guerillas; but woe unto the people who seek to expend their wild passions in such a manner, for there is but one dreadful result!

Some soldiers took the news calmly; some were even pleased. Many began to call for revenge, and a few headed for Raleigh carrying torches, intent on burning the place. Fortunately, the mob was not large, and an officer, sitting on his horse in the road, threatened to shoot any man who failed to go back to camp, which they did. The citizens had a sleepless night, fearful of trouble. In a tragic incident, one of many such during the war, a soldier shot to death a civilian who voiced "satisfaction" at Lincoln's assassination.

Johnston, after his talks with Sherman, asked Breckinridge by telegram to join him as soon as possible. The secretary of war received the message the same day, at Lexington, and immediately returned to Greensboro, bringing Reagan with him on the orders of Davis. They arrived in Hillsboro early on April 18. In his capacity as a cabinet officer, Breckinridge authorized Johnston to negotiate the surrender of all Confederate armies. With that as an objective, the three men discussed specific terms that might be acceptable to both sides. Reagan sat down to put them in writing while Johnston left to resume his discussions with Sherman at the Bennett house. Johnston told Sherman that he now had authority for a complete surrender. He wanted, however, a statement regarding the political rights of his officers and men, as a means of getting their acceptance. Sherman pointed out that officers below the rank of colonel were, upon taking an oath of allegiance, protected by Lincoln's 1863 Amnesty Proclamation, and that the terms afforded by Grant at Appomattox provided amnesty for everyone who was paroled, including Lee himself. But this did not satisfy Johnston.

Breckinridge was then allowed to join the meeting, not as a member of the cabinet but as a CSA general. There is a story, which is probably apocryphal, since it was written thirty-four years later by a man who was not present, that Sherman had a bottle of bourbon in his saddlebags and offered a drink to the two Confederates, who gratefully accepted. Later, absorbed in the important issues being addressed, Sherman took a second drink himself without offering them another. According to this story, Breckinridge was so annoyed that he afterwards complained to Johnston that "Sherman is a hog, Yes, sir, a hog! Did you see him take that drink by himself? No Kentucky gentleman would ever have taken away that bottle. He knew how much we needed it. Needed it badly."

Memorandum, or Basis of Agreement

Johnston and Breckinridge, who were well-educated and experienced men, negotiated persuasively, citing constitutional and international law as well as the rules of war and rebellion. At last Sherman pushed his chair back and asked, rhetorically: "See here, gentlemen, who is doing the surrendering anyhow? If this thing goes on, you'll have me sending a letter of apology to Jeff Davis." At this point a messenger arrived with the memorandum prepared by Reagan. They handed it to Sherman, who read it, thought about it for some time, and then wrote his own version:

> Memorandum, or basis of agreement, made this 18th day of April, A. D. 1865, near Durham Station . . .
>
> 1. The contending armies now in the field to maintain their status quo, until notice is given by the commanding General of either one to its opponents, and reasonable time, say forty-hours, allowed.
>
> 2. The Confederate armies now in existence to be disbanded and conducted to the several State capitals, there to deposit their arms and public property in the State Arsenal, and each officer and man to execute and file an agreement to cease from acts of war, and abide the action of both Federal and State authorities. The number of arms and munitions of war to be reported to the chief of ordnance at Washington City, subject to future action of the Congress of the United States, and in the mean time to be used solely to maintain peace and order within the borders of the States respectively.
>
> 3. The recognition by the Executive of the United States of the several State governments, on their officers and Legislatures taking the oath prescribed by the Constitution of the United States; and, where conflicting State governments

have resulted from the war, the legitimacy of all shall be submitted to the Supreme Court of the United States.

4. The establishment of all Federal courts in the several States, with powers as defined by the Constitution and laws of Congress.

5. The people and inhabitants of all States to be guaranteed, so far as the Executive can, their political rights and franchises, as well as their rights of person and property, as defined by the Constitution of the United States and of the states respectively.

6. The Executive authority of the Government of the United States not to disturb any of the people by reason of the late war, so long as they live in peace and quiet, abstain from acts of armed hostility, and obey laws in existence at any place of their residence.

7. In general terms, war to cease, a general amnesty, so far as the Executive power of the United States can command, or on condition of the disbandment of the Confederate armies, the distribution of arms, and resumption of peaceful pursuits by officers and men, as hitherto composing said armies. Not being fully empowered by our respective principals to fulfill these terms, we individually and officially pledge ourselves to promptly obtain necessary authority, and to carry out the above programme.

This ill-conceived document was intended to settle delicate matters that clearly belonged to the civil government, not to the military command. In effect, it recognized the Confederacy, left the states armed, deprived the president and Congress of responsibility for setting reconstruction policy, and possibly provided for repayment of Confederate government debt. The statement about "rights of person and property, as defined by . . . the states" could be interpreted to mean that slavery would remain, though the two Confederates had told Sherman they thought slavery was "as dead as anything can be." Whether they meant that or not, it could not affect how others would understand the two words. The proposal is all the more astonishing because Sherman, thinking about the approaching surrender that would conclude his successful campaign, had written to his brother-in-law: "You need not fear my committing a political mistake, for I am fully conscious that I will imperil all by my concessions in that direction."

In retrospect, it hardly seems possible that Sherman made the proposal, let alone expected it to be approved. Yet expect it he surely did. Several explanations are plausible. One is that he understood Lincoln's policy of leniency toward the South and prompt restoration of the Union, expressed at the City Point meeting, without grasping the subtleties of how it was to be achieved. Or perhaps, flush with the fame and public approbation of his recent campaign, he hoped to be remembered as the general who obtained the surrender of the entire remaining Confederate army and restored the Union. Or, at a more basic level, he may simply have been the victim of his impulsive nature; overly generous in victory after the widespread destruction and despair he had been compelled to inflict on the South.

The Generals Await a Decision

While waiting for copies to be made, the generals went out into the yard. In the falling light of evening, they discussed the death of Lincoln. It was news of both political and personal significance to Breckinridge. On the political level, it was Lincoln who had defeated him for the presidency in 1860. On the personal level, Lincoln had died in the house where Breckinridge had lived when he was a Congressman, perhaps in his very room. Sherman took Breckinridge aside and advised him that, for his personal safety, he should leave the country as quickly as possible.

Sherman also issued Special Field Orders No. 58 on April 19:

> The commanding general announces to the army a suspension of hostilities and an agreement with General Johnston and other high officials, which, when formally ratified, will make peace from the Potomac to the Rio Grande. . . . Each army commander will group his camps entirely with a view to comfort, health, and good police. All the details of good military discipline must still be maintained. . . . The fame of this army for courage, industry, and discipline is admitted all over the world; then let each officer and man see that it is not stained by any acts of vulgarity, rowdyism, or petty crime. The cavalry will patrol the front line.

Sherman and Johnston sent copies of their memorandum of agreement to their governments. Sherman dispatched Major Henry Hitchcock with his copy on the morning of April 20, with covering letters to Grant and Halleck. To Grant he wrote:

> If you will get the President to simply indorse the copy, and commission me to carry out the terms, I will follow them to the conclusion. You will observe that it is an absolute submission of the enemy to the lawful authority of the United States, and disperses his armies absolutely; and the point to which I attach most importance it, that the dispersion and disbandment of these armies is done in such a manner as to prevent their breaking up into guerilla bands. . . . Both Generals Johnston and Breckinridge admitted that slavery was dead, and I could not insist on embracing it in such a paper, because it can be made with the States in detail.

Reinforcing the naivete that the proposal itself evidenced, he asked Halleck to "influence [the president], if possible, not to vary the terms at all, for I have considered every thing, and believe that, the Confederate armies once dispersed, we can adjust all else fairly and well."

Breckinridge left immediately for Charlotte with the Confederate copy. When he arrived, Davis asked if the news of Lincoln's death were true, and Breckinridge confirmed that it was. The president then called a meeting of his cabinet and asked each member to give him an opinion in writing as to whether or not to accept the proposed agreement. Breckinridge recommended that Davis surrender and disband all remaining Confederate forces, fearing that otherwise the conflict was "likely to lose entirely the dignity of regular warfare. Many of the States will make such terms as they may; in others, separate and ineffective hostilities may be prosecuted, while the war, wherever raged, will probably degenerate into that irregular and secondary stage out of which greater evils will flow to the South than to the enemy." Davis, he said, should recommend to the state governments that they accept those items for which he felt he lacked authority to act. Once again they were confounded by the old, ambiguous issue of state sovereignty, this time in the face of widespread disorganization, poor communication, and Federal occupation.

For the generals and their armies, there was nothing to do now but wait for word from their "principals." In the Confederate camp, rumors circulated that the war was over, so Johnston issued a general order that only a "suspension of arms" was agreed to. His soldiers deserted at an increasing rate, while discipline virtually collapsed among those who remained. The men got drunk, gambled, and fought among themselves. Governor Vance was unable to maintain civil authority as roving gangs stole and destroyed property and even stopped and robbed trains carrying supplies to Johnston's army.

Stoneman's Cavalry Raid

In the western part of the state, hostilities were not yet suspended: Union cavalry was aggressively destroying military property, bridges and railroads. On January 15, Grant had written to General George H. Thomas, the Virginian who commanded the Union Army of the Cumberland, headquartered in Nashville, and suggested a cavalry raid that "might penetrate South Carolina well down toward Columbia, destroying the railroad and military resources. . . . Three thousand cavalry should be sufficient force to take [since] this expedition goes to destroy and not to fight battles." Thomas assigned the mission to General George Stoneman, who began assembling scattered units and collecting additional men and horses, as well as 600 more Spencer carbines. This proved to be time-consumingly difficult (or, as Grant thought, Stoneman was not sufficiently energetic) and when the raid had not started by late February Grant ordered it redirected to southwestern Virginia, since by then Sherman's army had passed through South Carolina.

The expedition finally left Knoxville on March 20. Its purposes were to prevent reinforcement of Lee and Johnston, to destroy supplies that their armies badly needed, and to disrupt rail lines to hinder withdrawal to the west if either Confederate general should decide to do that. Under Stoneman, General Alvan C. Gillem was in command of the Sixth Cavalry Division. It consisted of three brigades, each of which had three regiments. The plan was to travel light, so the train was composed of only one wagon, ten ambulances and a four-gun battery of artillery. Each man carried five days rations, a one-day supply of corn for his horse, and four horseshoes. The intent was to live off the country, and for a month the division was able to do that, since no army had passed through this area before.

Gillem's cavalry moved along the edge of the Blue Ridge to Lynchburg, and made the East Tennessee and Virginia Railroad south of there useless. On April 9, the day of Lee's surrender, they struck the Danville-Greensboro road, by which Lee could have united his troops with those of Johnston had he escaped Grant. The troopers burned a railroad bridge shortly after the train carrying Davis and the cabinet passed over it on the way to Greensboro. On April 12, the Union cavalry fought the only engagement of the raid, a relatively light encounter with a scratch force at Salisbury, North Carolina. They took the town, where large quantities of weapons, ammunition, clothing and blankets were stockpiled. After burning these stores and capturing 1,300 prisoners, eighteen field guns and 10,000 stand of small arms, they moved on to Lynchburg. Southwest of there they destroyed railroad bridges and trestles for more than a hundred miles and tore up rails and ties for twenty miles east of New River. They then retired to Hendersonville, North Carolina. On April 23, on the way to Asheville, they received notice of the Sherman-Johnston armistice of April 18.

April 26: Surrender at Last

When the proposed agreement between Johnston and Sherman reached Washington on April 21, it was immediately shown to Johnson. The new president had been elected in 1843 as a Democrat to the House of Representatives, where he served for ten years. He entered the Senate in 1857. A serious and unimaginative man, he held strong beliefs. In the 1860 election he supported Breckinridge. When Tennessee seceded he did not resign from the Senate, and Lincoln appointed him military governor of Tennessee in 1862. He was Lincoln's candidate for vice-president in 1864 on the National Union ticket, combining Republicans and War Democrats. He supported Lincoln's plan for compassionate reconstruction of the secessionists.

The Sherman proposal was entirely unacceptable to the president and the cabinet, and was promptly rejected. Sherman was subjected to severe criticism for making the proposal. Grant hurried south to appease Sherman, arriving while the latter was still in bed on the morning of April 24. As Grant later remembered it, "I told him that I wanted him to notify General Johnston that the terms which they had conditionally agreed upon had not been approved in Washington, and that he was authorized to offer the same terms I had given General Lee. I sent Sherman to do this himself. I did not wish the knowledge of my presence to be known to the army."

At 6:00 A.M., Sherman wrote briefly to Johnston: "You will take notice that the truce or suspension of hostilities agreed to between us will cease in forty-eight hours after this is received at your lines, under the first of the articles of agreement." At the same time he wrote a second note to Johnston:

> I have replies from Washington to my communication of April 18th. I am instructed to limit my operations to your immediate command, and not to attempt civil negotiations. I therefore demand the surrender of your army on the same terms as were given to General Lee at Appomattox, April 9th instant, purely and simply.

In Charlotte, meanwhile, Davis did not refer the proposed agreement to the "sovereign states," since it was patently impossible to do that. He concluded that, while it "would not have all the binding force of a treaty, it secured to our people the political rights and safety from pillage, to obtain which I proposed to continue the war." So, with the concurrence of his "constitutional advisers" (the cabinet), he wired Johnston on April 24 that "Your action is approved. You will so inform General Sherman; and, if the like authority be given by the Government of the United States to complete the arrangement, you will proceed on the basis adopted."

Just after Johnston received this, he received the messages from Sherman. Johnston then consulted by telegraph with Davis, who told him to disband his infantry and have it reassemble later, somewhere, and to organize his cavalry into an escort for the president. The army, however, was without any discipline and was literally falling apart: as many as 8,000 men had deserted in the previous week. Johnston decided to ignore Davis's instructions. At noon on April 26, Sherman and Johnston again met at the Bennett house and discussed the awkward situation. General Schofield, who accompanied Sherman, waited outside while the principals talked.

Johnston resisted accepting the Lee-Grant terms, saying that hungry men had been released on the countryside and many of them had become robbers. He was concerned about feeding his men. Much of the food that the Confederates had been collecting at warehouses in North and South Carolina had been consumed or wasted by fugitives from the Army of Northern Virginia, but Johnston had believed that enough was left to feed his army for several weeks. He now discovered that the depots had been plundered by crowds of fugitives and local people. Schofield was called in and pointed out that his army was to remain to occupy North Carolina. He would be able to handle problems of civil disorder. As to food, he would arrange for 250,000 rations if the Confederates would transport them by rail from Morehead City. With this problem solved to Johnston's satisfaction, the final agreement read:

Terms of a military convention entered into this 26th day of April, 1865, at Bennett's house, near Durham's Station, N. C., between General Joseph E. Johnston, commanding the Confederate Army, and Maj. Gen. W. T. Sherman, commanding the United States Army in North Carolina.

1. All acts of war on the part of the troops under General Johnston's command to cease from this date.

2. All arms and public property to be deposited at Greensborough, and delivered to an ordnance officer of the United States Army.

3. Rolls of all the officers and men to be made in duplicate, one copy to be retained by the commander of the troops, and the other to be given to an officer to be designated by General Sherman, each officer and man to give his individual obligation in writing not to take up arms against the Government of the United States until properly released from this obligation.

4. The side arms of officers and their private horses and baggage to be retained by them.

5. This being done, all the officers and men will be permitted to return to their homes, not to be disturbed by the United States authorities so long as they observe their obligation and the laws in force where they may reside.

Johnston and Sherman signed the surrender document, which had taken thirteen days to complete since the first letter was sent, and Grant approved it. Johnston and Schofield signed a supplemental agreement, spelling out important related matters:

1. The field transportation to be loaned to the troops for their march to their homes, and for subsequent use in their

industrial pursuits. Artillery horses may be used in field transportation, if necessary.

2. Each brigade or separate body to retain a number of arms equal to one-seventh of its effective strength, which, when the troops reach the capitals of their States, will be disposed of as the general commanding the department may direct.

3. Private horses, and other private property of both officers and men, to be retained by them.

4. The commanding general of the Military Division of West Mississippi, Major-General Canby, will be requested to give transportation by water, from Mobile or New Orleans, to the troops from Arkansas and Texas.

5. The obligations [i. e., paroles] of officers and soldiers to be signed by their immediate commanders.

6. Naval forces within the limits of General Johnston's command to be included in the terms of this convention.

It was understood that soldiers could take away horses and mules owned by the Confederate army, as Grant had permitted at Appomattox, and that some additional animals would be provided. The only real difference between Durham Station and Appomattox was that, as a defense against brigands and guerillas, units were allowed to keep one-seventh of their rifles.

Back at Raleigh, Sherman received a telegram from Stanton, rebuking him for the original proposal. It was handed to him while he was meeting with some of his officers in the governor's house in Raleigh. General Carl Schurz described Sherman's reaction. He:

> paced up and down the room like a caged lion and, without addressing anybody in particular, unbosomed himself of an eloquence of furious invective which for a while made us all stare. . . . He berated the people who blamed him for what he

had done as a mass of fools, not worth fighting for, who did not know when a thing was well done. He railed at the press, which had altogether too much freedom; which had become an engine of vilification; which should be bridled by severe laws.

The next day Johnston notified the state governors by telegram of the agreement:

> The disaster in Virginia, the capture by the enemy of all our workshops for the preparation of ammunition and repairing of arms, the impossibility of recruiting our little army opposed to more than ten times its number, or of supplying it except by robbing our own citizens, destroyed all hope of successful war. I have made, therefore, a military convention with Major-General Sherman, to terminate hostilities in North and South Carolina, Georgia and Florida. I made this convention to spare the blood of the gallant little army, to prevent further sufferings of our people by the devastation and ruin inevitable from the marches of invading armies, and to avoid the crime of waging hopeless war.

On his part, Sherman issued Special Field Orders No. 65 on April 27, announcing that there was:

> a final agreement with General Johnston which terminates the war as to the armies under his command and the country east of the Chattahoochee. . . . Captain Myers, Ordnance Department, U. S. Army, is hereby designated to receive the arms, &c., at Greensborough, and any commanding officer of a post may receive the arms of any detachment and see that they are properly stored and accounted for. General Schofield will procure at once the necessary blanks, and supply the other army commanders, that uniformity may prevail. . . . Army commanders may at once loan to the inhabitants such

of the captured mules, horses, wagons, and vehicles as can be spared from immediate use, and the commanding generals of armies may issue provisions, animals, or any public supplies that can be spared, to relieve present wants and to encourage the inhabitants to renew their peaceful pursuits.

Sherman wrote to Johnston, sending a copy of this order, which he said gave Schofield "full and ample power to carry into effect our convention." He said he had instructed Schofield to let Johnston have 250,000 rations: "We have abundance of provisions at Morehead City, and if you send trains here they may go down with our trains." Then he dealt with economic matters. "I can hardly estimate how many animals fit for farm purposes will be 'loaned' to the farmers, but enough, I hope, to insure a crop. I can hardly commit myself how far commerce will be free, but I think the cotton still in the country and the crude turpentine will make money with which to procure supplies."

On the same day, Sherman wrote to General James Wilson in Macon, telling him:

> I regard the war as over, but it is well to be prudent and cautious, as there is much danger of some of the discharged soldiers of both armies infesting the country as robbers. If you encounter any of these either punish them with extreme severity or carry them where the civil authorities of an organized State can try and punish.

General Schofield's Regime

General William Hartsuff went, with nine staff officers, to Johnston's headquarters in Greensboro on April 30. He found the Confederate army scattered along the railroad from Hillsboro to Charlotte, a distance of 130 miles. The main part was in the vicinity of Greensboro. He began issuing paroles on May 1, and by two days later had issued 36,971. Hartsuff thought that, including the part of the cavalry who went off with Wheeler and Hampton, and those soldiers who went home after the cease-fire without being paroled, the total number of men surrendered was about 50,000. He reported:

> General Johnston tried to faithfully carry out the terms of agreement between himself and Major-General Sherman, but the terribly demoralized condition of the army, resulting from its being hastily disbanded, rendered it exceedingly difficult for him to control it. I think it would have been entirely disorganized but for the anxiety of the men to receive their paroles before going home.

Schofield signed the paroles for Johnston himself and each of the officers of his staff. On May 3, the stacking of arms was completed. The remaining men of the three infantry corps and some of the cavalry then began the march to Salisbury, fifty miles to the southwest. From there they found their ways home, the majority of them across the Appalachians.

The men under Johnston's command in the four southeastern states were gradually surrendered and dispersed. In Florida, the surrenders were not completed until June. Johnston's final orders, revealing his sensitivity to the problem of returning soldiers to civilian life and of avoiding disorder and brigandage, appealed to the best instincts of his men:

> I earnestly exhort you to observe faithfully the terms of pacification agreed upon; and to discharge the obligations of good and peaceful citizens, as well as you have performed the duties of thorough soldiers in the field. By such a course, you will best secure the comfort of your families and kindred, and restore tranquility to our country.

Very early in the morning of April 29 Sherman, still smarting from the statements made by Stanton a week earlier, which included insinuations that he had not made adequate efforts to find Davis, wrote perceptively (and alluding to the rumors of a huge Confederate treasure) to Grant's chief of staff:

> If he wants to hunt down Jeff. Davis or the politicians who had instigated civil war, let him use sheriffs, bailiffs, and catch-thieves, and not hint that I should march heavy columns of infantry hundreds of miles on a fool's errand. The idea of Jeff. Davis running about the country with tons of gold is ridiculous. I doubt not he is a beggar, and who will say that if we catch him he will be punished. The very men who now howl the loudest will be the first to intercede.

He then left for Charleston, while the troops of two of his armies began the march north to Richmond and Washington.

The Army of Ohio, comprising the 10th and 23rd Corps and the Third Cavalry Division, approximately 30,000 men, remained in North Carolina. Schofield, headquartered in Raleigh, was appointed to implement the surrender terms with Johnston, who was in Greensboro. He was then to exercise Federal authority until the president and Congress determined reconstruction policy. Schofield was a West Pointer, class of 1853, who was posted to the artillery. He was awarded the Medal of Honor for his actions in the Wilson's Creek battle, and commanded the 23rd Corps in Tennessee. He was later to serve as secretary of war in 1868-69, and as commander-in-chief of the U. S. Army from 1888 to 1895.

On April 27, in General Orders No. 31, Schofield announced "that hostilities within this State have definitively ceased; that for us the war is ended."

> It is now the duty of all to cultivate friendly relations with the same zeal which has characterized our conduct of the war,

that the blessings of the union, peace, and material prosperity may be speedily restored to the entire country. It is confidently believed and expected that the troops of this army and the people of North Carolina will cordially unite in honest endeavors to accomplish this great end.

Schofield assured the citizens that they would be protected and treated kindly, but that anyone who disturbed the peace would be severely punished by martial law. Troops, subject to "perfect discipline and good conduct," would be stationed throughout the state to secure the interests of the U. S. Government and to protect the people until a civil government could be established. People who had been "deprived of their animals and wagons by the hostile armies will be temporarily supplied, as far as practicable, upon application to the nearest provost-marshal, by loans of the captured property . . . The needy will also be supplied, for the time being, with subsistence stores from the commissary department. . . ."

Probably the most important issue that required prompt resolution was the status of the Negroes. Schofield regarded Lincoln's 1863 Emancipation Proclamation as a military order to the army to free all the slaves in seceded states as rapidly as military operations brought them within army control. They were clearly in the army's control in North Carolina, so he considered the freedom of slaves in the state to be an accomplished fact. When some citizens seemed uncertain about the situation, he issued, also on April 27, General Orders No. 32:

> To remove a doubt which seems to exist in the minds of some of the people of North Carolina, it is hereby declared that . . . all persons in this State heretofore held as slaves are now free, and that it is the duty of the army to maintain the freedom of such persons. It is recommended to the former owners of the freedmen to employ them as hired servants at

reasonable wages; and it is recommended to the freedmen that when allowed to do so they remain with their former masters and labor faithfully so long as they shall be treated kindly and paid reasonable wages . . . It is not well for them to congregate about towns or military camps. They will not be supported in idleness.

With regard to the surrender terms, there was still a problem with the Confederate cavalry, which had scattered rather than concentrate at Greensboro. On April 28, Johnston wrote to Sherman to say that some of his cavalry was moving westward from Hillsboro, and that he had ordered his division commander on the Yadkin River to intercept them as well as stragglers. "I regret the movement of these troops," he said, "fearing it may embarrass me in settling matters in Georgia and South Carolina." Later the same day he wrote again to say that "Some 3,000 cavalry was collected near Charlotte and on the Catawba. . . . The commanding officer expressed his readiness to obey the terms of the convention. . . . I hope and believe that there will be occasion for severities to none but members of bands of robbers now existing in many parts of the country." He thanked Sherman for his "enlightened and humane policy," and for the "generous offer of food for the troops." On April 30, Schofield notified Johnston that "the failure of so large a portion of your troops, especially cavalry, to comply with the terms of the convention will give us no little trouble, and keep the country in a disturbed condition for a long time." Schofield sent another copy of the supplemental terms to Johnston (who had lost his) and agreed to a modification that Johnston had asked for. Gradually, the cavalry units disbanded and the men returned to their homes.

THE NEED FOR A POLICY

Schofield, feeling the need to understand the political form that reconstruction was going to take, wrote to Sherman on May 5. He said, he thought it would be wise to open the state to trade at once, and continued:

> I hope the government will make known its policy as to organization of State governments without delay. Affairs must necessarily be in a very unsettled state until that is done. The people are now in a mood to accept almost anything which promises a definite settlement. What is to be done with the freedmen . . . is the all-important question. It requires prompt and wise action to prevent the negro from becoming a huge elephant on our hands.

Two days later, with the matter of how North Carolina was to be governed on his mind, he wrote to Halleck, in response to a dispatch from the chief of staff concerning slavery. He said:

> I have not recognized in any way any of the civil officers of the State -- not being willing to act in such matters in the absence of any indication of the policy of the government. . . .
> I desire to suggest that the sooner a military governor is appointed for this State, and steps taken to organize a civil government, the better. . . . I think it would be eminently wise to retain in office justices of the peace, sheriffs, and other inferior officers who may prove to be loyal and worthy. . . .
> The proper care of the freedmen should be provided for by State legislation as soon as possible.

On May 15, Schofield issued a ten-paragraph set of "rules . . . for the government of freedmen in North Carolina until the restoration of civil government."

Earlier, on May 10, he wrote a letter to Grant, expressing his views concerning the policy that ought to be pursued in re-establishing state government. He had received a letter from Chief Justice Salmon P. Chase, who proposed that an older state constitution, rather than the one in force at the time the state seceded, be used in determining the right of suffrage. Schofield objected to this for two reasons. The first was that the constitution as it existed prior to the rebellion was still in force: only the people could alter it. This was a positive, legal argument. The second was a normative, judgmental one: the freedmen should not be granted the suffrage. (The old constitution excluded slaves from voting; since there were no longer any slaves, Negroes would be able to vote). Schofield's view derived from his belief in

> the absolute unfitness of the negroes, as a class, for any such responsibility. They can neither read not write. They have no knowledge whatever of law or government. They do not even know the meaning of the freedom that has been given them. . . . It is true they are docile, obedient, and anxious to learn; but we certainly ought to teach them something before we give them an equal voice with ourselves in government.

He pointed out that nearly all of the Unionists in the state were content with the abolition of slavery, but not with political equality. "After careful consideration of all the questions involved," he proposed that a military governor be appointed, with command of all the troops. The governor should declare the constitution and laws that were in force "preceding the pretended Act of Secession . . . to be still in force." He should appoint peace officers, to serve until a new civil government can be organized, and order the enrollment of voters, the qualifications being those prescribed by the state laws, and the taking of the amnesty oath. That done, he should call an election for delegates to a convention, the acts of which would be submitted to the people for their ratification or rejection, a governor and legislators to be elected at the same time. He said he would expect the convention to repudiate the doctrine of secession and to abolish slavery.

> If, however, they should fail to do this, I would regard them as having violated their oaths, would dissolve the convention, and hold the State under military government until the people should come to their senses. I would have a lawful popular government or a military government.

As Schofield attempted to restore a functioning government on a constitutional, pre-war basis, and in a way that was consistent with the outcome of the war, former Governor Vance persisted in his unwillingness to accept that result. On May 9, at the direction of President Johnson, Schofield ordered his arrest. A provisional governor, William H. Holden, was appointed before Schofield was called by Grant to come to Washington in June for talks. He was subsequently ordered to Texas to assume control and direction of the military measures to be adopted to cause the French to evacuate Mexico. His sensible way of restoring order, based on established law, was not adopted by the Republican administration, either in North Carolina or elsewhere. Instead, the South was subjected to the ordeal of twelve years of radical reconstruction, the unforeseen, but not necessarily inevitable, consequence of surrender.

Chapter 8

Surrenders in Alabama, Georgia and Florida April-May 1865

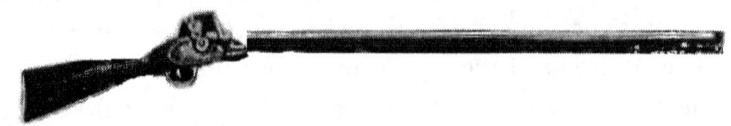

Canby Assaults Mobile

The offensive in Alabama ordered by Grant began in late March. It consisted of two large-scale movements. One was a combined operation by the U. S. Army and Navy to capture Mobile and defeat the Confederate forces in the region. The other was a cavalry campaign southeastward across Alabama, to crush or disperse Confederate forces and destroy munitions manufacturing plants. Of these two campaigns, the first to get under way, though by only a few days, was that of General Edward R. S. Canby, West Point 1835. Grant's orders to him were to take Mobile or, if that proved not to be feasible, to move directly on Montgomery. Canby's plan was to reduce the two Confederate strong points of Spanish Fort and Fort Blakely, on the east side of the bay opposite Mobile. The city would then be indefensible.

To do this Canby had an army of 49,000 men. The larger part of his force, 32,200 men, was encamped at Mobile Point and Dauphin Island. It consisted of General Gordon Granger's 13th Corps of 13,200 and General A. J. Smith's 16th Corps of 16,000. They were supported by an Engineer Brigade of 1,500, a siege train of 1,200, and 300 cavalry scouts. The other part of his force, 12,800 men, was at Pensacola under General Frederick Steele: 5,000 in General John P. Hawkins's First Division U. S. Colored Troops; 5,200 in two brigades of the 13th Corps under General C. C. Andrews; and 2,600 in General Thomas J. Lucas's cavalry brigade. In New Orleans, General Benjamin H. Grierson was preparing an additional cavalry brigade of 4,000. Canby was supported by a naval task force, to provide transportation and bombardment.

The Confederate District of Alabama, Mississippi and East Louisiana was commanded by General Richard Taylor. A graduate of Yale College, he was the owner of a large plantation in Louisiana. The son of former President Zachary Taylor, he was also the brother-in-law of Jefferson Davis. His headquarters was at Meridian, Mississippi, 125 miles north of Mobile. The Confederate officer in command at Mobile was General Dabney H. Maury, a Virginian and an 1846 graduate of West Point. He had designed the city's defensive works and understood their strengths and weaknesses well. Food supplies were adequate for a siege, but ammunition was limited. There were only about 8,000 infantry and artillery soldiers, plus 1,500 cavalrymen, who were of little use in resisting a siege.

An enormous logistical effort was required to transport and supply Canby's huge force. A base was established on the east side of the bay at Starke's Landing, five miles below Spanish Fort. There six wharves, 300 to 500 feet long, were constructed in five days by the 96th and 97th U. S. Colored Engineer Regiments. Over these docks all supplies and ordnance were brought in, and sick and wounded Union soldiers and Confederate prisoners were evacuated. The engineers also improved or built the roads over which supplies were transported to the regiments in the line. The navy protected and assisted the fleet of vessels that brought in ammunition, food and supplies during the twenty-five days of the campaign.

> ### ORDER OF BATTLE
> Army of West Mississippi: Canby
> 13th Corps: Granger
> 1st Division: Veatch
> 2nd Division: Andrews*
> 3rd Division: Benton
> 16th Corps: Smith
> 1st Division: McArthur
> 2nd Division: Garrard
> 3rd Division: Carr
> "Pensacola" Corps: Steele
> 1st Division: Hawkins
> *Two brigades: Andrews
> Cavalry: Lucas/Grierson

On March 20, Steele's corps started cross-country from Pensacola for Mobile Bay. There was sporadic Confederate resistance, with an engagement at Bluff Springs on March 25 that resulted in the taking of 120 prisoners, including a general. The area through which the corps passed was almost destitute of food and forage, but supplies were found at several locations and detachments that searched the countryside for cattle were able to bring in some beef on the hoof. The movement was slowed by the poor condition of the roads, the need to cross many streams at high water, and several storms. In eleven days, Steele covered 100 miles, for seventy of which the road ran through swamps and quicksand, and for fifty of which corduroy had to be laid and bridges built. On March 31, the force arrived at Stockton, where they received badly needed supplies sent by Canby. The next day, they encountered and engaged a strong force of infantry and cavalry.

Canby planned first to reduce Spanish Fort, which had an elaborate system of defenses and was manned by 1,900 soldiers under General Randall L. Gibson. Canby would then take Fort Blakely, a few miles to the north. On March 17, 13th Corps, with a train of 321 wagons, marched to Dannelly's Mills. One brigade of 16th Corps was landed at Cedar Point on the west (Mobile) side of the bay, to appear to threaten the city from there, though the terrain was unfavorable. The next day most of 16th Corps was moved up by water, but heavy rains delayed completion of the concentration until March 24. Two days later the advance guard of 13th Corps engaged the Confederate skirmish line a mile from Spanish Fort. The next day Veatch's and Benton's divisions formed in line at the edge of a wood, up to which the defenders had felled all trees for more than half a mile in their front. Within a few days McArthur's and Carr's divisions of 16th Corps were in position on their right. The four divisions faced west toward a heavily fortified line two miles in length, with three strong-points: Fort Alexis on the left, Redoubt McDermott in the center and Red Fort on the right. The Confederates had six heavy guns, fourteen field pieces and twelve Coehorn mortars.

The infantrymen began digging emplacements for the artillery, and field batteries were in place by March 28. They also excavated a system of parallel and sap trenches that eventually extended for 10,500 yards. For several days 16th Corps was subjected to heavy shelling from three Confederate gunboats and from Batteries Huger and Tracy, located on islands between and to the rear of the two large forts. A few days later, Union troops sited eight, thirty-pounder Parrotts and two Whitworth guns on a bluff. They reduced the fire from the batteries and drove away the gunboats. On April 4, the Union troops replaced the bridge over the bayou between Spanish Fort and Fort Blakely, which had been destroyed by the Confederates. By now thirty-eight siege guns (including six twenty-pounder rifles and sixteen mortars) and thirty-seven field guns were in position to shell the fortifications.

Bombardment began at 5:00 P.M. on March 30 and continued for two hours, but could not be maintained because of the difficulty of bringing up ammunition over the poor roads. Firing was continued at thirty-minute intervals during the night, and was resumed over the next four days whenever ammunition was available. On April 8, when some of the Union trenches were as close as 200 yards to the fort, the final assault was launched. Under cover of a sustained artillery bombardment at 5:30 P.M., two companies of the Eighth Iowa Infantry of Carr's Division advanced over marshy ground on the Confederate's extreme left, affected a lodgment, and gained a position from which they could enfilade 300 yards of the position. It was helpful that the part of the line they entered consisted of a series of unconnected small pits, which could be attacked in detail. The commander of the regiment reported that

> We here witnessed the spectacle of dying in the last ditch, as quite a number of the rebels refused to surrender and were shot in their ditches, and on the other hand quite a number of them who were taken prisoners ought, in justice to our men, to have been killed, as they would first fire at our men after being ordered to surrender, then throw up both hands and surrender.

The Iowans quickly seized several guns and turned them on the defenders. Despite the darkness, other troops of Carr's division poured in, captured the two miles of entrenchments and took 600 more prisoners. As the fort was overrun, two-thirds of the garrison escaped by way of a narrow causeway to Battery Huger and from there to Fort Blakely. Artillery, ordnance stores and supplies were abandoned. Canby assigned a brigade to take charge of Spanish Fort.

Fort Blakely Falls

Fort Blakely, where General St. John R. Liddell was in command of 2,300 infantry and 300 artillerymen, was now to be taken. On the evening of April 1, the First Division U. S. Colored Troops had arrived from Pensacola and was met by badly needed supplies. After a skirmish with the Confederates on April 2, they established themselves on the right in front of the fort, while the two brigades of Andrews's division took position to their left. Veatch's division then occupied the ground to the left of Andrews, and Garrard's division formed the left end of the Union line. As each division came into position the men promptly began digging parallel and approach trenches, 500 to 800 yards from the fort, working day and night. The ground was very hard, and one officer asked for more picks, observing "the shovel is a poor instrument without a greater number of picks to assist it." The Confederates put up stubborn resistance as the Union troops suffered from enfilading fire from gunboats. Four thirty-pounder rifles, which were with difficulty put into position by the afternoon of the April 8, severely damaged and drove off the boats. Orders were issued to move twenty-eight siege guns and sixteen mortars from their Spanish Fort positions. With two divisions in reserve, Canby was ready to attack.

The Confederate line extended for two-and-a-half miles, with nine strong redoubts connected by rifle pits and protected by palisades and torpedoes [mines]. The Union line was four miles long, enveloping the flanks of the fort. At 5:30 P. M. on April 9, as Lee surrendered in Virginia, the four Union divisions, more than 20,000 strong, assaulted and captured the fort. "With a gallantry to which there were no exceptions," Canby wrote in his after-action report, "the troops pressed forward under a heavy fire of artillery and musketry, passing over exploding torpedoes, networks and abatis, and assaulted and carried the enemy's works in about twenty minutes." Two hundred officers and 3,500 men were captured, only a few of them by the Negro division because the Southern soldiers, uncertain of what might otherwise happen to them, ran to the white troops to surrender.

Batteries Huger and Tracy held out. Cavalry was sent up the river to collect boats so that troops could be moved to the island between the batteries and Mobile, to cut communications between them. On April 10, additional guns were positioned to bear on the two batteries, and a boat expedition was planned for a night attack. Both works were abandoned at 10:00 P.M. and their magazines blown up. Maury began to evacuate Mobile that night. Ordnance and quartermaster stores, including light guns, were loaded on steamers and taken up the Tombigbee River. Commodore Edward Farrand, commander of the Confederate naval forces, led the armed vessels and steamers up the river, planting torpedoes as they went. These and other mines caused the sinking of six Federal vessels, two of which were lost after the surrender. Most of the commissary stores were turned over to the mayor for distribution to the people of the city. Much of the cotton that had accumulated at the port was burned, as required by Confederate government policy. Some of the infantry marched up the dirt road to Medina with a wagon train, while others were transported by train. The evacuation was completed on the morning of April 12, four years to the day after the attack on Fort Sumter and the day after Taylor learned of the fate of the Army of Northern Virginia.

On April 11, two divisions of 16th Corps, carrying five days rations, were ordered to cross Mobile Bay. They boarded transports at Starke's Landing at 2:00 A.M. on April 12 and disembarked at Catfish Point, five miles below Mobile, at 10:30. Mayor William Slough went out to the Union fleet under a white flag to surrender the city. He declared that the Confederate army had evacuated Mobile and that no resistance would be offered to its occupation. Granger arrived on the transport *General Banks* just as the head of the Federal column marched peacefully into the city at noon.

Union losses in the Mobile campaign were 232 killed, 2,123 wounded, and forty-three captured or missing. The number of Confederate casualties is not known, but fragmentary reports indicate at least 300 killed and more than a thousand wounded. The provost marshal accounted for a total of 4,924 prisoners, including four generals, 304 other officers and 4,616 enlisted men. Large quantities of naval stores (including 25,000 barrels of resin and turpentine) and army supplies, 231 artillery pieces, and 20,000 bales of cotton, were captured. On the same day, Wilson took Montgomery and Sherman entered Raleigh.

On April 13, Smith's 16th Corps began its march to Montgomery, unaware that the city had been occupied the day before. On April 17, General Grierson left Blakely with 4,000 cavalrymen in two brigades. They joined Smith on April 22 at Greenville, where they learned that Columbus had been captured. Grierson turned east to Eufaula, Alabama, to be in position to cooperate with Wilson in taking Macon, but stopped when he learned of the armistice. He then headed for Montgomery. From there he was ordered west to watch the crossings of the Black Warrior and Tombigbee Rivers with a view to capturing Jefferson Davis, who might be fleeing toward the Mississippi. On this long march Grierson took the surrender of, and paroled, more than 10,000 men.

Wherever he found Confederate commissary stores that his men could not use, he distributed them to the poor. He reported:

> The country is filled with bands of armed marauders, composed mostly of deserters from the late rebel armies, who have returned to find their families suffering from the neglect and persecution of the wealthy leaders. . . . The poor people, including the returned Confederate private soldiers . . . are, as a general thing, now loyal; but the far greater portion of the wealthy classes are still very bitter. . . .

Smith's infantry arrived in Montgomery on April 26.

WILSON'S EXPEDITION

Early in 1865 the strength of General George H. Thomas's Cavalry Corps had been reduced when General Judson Kilpatrick's Third Cavalry Division was transferred to Georgia as part of Sherman's army for the march north. Then, on February 12, the 5,000 men of the Seventh Cavalry Division, under General Joseph F. Knipe, were ordered by boat to New Orleans to join

Canby's army. The Sixth Cavalry Division under General George Stoneman was scattered in Tennessee. The remaining four divisions were encamped along the Tennessee River in the vicinity of Gravelly Springs, in the northwest corner of Alabama, and at nearby Eastport, in the northeast corner of Mississippi. The location was desirable because supplies could arrive by steamboats coming up the river to the head of navigation at Eastport, and because the terrain was such that there were large areas available for drill grounds.

The officer in command was General James H. Wilson, a twenty-seven-year-old graduate of West Point, where he ranked sixth in the class of 1860. He was self-confident, aggressive, and a believer in firm discipline and rigorous training. He devoted January and February to systematic practice in riding, in the use of arms, and in learning to maneuver and advance in column of twos. He decided to replace the standard single-file advance with this formation because it reduced by half the length of brigade columns and improved command and control.

The traditional roles of cavalry were scouting, screening, and massed charge against infantry. The probability of a successful charge by cavalry was reduced after the War Department decided, in 1861, to equip the infantry with rifles. These weapons, firing canoidal bullets (called Minie balls), had a range four times greater, and were considerably more accurate, than smooth-bore muskets. Horsemen, and for that matter infantrymen, attacking infantry armed with rifles were at a serious disadvantage. Moreover, both cavalrymen and horses (which typically cost about $150) were not well trained, and neither could be relied on to perform well in a charge.

Most of Wilson's men were armed with Spencer carbines, which had come into general use in 1863 by order of Lincoln, reversing a War Department decision not to buy them for fear the men would fire too many rounds (at the enemy!). This weapon, invented in 1860 by twenty-seven-year-old Christopher Spencer,

The Beginning and the End.

was a seven-shot repeater with a tube in the stock that fed .52 caliber copper rim-fire cartridges. Pre-loaded tubes could easily be inserted to replace empty tubes, so a man firing a Spencer could get off seven shots in half a minute, while an opponent fired only one from a muzzle-loader. Besides the carbines, the cavalrymen carried revolvers, and had recently been issued new thirty-five-inch sabers, five inches shorter than the old dragoon sabers, and nearly straight.

Wilson believed that the best way to use cavalry was to travel rapidly, then for the men to fight dismounted, where they were less exposed and their fire was more accurate. Cavalry was, in effect, mounted infantry, a concept introduced a year earlier by Colonel John T. Wilder, who formed four regiments of Spencer-equipped, horse-riding infantry into what was known as the Lightning Brigade. The assault made by Wilson's dismounted cavalry at Nashville had been essential to the Union victory there in December. But the cavalrymen maintained the capacity for mounted charges in the right circumstances.

Wilson's corps comprised three divisions, each of which had two brigades. The First Cavalry Division was led by General Edward M. McCook, with General John T. Croxton and Colonel Oscar H. LaGrange as brigadiers. General Eli Long commanded the Second Division, whose brigadiers were Colonels Robert H. Minty and Abram O. Miller. Generals Andrew J. Alexander and Edward F. Winslow were the brigadiers in General Emory Upton's Fourth Division. (The 6,000 men of the Fifth Division, under General Edward Hatch, were left behind because of a shortage of horses). Attached to each division was a battery of four twelve-pounder field guns. There was also a brigade of infantry with the corps. An engineer battalion was equipped with thirty canvas pontoons and lumber to complete a bridge up to 400 feet long. This material was carried in fifty wagons, each pulled by a team of six mules. There was also a train of supply wagons.

Wilson planned to start the campaign on March 5, but heavy rains lasting for two weeks made that impossible. Finally, after "Reveille" at 3:30 A.M. on March 22, soldiers fed themselves and their horses. At 5:00 A.M. bugles sounded "Boots and Saddles," men hurried to the horse lines and mounted, and the largest cavalry force in American history, 12,500 horsemen and 1,500 infantry, headed south into Alabama. On each saddle were two horseshoes, one hundred rounds of ammunition (including ten pre-loaded tubes), five days rations for the man, and feed for the horse for one day.

The expedition was intended to accomplish two things. The first was to engage and destroy the Confederate forces in the northern half of the state and prevent them from supporting General Taylor's army while it was being attacked by Canby. The second was to destroy the munitions works and facilities that supplied the Confederate army: the area from Columbus, Georgia to Meridian, Mississippi was rich in iron ore and coal. The extensive industrial capacity developed by the Confederates in the region had been virtually untouched by the war. Grant wished to deny this area to the Confederacy as a well-supplied redoubt for continued resistance. He suggested to Thomas in January that Wilson conduct a "demonstration" into Alabama with about 5,000 men. This would have been a raid in the sense of a swift incursion followed by a return to base, but Wilson proposed an expedition on a larger scale, with Georgia as a destination: a movement similar, in effect, to Sherman's "march to the sea." This plan was approved, and Grant recommended that Wilson, who was a protégé of the general-in-chief, be in independent command. In fact, Wilson would necessarily be independent, since the plan was for the cavalry to sever communications with its base and live off the country for as long as sixty days.

Atypically for the Civil War, secrecy was maintained and the men only learned on the day of departure that the immediate objective was the town of Selma. Wilson began his advance on three roads, so as to confuse the defending force, commanded by the formidable General Nathan B. Forrest, as to his intentions. Forrest's headquarters was on the Mobile and Ohio Railroad near West Point, Mississippi, and he had 10,000 men at various locations in the vicinity. His task was to defend against possible incursions from the Mississippi River, from the south by Canby, and from the north by Wilson. His dispositions were, as it turned out, least well placed with regard to the threat from Wilson. He did not begin to move any of his men until March 28, when Wilson's destination became apparent.

For the first hundred miles or so Wilson's troops marched through a hilly, barren, gravelly region of dense oak and pine forests. Because the roads were few and poor and the ground was muddy from heavy rains, much effort was devoted to corduroying roads and to keeping wagons moving. Forage and food were scarce, but there was no opposition, since the Confederates were still unaware of the expedition. On March 30, at the village of Elyton (present Birmingham) Wilson destroyed several factories. The next morning he detached General Croxton's brigade of 1,500 to attack Tuscaloosa, fifty miles to the southwest. The main force, finding no bridge or usable ford on the Cahawba River, crossed on a railroad trestle. Railroad ties were laid down to make a narrow roadway on which the troopers could lead their horses across. At the center of this hazardous passage the trestle was a hundred feet above the stream. But the crossing was made without loss and they rode on, reaching Montevallo on March 31. There they destroyed the Red Mountain, Bibb County and Columbiana iron works, the Cahawba Valley Rolling Mills, and cotton gins and collieries.

It was there that the first of Forrest's men formed a line of battle. General Upton attacked and drove them back to a second line of defense about six miles to the south. On April 1, at Ebenezer Church they were again opposed by about 3,000 men under Forrest. General Long's men attacked, quickly supported by Upton who came up on their left. In both cases, six mounted regiments charged successfully with sabers against infantry and dismounted cavalry. They took nearly 400 prisoners and captured three guns. As they went into camp at Plantersville, they had the good fortune to capture a courier with dispatches that revealed the position of each of Forrest's divisions and brigades as they moved eastward from West Point to intercept Wilson and protect Selma. Two of Forrest's divisions, those of General James R. Chalmers (3,500 men) and General William H. Jackson (2,500 men), were passing through Tuscaloosa, headed east to engage the Federal force.

Wilson dispatched General McCook with LaGrange's brigade to join Croxton's brigade and to destroy the bridge over the Cahawba River before the Confederates could cross. LeGrange's 1,200 men marched from Randolph to Centerville, secured and crossed the bridge, and continued west to Scottsville, ten miles beyond the river. There they destroyed a factory, a mill, a bridge and the niter works. Unable to contact Croxton, and facing Jackson's division, estimated to number 3,000, the brigade withdrew on April 2 to Centerville. They burned the bridge, preventing Jackson from joining Forrest in time to help him. While marching to Plantersville, on the way toward Selma, McCook and LaGrange received orders to return to Randolph and escort the wagon train to Selma. Meanwhile Croxton, who knew of the presence of the Confederates through his scouts and skirmishers, maneuvered around them toward his objective, his presence on their flank slowing their movement.

THE CAPTURE OF SELMA

Wilson's luck continued when an English engineer who had worked on the Selma defenses was captured. He sketched a detailed plan, as a result of which Wilson understood the city's fortifications better than Forrest did, and on the basis of which he planned his attack. Selma's extremely formidable defensive line was shaped like an inverted U, making a loop around the city from the river on the west to the river on the east. The flanks were covered by marshy ground. At the northern curve of the loop was a field of abatis 200 yards deep, then a row of chevaux de frise. Next came a wooden palisade, about six feet high. On the inside of this was a ditch five feet deep and ten feet wide, with sharpened stakes in the bottom. The earth from this ditch had been mounded on the town side, so that there was a steep bank rising from the ditch. A firing platform ran along the inside of this bank. There were a number of redans to allow for enfilading the ditch with rifle fire. Cannons were mounted in twenty-four large bastions. Forrest posted the militia along the flanks, where attack was thought to be least likely. In the center was a brigade of 1,400 veterans under General Frank C. Armstrong. The Confederates had perhaps 4,000 men altogether, but many of the defenders were old men or boys, conscripts with no combat experience, for every male was pressed into service, including lawyers, judges, doctors, preachers, and firemen. Moreover, the fortifications were designed to be manned by 10,000 defenders.

Wilson planned to launch his attack just as it was getting dark on April 2. Upton was to send 300 men against the northeast side as a feint. Long, when he heard firing from this attack, was to make the main assault from the northwest, using 1,550 men of his two brigades. They would advance dismounted in a single line, supported by a four-gun battery firing from a low hill. However, in late afternoon about 500 Confederate cavalrymen attacked Long's supply wagons. Long sent reinforcements to his wagon guard but decided that, with enemy troops in his rear, it was too risky to delay the attack. At 5:00 P.M., therefore, when it was still bright daylight on a clear day, Long ordered his brigades to charge, leading the assault in person. First they had to cross 600 yards of open field. Then pioneers with axes cut ways through the abatis and the palisade as the rapidly advancing Federals received canister fire from twenty guns. The men scaled the earth mound on one another's shoulders, and within twenty minutes were in possession of the works. Union losses were forty-two killed and 270 wounded.

Taylor left the city by train about 3:00 P.M. As the attack culminated, some Confederate military people fled, including Forrest. But many others failed to escape: 2,700 men were taken prisoner, with 150 officers. Other prizes included 2,000 horses and mules, thirty-two guns in position, seventy-two guns in the manufacturing plants, 66,000 rounds of artillery ammunition, and 14,000 pounds of gunpowder. The munitions were dumped in the river and the arsenal, machine shops, rolling mills, foundries and other production facilities, covering twenty acres along the river, were burned. The railroad bridge was also destroyed.

In the commercial part of the city, freed slaves looted shops and stores, and fires were started in the residential parts. Forrest had ordered the whiskey in the city to be destroyed, but the Federal troops soon got drunk and, despite strict orders against it, plundered without restraint, taking especially silver and jewels. An excess of 500 horses and mules that the army did not need were shot, to prevent them from being used later by the Confederates. Their carcasses were thrown into the river or left lying in the streets. Within days the stench of their decay was fearful. The fall of Selma occurred (unknown to Wilson, of course) on the same day that Lee evacuated Petersburg and Richmond.

Croxton's brigade, meanwhile, continued its mission to Tuscaloosa. After a forced march of thirty-five miles on April 3, it crossed the Black Warrior River forty miles above Tuscaloosa, at Black Rock Shoals, the men using the ferry while the horses, three of which drowned, swam. Undetected, and guided by several local Negroes, they reached Northport, on the other side of the river from the city, at 10:00 P.M. Just after midnight on April 4, they rushed and captured the pickets at the bridge. As they started across, they found that many planks had been removed, and the noise they made in replacing them gave the alarm. There was a brief fire fight with the defenders, about 300 cadets and some militia. Resistance quickly collapsed and seventy-three prisoners were taken. A foundry producing cannon, a factory making broad-brimmed hats for soldiers, and an army training school at the Alabama Military College were destroyed, as were fifty wagons, three guns, and quantities of harness. The Confederates were able to burn several hundred bales of cotton and some of their supplies. After obtaining bacon and other food for his men, taking horses from the government stables, and burning the bridge, Croxton turned north again, to avoid contact with the Confederates who were still west of the Cahawba.

The Surrender of Taylor

Following the fall of Mobile, Taylor's plan was for Maury's survivors to join the 3,500 soldiers remaining under Forrest. The 8,000-man army would fight its way across Georgia and South Carolina to join forces with Johnston in North Carolina. But this movement did not begin before the news of the Sherman-Johnston proposed agreement of April 18 reached Alabama on April 25. Canby and Taylor arranged to meet on April 30 in a house near the railroad tracks at Magee's Farm, fifteen miles north of Mobile. Taylor, using the fastest means of transport available to him, a railroad handcar powered by two Negroes, arrived with a single aide, Colonel William M. Levy. Canby was waiting for them escorted by a cavalry brigade with a military band and many officers. The two generals met and quickly arranged a truce, which could be ended by either party on forty-eight hours notice, while they waited to hear the outcome in North Carolina. Taylor described the scene that followed:

> We then joined the throng of officers, and although everyone present felt a deep conviction that the last hour of the struggle approached, no allusion was made to it. Subjects awakening memories of the past, when all were sons of a loved, united country, were, as by the natural selection of good breeding, chosen. A bountiful luncheon was spread, of

which we partook, with joyous popping of champagne corks for accompaniment, the first agreeable explosive sounds I had heard in years. The air of "Hail Columbia," which the band struck up, was instantly changed by Canby's orders to that of "Dixie"; but I insisted on the first, and expressed a hope that Columbia would be again a happy land, a sentiment honored by many libations.

The two generals returned to their headquarters at Mobile and Meridian. Several members of the Confederate Congress came to Taylor's camp, seeking advice (and perhaps protection). He told them to go home, submit to the inevitable, and resume their peaceful occupations. On May 1 both generals learned that the proposed agreement had been rejected and that Johnston had surrendered on April 26. Canby promptly notified Taylor that their truce would end in forty-eight hours. Taylor then told Canby that he wished to negotiate with him for the surrender of all the forces under his command, and the naval commander wished to do the same. Taylor later wrote,

> The military and civil authorities of the Confederacy had fallen and I was called to administer on the ruins as residuary legatee. It seemed absurd for the few there present to continue the struggle against a million of men. We could only secure honorable interment for the remains of our cause.

On May 4, the two generals met again, this time at Citronelle, thirty miles north of Mobile, and signed a document of surrender. The terms were similar to those accepted by Lee and Johnston, though several items were stated more explicitly. The complete text follows:

> Memorandum of the conditions of surrender of the forces, munitions of war, &c., in the Department of Alabama, Mississippi, and East Tennessee, commanded by Lieut. Gen. Richard Taylor, C. S. Army, to Maj. Gen. Edward R. S.

Canby, U. S. Army, entered into on the 4th day of May, 1865, at Citronelle, Ala.

I. The officers and men to be paroled until duly exchanged, or otherwise released from the obligations of their parole by the authority of the Government of the United States. Duplicate rolls of all officers and men surrendered to be made, one copy of which will be delivered to the officer appointed by Major-General Canby and the other retained by the officer appointed by Lieutenant-General Taylor; officers giving their individual paroles and commanders of regiments, batteries, companies, or detachments signing a like parole for the men of their respective commands.

II. Artillery, small-arms, ammunition, and all other property of the Confederate Government to be turned over to the officers appointed for that purpose on the part of the Government of the United States. Duplicate inventories of the property surrendered to be prepared, one copy to be retained by the officer delivering and the other by the officer receiving it, for the information of their respective commanders.

III. The officers and men paroled under the agreement will be allowed to return to their homes, with the assurance that they will not be disturbed by the authorities of the United States so long as they continue to observe the conditions of their paroles and the laws in force where they reside, except that persons residents of Northern States will not be allowed to return without permission.

IV. The surrender of property will not include the side arms or private horses or baggage of officers.

V. All horses which are, in good faith, the private property of enlisted men will not be taken from them; the men will be permitted to take such with them to their homes, to be used for private purposes only.

VI. The time and place of surrender will be fixed by the respective commanders, and will be carried out by the commissioners appointed by them.

VII. The terms and conditions of the surrender to apply to officers and men belonging to the armies lately commanded by Generals Lee and Johnston, now in this department.

VIII. Transportation and subsistence to be furnished at public cost for the officers and men after surrender to the nearest practicable point to their homes.

Taylor pointed out that there were thousands of bales of cotton, belonging to the Confederate government, near the Tombigbee River east of Meridian. He thought it appropriate that he protect this property and turn it over to the U. S. Government, as the successor to the Confederacy. Canby said that he would send a Treasury agent from New Orleans to take possession. The two generals then discussed the condition of the country before parting. On May 8 at Meridian, Taylor received the Federal officers appointed by Canby to take the paroles of his men and to issue receipts for the Confederate stores of which they took possession.

Forrest was encamped fifty miles northeast, at Gainesville, Alabama, with about a thousand men. They talked of refusing to sign paroles and instead going to Mexico. Forrest, however, after a night of tortured thought, decided to surrender. This convinced the men, who signed paroles on May 9. In his farewell to the troops he said:

> That we are beaten is a self-evident fact, and any further resistance on our part would be justly regarded as the height of folly and rashness. . . . Reason dictates and humanity demands that no more blood be shed. . . . The terms upon which you were surrendered are favorable, and should be satisfactory and acceptable to all. They manifest a spirit of magnanimity and liberality on the part of the Federal

authorities which should be met on our part by a faithful compliance with all the stipulations and conditions therein expressed. . . . Civil war, such as you have just passed through, naturally engenders feelings of animosity, hatred and revenge. It is our duty to divest ourselves of all such feelings. . . . The attempt made to establish a separate and independent confederation has failed, but the consciousness of having done your duty faithfully and to the end will in some measure repay for the hardships you have undergone.

WILLFUL DESTRUCTION OF UNION AMMUNITION

By Cavalry Corps Special Field Orders No. 30, issued on May 4 at Macon, Upton was to receive the surrenders at Augusta; McCook at Tallahassee; Croxton at Macon; Colonel B. B. Eggleston at Atlanta, and Major M. H. Williams at Milledgeville. The assistant adjutant general who wrote the order was not as particular as Grant and Lincoln about not recognizing the Confederacy. It said that "All officers and civilians, including tax-gatherers in kind, holding office under the Confederate States Government, having in charge engineer, ordnance, quartermaster's, commissary, or medical stores are hereby directed to report immediately to these headquarters the amount of property on hand, and to guard it until in can be turned over to the officers of the proper staff department." Having dealt with matters of surrender, the orders concluded with an admonition:

> A large amount of Spencer munition having been destroyed in direct violation of existing orders by the First Ohio Cavalry on the night of the 3rd of May, 1865, by throwing cartridges in the fire, and thereby endangering the lives of the men in the adjoining camps, it is therefore ordered: First. That each commissioned officer . . . be charged $10 on the muster and pay rolls at the next muster of the regiment, to pay for the ammunition destroyed. Second. That each enlisted

man . . . be charged $5. . . . This order is found to be necessary to protect the Government of the United States from losses on account of willful destruction on the part of enlisted men and gross neglect on the part of the officers.

Arrangements had to be made for a number of local surrenders as word spread through the area commanded by Taylor. On May 8, Major M. E. Johnston of the 25th Alabama Cavalry Battalion sent a brief letter to Granger. He said he had received a demand for the surrender of the forces under his command, but that no terms were stated. If the terms were acceptable he was prepared to surrender at any time and place after Wednesday [May 10]. He explained that his men were mostly south of the railroad and that he could get a greater number of them together if Granger's forces would stop north of the railroad. Granger replied on the same day, explaining he had previously asked Colonel Mead [presumably Johnston's superior] to surrender his forces on the terms granted to Lee and Johnston, but that Mead had refused, saying he saw no military necessity to do so. Granger had therefore issued an order declaring Mead and any soldiers who adhered to him to be outlaws. Granger was now willing to alter his order so that it did not apply to the men of the 25th Battalion. If Johnston accepted, his surrender would be received at noon on May 11 at Trough Spring. Johnston replied the next day, accepting the terms.

Taylor remained at Meridian until the last man of his command had departed, then went to Mobile, headed home. The Confederate money he had was worthless and he did not know how he would be able to get there. Fortunately, Canby and his staff were about to leave for New Orleans, and agreed to take Taylor and his two horses along on their steamer. Taylor afterwards wrote that he "had on various occasions seen General Canby on matters connected with the surrender and recall no instance in which he did not conform to my wishes. Narrow perhaps in his view, and harsh in discharge of duties, he was just, upright and honorable."

A postwar disaster struck Mobile on May 25. According to the Inspector-General, at 3:00 P.M. that day "a terrific explosion of twenty tons of captured powder shook the foundations of the city, followed immediately by a heavy rumbling explosion of shells and fixed ammunition and a shower of shot, shell, grape, and canister, and pieces of stone and brick. A dense column of smoke arose...." The explosion, of unknown cause, occurred while a detail from the U. S. Colored Troops was transferring ammunition from the railroad to a warehouse. Uncontrolled fires burned buildings in more than six acres of the city. Much of the army's stores and forage were destroyed, as were two steamers coaling at the wharf. Casualties were estimated to be 500 Union soldiers, paroled prisoners and civilians.

FROM MONTGOMERY TO WEST POINT

At Selma, Wilson prepared to move on Montgomery. Colonel Minty took command of the Second Division, replacing Long, who had been severely wounded in the head while leading the charge. La Grange's brigade of McCook's division rejoined the main force on April 5. The whereabouts of Croxton's brigade was still unknown. Wilson was anxious to notify Canby of the capture of Selma, but reluctant to send cavalrymen 150 or more miles overland to Mobile. He found a middle-aged Negro named Charles Marven who was willing to take a message down the river, by which the distance was about 300 miles. Marven left on April 4, traveled day and night, and delivered the message to Canby four days later. At Wilson's request, Canby gave him $200 for this service.

All the dismounted men of Wilson's corps, as well as servants, were now riding captured horses. From among the many freed Negroes Wilson recruited three mounted regiments and assigned one to each division. These men served effectively as supply train guards, teamsters and road builders. In hopes of solving the problem of what to do with his many prisoners, Wilson met with

Forrest at the village of Cahawba on April 6. Forrest was unwilling to make an exchange, but did ease Wilson's mind about where Croxton's brigade was by telling him it had burned Tuscaloosa.

Meanwhile, at Selma, Hubbard's engineers built a floating bridge across the Alabama River, which was 850 feet wide at that point. They used their thirty canvas pontoons, plus six that they built of lumber, which they cut themselves. The pontoons were anchored to barges tied to each shore, and secured to heavy pieces of machinery on the banks. The river was rising and the current was strong, so skiffs patrolled upstream to ward off floating logs which, with the high water, broke the bridge three times while it was being put in place. Unaware that Lee was surrendering as they moved, the cavalry began to cross on the afternoon of April 9, and all were on the south side by the next morning. Light for the troopers crossing in the dark was provided by burning buildings, set afire for that purpose. Only half of the canvas pontoons were carried in the train because the rivers to the east were not as wide. The others, along with the wooden ones built on-site, were destroyed.

The cavalry was now in a rich land, bountiful with forage and provisions. The decision to live off the country worked as well for Wilson as it had for Sherman. On the morning of April 10, as Sherman's army deployed against Johnston, Wilson started for Montgomery. LaGrange's brigade of McCook's First Division was in the lead, followed by Upton's Fourth Division. The Second Division, now commanded by Minty, followed in the rear, in charge of the wagon and pontoon trains. Because of the swampy nature of much of the route, and the poor condition of the roads, Minty had to corduroy at many places and repair several bridges, using planking obtaining by tearing down a barn.

LaGrange's brigade covered thirty miles the first day, exchanging fire almost continuously with Confederate forces along the way. At 4:40 A. M. on April 12, after a slight skirmish with the

Confederate rear guard, the Fourth Kentucky Cavalry entered the former Confederate capital, Montgomery, and received its surrender. The Confederates burned 85,000 bales of cotton and retreated toward Columbus, Georgia. The Union provost guard preserved good order during the two days the troops stayed. On April 13, after a heavy skirmish with cavalry, a detachment captured and brought to the city three steamboats with their cargoes of cotton, bacon, salt and corn. Before leaving, the regiment destroyed the three steamboats; the arsenal containing 20,000 stand of small arms; the niter works; a locomotive and twenty cars; two railroad depots; a car-wheel foundry; a machine shop, and twenty pontoons.

On April 14, LaGrange left the city and marched east, covering thirty-eight miles while conducting a running fight and capturing a hundred prisoners. The brigade, following the Montgomery and West Point Railroad, moved twenty-seven miles the following day, rebuilding a bridge on the way, and bivouacked at Auburn. On April 16, they broke camp at 2:00 A.M., passed through Opelika, captured a train of fourteen wagons, and arrived at West Point, Georgia, at 10:00 A.M. Their objectives were the turnpike and railroad bridges at this village on the Chattahoochee thirty miles north of Columbus, just at the point where the river becomes the border between the two states. The Confederates, under General Robert C. Tyler, had constructed a small redoubt, thirty-five yards square, surrounded by a ditch twelve feet wide and ten feet deep and equipped with two light guns and a thirty two-pounder. The defenders were 265 militia and artillerymen. When the first two Federal regiments arrived on the scene, they seized the bridges, preventing reinforcements from crossing to the west side of the river to support General Tyler.

La Grange bombarded the fort with his artillery until 1:30 P.M., when the other two regiments of the brigade arrived. He then assaulted the fort from three sides, bridging the ditch with boards taken from nearby houses. Tyler, three other officers and fourteen men were killed, and twenty-eight wounded, before the fort surrendered. Union losses were seven killed and twenty-nine wounded. McCook ordered the destruction of nineteen locomotives, 340 rail cars loaded with commissary and quartermaster stores, and large quantities of machinery, leather and other supplies. Sixteen prisoners were paroled to nurse the wounded, who were to be cared for by the Confederate surgeons. Seven hogsheads of sugar, 2,000 sacks of corn, and five tons of bacon were left in charge of the mayor to provide food for men of both sides in the hospital, any excess to be distributed among the poor.

The Arsenal City of Columbus

Upton's and Minty's divisions had taken parallel roads toward Columbus. On the afternoon of April 16, Upton arrived in front of the defenses of the small town of Girard (present Phenix City), on the Alabama side of the river. Mill Creek, which empties into the river near the center of town, flows through a valley about a mile wide, with a ridge on each side of it. There were three bridges: a road span at the lower end of town and road and railway spans about three-quarters of a mile above. There was also a bridge three miles above, at Clapp's Ferry. The lower bridge was defended by a rifle pit and three pieces of artillery. The upper bridges were defended by two redoubts connected by a range of rifle pits about three-quarters of a mile long, extending across the upper ridge. The guns in the lower redoubt, six twelve-pounder howitzers and four ten-pounder Parrotts, swept the valley. The upper redoubt contained four guns, commanding the Summerville road (which ran northwest). Five guns swept the railroad and two the upper road bridge, making twenty-four guns in all. There were about 2,700 infantrymen in the works.

Alexander's brigade arrived near the lower bridge at 2:00 P.M., but met heavy rifle and canister fire and found that the span had been set afire. Upton then placed Alexander along the crest of the lower ridge and sent Winslow's brigade to the Summerville road on the upper ridge. Winslow's attack began at 9:00 P.M. when six companies on foot charged to open a breach in what was thought to be the main Confederate line, so that two mounted companies could ride through to the bridge. It turned out that there was a second line of defense. The cavalry got through, however, because, in the dark, the Confederates thought they were their own men. Realizing they were behind the line, they returned to the Union position. The main line was then assaulted and penetrated by an impetuous charge that gave the defenders no time to react. The Union troopers turned to the right behind the line, seized the lower redoubt, and followed the retreating Confederates across the bridge, capturing two howitzers loaded with canister at the far end.

By 10:00 P.M., Columbus, a city of 12,000 people, was in Union hands. Upton's division took 1,500 prisoners and sixty-eight guns, at a loss of thirty men killed and wounded. Among the quartermaster stores that were destroyed, issued to Union troops, or given to Negroes, were 4,500 Confederate uniforms, 5,890 yards of army jeans, 1,000 yards of osnaburgs, 8,820 pairs of shoes, 4,750 pairs of cotton drawers, 1,700 gray jackets, 4,700 pairs of pants, 2,000 pairs of socks, 4,000 tin cups, 2,000 tin plates, 960 wooden buckets, 20 telegraphic instruments, 400 shirts, 375 hatchets, 650 gray caps, 400 wall tents and flies, 1,000 axes and helves, 400 spades and shovels, and fifteen boxes of carpenters tools.

Winslow, who was left in command of the city, said:

> No private buildings in Columbus were destroyed [but] more than 5000 employees were thrown upon the community for their support. . . . . There are thousands of almost pauper citizens and Negroes, whose rapacity under the circumstances of our occupation, and in consequence of such extensive destruction of property, was seemingly insatiable. The citizens and Negroes formed one vast mob, which seized upon and carried off almost everything movable, whether useful or not. Four bridges over the Chattahoochee River, at and near

Columbus, were thoroughly destroyed, one (old) by the enemy and three (including the railroad bridge) by our troops.

It is commonly believed that one of the reasons the North won the Civil War was because of its superior industrial strength, and this is true. It is nevertheless worth noting the impressive extent to which the South managed to create significant industrial capacity in only four years. A partial list of the facilities destroyed in Columbus, as reported by Winslow, attests to the Confederate achievement:

> Railroad depot: Three large warehouses containing 20,000 sacks of corn [and] an immense amount of quartermaster's property. . . . a large number of caissons and limbers. . . . 13 locomotives, 10 passenger, 45 box, 24 flat, and 9 coal cars; 1 round house and machine-shop.
>
> Naval Armory: One small rolling-mill . . . 40 horsepower; . . . 2 sets of rollers, and 3 furnaces, capable of making 4,000 pounds of iron per day. One new rolling mill nearly completed — one 150-horsepower engine, intended to roll railroad and boiler-plate iron; 3 large furnaces. . . . One machine-shop — 2 engines, 45-inch cylinder, nearly completed; 3 small and 2 large planers; 16 iron lathes. . . . All lathes and planers had full sets of tools. One blacksmith shop containing 10 forges. . . . Foundry, boiler-shop, copper-shop, and their contents.
>
> Navy Yard: Containing brass foundry, boat-building house, and machine-shop, with hot-air furnace. . . . 1 blacksmith shop and tools.
>
> Niter Works: Two hundred hands were here employed.
>
> Muskogee Iron Works: Consisting of foundry, machine-shop, small-arms manufactory, blacksmith shop (30 forges), a large saddler's shop, with tools, and 100 sets of flasks; one engine, 30-horsepower.

- C. S. Arsenal: Consisting of machine-shops, foundries . . . 2 furnaces, a large amount of machinery and war material; blacksmith shop (16 forges).
- Two powder magazines: Thirteen thousand pounds of powder, 4,000 loaded shells, 81,000 rounds of ammunition for small arms, and large quantities of rockets, fuses, &c.
- [Three oilcloth factories: capable of making 10,700 yards per day of jeans and other cloth.]
- Columbus Iron Works: Sabers, bayonets, and trace-chains were here made; 1,000 stand of arms found.
- Hainan's Pistol Factory: This establishment repaired small-arms, made locks, and was about ready to commence making revolvers similar to Colt.

Another example of the Confederate ability to built modern weapons was the nearly finished iron-clad ram, *Jackson*, which had been under construction for three years. This vessel, 250 feet long and forty feet wide, was made of live oak, with a hull two feet thick. There were two engines, fired by four boilers, which turned a screw propeller seven and a half feet in diameter. The two-inch armor plate was applied in two layers. The battery consisted of six seven-inch rifled Parrott guns, made in Richmond. The ship was destroyed.

COBB SURRENDERS MACON

Minty, who had been ten miles behind Upton and who had not taken part in the Columbus battle, arrived there at 7:00 A.M. on April 17. He now left the trains in charge of Upton, and late that day, ordered two of his regiments to start on an all-night march. His objective was to reach the Flint River early on April 18 and secure the double bridge there -- two spans, on opposite sides of an island. An advance battalion arrived shortly after daybreak, charged across the bridges at a gallop and captured most of the defenders, five guns, and thirteen wagons loaded with machinery. The rest of the division arrived a few hours later, having marched sixty-three miles in a day and a half. The next day Minty destroyed three large cotton mills at Thompson.

On April 20, Minty and his troops started on the road to Macon at 3:00 A.M. The lead regiment, the 17th Indiana Mounted Infantry, was commanded by Lieutenant Colonel Frank White. At Spring Hill, twenty-one miles from Macon, the four companies of the advance guard met and drove back a force of about 400 Confederates. They moved on to the bridge over Tobesofkee Creek at Mimm's Mill, where they encountered a force of about 300 men, in line of battle, who had set the bridge afire. The cavalry rode part way across, to the point where the planking had been torn up, then dismounted and crossed on the burning stringers. They drove off the defenders, who threw away about a hundred rifles as they fled. White set his men to work putting out the fire, and the rest of the regiment crossed as soon as the flames were under control.

When in sight of the bridge at Rocky Creek, White saw that the Georgians were trying to set it afire. His troopers drove them back to a line of palisades across the road, some of which they tore down. Behind it they found fortifications on both sides of the road. The Union officers demanded their surrender, saying that two divisions of cavalry were approaching. The commanding officer was not present, but subordinate officers agreed to surrender their commands and the 500 or so soldiers gradually lay down their arms.

White continued toward Macon. About eleven miles from the city he was met by General Felix H. Robertson and some other officers under a flag of truce. Robertson, a Texan, had been at West Point with Wilson. He bore a letter from General Howell Cobb, commander of the Georgia Reserve, addressed to "The Commanding General, United States forces." He told White that a truce had been agreed to on April 18. White replied that he knew nothing about a truce and referred the letter to Minty, who was close behind. Minty sent a courier with a copy to Wilson, and suggested to Robertson that he return to Macon to await a reply. Robertson insisted on something in writing, so Minty composed the following letter:

> General: I have received the despatch from General Cobb and have sent it by special messenger to Major-General Wilson, a few miles in my rear. As there may be some delay in receiving an answer, it is necessary for you to return immediately to Macon, to which place General Wilson's reply will be forwarded. I have directed the officer commanding my advance to move forward five minutes after this is handed to you.

White, concerned that this might be an attempt to delay his advance, gave the flag five minutes to get out of the way, then continued at the trot. He soon overtook the flag and the defeated soldiers from the Tobesofkee, who were slowly retreating. It was nearly sunset, and he did not want to call a halt outside the Macon defenses, nor to allow the Confederates to destroy the remaining bridges, all of which he was able to save by his rapid advance. Cobb's letter, meanwhile, had reached Wilson at 6:00 P.M., when he was about nineteen miles from Macon. He rode to the front to meet with Robertson, unaware that that officer had returned to Macon.

White had advanced several blocks into the town when he was met by another flag of truce and told that Cobb would surrender. He went to Cobb's headquarters and took formal possession, then posted patrols and camped the 17th Indiana in the courthouse square. Five generals, 345 other officers and 1,843 enlisted men became prisoners of war. When Wilson arrived, about 8:30, he found that White was holding the town garrison in the stockade pen which had been used for Federal prisoners. Wilson met with Cobb, who protested that the Federals ought to withdraw to the point at which they had been told of the armistice. Wilson declined to do so, saying he had no notification from his command of an armistice. But Cobb insisted that they should return to what he called the status quo ante. Wilson reasoned that there would only be a truce if Lee had surrendered. He asked if that were so, but Cobb refused to answer. Wilson then turned to one of the other officers, General Gustavus W. Smith, whom he had met at West Point, and asked the same question. Smith replied that yes, Lee had surrendered at Appomattox. Wilson then released the five generals to their quarters on their paroles.

The next day at 6:00 P.M. he received a message from Sherman, through Johnston via the Confederate telegraph that he had arranged "for a universal suspension of hostilities looking to a peace over the whole surface of our country." Wilson was to "desist from further acts of war or devastation until you hear that hostilities are resumed." Wilson installed his headquarters at the Lanier Hotel. White established street patrols and assured the safety and control of the town population (8,247). The main problem to be dealt with was finding food for 10,000 men and forage for nearly 20,000 horses and mules. Cobb and the others, accepting defeat, became cooperative and directed the Federals to the places most likely to supply their needs.

CROXTON REJOINS THE CORPS

Croxton's brigade had been out of contact with the rest of the Cavalry Corps while it was capturing Selma, Montgomery, West Point, Columbus and Macon. The brigade had operated independently since March 30. On April 5, after destroying the military property in Tuscaloosa, Croxton and his 1,500 men returned to the Northport side of the river, burned the bridge, and marched to the village of King's Store. The next day he heard from fugitives that Selma had been taken. Later in the day he was attacked at Bridgeville by a force that he estimated to number 2,800, and lost thirty-four men. He returned to Northport, but left again on April 8, camping for three days about twelve miles north while trying to establish contact with McCook. He continued north along the Black Warrior, looking for a place to get to the east side of the flooded river. The brigade was in hilly, wooded country, where food and forage were scarce. On April 15, fourteen miles north of Elyton, the men crossed the Sipsey Branch in canoes while the horses swam. The brigade continued slowly eastward toward Georgia, following a route roughly a hundred miles north of that taken by the rest of the Cavalry Corps.

A week later, around sundown on April 22, the brigade reached Talladega, where it was engaged by seventy men of the 48th Alabama Infantry. After brief skirmishing, the Alabamans fell back before the much larger Union force. Croxton burned the railroad depot, a conscript camp, niter sheds and the county jail. As elsewhere, despite orders to the contrary, silverware, watches, jewelry, horses, mules and other valuables were taken by the Federal troops. After four years of warfare, many men felt no compunction about stealing the property of secessionist civilians, or even in some cases about physically abusing them. The brigade moved on to burn railroad bridges and tear up tracks, attacked from time to time by bushwackers.

At the village of Blue Mountain (present Anniston), General Benjamin J. Hill commanded a small Confederate force that attempted to slow the brigade's advance. After a brief skirmish, he fell back and his men dispersed. On April 23, near Munford's Station, the last engagement east of the Mississippi River took place. Two Federal soldiers and one Confederate, A. J. Button, were the last to die in combat. There were, in addition, several civilian deaths, caused by charging horses, among people who had gathered to watch the fight. The Federals went on to destroy the Oxford Iron Works, which had produced up to twenty tons a day of high-quality iron. This iron had been shipped by rail to the Confederate ordnance works at Selma, where it was made into plates, machinery, cannon and shells. On April 26, the brigade reached the Chattahoochee River, and on April 28, crossed the Flint River at Flat Shoals. The next day, near Newnan, Georgia,

Croxton reestablished contact and learned of Lee's surrender, the death of Lincoln, and the Johnston-Sherman armistice. Croxton's brigade, which had operated for thirty days and covered 653 miles without receiving any word from the rest of the Cavalry Corps, arrived in Macon on May 1.

In the month-long cavalry expedition, ninety-nine Union soldiers were killed in action, 598 wounded and twenty-eight reported missing. Confederate losses are not accurately known because unit commanders typically did not submit reports for the final days of the war, but Wilson reported that he had taken 6,820 prisoners. Senselessly, 255,000 bales of cotton had been destroyed: 120,000 burned by the Confederates and 135,000 by the Federals. Officers and men proudly claimed the trophies they captured, a matter of great importance to them. LaGrange, for example, reported the following:

> 1. The Palmetto flag carried by Buford's brigade; 2. Colors (blue silk with inscription) of Clanton's brigade; 3. U. S. garrison flag (inscription Montgomery True Blue); 4. Two U. S. flags (regimental colors) captured by enemy near Etowah Creek, Georgia; 5. Flag of Dixie Rangers; 6. The garrison flag of Fort Tyler at West Point. . . . Other trophies, as arms, horses, &c., captured by the brigade have, in accordance with established usages in the cavalry, been appropriated by the captors.

Vodges Awaits Instructions

General Quincy A. Gillmore was the senior Union officer in the southeast, and head of the Department of the South, which encompassed South Carolina, Georgia and Florida. His headquarters was at the large Union base on Hilton Head Island, South Carolina. Gillmore, who ranked first in the West Point class of 1849, had been assigned to the Corps of Engineers. In 1862 he was responsible for the thirty-hour bombardment that forced the Confederates to surrender Fort Pulaski, and for the subsequent attack on Battery Wagner, after which he commanded the 10th and 19th Corps. General Edward P. Scammon was in charge of the Union District of Florida, headquartered in Jacksonville, where General Israel Vodges commanded the Fourth Separate Brigade. This unit consisted of two regiments of white troops, the 17th Connecticut and the 1st East Florida Cavalry, and the 3rd and 34th U. S. Colored Troops. Vodges, whom the reader may remember from his role at Fort Pickens in 1861, was a West Point graduate of 1837 who had served as an artillery officer and as an instructor at the military academy for twelve years, and who had seen service against the Seminole Indians. He was captured by the Confederates in an engagement on Santa Rosa Island in October 1861 and held prisoner for ten months. In the spring of 1865 there was no active fighting in the Jacksonville area, but the Union forces maintained a picket line several miles west of the city. Communications with Hilton Head were by sea.

The Confederate commander was General Samuel Jones, an 1841 graduate of West Point. He served in the artillery for twenty years until he resigned in April 1861. He had experience as a division and corps commander before being assigned, on February 2, 1865 to head the Confederate District of Florida. On March 27, General Jones wrote to General Scammon, asking that the Federals receive several thousand Union prisoners. Scammon referred the matter to Gillmore, who decided on April 3 that no prisoners would be received until he had instructions from Grant. Meanwhile, 3,000 Federal prisoners left Andersonville on April 4, 5 and 6, by train to Albany. They were then marched by way of Thomasville, Georgia to Monticello, Florida, a distance of about eighty miles. Jones wrote to Vodges on April 22, saying that, "By a cartel for exchange of prisoners, agreed on between Lieutenant-General Grant and the Confederate Government, Mobile and other points were designated as points of exchange." Since it was impracticable to send "some 3000 or 4000" prisoners to Mobile, could he not deliver them on parole "subject to future adjustment with your Government?" He added that "It is nothing more than humanity would dictate that you should receive them within your lines. My officer will await your answer a reasonable time."

A responsible officer, one of whose principal duties is to see that troops are well cared for, and who had himself been a prisoner, would be expected to promptly accept them. Jones claimed that exchange had been resumed and, more importantly, offered to parole the men without exchange. Besides, the truce with Johnston, following Lee's surrender, made it apparent that the end of the war was near. Vodges did not reply until the next day, when he said that he would agree to a temporary suspension of hostilities, but could not give an answer regarding the prisoners until he communicated with the department commander, which would take about three days.

From Tallahassee, Jones had telegraphic communication via Macon and Augusta to Greensboro, so he was receiving news of developments more quickly than the Federals were. On April 23, he sent Vodges a copy of the telegram by which he learned of the armistice:

> It is announced to the army that a suspension of arms has been agreed upon, pending negotiations between the two Governments. During its continuance the two armies are to occupy their present positions. . . . The armistice . . . applies to your command and the forces opposing you. Publish it and communicate it to the army.

Jones said that the prisoners were now on the road to Lake City and asked that they be received "pending the armistice." He then asked Vodges whether "a due observance of it on your part [will] permit you to receive on any of your vessels or within your lines any negroes escaping from their masters . . . ?"

That same day Vodges wrote to Department of the South headquarters requesting "an early answer and instructions" in regard to the prisoners. He suggested that a boat to sent to transfer them to Hilton Head and asked that rations be sent for them, adding "I presume they must have endured much suffering and are much reduced, and humanity would require that they be received." But he, the general in local command, declined to receive them.

On April 25, Jones and Vodges met at the village of White House, ten miles west of Jacksonville. Jones said that the prisoners were now between Lake City and Baldwin, which was only ten miles west of where they were meeting, and that the men were "very much exhausted." Jones again offered to parole them, leaving the matter of exchange to be dealt with later. Vodges, who was a by-the-book bureaucrat, again replied that he was still waiting for instructions. Jones once more brought up the matter of Negroes. He wanted to know if escaped slaves would be received within the Union lines, and if persons within the lines would be allowed to go out for the purpose of inducing slaves to come into the Union lines.

Vodges referred the question to headquarters on April 26, with this recommendation: "It appears to me that good faith requires that we should not send our agents . . . to offer any inducements to the negroes to leave. At the same time such as voluntarily leave and effect, unaided by us, their escape should be received as hitherto. . . . Before taking action in this case I await the decision of the major-general commanding." He then returned to the subject of the prisoners. "I think under the circumstances it would be best to receive them, but the instructions of the major-general commanding to my predecessor do not appear to leave any discretion on my part. I request early instructions." He then took the initiative to the extent of sending Jones an "official copy" of the order for suspension of hostilities, adding that "in regard to the several inquiries propounded by you to me yesterday, I am at present unable to answer. . . ."

On April 28, Vodges received a message from Confederate Colonel George C. Gibbs at Baldwin:

> I have the honor to inform you that by order of Major-General Jones, commanding District of Florida, I have

brought to this place about 3,400 prisoners of war. . . . All are on parole of exchange. Among them are about 300 who cannot make the march to Jacksonville. I find the transportation here is very limited, and I respectfully suggest that you furnish wagon enough to carry these disabled men to your lines.

On May 1, Vodges wrote to Jones to say that he had been authorized by the commanding general to receive the officers and soldiers held as prisoners. He would have the provost marshal receipt for them at 10:00 A.M. May 3 at White House. He then notified Jones of the end of the armistice. "Hostilities will accordingly recommence in twenty-four hours after this notice has been given at your outpost. These hostilities, if you accede, will not interfere with the transfer of receipts in respect of the prisoners. . ." Jones received the letter too late to make the proposed date, but wrote to say that he would have an officer there on May 4. In a later message, he said he had received from Macon an informal message that he believed to be genuine. No copy has been found, but presumably it told of Johnston's surrender and possibly the approach of McCook. He said, "I would rather surrender my command to you than to any other U. S. officer in my vicinity."

On May 5, Jones wrote that, in order to disband the Confederate troops in Florida, as provided in the military convention "believed to have been entered into" at Durham Station, he was going to collect the arms in the hands of his troops and turn them over to designated U. S. officers, together with muster rolls. "I pledge my word," he said, "that I will do all in my power to effect the disarming and disbanding of the troops in the way best calculated, in my judgment, to promote the interest of the community . . . and of the United States." Vodges replied, "not having as yet received any instructions in the case, I am unable to give you any answer. I will, however, take the earliest opportunity of communicating your wishes to Major-General Gillmore . . . whom I see by the communication you so kindly forwarded to me is authorized to receive the surrender of all troops and munitions of war in the Department of the South." Jones was offering his sword, and Vodges was declining to accept it!

On May 6, Vodges wrote yet again to Department of the South headquarters, saying, "No blanks or instructions have been received by me. I request that they be forwarded as soon as possible." He then asked whether the commanding general intended for him to occupy Tallahassee. He said that Jones had told him, "he has had some difficulty in reconciling his troops to the surrender" and that "if it was decided to send troops there that white troops be sent." Vodges continued that, "at least temporarily," white troops should be sent, because "Florida presents many facilities, both in the nature of the country and the character of the inhabitants, for a guerilla war. I think great caution should be exercised . . ." Finally, Vodges said that Jones had asked if he could have transportation for himself and his family to his home in Petersburg, Virginia, and for his staff officers to their homes. Gillmore, apparently with a sound understanding of his subordinate, wrote to Vodges on May 8, telling him to give every man he paroled a certificate and to

> demand from General Jones a delivery to yourself of all arms and property in the possession or under the control of himself or the rebel officers and forces under his command. . . . All acts of warfare must cease and good behavior is expected and demanded of all persons in Florida. . . . While we are to be humane toward surrendered enemies, these men are still rebels to whom any forgiveness is an act of grace and not of justice. . . . After General Jones has surrendered he will be furnished transportation to Fortress Monroe, Va., en route to Petersburg, Va.

About this time the exhausted prisoners from Andersonville finally entered the Union lines. Vodges, although he had asked that supplies be sent for the relief of the prisoners, was still not prepared to provide them with the food, blankets and other basics that they needed and deserved. The men of the Fourth Separate Brigade, appalled by the condition of the prisoners, collected spare clothing and other gear, and some local merchants provided much-appreciated tobacco.

Jones Surrenders at Tallahassee

General McCook, commander of the First Cavalry Division, was one of seventeen closely related McCooks, four of whom became generals, who served in the Union army and navy. He gave up his law practice in 1861 to join the regular army, but soon transferred to the volunteers. He fought in the Atlanta campaign and, more recently, in the sweep across Alabama to Macon. Wilson ordered him to receive the surrender of Jones and to take possession of Tallahassee, the only capital of a seceded state except Texas that was not in Union hands. He was to arrest soldiers who had not been paroled, deal with officials and newspapers that were not cooperating, protect government property, and prohibit meetings in order to allay public excitement. McCook headed south from Macon on May 5 with 500 men of the 2nd Indiana and 7th Kentucky Cavalry regiments, moving by rail the 100 miles to Albany, where he paroled several hundred prisoners.

On May 9, his column marched to Thomasville, where he learned that, the night before, a group of citizens and soldiers had seized a railroad train and stolen 70,000 pounds of bacon plus a lot of corn and forage belonging to the Confederate government. He sent a special train with a hundred men in pursuit and succeeded in capturing some of the ringleaders and recovering two carloads of forage. McCook proposed to Wilson that he turn the offenders over to the civil authorities, who he believed would deal severely with them. When the 4th Kentucky Cavalry joined McCook in Thomasville, he ordered it to remain there and patrol the area in search of Jefferson Davis. He also left fifty men of the 7th Kentucky to parole prisoners and receive public property.

McCook reached the Florida capital on May 10. With a staff of five, he rode unescorted into the city and established headquarters in a private residence. The two regiments arrived the next day. Jones surrendered the approximately 8,000 Confederate troops in the state and the U. S. flag was raised over the state house. Federal officers began issuing paroles, and 7,200 men were released at Tallahassee by June 1. Within a week after that, all organized units had been surrendered. On May 12, one of McCook's officers went to St. Marks, on the Gulf of Mexico twenty miles south of the capital. He received the surrender of Fort Ward and paroled the officers and crew of the gunboat *Spray*. McCook arranged for a steamer to stop at St. Marks to transport those Confederate officers who were from other states, and who were without funds to get home, to Mobile. He also ordered five days rations issued to refugees from Pensacola, partly to encourage them to go home.

The military property surrendered included forty artillery pieces with 10,000 rounds of ammunition, 2,500 rifles with 121,900 rounds, and 325 pikes and lances. There were also 63,000 pounds of lead, 700 pounds of musket balls, 2,000 pounds of niter, and other munitions. Supplies of food included bacon, corn, salt, sugar and syrup. There were 1,200 cattle, as well as eighty mules and seventy horses. The army used some of these to barter for corn and forage, while the others were loaned to farmers and other civilians for use as draft animals.

Vodges, meanwhile, unaware of what had happened, wrote to Jones on May 12. After telling him that "instructions have been received," he spelled out the details of surrender and enclosed a copy of the parole certificate. The next day Vodges learned from a Confederate officer that McCook had received the surrender of Confederate forces in Tallahassee. He wrote in exasperation to McCook, enclosing a copy of the instructions from Gillmore "directing me to receive the surrender of General Jones and all the forces under his command. I have also received the proper blank rolls and certificates of parole. . . . I have the honor to request you to desist from further proceedings," he said "in the matter of surrender of troops within the limits of this command, as that duty has been delegated to me."

Many of Jones's men had already been paroled by the time Vodges's letter arrived. McCook replied on May 14, saying that he believed "my action cannot in any way embarrass you in exercise of your administrative duties." He thought the timing of his arrival had been opportune, because "mobs of citizens and soldiers throughout the whole country were engaged in breaking open the public store-houses and appropriating their contents." He said he had no desire to interfere with any duties assigned to Vodges, but that he was acting on Wilson's orders and would sent a copy of Vodges's letter to Wilson.

This bureaucratic hassle had no effect on the termination of hostilities. Vodges, in fact, still had a role to play. On May 15, he wrote to the officer commanding the Confederate troops at Baldwin, proposing to receive their surrender. The following day he reported that he had found it necessary to use seventy-five men of the 3rd U. S. Colored Troops to guard the property to be surrendered, and had cautioned them to confine themselves to that duty and to preserve the strictest discipline. He had learned that there were also some men at Lake City and Waldo and said he would assure that they were paroled in proper form.

McCook, meanwhile, had returned to Macon. In his report he said:

> I had no collision with any of the authorities except the ecclesiastical. The pastor of the Episcopal Church in his public services omitted the customary prayer for the President of the United States. I thought it my duty to Christianize him, if possible, and succeeded in convincing him of the error of his way by a communication, a copy of which I have the honor to inclose. He prayed for the President that afternoon.

McCook had written, on May 21, to Pastor W. J. Ellis, pointing out that in his service that day he had

> omitted the usual prayer for the President of the United States. Although it may be inconsistent with your personal feelings to offer this prayer, yet as it is part of the formula prescribed by the bench of bishops . . . I must request that in future you will either include this customary prayer or the church be closed. . . I should think that your sense of Christian propriety might have suggested that as the professed vice-regent of Him who taught peace on Earth and good will toward men, you are in duty bound to soothe any feeling of irritation existing in your community, instead of endeavoring to keep it alive.

Civil authority in the state had virtually collapsed after word arrived on April 30 of the Johnston-Sherman agreement ending hostilities in the Carolinas, Georgia and Florida. Governor John Milton, apparently believing that the cause was lost, had committed suicide. On May 13, in an attempt to restore stability and order to public life in the state, A. K. Allison, who had succeeded Milton as governor while the state was still under the Confederacy, proclaimed himself acting governor and called the legislature into special session on June 5. Similar calls were issued in Georgia and South Carolina. To deal with the situation, Gillmore issued Department of the South General Orders No. 63 on May 14. It stated that the proclamations, calling the state legislatures to convene, by A. G. McGrath of South Carolina, Joseph E. Brown on Georgia and A. K. Allison of Florida, each one "styling himself governor," were null and void, since those men were believed to be "disloyal to the United States, having committed sundry and divers acts of treason." The orders proclaimed

> that the people of the black race are free citizens of the United States; that it is the fixed intention of a wise and beneficent Government to protect them in the enjoyment of

their freedom and the fruits of their industry, and that it is the manifest and binding duty of all citizens, whites as well as black, to make such arrangements and agreements among themselves for compensated labor . . . the Government will not extent pecuniary aid to any persons, whether white or black, who are unwilling to help themselves.

For the time being, civil and military authority was vested in the U. S. Army. It was required to play, as it has been in so many other instances, a political role in Florida, as well as elsewhere in the former Confederacy. It performed this function well, considering that the Federal government had not yet established a coherent reconstruction policy, and that the situation regarding the status of the former slaves was "vexatious." Gillmore put Vodges in command of the entire District of Florida, and Vodges issued General Orders No. 22 on May 24 as "instructions . . . for the guidance of all concerned." The main provisions were:

First. Martial law is, until otherwise directed by competent authority, the only law recognized as existing within the limits of this command. All proceedings at law, acts, or deeds, based on the authority of the so-called Confederate Government, or of the State of Florida as one of the members of that Government, are null and void . . . Second. Lawyers, practicing physicians, and minsters of the gospel exercising the functions of their respective professions will be required to take the oath of allegiance . . . Third. All authorized traders are required to take the usual oath of allegiance, and to conform to the regulations of the Treasury Department as well as the police orders . . . People are to be encouraged to being their produce, &c., for exchange. . . . Fourth. The freedom of the blacks having been fully declared by the President of the United States, no rules or regulations will be adopted interfering with their hiring themselves to whom they may be inclined. It is recommended to them to remain, as far as possible, with their late masters, the latter recognizing them as freemen and fully compensating them for their labor. In no case will they be allowed to remain in idleness at the expense of the Government. . . .

Since McCook and his men had been recalled by Wilson, Vodges assigned ten companies of the 17th Connecticut and 3rd U. S. Colored Troops to duty in Tallahassee. He then occupied all the towns, using both white and Negro troops. At first, Union men tended to doubt the loyalty of the Southerners, while many Southerners feared that they would be outrageously treated. But mutual trust was soon established, despite the arrest of Allison, former navy secretary Mallory, and former senator David L. Yulee, and life began to return to normal. Large landowners and small farmers planted crops, commerce and industry resumed their regular course, returning soldiers found jobs, and most of the former slaves did the work they had done before, but now for wages.

On May 27, the Jacksonville Clarion Union printed a dispatch from Tallahassee, dated four days earlier, that is probably no more inaccurate than other stories carried by the newspapers in those (and these) days:

> Brig. General McCook commands here. His course thus far has been eminently satisfactory. The best of feelings prevails between the soldiers of his command and the inhabitants. Nearly all of General Jones men have now been paroled and are returning to their homes . . . Large numbers of paroled men from Johnston's army are returning every day from Carolina. The spirit manifested by these paroled prisoners and people generally throughout the state is to be quiet and orderly. It is universally admitted by one and all that the Southern Confederacy is no longer in existence.

President Davis is Captured

Existence of the Confederacy may be regarded as having ended on May 10, at a village 110 miles north of Tallahassee. Before leaving Charlotte on April 26, the Confederate cabinet met for the last time, after which the attorney general and the secretary of the treasury resigned. Breckinridge, who was, it will be recalled, a general as well as secretary of war, was now in command of the escort. It numbered about 2,500 men from five Kentucky, Tennessee and South Carolina cavalry brigades -- made up of remnants of regiments many of which had less than a hundred men. The party crossed the Catawba River by ferry, headed, by way of Georgia, for General Taylor's army in Mobile and ultimately General Kirby-Smith's in the Trans-Mississippi.

They reached Abbeville, South Carolina, on May 2. At 4:00 P.M., at the mansion of Armistead Burt, Davis met with the four brigadiers and a colonel who were commanding the cavalry units. The members of the cabinet did not attend the meeting, though Breckinridge was there in his capacity as a general. Davis told them that he intended to form "some definite plan upon which the further prosecution of our struggle shall be conducted." He then asked for their opinions. Unanimously, they said that the war was over and that it was futile to continue hostilities. Guerilla warfare would impose an intolerable burden on the Southern people, many of whom were destitute.

Discouraged, Davis went to bed for much-needed rest. Several hours later Breckinridge woke him to say that Federal cavalry patrols were nearby. He told Davis that volunteers from the escort would continue to protect him, but that would be their only purpose: they would no longer be attempting to join the other Confederate armies. On May 3, the men of the escort who were guarding the wagons carrying the specie were paid off, since it was likely that they would soon decide to take it. The remaining specie was then disbursed: the largest part, about $200,000 belonging to

Richmond banks, was placed in the vault of a local bank. Secretary of the Navy Mallory and Secretary of State Benjamin left, to attempt to escape separately. On May 4, at Washington, South Carolina, Breckinridge disbanded the Confederate War Department. Meanwhile, the president's party moved on southward. On May 8, Davis and his wife were reunited.

In Macon on April 27, Wilson received word via the Confederate telegraph of Johnson's surrender the day before. It appeared, however, that Davis, although he was commander-in-chief of the Confederate army and navy and was within the territory covered by the terms, did not consider himself bound by them. In his *Memoirs*, Grant wrote, "Mr. Lincoln, I believe, wanted Mr. Davis to escape, because he did not wish to deal with the matter of his punishment. He knew that people were clamoring for the punishment of the ex-Confederate president, for high treason. He thought blood enough had already been spilled to atone for our wickedness as a nation." Secretary of War Stanton did offered a $100,000 reward for the capture of Davis, who was suspected of complicity in Lincoln's assassination.

Union cavalry conducted a widespread search. Wilson ordered Upton to take two regiments by rail to Augusta, to cover the bridges, fords and ferries of the Savannah River and the area to the south of the town. Winslow was told to march to Atlanta with 4,000 men for the same purpose, in case Davis should travel westward through north Georgia. To try to locate the Davis party, which was known to have a cavalry escort, Lieutenant Joseph Yeoman and twenty men of the First Ohio Cavalry dressed in captured Confederate uniforms and rode into an area where Davis was thought to be. They were able to join his escort, which was composed of cavalry units that had not served together and did not know one another. Yeoman hoped to be able to capture and remove Davis, but the escort was, as already noted, dismissed at Washington, and he and his platoon left when the others did.

On May 6, Wilson ordered Lieutenant Colonel Henry Harden and 150 men of the First Wisconsin Cavalry to search in the direction of Dublin. Wilson believed that Davis was headed for Florida, rather than Alabama (although Davis said years later that he was trying to get to Taylor). The next day, May 7, Wilson dispatched Lieutenant Colonel Benjamin D. Pritchard of the Fourth Michigan Cavalry with 135 men. On May 9, about eighty miles south of Macon, Pritchard learned that the Davis party was a mile and a half north of Irwinville on the Abbeville road. He approached during the night from the south, but sent a detachment around to the north to block possible escape in that direction. These men ran into Harden's troopers who were approaching from the north. Each regiment was unaware of the presence of the other. In the darkness they mistook one another for Confederates. An exchange of fire killed two soldiers and wounded an officer and three men.

Lieutenant Julian G. Dickinson of the Fourth Michigan was the first to recognize Davis, who hurriedly fled from his tent wearing a waterproof cloak and a long black shawl. This led to the allegation, probably not true, that he was trying to escape dressed as a woman. Davis arrogantly demanded to know which of the colonels was in command. Since neither knew the other's date of rank (their regiments were from different divisions), they were unable to say. But they assured Davis that he was nevertheless a prisoner. Also captured were Postmaster-General Reagan, three colonels, four other officers and thirteen soldiers. The civilians were Mrs. Davis, her sister, four children, and half a dozen Negro servants and teamsters.

They were taken to Macon, arriving there on May 13. Davis and Wilson met at the latter's quarters, where they talked amicably, discussing West Point professors and graduates known to both men. Davis made comments about a number of Confederate generals, some positive, others not, and clearly expressed his strong dislike for President Johnson. A few hours later he and his party left on a special train, preceded and followed by two other trains, each of which carried 400 soldiers: Wilson was taking no chances with regard to an attempt to recapture Davis, unlikely as that was.

When the train reached Augusta, they found that Upton had captured Vice-president Stevens. He was added to the party, even though he and Davis were not on speaking terms. Wheeler was also captured, carrying a forged parole but claiming he was not trying to escape. He too was sent along. The captives were taken down the river to Savannah, then by ship to Fort Monroe, Virginia. Davis was imprisoned there until he was released in 1867. He was never charged with treason, though he was included in the indictment regarding the assassination of Lincoln, in which he played no part. Ordinarily, the surrender of the head of state of an enemy nation would be a significant event in the ending of hostilities. This was hardly so in the case of Davis, since nearly all the forces of the seceded states had by now surrendered, and he had been unable to effectively exercise command as the Confederacy disintegrated.

CHAPTER 9

SURRENDERS WEST OF THE MISSISSIPPI APRIL–MAY 1865

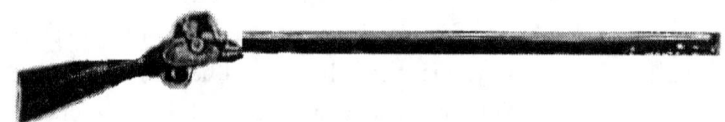

POPE PLANS AN OFFENSIVE

On April 8, General John Pope, commanding the Military Division of the Missouri in St. Louis, wrote a long letter to Grant. He was responding to a suggestion made by the general-in-chief on March 21, that he plan an offensive into Texas. Pope began by saying that he had 17,000 effectives, 7,000 of whom were cavalry for which he needed 5,000 horses, and that he had supplies on hand for six months. He estimated that General Kirby-Smith's army numbered nearly 60,000, based in Camden and Fulton, Arkansas, and in Lewisville and Shreveport, Louisiana. General Pope proposed to move through Arkansas in three columns, crossing the Red River near Clarksville, Texas. He hoped to do this before the Confederates figured out where he was headed, which was to Marshall, Texas. "This plan of operations, if successful," he said, with a hint of pessimism, "will secure results completely decisive, so far as concerns the Trans-Mississippi army of the rebels." He thought, with a hint of optimism, "if they deliver battle at all they will do so near Marshall." Otherwise, the Union force would sever the Confederate supply line. Pope proposed that he then move on Washington, Texas, from where he would threaten Houston, Galveston and Austin.

Pope told Grant that he would need an additional 30,000 men,

> Western men, accustomed to make long and rapid marches, and to live without grumbling or discouragement on short rations.

He would also need "about 3,500 wagons with mules and harness complete, and a good light pontoon train." He thought he could not commence this movement until June 1. For one thing, the rivers were in flood and difficult to cross in May. He also wanted to wait until the corn and wheat crops were well advanced, since the army would be depending on the country for food. He planned to use a mounted force, consisting partly of loyal Cherokees, to drive the cattle of the hostile Choctaws and Chickasaws to the army, to furnish it with meat. As for the cavalry, artillery and wagon animals, there would be ample grazing in the flat prairie country through which they would be traveling. He added, tactfully, that he would,

> Be greatly obliged to you for any advice or any suggestions which you think may be useful to me in the proposed operations.

Grant did not read this letter before Pope heard, on April 10, of Lee's surrender. He then sent Grant a brief message saying that the operation would presumably not now be necessary, and asking whether he should send a copy of the message about Lee's surrender to Kirby-Smith and "demand the surrender or dispersal of his army?" It was an important question, since Kirby-Smith's Army of the Trans-Mississippi, headquartered at Shreveport, was one of the three remaining Confederate forces (the others being Johnston's and Taylor's).

On the Red River in Arkansas, there were fifteen Confederate transports and two warships, the *Merite* and the *Missouri*. The latter was under construction as a six-gun iron-clad on which some hull armor had been installed, but it was months away from being completed. At Shreveport was an unarmed 206-foot side-wheeler, the *William H. Webb*. Lieutenant Charles W. Read, a graduate of the U. S. Naval Academy's class of 1860, took command of the *Webb* on March 31. He found that the vessel was "totally unprepared for the service upon which I was ordered to take her, without a single gun on board, little or no crew, no fuel, and no small-arms." Read took the *Webb* down river to Alexandria on April 7, and began fitting it for combat. Kirby-Smith helped by having the army supply a thirty-pounder Parrott rifle for a bow pivot, and two small iron twelve-pounders that were placed aft. There were also five 100-pound torpedoes, one of which was mounted on a spar.

Lieutenant Read recruited and trained a crew of sixteen officers and fifty-one men at Alexandria. His orders were to take the ship to the Gulf of Mexico and operate as a raider against Union commerce. He had enough coal for one day of steaming, plus about 200 cords of wood, mostly pine knots, low-grade fuel, but it would suffice for another four days. There was also some turpentine. He loaded 190 bales of cotton, which were placed to shield the machinery and which he planned to exchange for coal when he reached Cuba.

The *Webb* got under way down the Red River about 4:30 A.M. on April 23, stopping to pick up a pilot, George Price. The intended route was through Atchafalaya Bayou into Berwick Bay, but this proved to be impracticable because the fully loaded boat drew too much water, ten feet. Read decided to continue on the Red River to its junction with the Mississippi. From there to the mouth of the Mississippi was 300 miles, with Union gunboats on station every few miles. The *Webb* reached the Mississippi at 8:30 P.M., displaying Federal recognition signals. One Union gunboat realized the *Webb* was a Confederate vessel and fired at her, but the shot missed by 400 yards.

To prevent word being sent ahead, Read arranged for the army to cut the telegraph wires as far down river as Placquemine. South of there he stopped every ten or fifteen miles for his crew to make additional cuts. About ten miles above New Orleans on April 24, Read flew a U. S. flag at half mast, to appear to be in mourning for Lincoln. The *Webb*, which had a top speed of twenty-five knots, managed to make it past the city, but not without being hit by three shots. One of them deranged the torpedo attached to the bow, swinging it around and under the vessel, which had to stop while the torpedo was cut loose. The gunboat *Hollyhock* pursued the *Webb* for twenty-five miles until it was recognized by the Union sloop-of-war *Richmond*, which fired a broadside. Read turned up river, but ran into the *Hollyhock*. Trapped between the two Federal vessels, he put the *Webb* aground. All hands but three escaped before the magazine exploded after the crew poured turpentine on the deck and set the ship afire. Fifteen crew members were captured by Negro infantrymen and taken to New Orleans, where they were paroled as part of Buckner's surrender on April 26.

Meanwhile, Pope continued to plan his elaborate offensive. On April 20 he wrote to General J. J. Reynolds, who commanded the 20,000 Union troops in Arkansas from his headquarters at Little Rock. After informing Reynolds (who had expressed doubts about the venture) that he was sending 5,000 cavalry horses, 2,000 Canadian ponies, and 3,500 wagons with teams, he went into the details about the offensive and posed the critical question:

> I think the operations I propose worth some risk and much labor. We must get over about 175 miles of desert and difficult country, depending upon our own resources. This distance can probably be traversed . . . in about twenty-five days. The question simply is, can we march an army of 50,000 men from the Arkansas [River] to the Red River (a distance, say, of 200 miles), carrying our own supplies, in view of bad roads and the ordinary questions of nature?

By this time Lee had surrendered, Mobile had been taken, and the Johnston-Sherman truce was in effect, but Pope still supposed that a large-scale operation might be required. He again wrote to Grant the next day, expressing confidence that between his offensive and "Canby's force at proper points in Texas the final surrender or dispersion of the rebel army under Kirby-Smith would be certain." He repeated his request for "Western troops accustomed to long marches and to half rations" and for "the very best and strongest mules and wagons." He would certainly need the strong mules: enclosed was a list of rations for forty days for 55,000 men, estimated to weigh 4,267,808 pounds and to require 2,133 wagons to transport.

Thompson Surrenders in Arkansas

Union General N. J. T. Dana at Vicksburg notified Confederate General W. F. Turner on April 26 of the April 18 truce between Johnston and Sherman. The two officers then entered into a truce of their own:

> An armistice is agreed upon between Major General Dana and Brigadier General Tucker subject to the approval of their respective superiors, the conditions of which are as follows:
>
> First. The cessation of hostilities shall be total, and the troops on each side shall remain in statu quo.
>
> Second. Either party reserves to itself the right to punish guerillas and other offenders against the peace, and to enforce the requisite police regulations within the limits of their respective commands.
>
> Third. Existing regulations of trade and intercourse shall continue as heretofore under a liberal construction of the present policy.
>
> Fourth. The armistice shall commence and be binding on both parties from and after the hour of 9 A.M. on the 28th instant.
>
> Fifth. This armistice shall terminate forty-eight hours after the receipt of notice by either party from the other of their desire to terminate it, or immediately after the notice of either party of the disapproval by the superiors of the other party agreeing hereto.

The second and third articles of the truce agreement, dealing with "offenders against the peace" and with "trade and intercourse," are interesting in that they address matters not mentioned in most of the surrenders. Two days later, word was received that the Federal government had rejected the North Carolina agreement, and Dana promptly notified Tucker that he was terminating their armistice.

The saga of General M. Jeff Thompson, Confederate commander in northern Arkansas, nicely illustrates the physical as well as diplomatic difficulties involved in making surrender arrangements. On April 25, Pope wrote to General Grenville M.

Dodge, commanding the Department of the Missouri at St. Louis, saying that "In relation to M. Jeff. Thompson, it is probable that guarded overtures made by the commanding officer nearest him might be useful." On the 30th, from Harrisburg, Arkansas, General Thompson wrote to General Reynolds in Little Rock, commenting on the request for his surrender which had by then been made, and which had suggested that he would be responsible for the deaths of "brave men" if he did not do so.

He told Reynolds:

> Being disposed to believe that you are actuated by philanthropic principles in making these propositions, or that you are acting in conformity to orders, I receive them in more kindness than I otherwise would, but I respectfully and most positively decline accepting your offer. While frankly admitting that the news that has reached me of the condition of the Confederate cause in Virginia is very discouraging, yet believing firmly in the justice of our cause and our ability to succeed in the course of time, I will march firmly on in the path of my duty until my Government or my superior officers shall bid me stop, which I hope and pray will never be until the Southern people are a free and independent nation.

Thompson added a P. S.,

> Allow me to express my sincere regret and horror at the manner in which President Lincoln came to his death.

Dodge, unaware of this exchange, sent Lieutenant Colonel C. W. Davis to personally obtain Thompson's surrender. It took Davis three weeks to accomplish this task. On April 30, accompanied by two staff captains and escorted by 200 men of the 17th Illinois Cavalry, he headed for Arkansas via Cape Girardeau. On May 5, the party arrived at Chalk Bluff on the Saint Francis River, which was in flood. Some of the men built a raft while others foraged.

Davis tried to learn the whereabouts of Thompson, and was told that his headquarters was at Harrisburg. Davis sent two letters to Thompson by different routes, hoping that at least one would reach him. One did, on May 7. Thompson replied immediately, saying that he would meet Davis at Gainesville or, if he arrived first, "up on the ridge" between there and Chalk Bluff. But one of the captains found Thompson before that, and returned to Chalk Bluff on May 9 with Thompson and four of his officers. Davis then delivered the letter that Dodge had written on April 29, which said, in part:

> The terms granted by Lieutenant-General Grant to General Lee will be given the forces under your command. By accepting these terms you will put an end to the further destruction of life and property in North Arkansas. To continue the struggle longer must be evident to you as useless. Should you not accept these terms . . . [your men] will immediately be declared outlaws, and no terms thereafter granted them.

Several long discussions followed. Thompson had doubts about whether he had the right to surrender a district and a force that were not surrounded or in danger of immediate capture. Davis gave him forty-eight hours to consult with his brigade commanders. Apparently they decided that they had the right, absent any other source of authority. When time expired at 5:00 P.M. on May 11, Thompson announced his decision to surrender. Wittsburg and Jacksonport were selected as the most convenient places of taking paroles, given the high stage of the rivers and the destitute condition of the country. Thompson expected to surrender about 5,000 men, all without anything to eat. Davis arranged for 50,000 rations so the Confederate soldiers could be fed while being paroled and on the way to their homes. A total of 7,454 (636 officers and 6,818 men) were paroled.

At least 175,000 paroles were signed by surrendered Confederate soldiers in 1865. Thompson's parole indicated that he was surrendering himself, since he was the officer in command:

> I, the undersigned prisoner of war, belonging to the army of the Northern Sub-district of Arkansas, having been, on the 11th day of May, 1865, surrendered by Brig. Gen. M. Jeff. Thompson, commanding said army, to Maj. Gen. G. M. Dodge, commanding the Department of Missouri, do hereby give my solemn parole of honor that I will not hereafter serve

in the armies of the so-called Confederate States, or in any capacity whatever against the United States of America, or render aid to the enemies of the latter until properly exchanged in such manner as shall be mutually approved by the respective authority.

M. Jeff. Thompson
Brigadier-General,
Missouri State Guard Commanding C. S. Troops,
Northern Sub-district of Arkansas
Done at Jacksonport, Ark., this 5th day of June, 1865

KIRBY-SMITH HOLDS OUT

Nearly two weeks after Lee surrendered, the news reached Shreveport. Confederate civilians and soldiers in the region were demoralized and realized the cause was lost. Nevertheless, there was sentiment in favor of sustaining the war among governors, newspaper editors, and other die-hards and romanticists. Mass meetings were held in support of continued hostilities. On April 21, Kirby-Smith published an address to the Army of the Trans-Mississippi, extorting the troops to continue to serve while presaging the likelihood of surrender:

> Great disasters have overtaken us. The Army of Northern Virginia and our General-in-Chief are prisoners of war. With you rests the hopes of our nation, and upon your action depends the fate of our people. . . . Show that you are worthy of your position in history. Prove to the world that your hearts have not failed in the hour of disaster, and that at the last moment you will sustain the holy cause . . . Stand by your colors — maintain your discipline. The great resources of this department, its vast extent, the numbers, the discipline, and the efficiency of the army, will secure to our country terms that a proud people can with honor accept, and may, under the Providence of God, be the means of checking the triumph of our enemy and securing the final success of our cause.

He was not the only officer extorting the troops and the people to rally to the cause. From Houston, General John B. Magruder called upon:

> The army and patriotic citizens of Texas to set an example of devotion, bravery and patriotism, worthy of the holy cause of liberty and independence . . . The Army of the Trans-Mississippi is larger, in finer order, and better supplied than ever. There are no navigable streams in Texas, therefore the enemy will be divested of the great power of steam . . . Crops have been bountiful; our armies can therefore be supplied in almost any part of Texas. There is no reason for despondency, and if the people of Texas will it, they can successfully defend their territory for an indefinite period.

On April 29, Governor Henry W. Allen of Louisiana told a crowd that all that was required was "a little patience and perseverance, bringing into requisition all of our available strength to secure the great end of the struggle, viz: the independence of our country." There was speculation that, now that Richmond had fallen, the capital of the Confederacy would be shifted to Texas, as indeed, Davis seems to have intended. Many imagined that the war could be continued indefinitely from there, and still hoped, desperately, for foreign recognition and assistance. It was proposed that an effort be made to contact Emperor Maximilian of Mexico and offer the services of the surviving Confederate forces in defending Mexico against the United States if it tried to force the French to withdraw.

Meanwhile, Pope sought to obtain Kirby-Smith's surrender by sending a mission "from which, I am constrained to say, that I expect little." He wrote two lengthy letters from his St. Louis headquarters on April 19. One was to Kirby-Smith. The other, consisting of detailed instructions, was to his chief of staff, Lieutenant Colonel John A. Sprague of the 11th U. S. Infantry. Sprague was to go to the Red River and deliver the letter to Kirby-Smith. Pope told Sprague that he must carefully bear in mind, and make clear, that the arrangement proposed in the letter was purely military and did not relate to civilians or civil affairs (something

Sherman had not born in mind in North Carolina on the previous day).

Sprague was not to object if Kirby-Smith or any of his officers preferred to go to Mexico without parole. If they decided to march off in an organized body, with their arms, to Mexico, he was not to commit the U. S. Government to any policy. "It might be well to allude to the assassination of the President and the deep feeling it has created throughout the United States, which feeling will undoubtedly be heavily visited on those who continue to resist the authority of the United States," Pope wrote. The only written agreement Sprague was to make was to be substantially the terms accorded to Lee. If Kirby-Smith were to accept the offer in Pope's letter, arrangements were to be made for taking paroles.

To deliver this message, Sprague traveled by steamer down the Mississippi. He arrived at the mouth of the Red River on April 24, and was later met by a boat on which were three officers who offered to carry the letter to Kirby-Smith. Sprague, however, said his instructions required him to deliver it in person, and he was allowed to do so at Shreveport. After pointing out that Lee had surrendered, that Johnston had agreed to terms with Sherman, and that Mobile was reported to have fallen, Pope's letter said that Grant had instructed him to offer Kirby-Smith the same terms given to Lee. Noting that the Confederate general would "be responsible for unnecessary bloodshed" if he failed to surrender, the letter continued:

> The duty of an officer is performed and his honor maintained when he has prolonged resistance until all hope of success has been lost. Any further continuance of hostilities simply leads to the certainty of inflicting upon a people, incapable of successful resistance, all the horrors of violent subjugation. Wisdom and humanity alike require that this contest, under the circumstances, be brought to an end without further suffering or shedding of blood.

Kirby-Smith explained to Sprague that his army was not surrounded, or even engaged, and that in any case he expected more liberal terms than Lee. He then wrote a letter to the governors of the three seceded states west of the river: Henry

Allen of Louisiana, Pendleton Murrah of Texas, and Harris Flanagin of Arkansas, and also to Thomas C. Reynolds of Missouri. It raised yet again the question of where the authority to surrender lay:

> The surrender of General Lee, and the perilous situation of the armies in North Carolina and Alabama, seem to preclude the possibility of successful resistance in the states east of the Mississippi. The army under my command yet remains strong, fresh, and well-equipped. The disparity of numbers, though great, between it and our enemies may be counterbalanced by valor and skill. Under these circumstances it is my purpose to defend your soil and the civil and political rights of our people to the utmost extent of our resources. . . . Since the evacuation of Richmond, the seat of government of the Confederate States has not been fixed, and it may be transferred to the western side of the Mississippi. It is impossible to confer with the President. . . I yet feel that I should carefully avoid any appearance of usurping functions not intrusted to my discretion. . . . I have therefore requested you to assemble in conference and [will] ask you to indicate such policy as you may deem necessary.

In preparation for the meeting, scheduled for May 13, Governor Reynolds prepared a memorandum on May 10. It was ambiguous in that it left unanswered the question of the means by which, in the circumstances, the "people and authorities" were to decide:

> The position of the Missourians both in the army and in civil life in this department is this: The people and authorities of the territory held by the Confederacy should decide whether they will continue the war. If it is to be continued, we will standby them faithfully to the last. Should the war be discontinued, we desire time and facilities and supplies to leave the country with our personal property.

Allen, Flanagin, Reynolds, and a representative of Murrah (who was ill) met at Marshall, Texas and advised Smith that he should "accept the following terms, in order that peace may be restored to the country." They then specified five terms. The first of which they probably knew would not be acceptable to the U. S. Government:

>First. The U. S. Authorities to grant immunity from prosecution for past acts to all officers and soldiers and citizens in the Trans-Mississippi Department.

>Second. On the granting of this immunity all resistance to the United States Government to cease.

>Third. The Confederate Army to be disbanded and its officers and soldiers be permitted to return to their homes, transportation to be furnished them as far as practicable.

>Fourth. Such officers and soldiers as choose will be permitted, without molestation, to leave the country, with or without their arms, in a reasonable time.

>Fifth. The same permission to be granted to citizens.

Until this time Kirby-Smith had no intention of surrendering. He believed that he was obliged to hold out until Jefferson Davis arrived. General Sterling Price, however, fearing what Kirby-Smith might agree to in the negotiations with Sprague, met with five other officers and proposed to arrest the commanding general. The facts concerning this incident are uncertain, but if carried out it would have been a coup d' etat, since Kirby-Smith was head of both the army and the Confederate government in the Trans-Mississippi. Nothing came of this plan, but it indicates the intensity of the long-standing differences between these two men on policy matters as well as personal grounds.

On May 15, Sprague was still in Shreveport waiting for the results of the conference. Kirby-Smith gave him his official reply to Pope's letter, but also a personal memorandum in which he told Sprague that Pope's terms were not what a soldier in his circumstances could accept. "An officer can honorably surrender his command," he said, "when he has resisted to the utmost of his power and no hopes rest upon his further efforts." He didn't contend that his army could accomplish its independence without assistance, and he conceded that the effusion of blood and devastation of the country should be avoided. But he discussed at length his views regarding honor and surrender. Then he asked that Governor Allen accompany Sprague to Washington "for the purpose of presenting to the proper authorities the terms for their consideration." Sprague declined to accede to this request.

In his official letter to Pope, Kirby-Smith said, perhaps a bit testily:

> Your propositions for the surrender of the troops under my command are not such that my sense of duty and honor will permit me to accept. I regret that your communication should have been accompanied with a threat, or that you should have supposed that personal considerations would have influenced me in the discharge of my duties.

Attached was a memorandum stating the five terms proposed by the governors. Kirby-Smith said he thought they were of "a character so reasonable under the circumstances that it is difficult to conceive of any objection being urged to them." In concluding, he made an argument for leniency and implied a threat of his own: "Many examples of history teach that the more generous the terms proposed by the victorious enemy the greater is the certainty of a speedy and lasting pacification, and that the imposition of harsh terms leads invariably to subsequent disturbances." The Confederate proposal was unacceptable to the Union.

Guerilla Warfare Ends

Before there were any surrenders west of the Mississippi, active fighting subsided, and the military authorities began addressing the problems that resulted from the disarray or collapse of the Confederate and state governments. On April 27, Pope replied to a petition from Dodge asking permission for "banishment to the South of disloyal families from certain counties in Missouri." Pope said,

> The banishment of residents of Missouri to the South is no longer admissible, if, indeed, it has ever been judicious or just. The Southern armies and State governments are now broken to pieces, and the object of the General Government is to restore peace and reinstate civil government in the Southern

States. It is clear enough that there are a sufficient number of disloyal men and lawless vagrants in those states already to make the attempt to restore peace very difficult.

Pope pointed out that, since Missouri had relatively few such men, it would be better to deal with them there than to transfer the problem elsewhere. Two days later Dodge instructed his district commanders on how to handle the large number of former Confederate soldiers who were on the way to, or had arrived at, their homes:

> All men who report from rebel armies who are deserters and have no charges against them for crimes release on taking amnesty oath. Give deserters a copy of the oath, which will be their protection as long as they keep laws of the United States.

Throughout the Civil War the Union army, and local militias and citizens, had the difficult task of contending with bands of irregular fighters. It was been suggested that the South might have won if it had fought a guerilla war rather than a conventional one. Certainly the consequences for civilians would have been dreadful, as the wartime events in Missouri attest. Moreover, guerilla warfare would have induced the North to quit only if it had been able to inflict suffering on Northern citizens. That would have required operations in the Northern states, precisely where there would not have been the support from local populations that guerillas require.

Guerilla fighting of the most appalling kind had been carried on during the four years of the Civil War and continued, as the war ended, throughout the swamps, forests, hills and back roads of the Trans-Mississippi. This unconventional warfare had been especially prevalent in Missouri, which officially remained in the Union, but where adherents of secession formed a separate legislature. It voted to secede, elected a governor, sent representatives to the Congress in Richmond, and raised a number of regiments for the Confederate army. Missouri was therefore a sharply divided state, and the warfare that developed and persisted was a vicious conflict between those who supported the Union and those who wished to be part of the Southern Nation. The guerillas ranged in character from partisan and irregular troops acting under military command to groups of bushwhackers and deserters who, under the guise of supporting the Confederate cause, committed robbery and murder for their own gain and satisfaction. For these men, war provided an opportunity and a justification for violence to persons and for theft and destruction of property.

In the spring of 1865, the war appeared to be over, but the situation prevailing west of the Mississippi River was ambiguous, since the Confederate forces had not surrendered. Vigilance was the order of the day. On April 27, Colonel S. B. Jones of the 78th U. S. Colored Infantry was told to send:

> A weekly mounted reconnaissance of fifty men . . . through Labadierville and Brule Texas and Landry to the Shell Bank, on Lake Verret, for the purpose of watching that section of the country and preventing any intended raids or thieving excursions. No regular day will be established for these scouts, as this would enable the enemy to ambush and perhaps defeat you.

Similar orders went out to other regiments, some stating that the purpose of the expeditions was "cleaning out the guerillas and jayhawkers." For a long time the U. S. Army performed many of the functions that would normally have been the responsibility of the police. The *Official Records* contain reports of hundreds of instances. Some excerpts:

> New Orleans, April 4: "Whitaker's gang of guerillas, or some rebel force, visited the Saint Emma Plantation, . . . coolly called up the overseer, and forcibly took from him thirty-seven mules. . . . This is evidently in pursuance of a system of the enemy to supply their army with draft animals.

> Farmington, Missouri, April 4: "Hilderbrand and his gang, numbering eight men in all, were at Hered's place, near Big River Mills, at daylight and took breakfast. . . . I immediately sent out two details . . .to intercept them. . . . They had about fourteen led horses. . . . About two miles from this place they ran in and took out an old black man, and killed him. . .

having traveled some forty miles, Sergeant Hood thought it advisable not to pursue farther."

Patterson, Missouri. April 18: "Scouts reporting fifteen guerillas on McKenzie's Creek, I immediately dispatched a scouting party of twenty men under Lieutenant Crane [of the Seventh Kansas] in pursuit, who surprised them in their camp, killing 4 and capturing 6 horses, together with a quantity of articles taken from the citizens, which have been returned to the proper owners."

Memphis, Tennessee, April 23: "Disembarking the Third U. S. Colored Cavalry at Randolph, Lieutenant Colonel Cook . . . captur[ed] one Wilcox, alias J. M. Luxton, who was in command of seven others, whom he was unable to capture. . . Arriving at Randolph, Wilcox, alias Luxton, was tried by drumhead court-martial and at 6:30 was, by my order, hung by the neck until he was dead, and left hanging as a warning to his brethren in crime. . . . Eight horses died from buffalo gnats."

By the actions of the U. S. Army, the organized guerillas were gradually disbanded. Most of the survivors in Missouri, Arkansas and Louisiana surrendered during May and June. The situation became clear to them after May 12, when General Dodge established the applicable terms. They would not be interfered with by the authorities, if they signed paroles and obeyed the laws. The nature of many of the acts they had committed, crimes not connected with the war, led to some being arrested by county sheriffs for murder and other serious charges.

Still, individuals, and small groups composed of former guerillas, militiamen, and deserters, including many released from jails, continued to be a public menace. They commonly became highwaymen who indiscriminately robbed civilians and returning soldiers, the latter often carrying their mustering-out pay. These soldiers sometimes received warning letters from home, recommending that they travel armed and in groups to defend themselves. Only limited help was available from the Federal government because the garrisons were withdrawn from small towns as the army demobilized. Protection depended, therefore, on the local authorities. This in turn meant a fierce struggle between the two sides to control the courts and other elements of local government. Both sides were willing to use violence, a legacy of the accumulated cruelty of the four preceding years.

Among the best known of the guerilla chiefs, notorious for his sacking of Lawrence, Kansas in 1863, was William C. Quantrill. Born in Ohio, he had rampaged across Kansas and Missouri since 1862. In early 1865, he was known to be in Kentucky. General John M. Palmer, in command of the Union forces in that state, sought to have him captured or killed, but an attempt in March failed. In April, a nineteen-year-old Confederate deserter named Edwin Merrill, who claimed to have known Quantrill in Kansas, offered to undertake his capture, and recruited thirty men to help. The plan was for these men to dress and conduct themselves as a guerilla band, so as not to appear to be Federal soldiers as they scoured the countryside looking for him.

Their search continued for nearly a month until May 10, when a Negro blacksmith told them that the man they were seeking was on the farm of James H. Wakefield near Taylorsville. On that rainy morning, Merrill and his men rode onto the farm, carbines and pistols at the ready, and surprised Quantrill, who was asleep with most of his companions in the barn. He and two of his men were shot as they tried to flee on horseback. Quantrill was hit in the left shoulder, the round ending up in his spine, paralyzing him. A second round took off his right index finger. Writing forty-four years later, W. E. Connelly described what happened next:

> [Some men] ran into the house for a blanket on which to bring him in, which they soon did, laying him on a lounge. Captain Merrill entered and talked with him. He repeated that he was Captain Clarke [Clarke was Quantrill's mother's maiden name] of the Fourth Missouri Cavalry. He did not wish to leave Wakefield's, and gave Captain Merrill his fine gold watch and $500 to allow him to remain. . . . By the military orders then existing, the life and property of Wakefield was forfeit for harboring the guerillas. Captain Merrill began to plunder the house, when Wakefield took him and his lieutenant aside, giving the captain $20 and the

lieutenant $10, which, supplemented with a jug of whisky, saved further depredations, and the hopeful command departed.

Terrill returned on Friday morning, May 12, and took his prisoner in a farm wagon to Palmer's headquarters in Louisville, arriving there the next day. He and his men were paid off by the army for their service. Quantrill was taken to the hospital of the military prison, then moved to a Catholic hospital, where he died of his wounds on June 6.

A Commander Without an Army

Kirby-Smith's situation steadily deteriorated as the men of his army deserted, frequently as individuals, sometimes as whole companies or even regiments. Reluctantly realizing that he would soon have no army to surrender, he turned from Pope to Canby, who was back in New Orleans after Taylor's May 4 surrender. On May 18, Kirby-Smith announced that he was moving from Shreveport to Houston, where his headquarters would be less exposed when the Federals attacked. He left two days later. During the week it took him to make the trip, discipline in the army collapsed. Probably as many as half of the troops simply went home. One officer wrote that his division would "lay down their arms at the first appearance of the enemy." Cavalry units dissolved themselves and one infantry company mutinied.

General Simon B. Buckner, Kirby-Smith's chief of staff, and General Sterling Price left Shreveport under a flag of truce and reached New Orleans on May 25. Taylor was waiting there for his family to join him when the two generals arrived. They told him that military affairs were in disarray, that many units of the army had disbanded, and that brigand mobs were roaming the country, stealing and destroying property. They invited him to join them in a meeting with Canby and his chief of staff, General Peter J. Osterhaus, on May 26. At this meeting the Confederates received the same terms as Lee, Johnston and Taylor. Key provisions of the nine sections of the surrender agreement read:

I. All acts of war and resistance against the United States on the part of troops under General Smith shall cease from this date.

II. The officers and men to be paroled until duly exchanged or otherwise released from the obligation of their parole by the authority of the Government of the United States. . . .

III. Artillery, small-arms, ammunition, and other property of the Confederate States Government, including gun-boats and transports, to be turned over to the officers appointed to receive the same. . . .

IV. The officers and men paroled under this agreement to be allowed to return to their homes, with the assurance that they will not be disturbed by the authorities of the United States so long as they continue to observe the conditions of their parole and the laws in force where they reside, except that persons resident in the Northern States, and not excepted in the amnesty proclamation of the President, may return to their homes on taking the oath of allegiance to the United States.

V. The surrender of property will not include the side arms or private horses or baggage of officers.

VI. All horses which are in good faith the private property of enlisted men will not be taken from them. The men will be permitted to take such with them to their homes, to be used for private purposes only.

VII. The time, mode, and place of paroling and surrender of property will be fixed by the respective commanders. . . .

VIII. The terms and conditions of this convention to extend to all officers and men of the Army and Navy of the Confederate States, or any of them being in or belonging to the Trans-Mississippi Department.

IX. Transportation and subsistence to be furnished at public cost to the officers and men (after being paroled) to the nearest practicable point to their homes.

The agreement was signed by the two staff officers, but Buckner made it clear that it needed to be officially accepted by Kirby-Smith. By this document about 18,000 men were surrendered in western Louisiana, Texas, Arkansas, Missouri and Indian Territory.

Canby, determined to accomplish the transition to peace as smoothly as possible, issued lengthy general orders on the same day informing his command of the surrender terms and describing the conditions to be observed in carrying them out.

> If the U. S. troops designated for the garrison of interior points should not have reached their destinations before the work of paroling is completed, suitable guards will be detailed for the protection of the public property. These guards, when relieved, will surrender their arms and be paroled. . . . When detachments are made for the purpose of protecting the inhabitants against jayhawkers and other lawless characters, and on all marches through the country, the conduct of officers and men must be such as to inspire the people with confidence and respect, and no depredations, however slight, or interference with the citizens in their lawful pursuits will be permitted. . . . Private property will not be interfered with unless required for "public use," and where this is necessary it will be taken in an orderly and regular manner. . . . Under the authority of the Executive order of April 29, 1865, all "well-disposed persons" who accept in good faith the President's invitation "to return to peaceful pursuits" are assured that they may resume their usual avocations, not only without molestation, but if necessary, under the protection of the U. S. troops, conforming to the regulations of the U. S. Treasury Department, and to the additional condition of not fabricating or dealing in articles contraband of war.

On May 30, Kirby-Smith published his last message to the army. He advised the men to return to their families and obey the laws. Now that his army was gone he wrote:

> Soldiers! I am left a commander without an army — a General without troops. You have made your choice. It was

unwise and unpatriotic, but it was final. You have voluntarily destroyed your organizations, and thrown away all means of resistance. The department is now open to occupation by your Government. The citizen and soldier alike, weary of war, are ready to accept the authority and yield obedience to the law of the United States. A conciliatory policy, dictated by wisdom and administered with patient moderation, will insure peace and secure quiet.

General John B. Hood was picked up on the same day by a Union patrol as he was about to cross the Mississippi to join Kirby-Smith. He had been covered by the Taylor surrender, but was nevertheless intent on getting to Texas and helping to continue the rebellion. He was paroled the next day.

On June 2, Kirby-Smith boarded the Union vessel *Fort Jackson* off Galveston and signed the document the two chiefs of staff had agreed to. He endorsed it: "Approved, understanding that by the provisions of this convention C. S. officers observing their paroles are permitted to make them homes either in or out of the United States." Kirby-Smith had $5,000 in gold that was to be delivered to Davis in Cuba, from where the president was expected to come to Texas. But surrender came before the gold left, and Davis never even got as far as Florida, let alone Cuba or Texas. Kirby-Smith used $1,700 to pay amounts due to five generals. He turned the remaining $3,300 over to Canby. The port of Galveston, which was under Union blockade, was surrendered on June 5.

THE FLIGHT TO MEXICO

To understand the relationship between the Confederacy and Mexico requires a brief historical review. In Europe, the Old Regime had been shaken by the French Revolution of 1789 and by the liberal uprisings of 1848. The aristocracy, determined to retain its power, believed it could reduce the rising threat of republicanism by restoring monarchy to the former European colonies in the New World. This was precisely what the Monroe Doctrine was intended to prevent. The potential break-up of the United States by the possible secession of the slave states provided an opportunity. After Lincoln's nomination in 1860, suggestions were secretly made by Southerners to European diplomats that, if the European powers were to recognize a yet-to-be-created Southern Nation, the scion of some royal family might become its king.

In Mexico, which won its independence from Spain in 1821, civil war had raged since 1855 between the conservative aristocrats and the liberal republicans. The forces of the latter were victorious and established their capital at Vera Cruz on May 4, 1858. With Benito Juarez as president, the republicans confiscated the large estates owned by the aristocrats and the Catholic Church. On April 6, 1859, the Buchanan administration recognized the republican government.

Although their interests were somewhat different, France, Austria and Britain saw an opportunity in Southern secession to again assert their influence in the Americas and to diminish the power of the United States. In particular, the French Emperor, Napoleon III, desired to establish in Mexico a Catholic dominion under French hegemony, to provide markets and raw materials. When, in the summer of 1861, Mexico suspended repayment of loans from France, Spain and Britain, those countries decided to intervene, under the guise of enforcing repayment. They landed troops at Vera Cruz on December 17, 1861. The Juarez government escaped, but continued to resist.

After the French designs became clear to the British and Spanish, those countries withdrew their contingents in April 1862. Adroitly, Napoleon nominated Archduke Ferdinand Maximilian, a Hapsburg, to be ruler of his Mexican Empire. Brother of the Austrian Emperor Franz Joseph, Maximilian was also the son-in-law of King Leopold of Belgium, who was the uncle of Queen Victoria of Britain. King Leopold, in a letter to Maximilian urging him to accept, plainly stated the political purpose: "to raise a barrier against the United States and provide a support for the monarchical-aristocratic principle in the Southern states." The grand strategy of the Europeans consisted of five sequential steps: (1) occupation of Mexico; (2) financial and military support for the Confederacy; (3) recognition of the Confederacy; (4) introduction of monarchy in the Confederacy; and (5) elimination of all republican governments.

French forces occupied Mexico City in June of 1862. Ten months later, with the support of Mexican conservatives, they proclaimed Maximilian Emperor and installed him and the Empress Carlota in the "Imperial Palace" of the former Spanish Viceroys. The French army of 30,000 men, aided by 6,000 Austrian soldiers, defeated Juarez, who continued to fight a guerilla war from along the Rio Grande. The Confederates were delighted to have a friendly government along their southern border. The European powers had hoped from the beginning to recognize the Confederacy, but refrained from doing so out of fear of war with the United States. The French presence in Mexico encouraged the hopes of the secessionists for recognition. They even dreamed of intervention by the French army, since the Emperor had designs on reclaiming New Mexico and California from the United States in the event of Confederate success. Supplies came across the Rio Grande throughout the war. The U. S. government, outraged by the French intrusion, was in no position to do anything other than protest through diplomatic channels and refuse to recognize the imperial government.

The situation had changed radically by the spring of 1865. On May 17 Grant ordered Sheridan to take command of the Military District of the Southwest, comprising all territory west of the Mississippi River and south of the Arkansas River. His mission was to break up or destroy Kirby-Smith's army. Sheridan, who saw no possibility of distinction in this assignment, protested. But Grant quietly informed him that it was to be a dual mission. As soon as Kirby-Smith surrendered, Sheridan was to be ready to move against the French. The United States, with a strong, seasoned army on the Texas-Mexican border, would be in a position to compel them to leave and thus to restore independence to Mexico, although Secretary of State Seward preferred doing so by diplomacy rather than force.

When Sheridan assumed control at New Orleans on May 29, he learned that Kirby-Smith's army had been surrendered the day before. He was annoyed that many of the Texas troops had refused to surrender. Instead, they disbanded to their homes, taking their arms and ammunition with them. Sheridan would now use his army of about 52,000 men to occupy Texas. The infantry force of 40,000 men consisted of 4th and 25th Corps, supported by 13th Corps. There were also two columns of cavalry: 5,000 men under General Wesley Merritt at Shreveport and 4,500 under General George A. Custer at Alexandria. They carried pontoon trains to cross streams on the line of march, and "to be able to cross the Rio Grande should the government decide to send troops in that direction." Moving all these units into position was difficult: the wharves at all the ports except Galveston had been destroyed, the railroads were in poor condition, and there was a shortage of potable water for the men and of coal for the locomotives and ships.

Along the Rio Grande, troops of 25th Corps were deployed up the river as far as Laredo. Because ships often could not cross the bar at the mouth of the river, Sheridan had a railroad built from Brazos Santiago to White's Ranch, a distance of eleven miles, to provide a secure means of supply. (It was later sold, he proudly reported, for $40,000 more than the cost of construction). Sheridan said, "the appearance of our troops and the knowledge that friends were on the border went like electricity to the homes and hearts of the Mexican people." Over the next year the Juarez forces gradually recaptured the northern towns and confined the European army to the Valley of Mexico. Sheridan's view was that "believing that the contest in our own country was for the vindication of republicanism, I did not think that that vindication would be complete until Maximilian was compelled to leave."

Grant also said that they should "look upon the French occupation of Mexico as part and parcel of the late rebellion in the United States, and a necessary part of it to suppress before entire peace can be restored." In a letter on June 19, he expressed to President Johnson his views about the situation:

> I regard the act of attempting to establish a monarchial government on this continent in Mexico by foreign bayonets as an act of hostility against the Government of the United States. . . . Matamoros and the whole Rio Grande under [Maximilian's] control has been an open port to those in

rebellion against the Government. . . . French soldiers have fired on our men from the south side of the river in aid of the rebellion. Officers acting under the authority of the would-be empire have received arms, munitions, and other public property from the rebels after the same has become the property of the United States.

Sheridan wrote to Grant from New Orleans on June 28, saying:

> The Kirby Smith and General Canby surrender was for the most part a swindle on the part of Kirby Smith and Company, as all Texas troops had disbanded or had been discharged and gone home. Kirby Smith, Magruder, Shelby, Slaughter, Walker, and others of military rank have gone to Mexico. Everything on wheels – artillery, horses, mules, &c. – have been run over into Mexico. . . . Representatives of the imperial government along the Rio Grande have encouraged this wholesale plunder of property belonging to the United States. . . . The French officers are very saucy and insulting to our people at Brownsville.

On July 5, he ordered General Gordon Granger, in command of the District of Texas, to

> Get your troops on the Rio Grande in readiness for active service. Caution them, however, against provoking hostilities, and demand the surrender of all public property run cross the Rio Grande since the first surrender.

The next day he wrote to the chief of staff.

> Affairs on the Rio Grande frontier are getting beautifully mixed up. . . . General Steele says the French officers and soldiers are very bitter against our people, and writes me that a grandson of Marshal Ney with 2,000 French cavalry is reported approaching Matamoras and . . . says he is going to invade Texas.

Tense as the situation on the border became, it did not result in a clash of arms with the French. Several Confederate generals, as well as other officers and enlisted men who had declined to sign paroles as part of the Trans-Mississippi surrender, went to Mexico, many hoping to join the French army and Maximilian (another lost cause). To the bitter end they believed that France would come to their rescue by going to war with the United States, thus giving them the opportunity to continue the fight for Southern independence. Others considered becoming mercenaries for Juarez. Near Corsicana, Texas, General Joseph O. Shelby told his division that the war was over and they could go home, but he was heading across the Rio Grande. He was followed by about 200 of his men. As they marched to San Antonio they picked up additional recruits, including two generals, Magruder and Price, the governors of Texas and Louisiana, other civilians, and eventually Kirby-Smith. By the time the party crossed the river on July 4 at Eagle Pass it comprised perhaps 500 people.

After arriving in Monterrey, most of the civilians left for Cuba and Brazil. Shelby and the rest of the soldiers continued to Mexico City, where they were not accepted into the army of Mexico because Maximilian realized that enlisting *gringos* was not a wise idea for someone as unpopular as he was. He offered the Confederate refugees land where they could establish colonies. The largest, seventy miles west of Vera Cruz, was called Carlota, after the Empress. Under the direction of Price, about 250 Southerners laid out a town and planted corn, tobacco and coffee. Because they lacked capital, suffered dysentery and tropical diseases, and found it hard to adapt to the Spanish life-style, this venture lasted little more than a year. After it was raided by a band of a thousand guerillas on June 1, 1866, many more colonists fled to foreign countries.

Discouraged, and perhaps homesick, those that did not flee soon came back to the United States. In November of 1866, Kirby-Smith was permitted by Grant to return on parole. He became president of a telegraph company, then chancellor of the University of Nashville. During the turbulent spring of 1867, Shelby, the leader of the exodus, left Vera Cruz on a U. S. gunboat. He resumed farming in Missouri, became involved in coalmines and railroads, and was appointed U. S. marshal in Kansas City. Before the United States took military action, the French appreciated the realities of the situation and Napoleon withdrew his troops in

March of 1867. Maximilian, not in the least beloved by the Mexican people, was executed by firing squad on June 19.

WAR WITH THE CONFEDERATE INDIANS

As the Civil War came to its conclusion, the civilized tribes of Indian Territory (present Oklahoma) reluctantly ceased to fight. Nominally independent, not really part of either the United States or the Confederate States, Indian Territory was a sort of quasi-state, which Congress established in 1834 for the thousands of Indians forced to surrender their homelands in the east. It was the home of the Five Nations, as they styled themselves: Cherokees, Choctaws, Creeks, Osages and Seminoles. They had constitutional governments, lived in houses, practiced agriculture, owned Negro slaves, and mostly supported Southern independence (as did the Chickasaws, who were not part of the Five Nations). They formed alliances with the secessionists and sent more than 3,000 Indians to serve in the Confederate army. At first two regiments were formed, then a brigade, and eventually a division. Late in the war it was commanded by General Stand Watie, who was three-quarters Cherokee (his mother was a Moravian, half white and half Indian). Born near Rome, Georgia in 1806, he was named Ta-ker-taw-ker, meaning "immovable" or "to stand firm," and was known as Stand. He moved from Georgia to Indian Territory, and eventually became principal chief of the Southern Cherokees.

By the winter of 1865, Federal forces were able to move nearly unopposed in Indian Territory, and many Cherokees had become refugees, without adequate food, clothing and shelter. When General Watie's soldiers, who had managed to obtain some supplies by raiding into Kansas, did the same thing in Texas, he had to intervene to prevent open conflict between Texans and Indians. Although Watie was able to obtain limited quantities of bread and other food at Boggy Depot, his men were on half rations by April.

The Federal government had offered the Plains Indians guns and ammunition in an unsuccessful attempt to convince them to support the Union cause. The Confederate Indians and the Plains tribes met in council at Camp Napoleon, on the Washita River. As far as the Plains Indians were concerned, their conflict with the whites had nothing to do with the Civil War. But the native peoples of the western prairies and forests realized that they could no longer afford to dissipate their strength in hostilities against one another: they needed to unite in order to deal effectively with the U. S. Government. Optimistically, and perhaps desperately, they entered into an agreement on May 26, which provided:

> Peace and friendship shall forever exist between the tribes and bands parties to this compact. . . . The tomahawk shall be forever buried. The scalping knife shall be forever broken. The warpath heretofore leading from one tribe or band to another shall grow up and become as the wilderness. . . . The parties to this compact . . . shall compose an Indian confederacy or band of brothers, having as its object the peace, the happiness, and the protection of all alike, and the preservation of our race. In no case shall the warpath be opened to settle any difficulty or dispute that may hereafter arise . . . All the difficulties shall be settled without the shedding of any blood. "An Indian shall not spill an Indian's blood."

After the surrenders of Lee, Johnston, Taylor and Kirby-Smith, sensible Southerners, Indians and whites alike, realized that the war had drawn to its inescapable close. While Colonel William A. Phillips assembled a force at Fort Gibson to prevent further raids by Watie, General James C. Veatch sought to secure the surrenders of the Indians. A Confederate general in the Indian Territory told Veatch "it is impracticable for [me] to surrender the members of the Indian nations . . . it would endanger [my] life to attempt it." As Veatch understood the situation:

> The Cherokees, Choctaws, Muscogees, Seminoles, Chickasaws, Reserve Caddos, Osages, and Comanches, or the parts of their tribes or nations that joined the rebel cause in the present war, did so as independent powers and allies of the rebels, and they claim their right to make terms of peace with the United States regardless of any terms of surrender agreed upon and accepted by the rebel authorities.

He was in favor of feeding the destitute Indians, of which there were estimated to be 15,500,

> who have lost what little they owned by the war, and have raised no crops the present season, and are left without any means of subsistence. . . . The citizens of Texas, near the Red River, are now sending them supplies as charitable donations, but prompted, no doubt, more by a sense of fear of marauding bands than from any real charitable feeling. . . . As a simple question of economy it is vastly cheaper to feed these people than to send troops there to keep them in order, or punish them for disturbing the country by stealing and marauding against their neighbors.

Veatch sent Lieutenant Colonel Asa C. Mathews of the 99th Illinois Infantry to Indian Territory, on a mission to obtain surrenders. On June 19, at the Choctaw capital, Doaksville, he met with Governor and Principal Chief Peter P. Pitchlynn, who agreed to surrender the Choctaw Nation. The treaty stipulated:

> All acts of hostilities on the part of both armies having ceased (by virtue of a convention entered into on the 26th day of May, 1865, between Maj. Gen. E. R. S. Canby . . . and General E. Kirby Smith . . .) the Indians of the Choctaw Nation here represented, lately allied with the Confederate States in acts of hostility against the Government of the United States, do agree at once to return to their respective homes, and there remain at peace . . . So long as the Indians aforesaid observe the provisions of this agreement they shall be protected by the U. S. authorities in their persons and property, not only from the encroachments on the part of the whites but also from the Indians who have been engaged in the service of the United States.

This agreement was to remain in force until the meeting of a grand council between the Indians and the U. S. government on September 1 at Armstrong Academy in the Choctaw Nation. Pitchlyn issued a circular announcement to the tribes, which said:

> It is the earnest desire of this people to have an honorable and lasting peace and to resume their former friendly

relations with the U. S. authorities. . . . There will be a grand council of all of the Indians of the prairies . . . to treat on the subject of a permanent and lasting peace. . . . There shall be an immediate cessation of hostilities. . . . Our late allies in war, the Confederate armies, have long since ceased to resist the national authorities; they have all either been captured or surrendered to the forces of the United States. It therefore becomes us as a brave people to forget and lay aside our prejudices. . . . Let reason obtain now that the sway of passion has passed.

Watie, with about a third of the army Indians, had hoped to conduct guerilla warfare, but finally understood the futility of resistance. Early on June 23, with a small column of Cherokee cavalry, he approached Fort Towson, twelve miles west of Doaksville. There, at the home of Robert M. Jones, a leading Choctaw citizen, Watie and Mathews met and negotiated terms. Two days later they signed a treaty, similar to that with Pitchlyn, which also recognized that there were likely to be bad feelings between Indians who had taken opposite sides in the war. The terms were extended to the Creeks, Osages and Seminoles, and Watie pledged to try to convince other Indians to lay down their arms. Watie was the last of the Confederate generals to surrender.

The Chickasaws, still not grasping that only simple surrender was acceptable, wanted to send delegates to Washington to negotiate a peace treaty. Governor Winchester Colbert, however, finally accepted the inevitable. On July 14, he surrendered to Mathews the Chickasaw Nation, along with the members of the Caddo, Comanche, and other bands known as Reserve Indians residing in that nation. The terms were identical to those with the Choctaws, except that the Chickasaws were to:

> Offer no indignity whatever, or commit any acts of hostilities against the whites or Indians of the various tribes who have been friendly to or engaged in the service of the United States during the war.

They were the last of the Confederate Indians to capitulate, fourteen weeks after Lee surrendered at Appomattox Court House.

War with the Plains Indians

Beyond the Mississippi and Missouri Rivers the U. S. Army had been engaged, throughout the Civil War, as it had been in previous years, in protecting white Americans as they pushed westward into territory inhabited by Indians. The missions of the army included guarding wagon trains, stagecoaches, settlements and telegraph lines, as well as building roads and bridges. The army was also to enforce treaty provisions and to give limited aid to Indians in need. When most of the regulars were engaged further east, several serious flare-ups, one of them in Minnesota in 1862, were handled by militias.

The pace of incursion increased in 1865, inevitably resulting in more conflict between the newcomers and the indigenous peoples. To make matters even worse, because of the severe scarcity of food during the winter of 1864, many Indians had starved. Driven by serious suffering, they attacked wagon trains and took what provisions they could find, though generally leaving the travelers alone. A series of small incidents gradually escalated until the governor of the Colorado Territory, John Evans, who was determined to eliminate the Indians entirely, organized a force expressly for that purpose, the Third Colorado Cavalry Regiment. Under the command of Colonel John M. Chivington, the recently recruited troops located a village of about 550 people of the Southern Cheyenne and Arapaho tribes at a place called Sand Springs. In a surprise attack at dawn on November 29, 1864 Chivington ordered his men to take no prisoners, to kill and scalp everyone. The soldiers killed about fifty men and more than a hundred women and children.

The result of this atrocity was open warfare that was neither guerilla nor conventional in nature. It was war between two peoples of vastly different cultures, standards and intentions. In retaliation for the Sand Springs massacre, a thousand Indians attacked Julesburg, Colorado on January 6, 1865, killing a dozen residents. Governor Evans beseeched Washington for regulars to assist in his campaign, and by May many regiments were deployed west of the 100th meridian. Considerable effort was required by both regulars and militia to guard emigrants as they journeyed across the plains and to attack Indians in their homelands. In addition, the army had to protect the surveyors and work crews of the Union Pacific Railroad, which began building westward from Omaha in the spring of 1865.

From St. Louis, General Dodge coordinated the disposition of cavalry and infantry along the wagon roads followed by pioneers on their way to the Oregon country, the Dakota territory, California, New Mexico and Nevada. Much of the action of these units consisted of the routine patrols and small-scale battles that we are familiar with through the movies, but the fighting steadily became more intense. After Indian attacks on the Overland Stage Road in Kansas and Colorado, troops were sent along the Platte, Sweetwater and Niobrara Rivers. Then, in June, a major drive into the northern plains and the Rocky Mountains was organized. Known as the Powder River Expedition, it was a movement similar in scope to Confederate and Union cavalry raids of the Civil War.

In the course of these campaigns, army troops were guilty of many instances of terrible treatment of the Indians, including murder. In other cases they tried hard to police the relations between the emigrants and the Indians, and to protect the Indians from attacks by whites. To some extent they dealt with the everyday needs of the Indians, whose ability to feed themselves was impaired by the encroachment of roads and settlements, often providing them with food, clothing and blankets. Many of the matters they dealt with were pathetic. Colonel Phillips wrote to his commanding officer from Fort Gibson on April 4:

> I employed all the spare forces of my command putting in crops or assisting the [Indian] refugees to put in crops. . . . There is great suffering among the refugees. I wish that a supply of garden seeds and sweet and Irish potatoes, for seed, could be obtained and sent at once.

Crops, however, were not the solution for the 9,000 or more gravely undernourished Indians at Fort Gibson. Attempts to relieve them with supplies of food were impeded by the terrible condition of the roads and because low water made it impossible for steamers to get up the river.

In New Mexico, a man named Miguel des Marais reported an instance of the sort of mundane problems the army had to deal with. He wrote to "Lieutenant Edgar, or any other picket officer at the Alamo Gordo:"

> My herders have just arrived here from my ranch, which is called La Turpentino. . . . They say there are twenty Navajo Indians there and have been there some eight or ten days, and are daily killing my sheep and cattle. . . . Will you, sir, be so kind as to send and take these Indians back to their reservation at once.

Despite efforts by humane officers to alleviate Indian suffering, and to control depredations by both Indians and whites, for the most part the Indians were either killed (more by disease and starvation than by gunfire) or driven onto reservations during the twenty years following the Civil War. They were inevitably defeated by the overwhelming forces of the United States as a nation, not a mere compact of states, in vigorous pursuit of its "Manifest Destiny" westward.

Chapter 10

The End: On the Water
April to December 1865

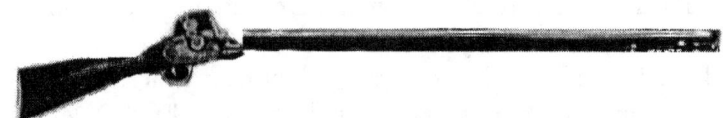

The Battle of Palmito Ranch

Two weeks before Kirby-Smith's army was surrendered, the last of the 2,265 engagements of the four-year war occurred on May 12 and 13 on the Mexican border in Texas. At the mouth of the Rio Grande, the Union navy maintained a small blockading force to hinder the export of cotton and the import of munitions and supplies. The army had about 950 men stationed on Brazos Santiago Island, commanded by Colonel Theodore H. Barrett. A Confederate force was stationed at Brownsville, thirty miles inland, under Colonel John S. Ford, whose superior officer was General James E. Slaughter. For some time the two sides had observed a de facto truce, neither seeing any purpose in combat, since Lee, Johnston and Taylor had surrendered.

On the afternoon of May 11, Barrett ordered 200 men of the 62nd U. S. Colored Infantry, under Lieutenant Colonel David Branson, to cross to the mainland and conduct a raid toward Brownsville. The objective, Barrett said later, was to obtain forage and horses. Other officers, however, thought it was to obtain fresh beef, and lumber to build barracks. Yet another officer believed, perhaps ungenerously, that Barrett hoped to achieve some measure of fame as the war ended. Whatever the real purpose may have been, the steamboat that was to take the men across from the northern end of the island broke down. They then marched two miles to the southern end and crossed through the shallows there. Each man was carrying a hundred rounds of ammunition and rations for three days. Despite a storm, which slowed their movement, the regiment was on the mainland by 9:30 P.M. They were joined by fifty unmounted men of the Second (U. S.) Texas Cavalry. About 2:00 A.M. they reached White's Ranch, where they found no Confederates. While two companies stood watch, the rest of the men slept until 5:30. When Mexicans on the south shore saw the union troops, they sent word to the Confederates.

The main feature of the terrain here was the river itself, which was on their left as they advanced westward. The ground was flat and sandy, with patches of grass, much chaparral and numerous bayous and lagoons. Company F, under Captain Fred E. Miller, led the advance toward Palmito Ranch, encountering a few scouts on the way. At Palmito they took three prisoners, two horses and four cattle. In mid-afternoon, a larger force of cavalry appeared, and Branson observed what he took to be threatening movements by Mexican soldiers across the border. Since he was in an exposed position and unsupported, he decided to retire, skirmishing continually on the way, to White's Ranch. From there he sent a report to Barrett at Brazos Santiago.

Barrett promptly dispatched 200 men from the 34th Indiana Infantry, under Lieutenant Colonel Robert G. Morrison, as reinforcements. The regiment arrived at White's Ranch around sunrise on May 13, bringing instructions for the Union brigade, now 450 strong, to again advance to Palmito Ranch. Meanwhile, the situation had been reported to Ford in Brownsville. Ford, angered by the Union's violation of the informal truce, gave orders organizing an attack force and went to see Slaughter. The general advised him to withdraw, citing the large number of desertions and the risk of a raid from across the river by Mexican bandits. The two officers argued about what to do, Ford shouting at Slaughter that he could retreat and go to hell if he wished. The men were his, Ford said, and he was going to use them to fight. The two officers then agreed to move against the Union expedition. Ford left Brownsville with about 300 cavalrymen and six twelve-pounder field guns.

Barrett arrived at White's Ranch and personally took command. He sent all disabled men and the prisoners to Brazos Santiago. While the 34th Indiana ate breakfast, he ordered the 62nd Colored and the Second (U.S.) Texas to advance to Palmito Ranch. They reached their destination at 8:00 A.M. After stopping for two hours to eat and rest, the men continued their advance toward Brownsville. With the Second Texas in the lead, it and the 62nd were opposed by about sixty Confederates under Captain W. N. Robinson. Meanwhile, Barrett ordered the 34th to move up to join the main body. When the troops arrived at noon, he sent part of them two miles along the bluff of the river. Lieutenant Charles A. Jones, in command of the detachment, suggested setting an ambush. The idea was to hide men in the thickets along the river, then send a decoy party into the open to lure the Confederates to attack. A line of infantrymen from the 62nd, who did not know of the plan, unexpectedly appeared. Jones asked them to move back, which they did. Then one of his own men fired prematurely and gave away the ambush.

Barrett now had a line consisting of the 34th on the left, the 62nd on the right, and the Second between them. The low rise of Palmito Hill was to the rear of the 34th. In mid-afternoon, the Confederate force, consisting of about 360 men under Ford, formed an L-shaped line of battle. Their main line was perpendicular to the river, with an extension on the left in order to outflank the Union right. Ford placed two guns in each segment of the line, with the other two in reserve. Although the movement was plainly observed from Palmito Hill, many of the Union troops were cooking dinner when the attack began. Barrett, who was surprised by Ford's aggressiveness, ordered the 34th to put out two companies as skirmishers, facing west, with the Second on their right. The 62nd deployed parallel to the river, facing north to meet the attack on the right flank. Confederate cannon fire, to which the Union forces were unable to reply, and the precariousness of their position, led Barrett to order his troops to withdraw.

Unfortunately, there was a bend in the river in back of the Union line. Their left flank was therefore exposed as they were forced to move across the front of the Confederate line before turning east. The withdrawal became disorderly when men of the 34th and the 62nd became intermixed for a time. In the confusion, the skirmishers of the 34th and most of the men of the Second were inadvertently left behind, and were taken prisoner. The 34th lost both its state and national colors. The national flag was hidden in the chaparral and found the next day by the Confederates. A soldier wrapped the state flag around himself and swam across to Mexico, from where it was eventually recovered.

With order restored, the 34th and the supply wagons marched first, followed by the 62nd and Captain Miller's Company F acting as the rear guard. Ford followed the Federals for seven miles, despite the poor condition of his cavalry and artillery horses, and Slaughter arrived with additional troops. The Confederates finally stopped their pursuit when the Union troops formed a defensive position at Cobb's Ranch, as the 34th crossed through the shallows to Brazos Santiago. What Barrett called "the last actual conflict between hostile forces in the great rebellion" had ended. "The last volley of the war, it is believed, was fired by the Sixty-Second U. S. Colored Infantry about sunset." At 4 A.M. on May 14, the weary 62nd waded across to the island. One Union soldier was killed in action, and one died of wounds. In addition, nine men were wounded. The 101 men taken prisoner were soon paroled. The Confederates suffered five men wounded. The fight was of no tactical or strategic significance. Why Barrett conducted this Union raid remains a subject of speculation.

The Plight of the Prisoners

OF the three million men who served in the armies and navies, 620,000 were killed in action or died of wounds, disease or other causes. Terrible privations were suffered by civilians, mostly in the Southern states. Less attention, however, has historically been given to the 408,608 men who were prisoners of war (193,743 Federals and 214,865 Confederates). The number of prisoners was larger than the number of men killed in battle. Neither side made an acceptable effort to provide the requisite sustenance and shelter for prisoners. The South's performance measured by deaths is worse than the North's: 15 percent, compared to 12 percent in the

North, a total of nearly 55,000 deaths. Given the greater resources available in the North, however, it would be reasonable to think its performance the worse of the two. What is clear is that the care provided by both sides for their prisoners was grossly inadequate.

Andersonville is surely the best known of the 117 Confederate prisons. Officially named Camp Sumter, it was located a mile and a half from Anderson Station on the Georgia Southwestern Railroad, fifty miles southwest of Macon. Opened in February 1864 on a sixteen-and-a-half acre site, later expanded to twenty-four acres, it was intended to have enough barracks for 10,000 prisoners, but none was ever built. The men lived in make shift huts and tents, or simply slept in the open, exposed to summer sun and winter rain. No attempt was made to organize the men inside the double stockade, which was designed both to keep the prisoners in and to prevent their being rescued by a Union cavalry raid. Food was meager: corn meal, peas and sweet potatoes when there was anything. The men scrounged whatever they could to eat, including swallows. Visitors were allowed to climb the guard towers and look down on the lousy, filthy, starving prisoners. Only four cities in the Confederacy had larger populations than Andersonville's peak of 32,899. In October 1864, the Confederates began transferring men to other sites and by the end of the year only 1,500 men remained. During the fifteen months of its existence, 329 men escaped, while 12,919 died.

Elmira, New York was the site of one of 106 Union prisons. The eight-acre site had been built as an army reception center, called Post Barracks, early in the war. There were thirty barracks, 100 by 22 feet, each able to hold 100 soldiers in double bunks. It was estimated that they could accommodate about 4,000 prisoners in triple bunks, and that another 1,000 men could be housed in tents. However, after the prison camp was opened in July 1864, 9,441 men were at one time packed in, and there were 2,933 deaths in the nine months the camp was in use. The barracks were poorly built, of green lumber, without plaster walls or ceilings, so they were very cold, especially during the three-and-a-half months when there was snow and ice on the ground that winter. Food consisted of small quantities of bread, rice, potatoes and salt pork, often supplemented by rats, which were plentiful. The men were fed in the mess halls twice a day, in three shifts each time. Near the Chemung River was a pond into which tons of urine and fecal matter drained, creating a condition that was both unsanitary and atrocious. Prisoners suffered from numerous diseases, many of which hardly exist today. Most deaths were caused by dysentery and diarrhea, but pneumonia, tuberculosis, smallpox, typhoid fever, scurvy, erysipelas and cholera were not uncommon. Outside the walls local entrepreneurs built two towers from which sightseers could, for ten cents, watch the prisoners.

By the end of 1864, the prisons of both armies had become like concentration camps. As many as twenty men died each day. The men's clothes were nothing more than rags, and they were invested with and attacked by vermin of all kinds: lice, cockroaches, bedbugs, flies, mosquitos. The monotony of camp life, combined with the dreadful conditions, resulted in an increase in violence. There were regular food fights over mere scraps, over uncontrollable tempers, and over turfs between soldiers from different regiments and states. In some cases, Confederate deserters were imprisoned with Union soldiers, and that was another source of conflict.

In the early stages of the war, captured men were commonly exchanged soon after the battles in which they were taken, so that there were few prisoners. The situation inevitably changed as the conflict progressed, and both sides began confining captured men in organized stockades or prisons for long periods. This was costly both in terms of the subsistence that had to be provided and the number of men that had to be assigned as guards. There were only two alternatives to holding prisoners. One was, of course, exchange. To limit the growing numbers, a formal agreement, called a "cartel," was adopted on July 22, 1862. It set ratios of exchange, for example, sixty privates for one general, ten privates for a colonel, and so on. The procedures for exchange were not, however, adequately defined. The cartel collapsed on April 17, 1863 over a disagreement regarding what to do about Negro soldiers. The Confederates maintained that these men were escaped slaves who should be returned to their owners. The Federals insisted that they were, just like white men, U. S. soldiers. The other alternative was to release prisoners on parole, that is, on their "word." A soldier signed a promise not to again serve in the armed forces of his country until he was properly exchanged. There was, however, no way to assure that men so released would not return to duty.

While the issue regarding Negro troops was the immediate cause of the cancellation of the cartel, Grant believed that it was to the advantage of the North, with its greater manpower, not to exchange prisoners. In February 1864, he stated his position:

> It is hard on our men held in Southern prisons not to exchange them, but it is humanity to those left in the ranks to fight our battles. Every man we hold, when released on parole or otherwise, becomes an active soldier against us at once either directly or indirectly. If we commence a system of exchanges which liberates all prisoners taken, we will have to fight on until the whole South is exterminated. If we hold those caught they amount to no more than dead men.

By early 1864, there were strong reasons for resuming prisoner exchanges. In addition to the moral issue posed by the suffering of the captives, as a result of the horrible conditions in the prisons, wives and other relatives and friends on both sides pressured their representatives to arrange for the return of the men. Besides, it was increasingly difficult for the military authorities to deal with the costs and problems of holding the prisoners. There were also political problems arising from the location of the camps. The governor of South Carolina, M. L. Bonham, wrote to Davis on October 29, 1864 asking him to "stop the proposed construction of the prison camp within four miles of [Columbia], where so much valuable Confederate and State property in now located. It seems to me there should be no prison camp within twenty or thirty miles of a State capital." Davis told the officer in charge "It is desirable to avoid conflict on such questions with the State authorities."

On December 31, 1864, General John H. Winder, commander of Confederate prisons east of the Mississippi, suggested to General Cooper that "there is no place that can be considered as safe from the operations of the enemy" and that "the rules of war authorize the party holding prisoners of war to parole them whenever they think proper to do so, provided the prisoner will accept the parole." He wanted to parole at least those men whose terms of enlistment had expired.

Colonel Robert Ould, a District of Columbia lawyer who had been a U. S. district attorney in Washington before the war, was the Confederate Commissioner of Exchange. From his office in Richmond, Ould was in regular contact with Grant, seeking a solution to the prisoner problem. In October, they concluded an agreement by which both sides could provide, in the words of Davis to his Congress, "necessary comforts to its own citizens held captive by the other." Food, clothing, blankets, tents and medicines could be supplied. Grant permitted the Confederates to ship 1,000 tons of cotton from Mobile to New York, where it could be sold and the money used, by a paroled CSA general, to purchase supplies. That was a beginning. The next step involved the exchange of prisoners suffering from serious illness or injury.

On February 2, as Grant reacted favorably to a proposal by Ould to resume formal exchanges, the general-in-chief notified Stanton:

> I am endeavoring to make arrangements to exchange about 3,000 prisoners a week. This is as [fast] and probably faster than they can be delivered to us. . . . I would like disabled troops sent first, as but few of these will be got in the ranks again, and as we can count on but little re-enforcement from the prisoners we get.

The intent was to exchange man for man, with the understanding, as before, that higher ranks counted for more than lower ranks. When, in a particular exchange, one side had more men to release than the other, the men were paroled subject to later exchange. This meant that a running record had to be kept of which side "owed" additional prisoners to the other. Considering that this was a time when records were all made with pen and ink, and the many locations at which exchanges were occurring, it is remarkable that the system worked as well as it did. The Confederates also were selective about which prisoners they released, sending first those whose enlistments had expired.

The matter arose again on February 16, when Grant wrote to Hitchcock:

> I see it stated in the papers that when some prisoners in the West were paraded to be sent forward for exchange, those who preferred Northern prisons to a return to the rebel service were invited to step to the front. I think this is wrong. Those who do not wish to go back are the ones whom it is most desirable to exchange.

The matter came to the attention of General Henry W. Halleck, the chief of staff, who expressed a different view to Stanton:

> First. It is contrary to the usages of war to force a prisoner of war to return to the enemy's ranks. If he declines to return, he is, in regard to his own Government, a deserter, and desertion from an enemy is always to be encouraged. Second. The President's proclamation encourages rebel soldiers to leave their ranks and resume their allegiance to the United States. To compel rebel prisoners who are willing to abandon the rebel cause . . . to return to the rebel ranks would not only be a violation of the usages of war, but an abandonment of the policy of the President's proclamation. . . . Third. The enemy has no claim whatever upon us to return such of his men as voluntarily choose to remain with us. Fourth. No rebel prisoner has during this war been returned to the enemy against his will. . . . Fifth. Most of the prisoners who have expressed an unwillingness to be exchanged are from . . . States now in or about to return to the Union. . . . I think that on a full consideration of this matter General Grant would be disposed to change his recommendation. It is much cheaper to feed an enemy in prison than to fight him in the field.

On February 22, the Confederates released for exchange Union soldiers held at Salisbury, North Carolina. Leaving behind those who could not move because of illness, weakness or being crippled, 2,000 men started on the fifty-mile march to Greensboro. Only

1,800 made it. Another group followed, and the assembled survivors, 5,149 in all, were taken by train to Wilmington. They entered the Union lines on March 24. In early April, a large number were released from the eight prisons in the Richmond area when that city was captured.

There were sharp disputes about the status of some prisoners. From Nashville on April 4, General Thomas wrote a letter of protest to General Taylor in Alabama, stating he heard

> that Capt. Hanchett, Sixteenth Illinois Volunteers (Cavalry) . . . is being tried by court-martial at Cahaba, Ala., on the charge of being a spy. Capt. Hanchett is an officer of the U. S. Army; has never been within Confederate lines, except in the performance of his duties as an officer with troops. Should he be convicted and punished as a spy, I assure you I shall make most ample retaliation.

THE SULTANA DISASTER

With the Confederate command system in a state of collapse, Union prisoners, for whom in many cases no food at all was available, were being turned over with minimal formalities. Ould designated Vicksburg as a central point for collection of prisoners. The two sides declared a neutral zone along the Black Lick River and established an exchange depot, called Camp Fisk, at Four-Mile Bridge, four miles from town. The prison commander was a Confederate officer; the guards were two companies of Union soldiers. Prisoners began coming to the camp from Cahaba, Alabama on March 22: 1,100 arrived that day and 1,300 three days later. They had traveled for twelve days and nights, by train to Montgomery, by steamboat to Selma, and on foot from there, many dying on the way. Others continued to arrive until there were about 5,500 men present. All were faint from malnutrition (they had been without food for three days) and most suffered from dysentery or other ills. The local Confederate exchange agent, Colonel H. A. M. Henderson, was strictly enforcing his instructions to release one Union soldier for each Confederate turned over to him. This proved to be impossible in the circumstances. He sought new orders from Ould, but that officer could not be reached because he was with the Army of Northern Virginia when it surrendered. Finally, on April 18, Henderson received word to release the Union men on parole, without exchange.

The Union officers in charge of the prisoners, Captain George A. Williams, an assistant commissioner of exchange, and his assistant, Captain Frederic Speed, were under orders to move the men north by steamboat as quickly as possible. Williams was away from the post on detached duty. Lieutenant Colonel Reuben B. Hatch, the chief quartermaster, and Captain W. F. Kerns, master of transportation, were responsible for selecting boats to transport the troops up river. The transportation system, comprised of both railways and waterways, was clogged with men headed homeward. The prevailing practice, ordered by Grant, was to pay $5 for enlisted men and $10 for officers for passage on steamboats. The boat captains took as many men aboard as possible, to maximize their profits. There was an opportunity for corruption on the part of the officers who selected which steamboats to use. In this case, Kerns believed that Speed had been bribed to put as many men as possible on the *Sultana*, while Speed accused Kerns of trying to divert the men to the *Pauline Carroll*, another steamboat which was also then at Vicksburg. Neither of the charges, which may have been based only on personal animosity, was ever proved.

On April 21, the *Henry Ames* left Vicksburg with 1,300 men on board, and on April 23, the *Olive Branch* carried 700. That same evening the *Sultana*, registered to carry seventy-six passengers in cabins and 300 on deck, arrived from New Orleans. The vessel, launched in February 1863, was 260 feet long, forty-two feet in the beam, and drew three feet of water. It was powered by four high-pressure boilers, each eighteen feet long and nearly four feet in diameter. The engineer, Nathan Wintrenger, had found a crack in one of the boilers, which were of a new type, easily clogged by the muddy water of the lower Mississippi. A boiler maker came on board to repair it. The captain and owner, J. Cass Mason, wanted to get under way as soon as possible. During a thirty-three-hour delay a temporary fix was made, good enough, it was thought, to enable the boat to complete the trip. While the work was being done, Mason tried to collect as many army passengers as possible, to be transported to the Jefferson Barracks in St. Louis.

In the absence of Williams, Speed made the loading decisions. At first he said he would send no men on that boat, but changed his mind: he would send about 500, the number for which the paperwork had been prepared. Colonel Hatch, however, suggested that he send more, with the paperwork to follow later. There was no accurate record of how many men remained at Camp Fisk, though one count put the number at 2,146: 552 from Ohio, 522 from Tennessee, 460 from Indiana, 420 from Michigan, 180 from Kentucky, twelve from West Virginia.

On April 25, the transfer of men to the *Sultana* began. Late in the day Speed and Williams (who had returned) thought that about 1,400 men had arrived on two trains, but a third train, of which they were not aware, carried an additional 400. Kerns became concerned that too many men were being put aboard and informed Hatch. The colonel, however, chose not to interfere. When the boat finally left it carried, in addition to 1,866 ex-prisoners, seventy civilian cabin passengers and a crew of eighty-five. The cargo included sixty horses and mules, a hundred or more hogs, and about a hundred barrels of sugar. Stanchions had to be placed beneath the upper deck because it was sagging in many places from the weight of the men. The boat was perilously overloaded, and some of the men were afraid that it might capsize. Most, in high excitement at the thought that they were on their way home, were oblivious to the danger.

The *Sultana* arrived safely at Memphis in the early evening of April 26. After unloading some cargo and picking up a few additional passengers, the boat crossed to Hopefield, Arkansas for coal, then continued northward. At about 2:00 A.M. it was eight miles north of Memphis, steaming through some islands called Paddy's Hen and Chicks, when a boiler exploded. A few people were killed by the blast or blown overboard, but most were not injured. However, fire broke out, and no organized effort was made to put it out. Within twenty minutes the entire boat was in flames, and those on board faced the choice of burning alive or jumping into the river, which was already full of struggling animals and people. Other passenger vessels as well as Union gunboats in the vicinity came to the rescue, but their efforts were hampered by the darkness and the fact that the river, in spring flood, was flowing very fast.

General William Hoffman, commissary general of prisoners, reported to Secretary of War Stanton in a letter dated May 19 as follows:

> I am of the opinion that the shipment of so large a number of troops (1,866) on one boat was, under the circumstances, unnecessary, unjustifiable, and a great outrage on the troops. . . . There were two other steamers at the landing during the day, both of which would have taken a part of the men, and there was therefore no necessity for crowding them all on one boat. . . . Both Captain Speed and Captain Williams acted under the impression that there were only about 1,400 men to be forwarded, but neither of them made any inspection of the boat to see whether there was room for every man to lie down. . . . I am satisfied that there was scant sleeping room for all the men when every part of the boat, from the roof of the "texas" to the main deck, was fully occupied. . . . The men were exceedingly anxious to return to their homes and were willing to put up with many inconveniences, but they felt that they were treated with unkindness and harshness when they were crowded together in great discomfort.

Estimates of the number who died in the explosion on the *Sultana* range from 1,238 to 1,547 to as high as 1,800. It was possibly the greatest marine disaster of all times: 1,642 people went down with the *Titanic*.

The Scapegoat: Captain Wirz

At General Wilson's headquarters in Macon, a letter dated May 7 arrived from nearby Andersonville. It was from Captain Henry Wirz, the officer in charge of the prisoners at Camp Sumter in the final months that it was in use. He explained that he was a native of Switzerland, a physician, who had immigrated to Louisiana. When war broke out he joined the Confederate army and was severely wounded in the right arm at the battle of Seven Pines. Unfit for field duty, he was put in charge of a prison at Tuscaloosa. In failing health, he went to Europe on furlough. On his return he was assigned to command the interior of the prison at Andersonville. He wrote:

> The duties I had to perform were arduous and unpleasant, and I am satisfied that no man can or will justly blame me for things that happened here and which were beyond my power to control. I do not think I ought to be held responsible for the shortness of rations, for the overcrowded state of the prison, . . . for the inadequate supplies of clothing, want of shelters, &c. Still I now bear the odium, and men who were prisoners here seem disposed to wreak their vengeance upon me for what they have suffered, who was only the medium, or, I may better say, the tool in the hands of my superiors. . . . My life is in danger, and I most respectfully ask of you help and relief.

He asked for a safe-conduct or guard to protect him and his family until they could return to Europe. Instead, he was arrested and taken under guard to Washington for trial.

The trial began, in the basement of the Capitol, on August 23. The court had obviously decided that he was guilty before the presentation of the evidence, most of which was hearsay, contradictory and irrelevant, and much of it suborned. The conditions at Andersonville, terrible as they were, had been little worse than in dozens of other prison camps, North and South, and those conditions could be blamed partly on the Federal abrogation of the prisoner-exchange cartel in 1863. Moreover, Wirz himself had lacked the resources to alleviate the suffering of the prisoners. The Northern public, excited by exaggerated reports of conditions and happenings at the Georgia camp, was hungry for revenge. As in other times and places, a scapegoat was required, and Wirz was unluckily marked for that purpose. He was found guilty after a two-month trial and was hanged on November 10, 1865.

Wirz was not the only person arrested as a result of the alleged mistreatment of Union prisoners. On May 3, Halleck wrote to Stanton as follows:

> It is ascertained that at least a part of the money sent from the North for the use of our prisoners of war was diverted to other purposes, and the evidence seems to implicate Robert Ould and his assistant, Hatch. I have arrested both, and shall keep them in prison till a full investigation can be made.

Stanton replied, "Your action in respect of Ould and Hatch is cordially approved. I hope . . . if their guilt be established that they will receive exemplary punishment." No guilt was established, for there was none. The provost marshal of the Department of Virginia convened a board in Richmond to investigate Ould and three others. The members of this board issued their report on July 25.

> We find that all money was taken from Federal prisoners on their being committed to Libby Prison . . . and turned over to [the] assistant quarter-master, together with invoices of the same, giving the name of each person to whom said money belonged. . . . From the funds which they had deposited prisoners were generally allowed $100 per month in Confederate money. The rate which they were allowed was generally $7 in Confederate money for one U. S. Treasury note. . . . When prisoners were exchanged the balance due them was generally paid them in kind . . . although there were rare instances in which they were compelled to take Confederate money . . . A thorough investigation of the whole system of keeping the money accounts of Federal prisoners has been made, and we find that the books . . . were systematically and correctly kept . . . we fully exonerate the [parties] from all charges of fraud or dishonesty.

This result was both more just, and more fortunate than that in the case of Wirz. Ould's performance in the difficult role of coordinating the exchange of prisoners was exemplary. It is deplorable that no Union officer of like competence and dedication was assigned a similar role by Grant. He never centralized responsibility for dealing with the prisoner problem.

ALL THE PRISONERS GO HOME

Given the gradual and piece-meal way in which surrenders occurred, there was considerable confusion about the status of individuals. The two main factors in determining when and how prisoners would be released were (1) whether they had surrendered individually in battle or had been surrendered by their commanders under defined terms (as with the Army of Northern Virginia), and (2) whether their homes were in one of the eleven states that had passed ordinances of secession or were in one of the states that had remained in the Union. (West Virginia, Kentucky and Missouri were special cases). A policy gradually emerged. Those from seceded states were allowed to return to their homes on regular parole, while those whose homes were in Union states were required to take an additional oath.

Tens of thousands of long-term prisoners, as well as soldiers who had recently surrendered, were released on parole and, when possible, given transportation home. The local commanders, who had not received explicit statements of policy, subjected those paroled to restrictions beyond those intended by Lincoln and Grant. In the Department of the Gulf, for instance, these instructions were issued:

> Prisoners of war on parole granted by competent authority are allowed to return "to their homes not to be disturbed by the U. S. authorities so long as they observe their parole, and the laws in force where they may reside." But they are to be regarded as prisoners of war. They will not be allowed to bear arms, to wear in public the uniform of the Rebel army, the uniform of the United States, or any distinctive badge of military service. They are not entitled to participate in the management of public affairs or to enter upon business pursuits.

On May 8, the U. S. War Department issued General Orders No. 85:

> Ordered, that all prisoners of war, except officers above the rank of colonel, who before the capture of Richmond signified their desire to take the oath of allegiance to the United States

and their willingness to be exchanged, be forthwith released upon their taking the said oath, and transportation furnished them to their respective homes.

On May 16, General James Barnes, in command of the Point Lookout, Maryland prison, wrote to Hoffman to call attention to the patients in the hospital there, and by implication to the pointlessness of not releasing all the men:

> There are in this hospital 1,859 men . . . Some 1,600 of them could be sent home with proper means of conveyance, say, by steamer, to the most advisable ports [Wilmington, Savannah and Mobile]. The oath of allegiance could be administered to them all, for they all are ready to take it and would be glad to be sent home. Many are disabled by loss of limbs and otherwise by wounds and the expense of taking care of them here is considerable.

Hoffman forwarded the letter to Grant and Stanton with this endorsement: "The [cost of] transportation of the men to their homes would soon be balanced by [saving] the expense of keeping them in hospital." The general and the secretary approved.

Grant responded to a letter from forty-nine Confederate officers confined at Fort Delaware. They asked that they be released "on taking the oath of allegiance to the Government of the United States." Many had been in confinement since the battle of Gettysburg, and many were crippled for life. On May 18, Grant wrote to Stanton:

> I hope early means may be devised for clearing our prisons as far as possible. I would recommend that all who come within the amnesty proclamation be allowed the benefit of it. By going now they may still raise something for their subsistence for the coming year and prevent suffering next winter.

Even though the Confederate army west of the Mississippi had not yet surrendered, prisoners were being released by Union authorities as rapidly as transportation and other arrangements could be made. No regular reports have been found for the Confederate prisons, but the rate of release can be inferred from the following table, which presents the total number of prisoners, at the end of each month, in the principal Federal prisons:

January	February	March	April	May	June	July
65,322	52,189	41,659	64,301	48,195	2,425	165

The sharp increase in April was caused by the prisoners taken in Virginia, North Carolina and Alabama before the surrenders there. During May and June, virtually all of the Confederate prisoners, 62,000 of them, were released. The prisoners remaining after early July were civilians, five of whom were still held when the reports end on October 31.

In December of 1863 and March of 1864, President Lincoln had offered pardons to certain classes of people, but few had taken advantage of it. Now, with the war over, President Johnson pardoned most Confederates on May 29:

> I hereby grant to all persons who have, directly or indirectly, participated in the existing rebellion, except as hereinafter excepted, amnesty and pardon, with restoration of all rights of property, except as to slaves . . . but upon the condition, nevertheless, that every such person shall take and subscribe the following oath . . . I, ------ ------, do solemnly swear (or affirm), in the presence of Almighty God, that I will henceforth faithfully support, protect, and defend the Constitution of the United States, and the Union of the states thereunder; and that I will, in like manner, abide by and faithfully support all laws and proclamations which have been made during the existing rebellion with reference to the emancipation of slaves: so help me God.

Those exempted from the pardon included officers of the Confederate government; men who left seats in the U. S. Congress to aid the rebellion; governors of seceded states; general officers of the Confederate army and navy; officers who resigned their U. S. commissions to evade duty in resisting the rebellion; Confederate officers who were educated at West Point or Annapolis, and eight other classes of persons. However, all of these could also be pardoned if they made application to the president, who promised,

"Clemency will be liberally extended as may be consistent with the facts of the case and the peace and dignity of the United States." On the same day the president ordered "That in all cases of military tribunals of imprisonment during the war the sentence be remitted and that the prisoners be discharged." Not all officers were clear on the meaning of the president's proclamation for the prisoners under their charge. One asked General Hoffman "whether or not it is the intention of the Government to release immediately all prisoners now held who are willing to take the oath." The answer was yes, that was the intention.

As the exchange of prisoners continued, it gradually became apparent that the process was pointless: the war was over, and the only sensible thing to do was to send all of the prisoners home. On May 31, Hoffman wrote to Grant, proposing such a program:

> To facilitate the release of prisoners of war without its being too much hurried . . . I would respectfully suggest that the commanding officers of the military prisons be directed to release, on their taking the oath of allegiance, fifty or more per day, taking those below the rank of general in alphabetical order . . . None to be discharged under this arrangement against whom there are charges of any kind . . . There are seventeen military prisons at which are confined over 50,000 prisoners, and at the rate of fifty per day it will take near sixty days to vacate the prisons. . . . There are a number of citizens in confinement without charges, and some against whom there are charges who have not been tried. Inasmuch as all who have been tried and sentenced to confinement during the war have been pardoned, it would seem that the prisoners above referred to might be released, with perhaps a few exceptions of those awaiting trial.

CIVILIAN PRISONERS

As Hoffman's proposal to Grant made clear, there were, in addition to the soldiers and sailors, a number of citizens still held prisoner, some of them private persons, some public officials. Many were in custody without being charged, since the writ of habeas corpus had been suspended during the war, amid great controversy, in both the United States and the Confederate States. Hundreds of persons suspected of disloyally aiding the enemy were arrested. Some were tried by court-martial; others were detained awaiting trial on specific charges, including blockade running. Most of them were minor figures in the conflict, although a few were notorious. Grant began resolving this practice, along with the release of military prisoners, when he issued orders as early as February 16 for:

> The release and exchange of all citizen prisoners now held by military authority, except those under charges of being spies or under conviction for offenses under the laws of war on both sides.

President Johnson's May 29 *Order of Amnesty and Pardon*, completed the matter.

However, even as most civilians were sent home, others were being arrested - the best known, being Jefferson Davis. As we have seen, he was taken, along with Vice-president Stephens, Postmaster General Reagan, Clement C. Clay and others, on the steamer *Clyde* to Fort Monroe, where they arrived on May 19. Within days, all of those aboard except Davis and Clay were transferred elsewhere: Stephens and Reagan to Fort Warren in Boston, others to Fort Delaware, Mrs. Davis and her children to Savannah, and the servants to Norfolk. Clay was detained because his name was included in the indictment of the people arrested in connection with Lincoln's assassination.

No one in Washington knew what was to be done with Davis, but it was clear that he must not be allowed to escape or to be killed, and orders were issued by Stanton and Halleck in excruciating detail. On May 22, General Nelson A. Miles was assigned responsibility for Davis, and was told by Stanton:

> At 1 P.M. you will proceed to bring Messrs. Davis and Clay from the Clyde to the engineer wharf; thence through the battery to their prisons in the fort.

Assistant Secretary of War Charles A. Dana, who hurried with Halleck to Fort Monroe, reported to Stanton that Davis and Clay had been transferred to their cells:

> The arrangements were excellent and successful, and not a single curious spectator was anywhere in sight. Davis bore himself with a haughty attitude. . . . The arrangements for the security of the prisoners seem to me as complete as could be desired. Each one occupies the inner room of a casement. The window is heavily barred. . . . A lamp is constantly kept burning in each of the rooms. The furniture of each prisoner is a hospital bed with iron bedstead, a chair, a table, and a movable stool closet. A Bible is allowed to each.

He explained that sentries were placed inside and outside the cell doors, as well as outside the outer door, in a line across access to the casements, and on the parapet overhead. An officer was on duty to check the prisoners every fifteen minutes. Before returning to Washington the next day, Dana instructed Miles that he was "authorized and directed to place manacles and fetters upon the hands and feet of Jefferson Davis and Clement C. Clay whenever [you] may think it advisable in order to render their imprisonment more secure." On the same busy day, Halleck issued regulations consisted of seven sections that provided detailed rules for security, including the following:

> 5. No person will be permitted to communicate with the prisoners verbally or in writing. No sentinel will be permitted to speak to them or to answer any questions. . . . In case of sickness the surgeon's visits will be accompanied by the field officer in charge. 6. The meals of the prisoners will be furnished from the kitchen of the guards and passed in by the officer on guard, but no servant or waiter will be permitted to enter the prison rooms . . . nor will any visitors be permitted to enter the fort without a pass from the commanding officer or superior authority.

Miles soon decided to place leg irons on Davis, loose enough to allow him to walk but not to run, but he did not manacle him. Within a few days the fetters were removed. Davis complained that they were not allowed prayer books or tobacco, and Stanton ordered that they be supplied.

It was soon clear that neither man had anything to do with the assassination (on the charge of which they had been indicted). A trial for treason would have involved many other people, as well as complex legal questions. It might even, conceivably, have resulted in a decision by the Supreme Court that the Confederate states had been right! So they were released, Davis by order of the president on May 13, 1867. He spent the rest of his life writing and speaking, arguing for the validity of the constitutional right to secede.

Eight civilians, seven men and one woman, were arrested in connection with the assassination of Lincoln: David E. Herold, G. A. Atzerolt, Lewis Payne, Mary E. Surratt, Samuel Arnold, Samuel A. Mudd, Michael O'Laughlin and Edward Spangler. They were taken into custody within days after the murder. The charges against them were heard, beginning on May 9, by a military commission. The indictment went to great lengths to explain why the accused were being tried by a court-martial, rather than by a judge and jury in a Washington court:

> For maliciously, unlawfully, and traitorously, and in aid of the existing armed rebellion . . . combining, confederating, and conspiring, together with . . . John Wilkes Booth, Jefferson Davis [and others] . . . to kill and murder, within the Military District of Washington, and within the fortified and entrenched lines thereof, Abraham Lincoln . . . President of the United States of America and Commander-in-Chief of the Army and Navy thereof . . .

All were found guilty, though not of all charges. The first four named individuals were sentenced to death, and were hanged on July 7 by the military. The others were sentenced to be "confined at hard labor in the military prison at Dry Tortugas, Fla.," Arnold, Mudd and O'Laughlin for life, Spangler for six years. The trial, conducted during a time of public outrage over the president's death, was hardly fair, but the demand for revenge had to be satisfied.

Runners and Raiders

On June 23, President Johnson proclaimed that the naval blockade of the South was at an end. Although it had never been fully effective, it had been recognized by all foreign nations, and had required the Confederacy to export its cotton and other products, and to import munitions and supplies, by ships running the blockade. It was apparent very early that sailing vessels were of limited usefulness, so steel-hulled steamers, designed to carry heavy loads, were specially built for the purpose. In the course of the war, nearly 300 ships, 136 of which were captured, were operated by the Confederate government, by state governments, and by private owners, both Confederate and foreign. They made a total of about 1,300 attempts to run the blockade, and more than a thousand of these trips were successful. They delivered from abroad 400,000 rifles, three million pounds of lead, and more than two million pounds of saltpeter. The South would have been unable to fight the war without the materials brought in by the blockade runners.

A major change in the logistics situation occurred in early 1865, when the port of Wilmington was closed by the capture of Fort Fisher on January 15, and when the port of Charleston was evacuated on February 17. With no Atlantic ports available, Lee's and Johnston's armies were cut off from foreign supplies. Large quantities of shoes, uniform cloth, blankets, meat and other goods that were waiting in Bermuda and Nassau for vessels to take them through the blockade were returned to England. English merchants were left, at war's end, with large unpaid debts. Attempts after the war to collect from the U. S. Government were, understandably, not successful.

The only port still open, though closely blockaded by the U. S. Navy, was far away: Galveston, Texas. Cotton could be collected there for export, and munitions and supplies transported from there to Kirby-Smith's army via the Galveston-Houston railroad. During April and May, at least a dozen blockade runners entered the port, bringing lead, saltpeter, and even a battery of breech-loading field guns. None of these supplies could, however, be sent east of the Mississippi River.

On May 22, as the end approached, General Magruder ordered the commanding officer in Galveston to arrange for the surrender of the port. The next day the second most successful of all of the Confederate blockade runners, *Denbigh*, arrived from Havana on her second round-trip in six weeks. The vessel was a 182-foot steamer built in 1860 in Birkenhead, England. Trying to enter the harbor, it ran aground (a not uncommon occurrence in those waters) on Bird Key and the crew abandoned it. The next morning Union gunboats pounded it with cannon fire, then burned the wreckage. On May 24, the *Lark*, another Birkenhead-build sidewheeler, but four years newer, arrived. Confederate soldiers removed the cargo as soon as the ship docked at the wharf. The *Lark* then took aboard the *Denbigh's* crew and steamed into the Gulf of Mexico, the very last of the Confederate blockade runners.

With resistance virtually ended on land, several Confederate ships were still at sea, looking for Union prizes. One was the new iron-clad ram *C. S. S. Stonewall*, built at Bordeaux and armed with a thirty-pounder Armstrong rifle. Although contracted for by the Confederate naval agent in Europe, Captain James D. Bulloch, the French government, recognizing that it had a serious problem with the United States over Mexico, prohibited the Confederacy from taking delivery and sold the ship to the Danish Navy, which promptly sold it to the Confederacy. The *Stonewall* sailed from Copenhagen in January under Captain Thomas Jefferson Page. Bulloch arranged for a meeting off the Brittany coast with a ship carrying men for the crew. After suffering damage in a storm, the ship stopped in Ferrol, Spain for repairs. Two Federal frigates, *U. S. S. Niagara* and *U. S. S. Sacramento*, waiting outside the harbor, declined to engage when the *Stonewall* sortied on March 24. The raider stopped at Lisbon for coal and started across the Atlantic on March 28, refueling again at Tenerife. Word from the U. S. Consul there prompted Secretary of the Navy Welles to write to Secretary of War Stanton on April 28:

Confederate River Defense Ram *Stonewall Jackson*

The rebel ram Stonewall left that island, where she obtained a supply of coal, on the evening of [April 1] and steamed rapidly to the south. It is believed that her destination is some point on our coast. The Stonewall is represented by all parties to be a very formidable vessel and to possess superior speed. It behooves us to be prepared against surprise and to adopt every precaution to prevent injury from her. The [Navy] Department has to-day advised all the squadrons and the navy-yards.

The *Stonewall* reached Nassau on May 6. Despite what "all parties" believed, the French had, obviously, not built a fast ship. It anchored in Havana on May 11. As rumors circulated that the ship was on its way to pick up Davis, Page heard of the surrenders of Lee and Johnston. Then, while he pondered what to do, news arrived of Taylor's capitulation and the capture of Davis. Faced with this information, and a squadron of U. S. warships patrolling outside the harbor, he sold the ship to the Captain General of Cuba on May 19 for $16,000 and used the money to pay off the crew. The Spanish sold the ship to the United States, which in turn sold it to Japan.

FINALE IN THE ALEUTIANS

The last shot of the war, which landed harmlessly in the ocean, was fired by the *C. S. S. Shenandoah* in late June. This ship was one of the Confederate sea raiders that had destroyed Union shipping throughout the war. These were fast cruisers, propelled by both steam and sail and designed to attack merchant vessels, which were usually unarmed. Two of the best known raiders were sunk by the U. S. Navy. On June 19, 1864, the *C. S. S. Alabama*, which had put in to Cherbourg for coal, left the harbor and was engaged and sunk by *U. S. S. Kearsarge* seven miles off the French coast. The raider *C. S. S. Florida* was in port in Bahia, Brazil when it was located by *U. S. S. Wachusett*. On the night of October 6, 1864 the Union ship entered the harbor, rammed and captured the raider, and towed it to Hampton Roads, Virginia. The protest of the Brazilian government was of no avail.

The *Shenandoah* was still at sea in June, its whereabouts unknown to the U. S. Pacific Squadron, which was searching for it. The Confederates, recognizing the importance of whale oil as a lubricant in steam engines and other machinery, decided to try to interrupt the Union supply of the oil. The *Shenandoah* was therefore intended to attack the New England whaling fleet in the North Pacific. The 1,160-ton vessel, originally named *Sea King*, was built in Glasgow. It was the last cruiser purchased by Bulloch. He arranged for the ship to clear from Liverpool under false papers, and for the supply ship *Laurel* to precede it to Funchal, on the Island of Madeira. On October 19, 1864, under the lee of a small island, guns, powder, shot and shell, equipment, supplies and coal were put aboard and the *Shenandoah* was commissioned as a Confederate warship. The crew consisted of ten veterans from the sunken *Alabama* and twenty-three mostly English and Scottish volunteers from the *Laurel*.

Captained by Lieutenant Commanding James I. Waddell, CSN, the ship headed south through the Atlantic Ocean, capturing and destroying nine ships. Rounding the Cape of Good Hope, Waddell sailed to Melbourne, where he put in for repairs and supplies. While there fourteen of the crew deserted. Additional seamen, perhaps as many as eighty, were recruited in violation of British law. Leaving Australia, he then proceeded to Lea Harbor in the Caroline Islands, where on April 1, he found four American whalers and burned them.

THE BEGINNING AND THE END. 399

Waddell then sailed north into the Sea of Okhotsk. On June 22, the *Shenandoah* chased the New Bedford bark *Jerah Swift* for three hours, then fired an across-the-bow warning shot, the last round of the Civil War, from a 32-pounder Whitworth rifle. That day he captured four whalers. One of the ships was carrying San Francisco newspapers with the information that Lee had surrendered, that the government had moved to Danville and that Davis had asked the people of the Confederacy to carry on the struggle. Waddell decided to carry on. He ransomed two of the whalers; the other two he burned after taking navigation instruments and charts and removing the crews, three men of which signed to serve on the *Shenandoah*. In the next few days he came upon eight more New Bedford ships. He ransomed a whaler named *Milo* for $50,000 and burned the rest.

Finally, on June 28, eleven weeks after Appomattox, the war came to an end off Amchitka Island in the Aleutians, where the Pacific Ocean meets the Bering Sea. On that day the *Shenandoah* took twelve more whalers, all but two of them from New Bedford. On one ship, the *James Murry*, he found that the owner was a widow with two children aboard. Her husband had died, and in order to preserve his body for burial at home she had it placed in a barrel of whiskey. Waddell ransomed this ship for $37,000 and sent it to San Francisco with the crews from the other eleven ships, all of which he burned. In the destruction of these twenty-two ships, no life was lost. Nine more men signed on to his crew, convincing him that they did not believe the war was over.

The *Shenandoah* then sailed toward San Francisco, where Waddell planned, ambitiously it would seem, on "entering the harbor . . . and laying the city under contribution [ransom]." From newspapers reports he believed that only one naval vessel, *U. S. S. Saginaw*, commanded by a man with whom he had served in the U. S. Navy, was in port. But he thought it prudent to first speak with a vessel coming from there. On August 2, he encountered a ship which had left San Francisco two weeks before. The log entry reads:

> Having received by the British bark Barracouta the sad intelligence of the overthrow of the Confederate

Government, all attempts to destroy the shipping or property of the United States will cease from this date, in accordance with the First Lieutenant . . . receiving an order from the commander to strike below the battery and disarm the ship and crew.

Rather than surrender in the United States, Waddell decided to sail 17,000 miles to Liverpool. Several of his officers, as well as members of the crew, fearful of being tried for piracy, tried to persuade him to go to Sydney, but he insisted on returning to England. After the ship rounded Cape Horn most of the officers again tried to convince him to make port, this time at Cape Town, and again he refused. On November 5, having circumnavigated the Earth in the previous thirteen months, and without communicating with another ship after the *Barracouta*, he entered St. George's Channel. The next morning, in his own words, he stated:

> The Shenandoah steamed up the River Mersey in a thick fog under the Confederate flag, and the pilot had orders to anchor her near H. M. ship-of-the-line Donegal, Captain Paynter, R. N. Shortly after we anchored a lieutenant from the Donegal visited us to ascertain the name of the vessel and gave me official intelligence of the termination of the American war. He was polite. The flag was then hauled down.

On November 8, the crew was interviewed by Captain Paynter. He asked each man his nationally, and when a number of men with Scottish brogues declared that they had been born in Mississippi, he accepted their claims. All of the men were released and taken ashore, the first time they had been off the vessel since Melbourne. The *Shenandoah* had captured thirty-eight ships, thirty-two of which were burned, and had taken 1,053 prisoners. Waddell estimated the value of the damage inflicted at $1,361,983. British customs took possession of the *Shenandoah*, which was turned over to the U. S. Consul on November 11. Later sold to the Sultan of Zanzibar, it is reported to have sunk after grounding on a reef in the Indian Ocean in 1879.

Slavery Abolished, the Nation Endures

Slaves in America gained their freedom, over much time, by half a dozen different means. One was by personal initiative: they simply ran away, often with the help of white people. Another was by manumission by owners: George Washington, for example, freed his slaves in his will. Still another, in the decades just before and after 1800, was by legislation in the states north of the Mason-Dixon line. The Civil War provided three additional ways. One was the seizure, as contraband of war, of property (crops, wagons, horses, slaves) of persons in rebellion against the United States. Slaves thus freed were known as "contrabands." Another was by Lincoln's *Emancipation Proclamation*, which freed slaves in the territory of seceded states occupied by the U. S. Army. Finally, slavery was ended everywhere in the United States by constitutional prohibition. On December 18, 1865, the Secretary of State declared the Thirteenth Amendment to the Constitution was in effect, after having been ratified by the necessary twenty-seven states.

> 1. Neither slavery nor involuntary servitude, except as a punishment for crime whereof the party shall have been duly convicted, shall exist within the United States, or any place subject to their jurisdiction. 2. Congress shall have power to enforce this article by appropriate legislation.

In the beginning, seven states provoked a Constitutional crisis by seceding because they believed their right to own slaves was threatened by the election of a Republican president. At great cost in human lives lost, property destroyed and expense incurred, the crisis was resolved. In the end, slavery was abolished.

From the perspective of the 21st Century, it is reasonable to assert that the essence of secessionist surrender was the giving up, however reluctantly, of the idea of state sovereignty, and the acceptance of the United States of America as a sovereign nation. The evidence is abundant. We dedicate ourselves to the United States as "one nation, indivisible." Indeed, we believe it is the greatest of nations. This is uncontested except by a marginal, sometimes irrational, few. Nearly all of us think of ourselves as

Americans. We travel on United States passports, serve in the armed forces of the United States, move freely from state to state, support the United States Olympic teams and obsess about national elections. We rely on the United States government to provide a host of services and payments that we would be distressed, no matter how we protest otherwise, to do without.

That it was not always so does not invalidate the observation that, had the problem of slavery not existed, no serious consideration of secession would have occurred. Such issues as the tariff, disposition of public lands, and the building of a transcontinental railroad were not sufficiently important to fight about. A sense of nationality had been growing steadily during the first sixty years of the 19th Century, and even those dedicated to secession were anxious to create a Southern Nation patterned on, if slightly different from, the then existing United States.

The economic and political conflicts of earlier times -- among sections, between employers and employees, foreign relations, education, immigration, transportation, taxes, benefits, subsidies — all are echoed in each new session of Congress. They will always be with us. The issues of the 1860s, however, were narrowly focused. The Southern Nation was based on the practice of Negro slavery and the idea of state rights. Its surrender led immediately to the end of the first and gradually to the diminishment of the other.

The relevant issue for our times needs to be plainly stated: the distribution, or balance, of governmental powers. Governments, whether national, state, county or municipal, do not have rights. Governments have powers. Only individuals have rights. The Tenth Amendment to the Constitution provides,

> The powers not delegated to the United States by the Constitution, nor prohibited by it to the States, are reserved to the States respectively, or to the people.

An intriguing unresolved question is, 'Which powers are, or ought to be, the preserve of the states, and which should be the preserve of the people; and if of the people, then how exercised?' In our republican democracy, we have achieved an imperfect but stable *modus vivendi*. We adjust the equilibrium from time to time, but most of us are largely satisfied with it. To the extent that we are not, then in our pluralistic nation it may be best if the situation remains ambiguous, elusive, or even indeterminate, as it was before 1861. The enduring lesson of the Civil War is that no political issue, however intractable and divisive, is amenable to solution by resorting to arms.

NOTES ON SOURCES

This is a popular essay that does not present novel points of view or propose controversial interpretations, so chapter notes have not been provided. There is, however, a complete bibliography for the benefit of readers interested in the scope of the research involved. I am greatly indebted to the Lehigh University Library, the Muhlenberg College Library, the Allentown, Pennsylvania Public Library, the Library of Congress, the Civil War Library and Museum in Philadelphia, the U. S. Army Military History Institute Library at the Carlisle Barracks, the State of Georgia Archives, and the Florida State Library.

The principal source of this book is *The Official Records of the Union and Confederate Armies in the War of the Rebellion*. Published between 1880 and 1901, it was reissued in 1985 by Historical Times, Inc. for the National Historical Society, Harrisburg, Pennsylvania. To use this immense work, the reader will need to understand its structure. It comprises four Series. Series I, Reports and Correspondence, consists of orders, after-action reports, letters and other documents for the two armies, arranged both by geographic areas and chronologically, beginning December 20, 1860 and continuing until after the war's end. Many of the 52 volumes consist of two or three parts, each of which is a separately bound book. In all there are 111 separately bound books in Series I. In the other three series, none of the volumes is divided into parts. Series II, Prisoners of War, consists of eight volumes; Series III, Union documents, consists of five volumes; and Series IV, Confederate documents, of three volumes. A reader interested in, for example, the battle of Antietam/Sharpsburg, would use the Series I volume that contains reports for Maryland in September of 1862, and the Series III and IV volumes for the relevant dates. The volumes used in writing *The Beginning and the End* were:

Series I - <u>Reports and Correspondence</u>

Vol. 1, South Carolina, Georgia, Alabama, Mississippi, Florida and Texas: November 1896-April 1861

Vol. 46, Northern and Southeastern Virginia, North Carolina, West Virginia, Maryland and Pennsylvania

Part 1, Reports: January 1-June 30, 1865

Part 2, Correspondence: February 1-March 23, 1865

Part 3, Correspondence: March 16-June 30, 1865

Vol. 47, North Carolina, South Carolina, Southern Georgia and Eastern Florida

Part 1, Reports: January 1-June 30, 1865

Part 2, Correspondence: February 1-March 23, 1865

Part 3, Correspondence: March 24-June 30, 1865

Vol. 48, Louisiana and the Trans-Mississippi States and Territories

Part 1, Reports, January 1-June 30, 1865 and Correspondence, January 1- March 31, 1865

Part 2, Correspondence, April 1-June 30, 1865

Vol. 49, Kentucky, Southwestern Virginia, Tennessee, Northern and Central Georgia, Mississippi, Alabama, and West Florida

Part 1, Reports: January 1-June 1, 1865 and Correspondence, January 1- March 15, 1865

Part 2, Correspondence, March 16-June 30, 1865

Vol. 51, Supplement, Maryland, Eastern North Carolina, Pennsylvania, Virginia and West Virginia

Part 1, Reports and Union Correspondence, Jan. 1-June 30, 1865

Part 2, Confederate Correspondence, January 1-June 30, 1865

Vol. 52, Supplement, Southwestern Virginia, Kentucky, Tennessee, Mississippi, Alabama, West Florida and Northern Georgia

Part 1, Reports and Union Correspondence, January 1, 1861-June 30, 1865

Part 2, Confederate Correspondence, January 1, 1861-June 30, 1865

Vol. 53, Supplement, South Carolina, Southern Georgia, Middle and East Florida, and Western North Carolina, January 1, 1861-June 30, 1865

Series II - Prisoners of War
Vol. 7, April 1- December 31, 1864
Vol. 8, January 1, 1865-May 16, 1867

Series III - Union Documents
Vol. 1, November 1, 1860-March 31, 1862 (1-77)
Vol. 4, January 1, 1864-April 30, 1865
Vol. 5, May 1, 1862-October 20, 1867

Series IV - Confederate Documents
Vol. 1, December 20, 1860 to June 30, 1862 (1-223)
Vol. 3, January 1, 1864 to May 3, 1865 (1130-1183)

Also of use to students of the Civil War, though of limited applicability to this book, is the companion series, *Official Records of the Union and Confederate Navies in the War of the Rebellion*, published between 1894 and 1917. Volume 4 was a useful source. The Official Records are the basis for more than half of the contents of this book. The other half is based on the 215 works listed in the bibliography. They are organized in three categories: (1) General and Special Histories, (2) Biographies, Memoirs and Papers, and (3) Encyclopedias and Compendiums.

Bibliography

General and Special Histories

Abel, Annie H., The American Indian as Slaveholder and Secessionist (1915)

Abel, Annie H., The American Indian as Participant in the Civil War (1919)

Anderson, Bern, By Sea and By River: A Naval History of the Civil War (1962)

Andrews, C. C., History of the Campaign of Mobile (1867)

Avery, Isaac W., The History of the State of Georgia from 1850 to 1881 (1881)

Ball, Douglas B., Financial Failure and Confederate Defeat (1991)

Barrett, John G., The Civil War in North Carolina (1963)

Barrett, John G., Sherman's March Through the Carolinas (1956)

Barton, O. S., Three Years With Quantrill: A True Story Told by His Scout John McCorkle (1992)

Bates, Samuel P., History of Pennsylvania Volunteers, 1861-5 (1869)

Bergeron, Arthur W., Jr., Confederate Mobile (1991)

Beringer, Richard E. and others, Why the South Lost the Civil War (1986)

Black, Robert C., The Railroads of the Confederacy (1952)

Boorstin, Daniel J., The Americans: The National Experience (1965)

Bragg, Jefferson D., Louisiana in the Confederacy (1941)

Brownlee, Richard S., Gray Ghosts of the Confederacy: Guerilla Warfare in the West, 1861-1865 (1958)

Brubaker, John H., The Last Capital, Danville (1979)

Buenger, James, Secession and the Union in Texas (1984)

Castel, Albert E., Civil War Kansas: Reaping the Whirlwind (1997)

Catton, Bruce, Never Call Retreat (1965)
Catton, William and Bruce, Two Roads to Sumter (1963)
Cauthen, Charles E., South Carolina Goes to War (1950)
Chadwick, French E., Causes of the Civil War (1906)
Clark, James C., Last Train South (1984)
Collins, Bruce, The Origins of America's Civil War (1981)
Connelly, Thomas L., Autumn of Glory: The Army of Tennessee, 1862-1865 (1971)
Coulter, E. Merton, The Confederate States of America, 1861-1865 (1950)
Craven, Avery, The Coming of the Civil War (1942)
Crawford, Samuel W., Genesis of the Civil War: The Story of Sumter (1880)
Cunningham, Frank, General Stand Watie's Confederate Indians (1959)
Current, Richard N., Lincoln and the First Shot (1963)
Daniel, Larry J., Confederate Cannon Foundries (1977)
Davis, Burke, The Long Surrender (1985)
Davis, Burke, Sherman's March (1980)
Davis, Burke, Our Incredible Civil War (1960)
Davis, Burke, To Appomattox: Nine April Days, 1865 (1959)
Davis, Jefferson, The Rise and Fall of the Confederate Government (1881)
Davis, William C., ed., Embattled Confederacy (1982)
Denney, Robert E., Civil War Prisons and Escapes (1993)
Dietz, August, The Confederate States Post Office Department (1948)
Dowdey, Clifford, The Land They Fought For (1955)
Dowdey, Clifford, Experiment in Rebellion (1946)
Dufour, Charles, The Night the War Was Lost (1960)
Eaton, Clement, A History of the Southern Confederacy (1954)

Elliott, James W., Transport to Disaster (1962)
Fellman, Michael, Inside War: The Guerilla Conflict in Missouri During the American Civil War (1989)
Filler, Louis, The Crusade Against Slavery, 1830-1860 (1960)
Fleming, Walter L., Civil War and Reconstruction in Alabama (1905)
Frazier, Donald S., Blood & Treasure: Confederate Empire in the Southwest (1995)
Gallagher, Gary W., The Confederate War (1997)
Gibson, Arrell M., The Chickasaws (1971)
Goff, Richard D., Confederate Supply (1969)
Goodrich, Thomas, Black Flag: Guerilla Warfare on the Western Border, 1861-1865 (1995)
Greene, Francis V., Campaigns of the Civil War: the Mississippi (1882)
Hendrick, Burton J., Statesmen of the Lost Cause (1939)
Hendrickson, Robert, Sumter: The First Day of the Civil War (1990)
Hansen, Harry, The Civil War (1961)
Hasseltine, William B., ed., The Tragic Conflict (1962)
Hasseltine, William B., Civil War Prisons: A Study in Psychology (1930)
Hattaway, Herman and Jones, Archer, How the North Won: A Military History of the Civil War (1991)
Hoehling, A. A. and Mary, The Last Days of the Confederacy (1983)
Hoehling, A. A. and Mary, The Day Richmond Died (1981)
Henry, Robert S., The Story of the Confederacy (1931)
Hunt, Cornelius E., The Shenandoah; or The Last Confederate Cruiser (1867)
Jenkins, Brian, Britain & the War for the Union, vol. 1 (1974)

Johnson, Rossiter, A Short History of the War of Secession, 1861-1865 (1889)

Jones, Archer, Civil War Command & Strategy: The Process of Victory and Defeat (1992)

Jones, Virgil C., The Civil War at Sea (1962)

Josephy, Alvin M. Jr., The Civil War in the American West (1992)

Karl, Dennis, Glorious Defiance: Last Stands Throughout History (1990)

Kelly, Orr and Kelly, Mary D., Dream's End: Two Iowa Brothers in the Civil War (1998)

Klein, Maury, Days of Defiance: Sumter, Secession, and the Coming of the Civil War (1997)

Knoles, George H., The Crisis of the Union: 1860-1861 (1965)

Lee, Henry, The Militia of the United States (1864)

Livermore, Thomas L., Numbers and Losses in the American Civil War, 1861-1865 (1880)

Lossing, Benson J., A History of the Civil War, 1861-65 (1912)

Mallett, John W., Work of the Ordnance Bureau of the [CSA] War Department (1870)

Marvel, William, Andersonville: The Last Depot (1994)

Mahon, John K., History of the Militia (1983)

McClellan, E. P., The Ghosts of Castle Pinckney (1998)

McPherson, James M., Battle Cry of Freedom (1988)

McPherson, James M., Ordeal by Fire: The Civil War and Reconstruction (1982)

McMillan, Malcolm C., The Disintegration of a Confederate State [Mississippi] (1986)

Meredith, Roy, Storm Over Sumter: The Opening Engagement of the Civil War (1957)

Meneely, A. H., The War Department, 1861 (1928)

Miller, Roy, Croxton's Raid (1979)

Moore, James, A Complete History of the Great Rebellion (1868)

Musicant, Ivan, Divided Waters: A Naval History of the Civil War (1995)

Nevins, Allan, The War for the Union: The Improvised War, 1861-1862 (1959)

Pollard, Edward A., The Lost Cause: A New Southern History of the War of the Confederates (1867)

Potter, David M., The Impending Crisis: 1848-1861 (1976)

Potter, Jerry O., The Sultana Tragedy (1992)

[Pratt] History of the National Guard of Indiana (1901)

Rader, Perry S., The History of Missouri (1922)

Robertson, John., ed., Michigan in the War (1882)

Roland, Charles P., The Confederacy (1960)

Rolle, Andrew F., The Last Cause: The Confederate Exodus to Mexico (1965)

Royster, Charles, The Destructive War: William Tecumseh Sherman, Stonewall Jackson, and the Americans (1993)

Schaff, Morris, The Sunset of the Confederacy (1912)

Schmidt, Lewis G., The Civil War in Florida (1991)

Schouler, William, History of Massachusetts in the Civil War (1868)

Schwab, John C., The Confederate States of America, 1861-1865: A Financial and Industrial History (1901)

Scott, John, Partisan Life with Mosby (1867)

Sewell, Richard H., A House Divided: Sectionalism and the Civil War (1988)

Smith, Ernest A., The History of the Confederate Treasury (1901)

Smith, Paige, Trial by Fire (1982)

Speer, Lonnie R., Portals to Hell (1997)

Stampp, Kenneth H., The Imperiled Union: Essays on the Background of the Civil War (1980)

Stampp, Kenneth H., And the War Came: The North and the Secession Crisis (1950)

Starr, Stephen Z., The Union Cavalry in the Civil War, vols. 1 and 3 (1985)

Stern, Philip Van Doren, Prologue to Sumter (1961)

Stern, Philip Van Doren, An End to Valor: The Last Days of the Civil War (1958)

Swanberg, W. A., First Blood: The Story of Fort Sumter (1957)

Thomas, David Y., Arkansas in War and Reconstruction: 1861-1874 (1926)

Thomas, Emory M., The Confederate Nation, 1861-1865 (1979)

Thomas, Emory M., The Confederate State of Richmond: A Biography of the Capital (1971)

Thompson, Heber S., The First Defenders (1910)

Thompson, Samuel B., Confederate Purchasing Operations Abroad (1935)

Todd, Robert C., Confederate Finance (1954)

Trudeau, Noah A., Like Men of War: Black Troops in the Civil War (1998)

Trudeau, Noah A., Out of the Storm: The End of the Civil War, April-June 1865 (1994)

Tyrner-Tyrnauer, A. R., Lincoln and the Emperors (1962)

Tzabar, Shimon, The White Flag Principle: How to Lose a War and Why (1972)

Vandiver, Frank E., Their Tattered Flags: The Epic of the Confederacy (1988)

Vandiver, Frank E., Basic History of the Confederacy (1962)

Vandiver, Frank E., Rebel Brass: The Confederate Command System (1956)

Watt, William J. and Spears, James R., Indiana's Citizen Soldiers (1980)

Weichmann, Louis J., A True History of the Assassination of Abraham Lincoln (1975 reissue)
Wert, Jeffrey D., Mosby's Rangers (1990)
Wesley, Charles H., The Collapse of the Confederacy (1937)
Wheeler, Richard, Witness to Appomattox (1989)
Williamson, James J., Mosby's Rangers (1896)
Winters, John D., The Civil War in Louisiana (1963)
Wise, Stephen R., Lifeline of the Confederacy (1988)
Wooster, Ralph A., The Secession Conventions of the South (1962)

Biographies, Memoirs and Papers

Alexander, Edward P., Fighting for the Confederacy: Personal Reflections (1907)
Baird, W. David, Peter Pitchlyn, Chief of the Choctaws (1972)
Buchanan, James, Mr. Buchanan's Administration on the Eve of the Rebellion (1865)
Capers, Henry D., The Life and Times of C. G. Memminger (1893)
Castel, Albert, General Sterling Price and the Civil War in the West (1968)
Chamberlain, Joshua L., The Passing of the Armies (1915)
Cleaves, Freeman, Rock of Chickamauga: The Life of General George H. Thomas (1948)
Connelly, William E., Quantrill and the Border Wars (1909)
Current, Richard N., Lincoln and the First Shot (1963)
Davis, William C., Jefferson Davis: The Man and His Hour (1991)
Davis, William C., Breckinridge: Statesman, Soldier, Symbol (1974)
Doubleday, Abner, Reminiscences of Forts Sumter and Moultrie in 1860-61 (1876)
Dowdey, Clifford, ed., The Wartime Papers of R. E. Lee (1961)
Durkin, Joseph T., Stephen R. Mallory: Confederate Navy Chief (1954)

Elliott, Charles W., Winfield Scott: The Soldier and the Man (1937)

Eisenhower, John S. D., Agent of Destiny: General Winfield Scott (1997)

Franks, Kenny A., Stand Watie and the Agony of the Cherokee Nation (1979)

Freeman, Douglas S., Lee's Lieutenants: A Study in Command, Vol. 3 (1944)

Freeman, Douglas S., R. E. Lee, Vol. 4 (1935)

Govan, G. E. and Livingood, J. W., A Different Valor: General Joseph E. Johnston, C. S. A. (1956)

Grant, Ulysses S., Personal Memoirs (1885)

Harris, William C., Leroy Pope Walker, Confederate Secretary of War (1962)

Heyman, Max L., Prudent Soldier: A Biography of Major General E. R. S. Canby (1959)

Horan, James D., ed., C. S. S. Shenandoah: The Memoirs of Lieutenant Commanding James I. Waddell, C. S. N. (1960)

Johnson, Timothy D., Winfield Scott: The Quest for Military Glory (1998)

Johnston, Joseph E., Narrative of Military Operations Directed During the Late War Between the States (1874)

Jones, John B., A Rebel War Clerk's Diary at the Confederate States Capital (1866)

Jones, Virgil C., Ranger Mosby (1944)

Kerby, Robert L., Kirby Smith's Confederacy (1972)

Klein, Philip, President James Buchanan (1962)

McFeely, William S., Grant: A Biography (1981)

Moore, John B., ed., The Works of James Buchanan, Vol. 11 (1960)

Nevins, Allan, ed., The Messages and Papers of Jefferson Davis and the Confederacy (1966)

Nicolay, John G. and Hay, John, Abraham Lincoln, A History, Vol. 3 (1890)

O'Flaherty, Daniel, General Jo Shelby: Undefeated Rebel (1954)

Parks, Joseph H., General Edmund Kirby Smith, C. S. A. (1954)

Proctor, Ben H., Not Without Honor: The Life of John H. Reagan (1962)

Randall, J. G., Lincoln the President, Vol. 1 (1945)

Reagan, John H., Memoirs (1906)

Reagan, John H., Report of the Postmaster-General to the President, April 29, 1861

Richardson, James D., ed., Messages and Papers of the Confederacy (1966)

Roman, Alfred, The Military Operations of General Beauregard in the War Between the States, Vol. 1 (1884)

Sandburg, Carl, Abraham Lincoln: The War Years, Vol. 1 (1939)

Schofield, John M., Forty-Six Years in the Army (1897)

Scott, Winfield, Memoirs of Lieut.General Winfield Scott, LL. D. (1864)

Sherman, William T., Memoirs of General William T. Sherman (1875)

Sifakis, Stewart, Who Was Who in the Civil War (1988)

Smith, Elbert B., The Presidency of James Buchanan (1975)

Symonds, Craig L., Joseph E. Johnston (1992)

Taylor, Richard, Destruction and Reconstruction (1879)

Vandiver, Frank E., Plowshares Into Swords: Josiah Gorgas and Confederate Ordnance (1952)

Warner, Ezra J., Generals in Blue (1964)

Warner, Ezra J., Generals in Gray (1959)

Welles, Gideon, Lincoln's Administration (1876-78)

Whitney, Grady, Braxton Bragg and Confederate Defeat (1969)

Wilson, James H., Under the Old Flag (1912)

Yearns, W. Buck, ed., The Confederate Governors (1985)

Younger, Edward, ed., Inside the Confederate Government: The Diary of Robert Garlick Hill Kean (1957)

ENCYCLOPEDIAS AND COMPENDIUMS

The War of the Rebellion: A Compilation of the Official Records of the Union and Confederate Armies (1880-1901) Official Records of the Union and Confederate Navies in the War of the Rebellion (1904)

Army Regulations of the Confederate States of America (1861)

Boatner, Mark M., The Civil War Dictionary (1959)

Bishop, Chris, and Drury, Ian, 1400 Days: The US Civil War Day by Day (1998)

Buel, Clarence C. and Johnson, Robert U., eds., Battles and Leaders of the Civil War, Vols. 1 and 4 (1884-1887)

Carter, Allan and Provorse, Carl, The World Almanac of the USA (1998)

Current, Richard N., ed., Encyclopedia of the Confederacy, 4 Vols. (1993)

Denney, Robert E., The Civil War Years: A Day-by-Day Chronicle of the Life of a Nation (1992)

Dyer, Frederick H., A Compendium of the War of the Rebellion (1908)

Evans, Clement A., ed., Confederate Military History, 12 Vols. (1899)

Faust, Patricia L., ed., Historical Times Illustrated Encyclopedia of the Civil War (1986)

Katcher, Philip, The American Civil War Source Book (1992)

Long, E. B., The Civil War Day by Day: An Almanac 1861-1865 (1971)

Matthews, James M., ed., The Statutes at Large of the Provisional Government of the C. S. A. (1864)

Matthews, James M., ed., Public Laws of the Confederate States of America (1864)

McClure, Alexander K., ed., The Annals of the Civil War (1879)

Moore, Frank, ed., The Rebellion Record, 12 Vols. (1861-1868)

Mosocco, Ronald A., A Chronological Tracking of the American Civil War (1994)

Schlesinger, Arthur M., ed., The Almanac of American History (1983)

Index

ABADIE, E H 86
ABBEVILLE, 336
ABBEVILLE ROAD, 338
ACT FOR THE ESTABLISHMENT AND ORGANIZATION OF A GENERAL STAFF 109
ACT FOR THE ESTABLISHMENT AND ORGANIZATION OF THE ARMY, 111
ACT TO AUTHORIZE THE CONSOLIDATION OF COMPANIES BATALLIONS AND REGIMENTS, 211-212
ACT TO AUTHORIZE THE ISSUE OF TREASURY NOTES, 122
ACT TO DECLARE AND ESTABLISH THE FREE NAVIGATION OF THE MISSISSIPPI RIVER, 149
ACT TO ESTABLISH THE TREASURY DEPARTMENT, 119
ACT TO ESTABLISH THE WAR DEPARTMENT, 109 109
ACT TO INCREASE THE MILITARY FORCES OF THE CONFEDERATE STATES, 213
ACT TO MODIFY THE NAVIGATION LAWS AND REPEAL ALL DISCRIMINATING DUTIES ON SHIPS OR VESSELS, 149
ACT TO PROVIDE FOR THE PUBLIC DEFENSE, 110
ACT TO RAISE MONEY FOR THE SUPPORT OF THE GOVERNMENT AND TO PROVIDE FOR DEFENSE, 110
ACT TO RAISE MONEY FOR THE SUPPORT OF THE GOVERNMENT AND TO PROVIDE FOR THE DEFENSE OF THE CONFEDERATE STATES OF AMERICA, 121
ACT TO RAISE PROVISIONAL FORCES, 110
AD Valorem Duty 121
ADAMS, 176 Capt 164 Charles Francis Ambassador To Britain 147 H A 163 James H 36 Prepared To Re-enforce Fort Pickens 175 Reluctant To Violate Agreement With Confederates 174
ADAMS EXPRESS COMPANY, Competition Of Postal Service 124
ALABAMA, 50-51 70 97 115 148 191 202 208 244 299-300 302 307 309 316 330 338 350 382 390 As Source Of Iron 106 Citronelle Conditions Of Surrender 308-310 Dates Of Occupation 94 Loans 500000 To The Confederate Treasury 121 Militia 63 75 Mobile 204 Montgomery 86 Montgomery Convention To Establish Southern Confederacy 23 Mount Vernon Arsenal 74 Offensive Ordered By Grant 292 Selma 204 University 100 117
ALABAMA MILITARY COLLEGE, 307

ALABAMA MISSISSIPPI AND EAST LOUISIANA DEPARTMENT, Rolls 209
ALABAMA RIVER, 314
ALAMO, 86
ALAMO GORDO, 372
ALBANY, 325 330
ALCOHOL, Destruction Of 222
ALEUTIANS, 399
ALEXANDER, Andrew J 301 Porter 233
ALEXANDER'S, Brigade 316
ALEXANDRIA, 201 342 363
ALLEN, Ethan 68 Gov 352 Henry 350 Henry W 348
ALLISON, 335 A K 333
ALLSTON, Charles 31 Col 32
AMBASSADOR, To Britain Carefully Chosen By Lincoln 147 To France Carefully Chosen By Lincoln 147
AMCHITKA ISLAND, 399
AMELIA COURT HOUSE, 220 225-226
AMELIA ISLAND, 61 202
AMELIA RIVER, 61
AMERICAN, Consul 69
AMERICAN BANK NOTE COMPANY, The 123
AMNESTY PROCLAMATION, 1863 271
ANDERSON, 7-11 16 19 26 35-38 41-47 56 137-138 141 150 155-156 177 179-181 183 185 188-189 227 Actions Accepted In North 39 Continues To Prepare Reports 182 Declares Two Batteries Of South Carolina Fired On Unarmed Vessel Bearing Flag Of US Gov 45 Defends His Case 29 Failure To Fire On Secessionists 44 Joseph R 115 Maj 39 151-152 168 Maj Agrees To Evacuate Fort Sumter 187

ANDERSON (cont) Message To Secretary Of War Cameron 190 Not Willing To Give Up The Fort 47 Numbering Reports To Avoid Interception Of Mail 6 Official Dispatches Read By Confederate Officials 182 Optimistic And Confident 41 Richard H 136 226 Robert 4-5 267 Robert Rejects Confederate Order To Surrender 184 Seals Letters With Red Wax To Expose Tampering 134 Staunch And Loyal Unionist 5 Troop Commander 17
ANDERSON STATION, 377
ANDERSONVILLE, 325 329 385-386 Prison Conditions 377
ANDREW, John A 161
ANDREWS, 294 297 C C 293
ANNAPOLIS, 151 390
ANNISTON, 323
APALACHICOLA, 202
APALACHICOLA RIVER, 60
APPALACHIAN MOUNTAINS, 285
APPOMATTOX, 244 246 249 270-271 279 282 322 399
APPOMATTOX COURT HOUSE, 235 237 239 241 369
APPOMATTOX COURT-HOUSE, 261 266
APPOMATTOX RIVER, 217 225 227-228
APPOMATTOX STATION, 228 230 235 238
ARKANSAS, 81 197 202-203 282 341 343-345 347 350 355 359 384 Convention Called 130 Dates Of Occupation 94 Fulton 340 Little Rock 204 Militia 80 North 346 Seceded 196 Slave State 79
ARKANSAS RIVER, 81 343 362

ARLINGTON HEIGHTS, 201
ARMESY, Maj Captured 252
ARMISTEAD, Burt 336
ARMSTRONG, 63 As A Prisoner Of War 64 Capt Indecision 62 Court Martial Of 66 Frank C 305 James 61 Surrenders The Navy Yard 64 Takes No Precautions Against Secessionists Approaching 64
ARMSTRONG ACADEMY, 368
ARMY, 160 Southern 115 Southern Inducements To Join 9
ARMY OF ALABAMA-MISSISSIPPI-LOUISIANA, 243
ARMY OF GEORGIA, 256
ARMY OF NORTHERN VIRGINIA, 208 210 216 227-228 230-231 237 239 243 246 257 264 280 298 347 383 388 Proposed Surrender 234 Rolls 209 Soldiers Given Parole Passes 241 Surrender Of 240 242 247
ARMY OF OHIO, 256 286
ARMY OF TENNESSEE, 208-209 211 243 256-257 259 264
ARMY OF THE CUMBERLAND, 277
ARMY OF THE JAMES, 207 257
ARMY OF THE NORTHERN SUB-DIVISION OF ARKANSAS, 346
ARMY OF THE POTOMAC, 207 220 257
ARMY OF THE TRANS-MISSISSIPPI, 208 243 336 340-341 347-348
ARMY OF WEST MISSISSIPPI, 294 13th Corps 294 16th Corps 294 1st Division 294 2nd Division 294 3rd Division 294 Brigades 294 Cavalry 294 Pensacola Corps 294

ARNOLD, Lewis G 71 Maj 73 174 Samuel 394
ARSENAL, Frankfort 115 Harper's Ferry 114 US 79
ARSENALS AND ARMORIES, 56 Differences Between 56
ARTICLE, Of War 23d 216
ARTICLES OF WAR, 231
ARTILLERY, Auburn Light 161 First 5 89 First Company E 2 26 First Company H 2 First US Company G 62 Fourth US Company H 194 German Company 31 Lafayette Company 31 Marion Company 31 Ringgold Light 193-194 Second Missouri 225 Second US 58 71 173 Second US Company F 79 Washington 58 76 Washington Company 31
ASHEVILLE, 278
ASHLEY RIVER, 30 33
ATCHAFALAYA BAYOU, 342
ATLANTA, 204 208 245 269 311 330 337
ATLANTIC COAST, 204
ATLANTIC OCEAN, 67
ATLANTIC PORTS, In Control Of Union 212
ATZEROLT, G A 394
AUBURN, 315
AUGUSTA, 58 183 204 255 263 311 326 337 339
AUGUSTA ARSENAL, Date Of Occupation 93
AUSTIN, 340
AUSTRALIA, 398
AUSTRIA, 361
BADGER, Joseph 251 Summary Of Situation 252
BAKER, Luther B 254
BALDWIN, 327 332
BALTIMORE, 194
BARK, Release 166
BARNES, James 389

BARNWELL, Robert W 36
BARRANCAS BARRACKS, 62 Date Of Occupation 93
BARRETT, 375-376 Theodore H 373
BATES, 155 169 Attorney-gen 154 Edward P Attorney-gen 147
BATON ROUGE, 76
BATON ROUGE ARSENAL, Date Of Occupation 94
BATON ROUGE BARRACKS, Date Of Occupation 94
BATTALION, 43rd 249
BATTERY, Huger 295-297 Tracy 295 297 Wagner 325
BATTERY WAGNER, 203
BATTLE OF, Bentonville 256 Buena Vista 98 Columbus 319 Five Forks 218 Five Forks Confederate Survivors At Sutherland's Station 221 Five Forks Union Victory 219 Gettysburg 389 Monterrey 98 Nashville 207 New Orleans 75 Sayler's Creek 258 Seven Pines 386 Shiloh 112 Wilson's Creek 286
BEAUREGARD, 155-156 178-179 181-182 184 186 189 264 Brigadier-gen 185 G T 140 Gen 190 262-263 P G T 210 Pierre G T 112 Prepared To Attack 183 West Point 1838 141
BELLE PLAIN, 254
BELLONA FOUNDRY, 116
BENJAMIN, 264 Judah P 101 Judah P Attorney Gen 101 Secretary Of State 263 337
BENNETT, 281 James 268 Lucy 268
BENNETT HOUSE, 271 280
BENTON, 294-295
BENTONVILLE, 255
BERING SEA, 399
BERMUDA, 395

BERRYMAN, O H 63
BERRYVILLE, 249
BERWICK BAY, 342
BEVERLY, 201 252
BIBB COUNTY IRON WORKS, 303
BIG RIVER MILLS, 354
BIRD KEY, 396
BIRMINGHAM, 303
BLACK, Attorney Gen 37 Attorney-gen Suggestions In Reply To Commissioners 37 Jeremiah Attorney-gen 35
BLACK LICK RIVER, 382
BLACK ROCK SHOALS, 306
BLACK WARRIOR RIVER, 299 306 323
BLAIR, 169 Austin 162 Montgomery Postmaster-gen 127 147 Postmaster-gen 151
BLAKELY, 299 Rifled Cannon 183
BLUE MOUNTAIN, 323
BLUE RIDGE, 217 251 278
BLUFF SPRINGS, 294
BOGGY DEPOT, 366
BONHAM, M L 142 379
BOOTH, John Wilkes 394 John Wilkes Reward Posted 253 Killed 254
BORDEAUX, 396
BOSTON, 44 71 179 392
BOSTON AND BANGOR STEAMBOAT COMPANY, 44
BOSTON HARBOR, 162
BRAGG, 166 175-176 Braxton 76 Braxton West Point 1837 163 Gen 164 Letter To Lt Slemmer 165
BRANNAN, 69-70 Capt 72 John M 68
BRANSON, 374 David 373
BRAZIL, 365 Bahia 398
BRAZOS ISLAND, 203
BRAZOS SANTIAGO, 85 89 363 375-376 Date Of Occupation 94

BRAZOS SANTIAGO ISLAND, 373
BRECKINRIDGE, 270-272 274 278 336 Congressman 275 Disbands Confederate War Department 337 John C Secretary Of War 210 Recommends Davis Surrender 276 Secretary Of War 220 263-264
BRIDGES, Vulnerable To Fire 107
BRIDGEVILLE, 322
BRIERWOOD COTTON PLANTATION, 98
BRITAIN, Attacks Mexico 361
BRITISH, Ministry 128 Vessel Barracouta 399
BRITISH EMPIRE, Recognition Of Confederacy Considered Act Of War To US Government 129 Unaware Of Lincoln's Policy One War At A Time 130
BRITISH FOREIGN SECRETARY, 212
BRITTANY COAST, 396
BROOKLYN NAVY YARD, Commandant Of 171
BROWN, 57 59 174 176 Gov 56 Harvey West Point 18 18 173 Joseph E 51 333
BROWNSVILLE, 364 373-375
BRULE, 354
BRUSSELS, Asked For Diplomatic Recognition 128
BUCHANAN, 14 24 28 35-36 42 44-45 47-48 64 74 79 81 89 92 97 151 155 158 160 192 197 264 Does Not Support Fort Sumter 40 James 13 James Leaves Office 143 Perceived Lack Of Authority 38 President 11 131 Reply To Commissioners 37 Submits Question Of Civil War To Congress 38 Sympathy For Southerners 39
BUCHANAN'S, Cabinet 11

BUCHANAN ADMINISTRATION, 361
BUCKNER, 359 Simon B 357 Surrenders 343
BUELL, 26 38 Don Carlos 10 Major 24-25
BUFORD'S, Brigade 324
BULLOCH, 398 James D 396
BUREAU, Of Conscription 210
BURKESVILLE, 217 258
BURKEVILLE, 216 218 243 Grant's Headquarters 229
BUTTON, A J 323
CADDO, 369
CAHABA, 382
CAHAWBA, 314
CAHAWBA RIVER, 303-304 307
CAHAWBA VALLEY ROLLING MILLS, 303
CALIFORNIA, 86 362 371
CAMBRIDGE, Arsenal Supplies 161
CAMDEN, 340
CAMERON, 181 Corrupt And Incompetent 146 Secretary Of War 152 178 180 190 194 Simon B Secretary Of War 146
CAMP ADAMS, Date Of Occupation 94
CAMP COLORADO, Date Of Occupation 95
CAMP COOPER, Date Of Occupation 94
CAMP FISK, 382 384
CAMP HUDSON, Date Of Occupation 95
CAMP NAPOLEON, 367
CAMP SUMTER, 377 385
CAMP VERDE, 85 Date Of Occupation 95
CAMP WOOD, Date Of Occupation 95
CANADA, 172 Threat Of Incorporation Into US 129

CANBY, 293-294 296-297 302-303 307-308 310 312-313 357 359 364 E R S 208 368 Edward R S 309 Edward R S West Point 1835 292 Maj-gen Commanding Gen Military Division Of West Mississippi 282
CANBY'S, Army 300 Forces 343
CAPE FEAR RIVER, 77
CAPE GIRARDEAU, 345
CAPE HORN, 400
CAPE OF GOOD HOPE, 398
CAPE TOWN, 400
CAPITOL, 194 223 258 Construction Of New Dome Of 169
CAPITOL SQUARE, 260
CAROLINA, 335
CAROLINAS, 204 333
CAROLINE ISLANDS, 398
CARR, 294-295
CARR'S, Division 296
CARTER, Hall 247
CASH, John C 175
CASS, Lewis Secretary Of State 35 Resigns 35
CASTING, Rodman Method 116
CASTLE PICKNEY, 55 Muskets For 16
CASTLE PINCKNEY, 2-3 6 15 20 25 Captured Soldiers Were They Prisoners Of War 31 Date Of Occupation 93 Description Of 1 31 Held By South Carolina Militia 134 Militia Take Over 30 Munitions 31 Muskets For 19 Raising The Secessionist Flag 30 Reliable Men 17 Secessionists Capture 30 Security From Attack 7 Steamer Reconnoitered 25
CATAWBA, 288
CATAWBA RIVER, 336
CATFISH POINT, 298
CATHOLIC HOSPITAL, 357

CAVALRY, 294 301 13th Pennsylvania 268 16th New York 254 17th Connecticut 325 17th Illinois 345 1st East Florida 325 25th Alabama Battalion 312 43rd Virginia Battalion 246 4th Kentucky 330 7th Kentucky 330 Cherokee 369 Confederate 288 371 Corps 256-257 299 311 322-324 Eighth Ohio 251 Federal 336 Fifth Division 301 First Division 219 301 330 First Ohio 311 337 First Wisconsin 338 Fourth Division 301 Fourth Kentucky 315 Fourth Michigan 338 Fourth Missouri 356 Gillem's 278 Largest Force In American History 302 Scouts 293 Second 89 Second Division 301 Second US 87 Second US Texas 374-375 Seventh Division 299 Sixth Division 277 300 Third Colorado Regiment 370 Third Division 219 286 299 Thirty-third Virginia 252 Union 278 371 Union Search For Davis 337
CEDAR POINT, 295
CENTERVILLE, 304
CENTRAL, America 172
CHALK BLUFF, 345-346
CHALMERS, James R 304
CHAMBERLAIN, 242 Joshua L 241
CHAPEL HILL, 267
CHAPMAN, 250 Col 251 George H 249 William H 247
CHARLES TOWN, 202
CHARLESTON, 3 5-6 10 13-14 28 30 38 42 46-48 58 62 81 83 108 134 136-137 139-142 152 155 161 170 178 183 201-204 255 286 395 Garrison 211 Harbor 37 Harbor Navigation Lights Extinguished 42

CHARLESTON (cont)
  Institute Hall Convention
  Gathering Place 22 Sees
  Federals As Unwilling To Fight
  44 US District Court Grand
  Jury 20 US District Court
  Grand Jury Resignations 21
  Ways For Ships to Approach 2

CHARLESTON ARSENAL, 19
  Forty Muskets Removed 18
  Issuing Of Fixed Ammunition
  For Small-arms 3 Occupation
  Date 93 Return Of Muskets 20
CHARLESTON BAR, 171
CHARLESTON HARBOR, 151
  Command Of 42 Federal Orders
  To Hold Forts 25 Re-supplying
  Garrison 177
CHARLESTON LIGHTHOUSE, 185
CHARLOTTE, 263 267 276 279 284 288 336
CHARLOTTESVILLE, 217
CHASE, 66 168 Col 65 165 Salmon
  P 267 Salmon P Chief Justice
  290 Salmon P Secretary Of The
  Treasury 146 Secretary Of The
  Treasury 154 William H 64
CHATHAM ARTILLERY, 57
CHATTAHOOCHEE, 283 315
CHATTAHOOCHEE ARSENAL,
  Date Of Occupation 93
CHATTAHOOCHEE RIVER, 317 323
CHATTANOOGA, 203
CHEMUNG RIVER, 378
CHERBOURG, 398
CHESNUT, 188
CHESTNUT, Col 184 James 21
  James Jr 183
CHEW, Robert S 178
CHISOLM, A R 183
CHIVINGTON, John M 370
CHRISTIAN, 332-333

CHURCH, Ebenezer 303
CINCINNATI, 146
CITADEL ACADEMY, 32
CITY, Point 217
CITY POINT, Meeting 274
CIVIL WAR 38 51 66 Half Of
  Cannons Made At Richmond 116
CLANTON'S, Brigade 324
CLAPP'S FERRY, 316
CLARKE, Capt 356 J H 247
CLARKE'S HOTEL, 249
CLARKSVILLE, 202 340
CLAY, Clement C 392-393
CLOVER HILL TAVERN, 241
CLYDE, 392
COAST, Guard Revenue Cutter
  William Aiken Turned Over To
  South Carolina 30
COBB, 322 Gen 321 Howell 97 320
  Howell Secretary Of The
  Treasury 35 97 Resigns 35
COBB'S RANCH, 376
COCKSPUR ISLAND, 56
COEHORN, Mortars 295
COINS, English Sovereigns 122
  Five-franc Pieces 122 Mexican
  Doubloons 122 Napoleons 122
  Spanish Doubloons 122
COLBERT, Winchester 369
COLORADO, 371 Julesburg
  Attacked 370 Territory 370
COLORED ENGINEER
  REGIMENT, 96th US 293 97th
  US 293
COLORED TROOPS, 378-379 34th
  US 325 3rd US 325 332 335
  62nd US Infantry 373 376 62nd
  375 78th US Infantry 354 First
  Division US 296 Negro 25th
  Corps 223 Third US Cavalry
  355 US 213 313 US First
  Division 293
COLT, Revolvers 319

COLUMBIA, 204 208 211 245 255 277 308 379
COLUMBIANA IRON WORKS, 303
COLUMBUS, 204 263 299 302 315 317-318 322
COLUMBUS IRON WORKS, 319
COMMERCIAL SIDE-WHEELER, Star Of The West 40
COMMERCIAL VESSEL, Star Of The West 41
COMMISSIONERS, Reply With Legal Brief 38
COMMITTEE ON RELATIONS WITH SLAVEHOLDING STATES OF NORTH AMERICA, 22
COMPROMISE, Crittendens 132
CONDITIONS, Of Surrender Agreed To 239
CONFEDERACY, 2 51 53 58 73 97 104-105 116 139 191 194 211 217 228 311 361-362 Abandon Capital 221 Army Description 111 Article Vi Section 2 Relationship With Union States 97 Better Prepared For War 197 Capital Of 348 Changes To Command Structure 210 Chief Of The Quartermaster Bureau 117 Compensation Obligation To Federal Government For Property Seized 55 Copies Union War Articles 112 Cut In Half By Union Control Of Mississippi 107 Depended On European Recognition 128 Desire To Capture Fort Pickens 176 Does Not Manufacture Steel 106 Epitaph Died Of State Rights 109 Establishes Army 142 Establishes Constitution 142 Establishes Navy 142 Establishes New Nation 109

CONFEDERACY (cont) Form A Of Slave-holding States 23 Government 90 Gunpowder Needs 113 Iron Works Delivery 115 Leaders Assert Separation From Union Would Be Peaceable 120 Lincoln Allowing Them To Initiate War 177 Memphis Foundry Gained If Border States Join 115 Mission To Be Recognized By Britain 116 Mission To Trade Arms For Cotton 116 Munitions To Be Purchased From European Countries 116 Nashville Foundry Gained If Border States Join 115 Navy 111 Needs Friendly Indian Territory Relations 130 No Longer In Existence 335 339 Not Wanting Confrontation With Federal Government 101 Orders Surrender Of Fort Sumter 183 Population 196 Population Of North Ominous 198 Provides Financing For New Nation 142 Provisional Congress 142 149 Provisional Forces 140-141 Radical Changes In Slavery Considered 212 Relies On Borrowing 121 Request For Terms 203 Requests Admission Into Family Of Independent Nations 128 Selects Leaders 142 Southern Convention To Establish 23 Supplies Description 117 Take Forty-nine Federal Troops And Properties 92 Taxation Policies 120 Treasury Duties 119 Use Of Slaves As Soldiers Authorized 213 Using Slaves As Soldiers 214 Wants Fort Pickens And Fort Sumter 150

CONFEDERACY (cont)
   War Articles 112 War Not
Ended By Lee's Surrender 240
Without Money Credit Or
Arms 265
CONFEDERATE, 51 168
   Achievements 318 Army To Be
Disbanded 351 Attack On Fort
Sumter 187 Battle Success 192-
193 Blockade Runners 396
Building Modern Weaponry
319 Cabinet Meets For Last
Time 336 Capital 202 Capital
Surrendered 315 Capitol
Danville 243 Capital Taken By
Union 224 Casualties 298 324
Chief Of The Commissary
Bureau 117 Commander 156
Commissioner Of Exchange 380
Congress 121 139 210 212-213
308 Congress Adjourns For
Last Time 214 Congress
Adjourns 211 Congress
Declares State Of War 195
Congress Military Powers 103
Congress Passes Resolution To
Obtain Fort Sumter And
Pickens 139 Congress Power
102 Congress Power To
Declare War 244 Congress
Told Lincoln Requires
Unconditional Submission 209
Constitution 103 114 213 244
Constitution Differences From
US Constitution 102
Constitution Regular Officers
Appointed 211 Constitution Use
Of US Bill Of Rights 104
Convention/congress 119
Forces 91 219 284 336
Government 99 123 309 325
Government Belief That Britain
Would Aid 105 Government
Belief That France Would Aid
105

CONFEDERATE (cont)
   Government Cuts Off Mail
Service To Fort Sumter 181
Government Foreign Countries
Dependent On For Cotton 105
Government Formation 66
Government Moves To North
Carolina 245 Government Not
Recognized By US 269
Government Not Recognized
By US Government 178
Government Organizing 134
Government Out Of
Communication With Army 267
Government Overthrow Of 399
Government Will Not Interfere
With Existing Contracts With
U S Government 126 Gunboats
295 Lines 259 Losses 201-204
Militiamen Enlisted For Twelve
Months 114 Money 259 Naval
Forces 298 Navy Organization
118 Ordnance Bureau Unable
To Use Virginia Weapons 116
Percent Of Officers Who Left
The Union Forces 13 Post
Office 103 Prisoners 293 321
Prisoners Released 390
Proposal 352 Provisional Army
Description 114 Provisional
Congress 109 Provisional
Constitution 97-98 Refugees
Flee To Mexico 365 Secretary
Of Navy 66 Seize Federal
Money 119 States 99 103-104
121 185 209 368 States
Government Terms Of
Surrender 358 States Of
America 91 Strategy 216
Surrender 271-273 Treasure
Rumors Of 286 Treasury 124
Treasury Estimates Property
Values 118 Treasury Removed
From Capital 221 Troops 328

CONFEDERATE (cont)
   Volunteers Enlisted For
   Duration Of War 114
   Volunteers Service And
   Description 110 War
   Department 113 119 War
   Department Disbanded 337
   War Materials Exempt Reasons
   121
CONFEDERATE DIPLOMACY,
   128 Commissioners Notify
   Foreign Leaders of Secession
   128 Commissioners To
   Washington 148 Important
   Matters Affecting European
   Actions 129 Issues Discussed
   With Lincoln 148 Negotiate
   Treaty Of Friendship
   Commerce And Navigation 128
   US Must Recognize
   Confederacy 149
CONFEDERATE DISTRICT OF,
   Alabama 293 East Louisiana
   293 Mississippi 293
CONFEDERATE POSTAL
   SERVICE, Challenges 125
   Hires US Postal Employees 125
   Importance Of 124 Operation
   Described 125 Railroads
   Reducing Cost 126 Rate
   Changes 126 Self-sustaining 127
   Source Of Stamps 127
CONFEDERATE STATES OF
   AMERICA, 98
CONFEDERATED, Southern
   Nation 96
CONFEDERATES, 106 163 166
   169 183-184 186 190 Fire On
   US Schooner 179
CONGER, E J 254
CONGRESS, 80 92 141 286 402
   Passes An Act To Authorize
   The Issue Of Treasury Notes
   123

CONGRESSIONAL, Delegation
   161
CONNECTICUT, 35 113 146
CONNELLY, W E 356
CONSTITUTION, 12 196 Of The
   US 83
CONSTITUTIONAL, Right To
   Secede 11
CONVENTION, To Act As
   Congress 98
COOK, Col 355
COOPER, 6 8-9 11 19 41 71-72 80
   85 137-138 Col Suggestions To
   Cut War Department 159 Gen
   269 379 Samuel 2 Samuel West
   Point 1820 112 Suggestions To
   Cut War Department 160
COOPER RIVER, 30
COPENHAGEN, 396
CORBETT, Boston 254
CORPS, 10th 255 286 325 13th 292-
   295 363 14th 256 258 15th 256
   16th 292 294-295 298 17th 256
   19th 325 20th 256 23rd 255 286
   24th 220 236 25th 363 2nd 217
   220-221 226-227 4th 363 5th
   217-219 226 236 242 6th 226-
   227 9th 220 Cavalry 256 311
   Confederate Third 220 First
   226 Gibbon's 24th 228 Gordon's
   228 Gordon's Second 235
   Griffen's 5th 228 Humphrey's
   2nd 228 Longstreet's 228
   Longstreet's First 235 Negro
   25th 223 Penscola 294 Second
   236 Smith's 16th 299 Third 226
   Wright's 6th 228
CORPS OF ENGINEERS, 1 5 10-
   11 13 17 30-31 58 67-68 141
   158 324 Office 34
CORPUS CHRISTI, 203
COSTE, N L 30
COTTON, Britain Sells To New
   England Mills For 60 Cents Per
   Pound 117

COTTON (cont)
  Important For Foreign Trade
    106 Important To British
    Ecomony 129 In Warehouses Of
    Britain 116 Purchased At 14
    Cents Per Pound 116 States 51
    172 States Gist Requests
    Secession 21 Tax Described 121
    Tax Did Not Meet Needs 122
COURT, Martial Of Armstrong 66
COURTS, New Discussed 52
CRAB BOTTOM, 252
CRAIG, 4 15 Col 14 60 H K 3
CRANE, Lt 355
CRAVEN, T A 69
CRAWFORD, Martin 148 Samuel
  W 189
CRIMEAN WAR, 98
CRITTENDEN, Senator Proposals
  131
CRITTENDEN PLAN, Voted On
  143
CROXTON, 307 311 323-324 Gen
  303 John T 301
CROXTON'S, Brigade 304 306 313-
  314 322
CS ARSENAL, 319
CUBA, 86 172 342 360 365 Captain
  General Of 397
CUMBERLAND COURT HOUSE,
  228
CUMBERLAND SOUND, 61
CUMMING, Alfred 58
CUMMINGS POINT, 32 139 141
  152 157 179 182 Armaments
  138 183
CUNNINGHAM, John 33
  Occupation Of US Arsenal 34
CURRENCY, States Even Counties
  And Cities Each Print Own
  Currency 123
CURTIN, Andrew 193
CUSTER, Cavalry Division 226
  George A 363 George A Third
  Cavalry Division 219

CUSTOMS, Collectors Remained
  But Had To Reduce Force By
  Half 121 Duties Collection Of
  154 Houses Taken By
  Secessionists 95
CUTTER, Ordered 39
DAKOTA, Territory 371
DALGREN, Gun 183
DANA, Charles A 393 N J T 344
DANA-TURNER TRUCE,
  Described 344
DANISH, Navy 396
DANNELLY'S MILLS, 295
DANVILLE, 208 222 226 228 245
  258 260 262-263 399 New
  Confederate Capitol 243
DANVILLE-GREENSBORO
  ROAD, 278
DARDINGKILLER, Sgt 78
DART, Henry 76
DARTMOUTH COLLEGE, 146
DAUPHIN ISLAND, 75 77 292
DAVIS, 100-102 112-114 116-117
  119 139-141 149 177 195 210-
  212 215 232 242 260-265 268
  270-271 276 278-280 336 339
  345-346 348 360 379-380 397
  399 C W 345 Captured 338
  Faults Of 99 Issued
  Proclamation 243 Jeff 269 272
  286 Jefferson 5 49 77 148 158
  244 293 299 330 351 392-394
  Jefferson C 16 Jefferson
  President Of The Confederacy
  89 Jefferson Provisional
  President 98 Jefferson Secretary
  Of War 98 Jefferson Touches
  On Possibility Of War 99
  Jefferson US Senator 98
  Jefferson US Senator Appointed
  Maj-gen Of State Army 50
  Jefferson West Point 1828 98
  Mrs 338 392 Now General-in-
  chief 245 President 209 240

DAVIS (cont)
   President Inaugural Address
     109 Reunited With Wife 337
   Sen 159
DAYTON, William L Ambassador
   To France 147
DEATONVILLE, 226
DEBUSSY, 20
DECATUR, 202
DECLARATION, Of War 245
DECLARATION OF THE
   IMMEDIATE CAUSES
   WHICH INDUCE AND
   JUSTIFY THE SECESSION
   OF SOUTH CAROLINA
   FROM THE FEDERAL
   UNION, 24
DELAWARE, 250 Refuse To Call
   Convention 131 Slave State In
   Union 197
DEMOCRATIC, Party Divided
   Nominating Conventions 49
DEPARTMENT, Of Alabama 308
   Of East Tennessee 308 Of
   Mississippi 308 Of Texas 88 Of
   The South 324 326 329 333
DEPARTMENT OF MISSOURI,
   346
DEPARTMENT OF RICHMOND,
   Rolls 209
DEPARTMENT OF THE GULF,
   388
DEPARTMENT OF THE
   MISSOURI, 345
DEPARTMENT OF VIRGINIA,
   387
DERBY, Elias Hasket 44 Suggestion
   For Improvement Of Battle
   Vessels 44-45
DERUSSY, 17-19 69 Col 16 R E 10
DESAUSSURE, 186 Lt Col 179
   Wilmot G 31
DESMARAIS, Miguel 372
DEVIN, Thomas C 219
DICKINSON, Julian G 338

DIEHL, Patricia S 13
DINWIDDIE COURT HOUSE,
   218
DISCUSSIONS, Between
   Secessionists And The President
   Cause Delay 49
DISTRICT OF COLUMBIA, 83
   380
DIX, John A 36
DOAKSVILLE, 369 Choctaw
   Capital 368
DODGE, 346 352-353 Gen 355 371
   Granville M 345
DOHERTY, Edward P 254
DOLLARS, Mexican 122 U S 122
DONEGAL, 400
DOUBLEDAY, 31 Abner 26
DOUGLAS, Henry 60
DRAFT, Reply To Commissioners
   37
DRY TORTUGAS, 67 176
DRY TORTUGAS HARBOR, 174
DUBLIN, 338
DUCY OF WURTTEMBERG, 101
DUNN, Col 60
DURHAM STATION, 266 268 272
   282 328
EAGLE PASS, 365
EARLY, Jubal A 217
EASTPORT, 300
ECONOMY, Southern Description
   118
EDGAR, Lt 372
EDISTO ISLAND, 202
EGGLESTON, B B 311
ELLIS, 78-79 John W 77 W J 333
ELYTON, 303 323
ELZEY, Arnold 58
EMANCIPATION
   PROCLAMATION, 287 401
EMPRESS, Carlota Installed In
   Mexico City 362
ENGINEER BRIGADE, 292

ENGLAND, 183 395 400
 Birkenhead 396 Slavery
 Abolished 116
ENGLISH, Engineer Captured 304
 Volunteers 398
ETOWAH CREEK, 324
EUFAULA, 299
EUROPE, 212 360
EUROPEAN, Diplomats 361
 Nations 108
EVANS, Gov 370 John 370
EWELL, 209 227 229 Richard S 226
FALMOUTH, 202
FARMINGTON, 354
FARMVILLE, 226-227 230 235 237
FARRAGUT, David G 40
FARRAND, Edward 63 298
FAUQUIER COUNTY, 250-251
FAYETTEVILLE, 79 202 204 208
FEDERAL, Attack 219 Authorities 223 Forces 26 163 217 227 324 Forces Casualties 220 Property Right To Defend 11 Sub-treasuries And Mints Available To The Confederacy 119
FEDERALS, 186
FIVE FORKS, 217-218
FLAG, American 43 179 Confederate 400 Dixie Rangers 324 Fort Tyler Garrison West Point 324 Montgomery True Blue 324 Of Truce 230 320-321 357 Palmetto 30-31 324 Stars And Stripes 190-191 Truce 234 247 Union 224 US 30 33 59 178-179 225 267 324 331 342 US Garrison 324 US Raised Over Raleigh 261
FLANAGIN, Harris 350
FLAT SHOALS, 323
FLINT RIVER, 319 323
FLORIDA, 21 50-51 70 100 108 148 163 173-174 191 194 210 244 283 324 328-329 331 333-334 338 360 Amelia Island 202

FLORIDA (cont)
 And Alabama To Seize Installations 62 And Civil Problems Between Fishermen And State 72 Apalachicola Arsenal Seized 60 Chattahoochee 60 Confederate District Of 325 Dates Of Occupation 93 District Of 327 334 Dry Tortugas 394 Federal Forts At The Keys 67 Forces 61 Fort Clinch 57 Fort Jefferson 169 Forts Seized 68 Gov Of 68 Gov Seizes US Property 71 Lighthouses 67 Mail Service Through Havanna 69 Militia 63 65 Monroe County And The Fishery 70 Resistance To Republican President 68 Saint Augustine 60 Seceded 71 Secession 63 State Of War With The US 64 Surrenders Completed In June 285 Tallahassee 204 Union District Of 325 Will Secede From Federal Gov 69
FLOYD, 5 16 20 24 26 28 36 39 79 Approves Authorization Of Muskets 15 Asked For Resignation 35 John B Secretary Of War 4 35 Secretary 14 Secretary Of War 116 159 Telegraph To Anderson 28
FOOTE, Andrew H Commandant Of The Brooklyn Navy Yard 171
FORD, 374 John S 373
FORD'S DEPOT, 218
FORD'S THEATRE, 268
FORREST, 304-307 314 Farewell To The Troops 310 Nathan B 303
FORSYTH, John 148
FORT ALEXIS, 295

FORT BARRANCAS, 61-62 Date Of Occupation 93
FORT BEAUREGARD, Surrendered 201
FORT BELKNAP, Date Of Occupation 95
FORT BLAKELY, 292 294-296
FORT BLISS, 91 Date Of Occupation 95
FORT BROWN, 90 Date Of Occupation 95
FORT CASWELL, 77-79
FORT CHADBOURNE, Date Of Occupation 95
FORT CLARK, 85 201 Date Of Occupation 95
FORT CLINCH, 57 Date Of Occupation 93 Description Of 61
FORT DAVIS, 91 Date Of Occupation 95
FORT DEFIANCE, 202
FORT DELAWARE, 389 392
FORT DONELSON, 202
FORT DUNCAN, 90 Date Of Occupation 95
FORT ESPERANZA, 203
FORT FISHER, 204 395
FORT GAINES, 75 203 Date Of Occupation 94
FORT GIBSON, 367 371
FORT GREGG, 220
FORT HATTERAS, 201
FORT HEIMAN, 202
FORT HENRY, 202
FORT INDEPENDENCE, 162 At Boston 71
FORT INGE, Date Of Occupation 95
FORT JACKSON, 76 202 Date Of Occupation 94
FORT JACKSON DATE, Of Occupation 93

FORT JEFFERSON, 68-69 71 173-174 Remains In Federal Hands 73
FORT JOHNSON, 2 5 47 79 141 185 Armaments 138 Capture Description 78 Date Of Occupation 93 Description Of 1 32 Held By South Carolina Militia 134 Sessionists Capture 32 Transfer Of Wives And Children To 26
FORT JOHNSTON, 136
FORT LANCASTER, Date Of Occupation 95
FORT MACOMB, Date Of Occupation 94
FORT MACON, 202
FORT MARION, Date Of Occupation 93 Description Of 60 Possession Of 61
FORT MASON, 87 Date Of Occupation 95
FORT MASSACHUSETTS, 77 Date Of Occupation 94
FORT MCHENRY, 194
FORT MCINTOSH, 90 Date Of Occupation 95
FORT MCREE, 61 Date Of Occupation 93
FORT MONROE, 26 40 116 392-393
FORT MORGAN, 75 204 Date Of Occupation 94
FORT MORRIS, Armaments 138
FORT MOULTRIE, 2 4-5 7 9 20 24 36 42 44 55 139 141 152 185 Abandonment Of 28 Arms Trained On Steamer 27 Barracks Destroyed By US 190 Date Of Occupation 93 Defence Against Attack 26 Description Of 1 6 Fires On Star Of The West 43 Guns Aimed At Fort Sumter 138 Held By South Carolina Militia 134

THE BEGINNING AND THE END. 433

FORT MOULTRIE (cont)
Instructions From War
Department 10 Living
Conditions 47 Movement From
With No Orders 28
Reminiscence Of Escape To
Fort Sumter 27 Secessionists
Capture 31 Sessionists Capture
32 Strengthening Of 8 Work
Being Done 19
FORT MOUTRIE, 179
FORT PICKENS, 61 100 150 163
165-168 170-171 175 178 325
Denies Confederacy The
Pensacola Harbor 176
Description Of 62-63 Federal
Possession Alarms Gov Moore
65 Reinforcement Advocated
169 Relief Of 173 Remains In
Union Hands During Civil War
66
FORT PIKE, 76 Date Of
Occupation 94
FORT POWELL, 203
FORT PULASKI, 8 56 58 202 324
Date Of Occupation 93 In
Federal Hands 57 Occupied By
Georgia Troops 57
FORT QUITMAN, 91 Date Of
Occupation 95
FORT SAINT PHILIP, 76 203 Date
Of Occupation 94
FORT SMITH, 203
FORT STEDMAN, 217
FORT STOCKTON, Date Of
Occupation 95
FORT SUMTER, 2-3 5 8-9 24 27-
28 31 35 39 41 44 46-47 56 81-
82 90 100 115 118 123 132 134
136 138 140-141 149 151-152
155 163 166-172 175 178 182
186 190-191 193 195 197 201
203 267 298 Ammunition And
Armament 9 Attacked By
Confederacy 185

FORT SUMTER (cont)
Authorization Of Forty
Muskets To Engineer Officer 14
Buchanan Duty To Defend 38
Condition Of 6 Considerations
For Withdrawing From 153
Description Of 1 Fails To
Protect The Star Of The West
43 Importance 25 Instructions
From War Department 10
Light Visible 42 Movement
From Fort Moultrie With No
Orders 29 Munitions 26
Muskets For 16 19 Nightly
Approaches Signifying Hostile
Intent 26 No Mail Service
Allowed 181 Offensive
Capabilities 139 Plans To Blow
Up If Taken 20 Re-
Enforcements 40 Reliable Men
17 Report Requesting Re-
enforcements 150 Security
From Attack 7 Steamer
Reconnoitered 25
Strengthening Of 19 Supplies
Provided By South Carolina
Gov 138 Surrender 188-189
Surrender Of 54 177 Surrender
Ordered By Confederacy 183
Surrendered 176 Surrendered
With No Loss Of Life 190 Title
Held By US 83 Unable To
Purchase Supplies 42 Women
And Child Removed 137
Women And Children Confined
To The Fort 136 Workmen
And Their Attitude 15
FORT TAYLOR, 68 71-72 174
Remains In Federal Hands 73
Targeted After Secession 69
FORT THOMAS, Jefferson 67
FORT TOWSON, 369
FORT TWIGGS, 77
FORT WALKER, 201
FORT WARD, 331

FORT WARREN, 162 392
FORT WHITWORTH, 220
FORT WINTHROP, 162
FORT ZACHARY, Taylor 67
FORTS, Defense Of 5 Federal
  Defense Of 12 Original Purpose
  2 Sixty-one Federal In 1861 55
FOSTER, 10-11 16-20 28 30 138-
  139 157 Capt 8 Describes Event
  Inside Fort Sumter 186-187
  John G 5
FOUNDRY, Bellona 116
FOUR-MILE BRIDGE, 382
FOUR-YEAR WAR, 373
FOURTH, Separate Brigade 325
  330
FOX, 153 155 172 177-178 186 Capt
  181 G V 171 Gustavus V Asst
  Secretary Of The Navy 151 Mr
  180 182 Naval
  Recommendations To Lincoln
  152
FOX'S, Squadron 185
FOX'S EXPEDITION, 171
FRANCE, 172 365 Attacks Mexico
  361 Occupies Mexico City 362
FRANKFORT ARSENAL, 115
FRANKLIN, 203
FRASER COMPANY, 183
FRASER TRENHOLM AND CO,
  117
FREDERICKSBURG, 202
FREE, Negroes 196
FREEMAN, As Hired Servants 287
FRENCH, 348 397 Coast 398
  Government 396
FRENCH REVOLUTION, 360
FRIGATE, USS Niagara 396 USS
  Sabine 163 USS Sacramento 396
FUCH'S BATTERY, 225
FUNCHAL, 398
GAINESVILLE, 310 346
GALVESTON, 89 91 340 360 363
  396
GARDEN KEY, 67

GARDNER, Col 3-4 John L 2 5
GARRARD, 294
GARRARD'S, Division 297
GARRETT, Richard 254
GAY, Joe 252
GENERAL, Assembly 161
GENERAL ORDERS NO 5, 89
GEORGIA, 5 35 50-51 53 55-57 59
  84 97 101 107-108 148 191 194
  208 210 244 283 288 302 307
  320 323-325 333 336-337
  Augusta 107 191 Augusta
  Arsenal Movement Of Troops
  To 34 Cartersville 107
  Dahlonega 60 119 Dates Of
  Occupation 93 First Volunteer
  Regiment 57 Fort Pulaski 202
  Forts Seized 68 Importance To
  Confederacy 52 Lighthouses
  Undisturbed 60 Militia 57
  Milledgeville 204 Rome 366
  Rome Foundry 115 Secedes 59
  University 100 Votes To Secede
  58 West Point 315
GEORGIA CAMP, 386
GERMAN, Lithographer Engraved
  Plates And Printed On
  Smuggled Stock 123
GERMANY, 101
GETTYSBURG, 242
GIBBON, 239 Gen 241
GIBBONS, John 220
GIBBS, George C 327
GIBSON, Randall L 294
GILLEM, Alvan C 277
GILLMORE, 325 329 331 333-334
  Maj-gen 328 Quincy A West
  Point 1849 324
GILMAN, Jeremiah H 62 Lt 63
GIRARD, 316
GIST, 29 William H 21
GLASGOW, 398
GOLD, And Silver Sent To Europe
  To Buy War Materials 122

GOLD (cont)
   And Silver Shortage Because Used For War Materials 122
GOLDSBORO, 204 215 255-256
GORDON, 236 239 242 Gen 226 John B Launches Night Attack 217
GORDON'S, Corps 228
GORGAS, Josiah West Point 1845 115
GOSPORT NAVY YARD, Largest Source Of Armaments 116
GOVERNMENT, 166 334 Federal 38 Of The United States 231 Transports 241 Wishing To Keep Harbor 42
GOVERNOR'S ISLAND, 40
GRAFTON, 201
GRAHAM, 259 William A 258
GRANGER, 294 298 312 Gordon 292 364
GRANT, 208 215-216 220-221 225 229 232-236 241-243 250-251 256 258 269-271 275 277 279 281 286 290-292 302 311 325 337 341 343 349 362-365 379-381 383 387-389 391-392 Gen 266 Letter To Lee 230 Letter To Lee Conditions Of Surrender 231 Letter To Sherman 217 Lt Gen 224 Lt-gen 346 U S 240 Ulysses S Orders Advance Of Troops 207 Writes Out Terms 237-238
GRAVELLY SPRINGS, 300
GREAT BRITAIN, 128 172
GREENBRIER RIVER, 252
GREENSBORO, 217 260-263 267-268 271 278 284-286 288 326 381
GREENSBOROUGH, 281 283
GREENVILLE, 299
GREGG, Maxcy 136
GRIERSON, 294 Benjamin H 293 Gen 299

GRIFFIN, 239
GUARD BOAT, General Clinch 26 Nina 26
GUERILLA WARFARE, 232
GULF, Preparations For A Strong Defense Of 71
GULF COAST, 88
GULF OF MEXICO, 61 67 69 91 108 331 342 396 Safety Of Seceding States 65
GULFPORT, 77
GUNBOAT, Hollyhock 343 Spray 331 US 365
GUNBOATS, Union 385 396
HAINAN'S PISTOL FACTORY, 319
HALLECK, 275-276 289 386 392-393 Henry W 247 381
HAMMOND, James H 21
HAMPTON, 201 266-267 285 Gen 259 Wade 257
HAMPTON'S, Cavalry 268
HAMPTON ROADS, 209 233 235 398
HANCHETT, Capt 382
HANCOCK, 247-250 Winfield S 246
HAPSURG, 361
HARDEE, 260 Gen 259 William J 257
HARDEN, Henry 338
HARDING, Capt 252
HARPER'S FERRY ARSENAL, 114
HARPERS FERRY, 201-202 Arsenal 195
HARRISBURG, 193-194 345
HARRISON, William H Authorized To Surrender Raleigh 260
HARRISONBURG, 202
HARTSUFF, 285 William 284
HASKINS, Joseph 76
HATCH, 387 Col 384 Edward 301 L M Quartermaster-gen 137 Reuben B 383
HATCHER'S RUN, 216

HAVANA, 67 72 166 244 396-397
HAWKINS, 294 John P 293
HAYNE, 49 81-82 Isaac W 46 Sent To Washington 47
HAYNES BLUFF, 203
HAZARD POWDER COMPANY, 113
HENDERSON, 383 H A M 382
HENDERSONVILLE, 278
HENDRICK, John J 78
HERED'S PLACE, 354
HEROLD, Captured 254 David E 394 David E Reward Posted 253
HIGH BRIDGE, 227
HIGH POINT, 262
HILDERBRAND, 354
HILL, 226 A P 220 Benjamin J 323
HILLSBORO, 267-268 271 284 288
HILTON HEAD, 325-326
HILTON HEAD ISLAND, 201 324
HIS, Excellency The Commander-in-chief 162
HITCHCOCK, 246 381 Henry 275
HOFFMAN, 389 Gen 391 William 87 385
HOLDEN, William H 291
HOLT, 82 Joseph Postmaster-gen 35 Secretary 65 81 89 Secretary Of War 59 150 Suggestions In Reply To Commissioners 37
HOOD, 208 John B 207 360 Sgt 355
HOPEFIELD, 384
HOUGH, Daniel 190
HOUSTON, 340 348 357 Sam 52 85
HOWARD, Oliver O 256
HUBBARD, 314
HUGER, Benjamin 4 Col 9 16 18
HUMPHREY, Andrew A 220
HUMPHREYS, 4 20 34 Capt 18 33 Concerned Over Safety Of Men 34 F C 3
HUNT, Capt 73 174 E B 68
HUNTERSVILLE, 252
HUNTSVILLE, 100 202

HUSE, Caleb West Point 117
ILLINOIS, 100 253 Ratifies Amendment 143
INDEPENDENT, State 196
INDIAN, Hostilities On The Plains 158 Ta-ker-taw-ker 366 Territory 359 366 368
INDIAN OCEAN, 400
INDIAN TERRITORY, Description 130
INDIANA, 147 330 384
INDIANOLA, 89-90
INDIANS, 370 Arapaho Tribe Attacked 370 Cherokee Become Refugees 366 Cherokee Cavalry 369 Cherokees 341 367 Cheyenne Tribe Attacked 370 Chickasaws 341 366-367 369 Choctaw 369 Choctaw Nation Surrenders 368 Choctaws 341 366-367 Comanche 369 Comanches 367 Confederate 366 369 Confederate And Plains Meet At Camp Napoleon 367 Creeks 366 369 Five Nations 366 Join Confederate Army 130 Muscogees 367 Navajo 372 Osages 366-367 369 Plains 366-367 Reserve 369 Reserve Caddos 367 Resolve To Be Bound By Brethren Of Southern States 130 Seminoles 366-367 369 Support Confederate States 366 Surrender 369
INDIANS FIVE CIVILIZED TRIBES, Cherokees 130 Chickasaws 130 Choctaws 130 Creeks 130 Seminoles 130
INFANTRY, 11th US 348 17th Indiana Mounted 320 20th Maine 242 17th Regiment 33 32nd Regiment 32-33 34th Indiana 374-375 48th Alabama 323 99th Illinois 368

INFANTRY (cont)
  Allentown's Allen 194 Defense
  Of Bays And Rivers 33 Eighth
  89 Eighth Company A US 87
  Eighth Iowa 296 First 89 First
  Company 1 US 87 First
  Regiment 32 First US 85
  Lightning Brigade 301 National
  Light 193 Ninth US 41
  Oglethorpe 58 Seventh US 194
  Sixth Massachusetts Volunteer
  Three Soldiers Killed 194 The
  German Rifles 32 Third 89
  Union Light 33 Washington
  Light 30 Zouave Cadets 32
INSPECTOR-GEN, 313
IRON-CLAD RAM, CSS Stonewall
  396 Jackson 319
IRWINVILLE, 338
ISLAND, Number Ten 202
ISLAND OF MADEIRA, 398
ISSUANCE, Of Stocks And Bonds
  To Earn Money 121
JACKSON, 50 59 203 203 Henry R
  58 William H 304
JACKSONPORT, 346-347
JACKSONVILLE, 108 202 325 327-328
JACKSONVILLE CLARION
  UNION, 335
JAMES, George S 185
JAMES ISLAND, 1 32 138 141
JAMES RIVER, 116 222 229
JAMES RIVER CANAL, 217 251
JAMESTOWN, 262
JAMISON, David F 22 David F
  Palmetto Republic Secretary Of
  War 136 Secretary 137
JAPAN, 397
JEFFERSON, 210 Thomas 157
JEFFERSON BARRACKS, 384
JETERSVILLE, 226
JOHNSON, Andrew Presidential
  Oath Of Office 267 Joseph Jr 32
  New President 278-279

JOHNSON (cont)
  President 291 338 363 390 392
  President Proclaims Naval
  Blockade At An End 395
JOHNSON'S, Surrender 337
JOHNSTON, 209 211 215-216 256-257 259 261-262 264-268 270-272 276 278 280 283-284 307 314 322 326 341 349 357 373 395 Albert S 112
  Cavalry Moving In The
  Carolinas And Georgia 288 Gen
  243 275 279 282 285 310 Joseph
  E 112 208 210 255 281 M E 312
  Surrender Of 308 367 397 West
  Point 1829 269
JOHNSTON'S, Army 225 236 249
  251 258 260 263 277 335
  Surrender 328
JOHNSTON-SHERMAN
  AGREEMENT, 333
JOHNSTON-SHERMAN
  ARMISTICE, 324
JOHNSTON-SHERMAN TRUCE,
  343-344
JONES, 326-329 331-332 Charles A
  375 Gen 335 Robert M 369 S B
  354 Samuel 325 Surrender At
  Tallahassee 330
JOSEPH, Franz 361
JOSEPH R ANDERSON AND
  COMPANY, 115
JUAREZ, 363 365 Benito 361
  Defeated 362
KANSAS, 356 366 371
KANSAS CITY, 365
KENTUCKY, 5 35 98 250 263 271
  336 356 384 388 Provides
  Regiments To Confederacy 197
  Refuse To Call Convention 131
  Slave State In Union 197
KERNS, 384 W F 383
KERSHAW, Joseph B 227

KEY WEST, 68 70-71 166 169 174
    176 Barracks Built By US Army
    67
KEYES, Erasmus D 170
KILPATRICK, 260-261 266 Gen
    259 H Judson 256 Judson 299
KILPATRICK'S, Cavalry 268
KING, Horatio Postmaster-gen
    Replaces Holt 35
KING'S STORE, 322
KIRBY-SMITH, 209 336 341-343
    348-349 351-352 357 359-360
    364-365 395 E 368 Edmund 208
    Gen 243-244 340 Published
    Address 347 Surrender Of 367
    Surrenders 362
KIRBY-SMITH'S, Army 212 373
KIRKWOOD HOTEL, 267
KNIGHTS OF THE GOLDEN
    CIRCLE, 86
KNIPE, Joseph F 299
KNOXVILLE, 277
LA TURPENTINO, 372
LABADIERVILLE, 354
LAGRANGE, 315 324 Oscar H 301
LAGRANGE'S, Brigade 304 313-
    314
LAKE CITY, 326-327 332
LAKE GREEN, 90
LAKE PONTCHARTRAIN, 76
LAKE VERRET, 354
LAMON, 181 Col 180 Ward
    Unauthorized Remarks 155
LANDRY, 354
LANIER HOTEL, 322
LAREDO, 363
LAWRENCE, 356
LAWTON, A R 57
LEA HARBOR, 398
LEE, 188 208-209 213 217 220 226
    228 230-231 233-234 237-238
    241 243 245 247 256 258 271
    277-278 306 308 312 322 357
    369 373 395 Capt 184 Custis
    227 Decides To Surrender 232

LEE (cont)
    Fitzhugh 218-219 236 Gen 235
    249-250 261-262 266 269 279
    310 346 Gen Surrender Of 350
    Letter To Davis 215 R E 218
    227 R E Letter To Davis 242
    Robert E 87 112 207 224 240
    Robert E Appointed To Fort
    Pulaski 56 Robert E General In
    Chief 210 Robert E Lt Corps Of
    Engineers 56 Robert E West
    Point 1829 56 S D 257 Stephen
    D 183 Surrender 246 252-253
    259 324 326 341 343 349
    Surrender Of 297 314 367 397
    399 Surrenders 347 W H F 218
LEE'S, Army 218 225 253 260 263
    Army Holds Richmond 216
    Defeat 264
LEE-GRANT, Terms 280
LEESBURG, 202
LEOPOLD, King Of Belgium 361
LEVY, William M 307
LEWISTOWN, 194
LEWISVILLE, 340
LEXINGTON, 270
LIBBY PRISON, 387
LIDDELL, Saint John R 296
LINCOLN, 21 30 51-52 79 147 150-
    155 160 166 169-173 176-178
    181 233 247 271 278 287 300
    311 342 388 401 Abraham 100
    195 394 Abraham Calls Forth
    The Militia 191 Abraham
    Inaugural Address 143
    Abraham Inaugural Address
    144-146 Abraham Inaugurated
    143 Administration 142 180 197
    And Political Problem 157 As
    Cause Of War 23 Assassination
    Of 339 Assembles Both Houses
    Of Congress 192 Death Of 253
    Declares Blockade Of The
    Confederate Court 108

LINCOLN (cont)
  Emotional Reaction To The
    Election Of 56 Fears Support Of
    Confederate Government 147
    First State Dinner 167
    Inauguration 53 Nomination Of
    361 One War At A Time Policy
    130 Orders Naval Blockade 194
    Policy Of Leniency Toward
    South 274 President 209 224
    256 390 President Assassination
    337 345 392 President Death Of
    267-268 270 276 324 President-
    elect 132 Problems With
    Republican Majority 148
    Refuses To See The
    Commissioners 149 Threat To
    British Empire Regarding
    Canada 129 Wish To Preserve
    The Union 23
LISBON, 396
LITTLE ROCK, 79 203 343 345
LITTLE ROCK ARSENAL, Date
  Of Occupation 94
LIVERPOOL, 183 398 400
LOMAX, Col 63
LONDON, 117 147 Asked For
  Diplomatic Recognition 128
LONDON ARMORY COMPANY,
  117
LONG, 305 313 Eli 301 Gen 303
LONGSTREET, 227 231-232 234
  236 239 James 226
LOOTING, Of Commissary
  Warehouses 222
LOUDOUN COUNTY, 250
LOUISIANA, 70 75 90 101 107 148
  191 194 203 348 350 355 359
  365 385 Alexandria 203 Baton
  Rouge 52 203 Dates Of
  Occupation 94 Declares The
  Union To Be Dissolved 52 Free
  And Independent State 52
  Grays 76 Guards 76 Legion 76

LOUISIANA (cont)
  Ordinance Of Immediate
    Secession 52 Shreveport 340
LOUISIANA MILITARY
  ACADEMY, 269
LOUISVILLE, 357
LUCAS, 294 Thomas J 293
LURAY, 202
LUXTON, 355 J M 355
LYNCHBURG, 208 216 226-228
  236-237 278
MACON, 57 204 263 284 299 320-
  322 324 326 328 330 332 337-
  338 377 385 Destruction Of
  Ammunition 311
MAFFITT CHANNEL, 2 138
MAGEE'S FARM, 307
MAGRATH, Andrew G 21 46
MAGRUDER, 364-365 Gen 396
  John B Published Address 348
MAIN SHIP CHANNEL, 2 32 179
  Partially Blocked 46
MAINE, 35
MALLORY, 118 264 335 Secretary
  Of Navy 337 Secretary Of State
  263 Sen 165 Stephen 66 Stephen
  R 100 Stephen R Secretary Of
  Navy 100
MANASSAS, 202
MANIFEST DESTINY, 372
MANN, A Dudley 128
MARCH TO THE SEA, 208
MARSHALL, 249 350
MARTIAL, Law 334
MARTINSBURG, 201-202
MARTS, Joseph 179
MARYLAND, 35 48 58 83 147 250
  Point Lookout 389 Ratifies
  Amendment 143 Refuse To Call
  Convention 131 Slave State In
  Union 197
MARYVILLE COLLEGE, 101
MASON, 384 J Cass 383
MASON-DIXON LINE, 401

MASSACHUSETTS, Coast Open
    To Attack 162 Gov 161
MATAGORDA BAY, 89
MATAMORAS, 364
MATAMOROS, 363
MATHEWS, 369 Asa C 368
MAURY, 298 Dabney H West Point
    1846 293
MAURY'S, Survivors To Join
    Forrest 307
MAXIMILIAN, 363-364 Emperor
    348 Emperor Installed In
    Mexico City 362 Executed 366
    Ferdinand 361
MAXIMILIAN'S, Army 249
MAYNADIER, Suggestions To Cut
    War Department 159 William
    158
MAYO, Joseph Mayor Of Richmond
    222 Mayor 223 Surrender Of
    224
MCARTHUR, 294-295
MCCOOK, 311 316 322 328 331-
    333 335 Edward M 301 Gen
    304 330
MCCOOK'S, Division 313 First
    Division 314
MCCULLOCH, Ben 86-87
MCDERMOTT, Redoubt 295
MCGOWAN, Capt 43 John 40
MCGRATH, A G 333
MCKENZIE'S CREEK, 355
MCKNIGHT, James 193
MCLEAN, Wilmer 237
MCLEAN HOUSE, 241
MCNEILL, Capt 252
MCSWEENEY, Daniel 137 Mr 136
MEAD, Col 312
MEADE, 31 228 242 George G 207
    Lt 27 Richard K West Point
    1857 30
MEDINA, 298
MEETING, To Negotiate Peace
    Requirements 209

MEIGS, 71 170-171 174 Capt 69
    173 Montgomery C 67 169
MELBOURNE, 398 400
MEMMINGER, 127 Arranges For
    Small Amount Of Money On
    His Own Credit 119
    Christopher G 101 Christopher
    G Secretary Of Treasury 101
    Discovers No Facility In South
    To Print Certificates 123
    Discovers No Paper Available
    For Certificates 122 Faces
    Question Of Providing Long-
    term Financing 120 German
    Immigrant 118 To Find
    Financing For The Confederacy
    118 Willing To Accept Bank
    Notes For Exchange Rate 122
MEMPHIS, 203 355 384
MERCER, Samuel 171
MERIDIAN, 203 302 308 310 312
MERRICK, T D 80
MERRILL, Edwin 356
MERRITT, 239 Wesley 363
MEXICAN, Forces 374
MEXICAN BORDER, 373
MEXICAN WAR, 5 76 86 98 100
    105 141 146 157 163 237 244
    263 269
MEXICO, 172 249 310 348-349 360
    364 376 396 Carlota
    Confederate Refugee Settlement
    365 Civil War 361 French
    Evacuation Of 291 French
    Occupation 363 Northern 86
    Vera Cruz 64
MEXICO CITY, 362 365
MICHIGAN, 35 384 Militia
    Neglected 162 Supports Union
    163
MIDDLE, Military Division 246
MILES, 393 Nelson A 221 392
    William P 188
MILITARY, Duty 8

MILITARY DISTRICT OF THE
   SOUTHWEST, 362
MILITARY DIVISION OF THE
   MISSOURI, 340
MILITIA, 158 17th Connecticut 335
   17th Indiana 321 Cape Fear
   Minute Men 78 Chasseurs 76
   Clinch Rifles 58 Company F 374
   Conshohocken Rifles 161
   Crescent Rifles 76 First
   Mississippi Rifles 98 Irish
   Volunteers 58 Logan Guards
   194 Meacher Guards 30
   Montgomery Guards 58
   Orleans Cadets 76 Richmond
   Hussars 58 Sarsfield Rifles 76
   Seventh Kansas 355 Sixteenth
   Illinois Volunteers 382 Vigilant
   Rifles 32 Yagers 76
MILL CREEK, 316
MILLEDGEVILLE, 51 57 311
MILLER, Abram O 301 Fred E 374
MILLER'S, Company F 376
MILLWOOD, 247 249-251
MILTON, John 333
MIMM'S MILL, 320
MINISTER, Of Foreign Affairs 129
MINNESOTA, 370
MINTY, 319-321 Col 313 Robert H
   301
MINTY'S, Division 316 Second
   Division 314
MISSISSIPPI, 35 65 70 77 98 101
   115 158 191 194 203 208 299-
   300 302-303 342 350 352 360
   379 389 400 Corinth 203 Dates
   Of Occupation 94 Natchez 203
   Second To Secede 50 Ship
   Island Evacuated 201 West
   Point 303-304
MISSISSIPPI MERIDIAN, 293
MISSISSIPPI RIVER, 76 90-91 107
   121 202 209 212 244 303 323

MISSISSIPPI RIVER (cont)
   349 354 362 370 395
   Unrestricted Navigation 148
MISSOURI, 147 224 250 350 352-
   353 355-356 359 365 388
   Convention Called 130 Provides
   Regiments To Confederacy 197
   Slave State In Union 197 State
   Guard 347
MISSOURI RIVER, 370
MOBILE, 74 166 201 208 282 292-
   293 295 297-298 308 312 325
   331 336 343 349 380 389
   Ammunition Explosion 313 Fall
   Of 307 Port Of 204
MOBILE BAY, 75 203 294 298
MOBILE POINT, 292
MONEY, Confederate Note
   Exchange 70 Dollars For One
   US Gold Dollar 123 North And
   South Issue Own Notes 122
   Paper Holds Little Value 122
   US Greenbacks First Legal-
   tender Papery Currency 147
MONROE DOCTRINE, 360
MONTERREY, 365
MONTEVALLO, 303
MONTGOMERY, 51 92 98 115 130
   139-140 142 181-182 204 263
   292 299 313-314 322 382
   Commerce Building 119
   Convention 52 96-97 Surrender
   315
MONTICELLO, 325
MONTREAL, 117
MOORE, 76 Andrew B 51 74
   Governor Of Alabama 65
   Thomas O 52 75
MORAVIAN, 366 School 100
MOREHEAD CITY, 280 284
MORGAN, 248 C H 246
MORMONS, 158
MORRIS ISLAND, 2 32 42-44 138
   141 186 188 190 203 Battery
   Opens Fire On Schooner 179
MORRIS ISLAND (cont)

First Directed Shot Fired On Fort Sumter 185 Home To Soldiers And Equipment 41
MORRISON, Robert G 374
MORRISVILLE, 266-267
MOSBY, 247-251 Guerilla Chief 246 John S 246
MOUNT VERNON ARSENAL, 74 Date Of Occupation 94
MUDD, Samuel A 394
MUNFORD'S STATION, 323
MURRAH, Pendleton 350
MUSIC, Boots And Saddles 302 Dixie 308 Hail Columbia 308 John Brown's Body 258 Marching Through Georgia 258 Reveille 302 The Girl I Left Behind Me 76
MUSKOGEE IRON WORKS, 318
MYERS, Abraham C Chief Of The Quartermaster Bureau 117 Abraham C West Point 1833 117 Capt 283 To Provide Supplies To The Army 117
NAPOLEON, 75 365 Iii 361
NAPOLEON ORDNANCE DEPOT, Date Of Occupation 94
NASHVILLE, 52 202 208 255 277 301 382 University Of 365
NASSAU, 395 397
NATIONAL, Union 191
NAVAL ACADEMY, 151
NAVAL ARMORY, 318
NAVAL HOSPITAL, Date Of Occupation 94
NAVY, Yard Capture Of 66 Yard Commander Of 62
NAVY YARD, 318
NEGOTIATIONS, Between Independent States And Federal Government 37 Termination Of 37
NEGRO, Blacksmith 356 Charles Marven 313 Division 297
NEGRO (cont)

Infantrymen 343 Labor 307 Slavery 402 Slaves Owned By Indians 366
NEGROES, 53 106 306 327 Constructing Protective Devices 138 Importation Of Under Confederate Constitution 103 Laws Governing In North Carolina 290 Receive Quartermaster Stores 317 Resolution Of Status 287
NEUSE RIVER, 261
NEVADA, 371
NEW, Bedford 399 Bern 208 England 146 398 Orleans 208 World 360 York 117 York Mail Service To Florida 69
NEW BERN, 196 202 255-256
NEW JERSEY, 112
NEW MEXICO, 86 362 371-372
NEW ORLEANS, 41 52 76-77 101 113 119 122 201 282 293 299 312 342-343 354 357 362 364 383 Customs House Taken By Secessionists 77 Mint Branch Taken By Secessionists 77 Naval Hospital 77
NEW RIVER, 278
NEW YORK, 28 36 40-41 43-44 59 91 101 123 137 147 152 171 173 177 185 380 And Printing Of Stamps 127 Elmira 377 St Germain Hotel 151 Wood Tries To Separate New York City From State 54
NEW YORK CITY, 5 11 53
NEW YORK HARBOR, 39
NEWNAN, 323
NEWPORT NEWS, 201
NEWSPAPERS, In Charleston Published Accounts Of The Secrecy 41 In New York Published Accounts Of The Secrecy 41
NEWSPAPERS (cont)

In Washington Published
Accounts Of The Secrecy 41
NEY, Marshal 364
NICOLAY, 150
NIOBRARA RIVER, 371
NITER WORKS, 318
NORFOLK, 171 177 196 201-202
257 392 Gosport Navy Yard
116
NORFOLK NAVY YARD, 26
NORTH, 53 Determined To
Preserve The Union 84
Galvanized By Fort Sumter
Attack 191 More Prepared For
War 108 More Prepared To
Fight A War 106 Outrage Over
Flag 44 Pacific 398 Peace Party
Growing 169
NORTH CAROLINA, 49 57 79 107
121 197 201 204 208 210 216
243 258 260 266 280 283 286-
287 289 307 344 349-350 381
390 Citizens Take Possession Of
Federal Property 77 Convention
Called 131 Durham Station 281
Goldsboro 208 Greensboro 245
New Bern 202 Roanoke Island
202 Salisbury 204 278 Seceded
196 Secession Of 79 State
Constitution 289 291 University
Of 258
NORTH CHANNEL, 2
NORTHERN, Prisons 253 States
192
NORTHERNERS, Advantages 105
NORTHPORT, 306 322
NORTHRUP, Lucius B Chief Of
The Commissary Bureau 117
NORTHWEST, 148
NORWICH MILITARY
ACADEMY, 146
O'LAUGHLIN, Michael 394
OAK ISLAND, 77
OGLETHORPE, Light Infantry 57

OGLETHORPE BARRACKS, 58-
59 Date Of Occupation 93
OHIO, 35 356 384 Gov 146 Ratifies
Amendment 143
OKLAHOMA, 366
OKLAHOMA TERRITORY, 130
OLD POINT COMFORT, 9 15 40
OMAHA, 371
OPELIKA, 315
ORD, 228 234 236 Edward O C 207
Gen 217
ORDER OF AMNESTY AND
PARDON, 392
ORDINANCES OF SECESSION,
250
ORR, James L 36
OSTERHAUS, Peter J 357
OULD, 382 Robert 380 387
OVERLAND STATE ROAD, 371
OWSLEY, Frank 109
OXFORD IRON WORKS, 323
PACIFIC OCEAN, 399
PADDY'S HEN AND CHICKS, 384
PAGE, 397 Thomas Jefferson 396
PALMER, John M 356
PALMER'S, Headquarters 357
PALMETTO REPUBLIC, 20 23
136 Knew They Could Not
Prevail Against United States
Alone 23 Population White
Slave And Free Black 23
PALMITO HILL, 375
PALMITO RANCH, 374-375
PAMAUKEY RIVER, 217
PARIS, 147 251 Asked For
Diplomatic Recognition 128
PARKE, John G 220
PARKER, William H 221
PARTY WHIG, 11
PATTERSON, 355
PAYNE, Lewis 394
PAYNTER, Capt 400
PEMBERTON, John C 194
PENDLETON, 232 239 William N
Chief Of Artillery 231

PENNSYLVANIA, 35 115 146 193-194 Governor 193 Nazareth 100
PENSACOLA, 61 67-68 70 108 163 166 168 170 172-176 185 208 293 296 331 Naval Yard 202
PENSACOLA HARBOR, 62 171 Seceding States Need Possession Of 65
PENSACOLA NAVY YARD, Date Of Occupation 93
PERRY, Gov 60 Madison S 50
PETERSBURG, 207 209-210 215-217 220-221 225 256-257 306
PETTIGREW, 31 Col 30 Johnston 29
PETTUS, Gov 77 John J 50
PHENIX, City 316
PHILADELPHIA, 115 152
PHILIPPI, 201 251
PHILLIPS, Col 371 William A 367
PICKENS, 28-30 32-34 45-47 49 136 140 155 179 181 Agrees To Allow Gov To Settle Conflict 47 Claims Not Informed Of Relationship Between South Carolina And The U S 45 Control Of Federal Buildings 34 Francis W 24 Gov 25 37 41 81 141 182 Gov Controls War Department 134 Uses Time To Build Up Batteries 47
PICKETT, 219-220 George E Engages Sheridan 218
PIERCE, Franklin 98
PITCHLYN, 369
PITCHLYNN, Peter P 368
PITTSBURG LANDING, 202
PITTSBURGH, 114
PLACQUEMINE, 342
PLANTERSVILLE, 304
PLATTE RIVER, 371
POCAHONTAS COUNTY, 251
POINT LOOKOUT PRISON, 389
POLK, President 146

POPE, 341 343-344 348-349 351-353 357 John 208 340
PORT HUDSON, 203
PORT ROYAL SOUND, 201
PORTER, 3 172 David D 170 F J 2 Lt 171
PORTSMOUTH, 202
POST BARRACKS, Prison Conditions 377
POSTAL, Service Discussed 52
POTOMAC, 275
POTOMAC RIVER, 202
POTTSVILLE, 193-194
POWDER RIVER EXPEDITION, 371
POWELL, E 60
PRESIDENT, Refuses To See Hayne 49
PRESIDENTIAL, Election 21
PRICE, 365 George 342 Sterling 351 357
PRIME, Frederick 77
PRIOLEAU, Charles K 183
PRISONERS, And Disease 378 Civilian 391 Military 392 Of War Conditions Of 376
PRISONERS OF WAR, 388 Released 388
PRISONS, Conditions Of 377-378 Exchange Of Men 379-382 Federal Number Of Inmates 390
PRITCHARD, Benjamin D 338
PRYOR, 185 188 Poisons Himself 189 Roger A 184
PULASKI, Casimir 56
QUANTRILL, 357 William C 356
QUEEN, Victoria Of England 361
RAILROAD, 255 Danville 217 East Tennessee And Virginia 278 Engineers Remain Loyal To Union 108 Galveston-Houston 395 Georgia Southwestern 377 Mobile And Ohio 303 Montgomery And West Point 315

RAILROAD (cont)
  Richmond And Danville 216
  225 Southside 216-218 226
  Southside Open To Federals
  220 Union Pacific 371
RAILROAD DEPOT, 318
RAILROADS, Growth Of And The
  Telegraph 124 Southern 175
RALEIGH, 78-79 204 256 260-261
  263 267-268 270 282 299
  Surrendered 259
RANDOLPH, 304 355
RANDOLPH COUNTY, 251
RAPPAHANNOCK RIVER, 254
RATIONS, Described 112 Same For
  Union And Confederacy 112
READ, 342 Charles W 341
READING, 193
REAGAN, 264 271-272 John H 101
  John H Postmaster-gen 124
  John H Postmaster-general 101
  Postmaster Gen 392
  Postmaster-gen 125-126 263
  Postmaster-gen Captured 338
  Proclamations 127
RECTOR, 80-81 Henry M 79
RED FORT, 295
RED MOUNTAIN IRON WORKS,
  303
RED RIVER, 340-343 348-349 368
REESE, C B 75
REEVE, 92 I V D 91
REGIMENT, First Volunteer
  Georgia 57 Second Alabama
  Volunteer 65
REILLY, Describes Capture Of Fort
  Johnson 78 James 78
RENO, Jesse L 74
REPUBLICAN, Administration 291
  Sen Proposes Resolution 167
REPUBLICANS, 147
REVENUE CUTTER, Dodge 89
  Harriet Lane 152 177 Henry
  Dodge Taken By Secessionists
  95

REVENUE CUTTER (cont)
  J C Dobbin Surrendered To
  Armed Civilians 57 J C Dobbin
  Taken By Secessionists 95
  Lewis Cass 75 Lewis Cass
  Taken By Secessionists 95
  Washington Taken By
  Secessionists 95 William Aiken
  29 William Aiken Taken By
  Secessionists 95
REVENUE SCHOONER,
  Washington Taken By
  Secessionists 77
REYNOLDS, Gen 345 J J 343
  Thomas C 350
RICE'S STATION, 226
RICHMOND, 116 123 127 175 197
  202 204 207 216 220-222 224-
  225 234 237 242 249 251 286
  306 319 337 350 353 380 382
  388 Capital Of Confederacy 196
  City Council 222 City Hall 224
  Fallen 257 Set On Fire 223
  Tobacco Warehouses Set On
  Fire 222 Under Martial Law
  224
RIFLES, Enfield 117 Yancey Able
  To Purchase 10000 117
RINGGOLD BARRACKS, Date Of
  Occupation 95
RIO, Grande 275
RIO GRANDE, 85 89 363-365 373
RIO GRANDE RIVER, 362
RIVER MERSEY, 400
ROANOKE ISLAND, 202
ROANOKE RIVER, 257
ROBERTSON, 321 Felix H 320
ROCKETTS LANDING, 223
ROCKFISH GAP, 217
ROCKY CREEK, 320
ROCKY MOUNTAINS, 371
ROMAN, Alfred 148
ROMNEY, 201
ROSSER, 219 Thomas L 218
ROST, Pierre A 128

RUFFIN, Edmund 185
RUSSIA, 172
SABINE, The 175
SAINT, Marks 331
SAINT CROIX, 101
SAINT EMMA PLANTATION, 354
SAINT FRANCIS RIVER, 345
SAINT GEORGE'S CHANNEL, 400
SAINT GERMAIN HOTEL, 151
SAINT JOHN RIVER, 61
SAINT LOUIS, 340 345 348 371 384
SAINT PETERSBURG, Asked For Diplomatic Recognition 128
SAINT PHILIP'S ISLAND, 201
SALADO CREEK, 86
SALEM, 249-250
SALISBURY, 262-263 285 381
SALURNIA, 91
SAN ANTONIO, 84-86 90-92 365
SAN ANTONIO ARSENAL, Date Of Occupation 94
SAN ANTONIO BARRACKS, Date Of Occupation 94
SAN FRANCISCO, 399
SAN LUCAS SPRING, 91
SAND SPRINGS, Massacre 370
SANDY HOOK, 190
SANTA ROSA ISLAND, 62 165 171 325
SAVANNAH, 8 57 59 108 179 185 202 204 208 255-256 339 389 392 Garrison 211 Guards 57
SAVANNAH RIVER, 56 58 337
SAYLER'S CREEK, 226 Disaster For The Army Of Northern Virginia 227
SCAMMON, Edward P 325
SCHNIERLE, Gen 18
SCHOFIELD, 281 284-285 287-288 290-291 At Goldsboro 215 Awarded Medal Of Honor 286 Gen 280 283 John M 208 256

SCHOFIELD (cont)
Letters To Sherman And Halleck 289 Wes Point 1853 286
SCHOONER, Horace 91 Rhoda H Shannon 179 Urbana 91
SCHURZ, Carl 282
SCOTT, 12 40-41 48 69 85 151 163 168 170 173 Advises Lincoln That Anderson Should Evacuate Fort Sumter 151 Evacuation Of Fort Sumter Inevitable 150 Gen 36 39 67 84 158 169 174-175 Gen Daily Reports Requested Of 172 Gen Issues Orders To Slemmer 62 Has Second Thoughts About The Warship 40 Orders Recruits To Fort Sumter 39 Winfield 5 11 Winfield General-in-chief 147
SCOTTISH, Brogues 400 Volunteers 398
SCOTTSVILLE, 304
SEA OF OKHOTSK, 399
SECESSION, As A Problem For Congress To Solve 48 Likely To Lead To War 23 Ordinance Of Drafted 52 States Other Than South Carolina 48 Sympathizers 28
SECESSIONIST, Sympathizers Attach US Militia 194
SECESSIONISTS, First Time Holding US Fort 31
SECOND, Division 313
SECRETARY OF INTERIOR, Vacancy 36
SECRETARY OF NAVY, 67 175
SECRETARY OF STATE, 172 253
SECRETARY OF WAR, 7 158 193 261-262 Order To Return Muskets 20
SEDDON, James A Secretary Of War Resigns 210

SELMA, 263 302 304 313-314 322-
    323 382 Fall Of 306
SEMINOLE INDIANS, 325
SEMINOLE WAR, 269
SEMINOLE WARS, 163
SEMMES, 114 Capt 116 Raphael
    113
SENATE, 142 167 213 278
    Committee On Military Affairs
    158
SEWARD, 168-169 171 174 178
    270 Complaints And Requests
    To President Lincoln 172 Fort
    Pickens Operation Delegated
    To 170 Policy Of Appeasement
    Toward The South 173
    Secretary Of State 142 149 209
    362 Secretary Of State Stabbed
    268 William H Secretary Of
    State 147
SHAD, 219
SHARPE, George H Asst Provost
    Marshall 241
SHELBY, 364 Joseph O 365
SHELL BANK, 354
SHENANDOAH VALLEY, 202 217
    246 251
SHEPLEY, George F 224
SHERIDAN, 219-220 226 230 236
    242 258 362-364 Gen 217 Philip
    H 208
SHERIDAN'S, Cavalry 218
SHERMAN, 211 216-217 243 249
    256 258-261 265-268 270-271
    274 277 282 284 286 288-289
    299 302 314 322 349 Advancing
    In The Carolinas 212 Advises
    Breckinridge To Leave Country
    275 At Goldsboro 215 Gen 280
    Issues Special Field Orders 257
    275 Maj-gen 283 285 Proposal
    Rejected 279 W T 281 West
    Point 1840 269 William T 208
    Writes Terms Of Surrender
    272-273

SHERMAN'S, Army 255
SHERMAN-JOHNSTON, Armistice
    278
SHIP, Island Mississippi 201
SHIPMENT, Of Supplies 177
SHREVEPORT, 341 349 351 357
    363
SHUTES FOLLY ISLAND, 30
SIBLEY, 91 C C 90
SIDE-WHEELER, The Lark 396
    USS Powhatan 171 William H
    Webb 341
SIMMONS, Seneca G 194
SIPSEY BRANCH, 323
SKILLEN, Ordinance Officer 30
SLAUGHTER, 364 374 376 James
    E 373
SLAVE, Labor For Food Crops
    Manufacturing And More 107
    States Hold Convention To
    Secede Together 49
SLAVERY, 96 402 Abolished 401
    Goals To Expand Into
    Southwest 86 Specifically
    Mentioned In Confederate
    Constitution 103
SLAVES, 106 196 244 Accounting
    Of Under CS Constitution 104
    Emancipation Of 390 Freed
    Looting City 306 Possible
    Insurrection 4
SLEMMER, 64 66 164-166 Adam J
    62 Lt 163 Protests And Will
    Not Surrender 64 Receives
    Truce Notice 65 Refuses To
    Surrender 65
SLOCUM, Henry W 256
SLOOP OF WAR, Brooklyn 40
    Ordered 39
SLOOP-OF-WAR, Richmond 343
SLOUGH, William 298
SMALLPOX, Outbreak Of 22
SMITH, 168 294 350 A J 292 Caleb
    Secretary Of The Interior 147
    Gen 358 Gustavus W 322 H 76

SMITH'S, 16th Corps 299
SMITHFIELD, 256 258-259
SMITHVILLE, 78
SNYDER, G W 16 Lt 10 27
SOUTH, 53 Aggressive Minority Wants War To Establish Southern Nation 149 Attitudes Toward Strength And War 108 Depends On North For Grain And Other Products 107 Depends On Northern Banks For Financing 118 Determined To Leave The Union 84 Energized By Capture Of Fort Sumter 191 Five Of Eight States Call Conventions Regarding Secession 130 Lacking Merchant Vessels 108 Newspapers Print Davis' Proclamation 243 Not Supplied To Fight A War 106 Railroad Capabilities 107 Railroad Locomotives Made In Richmond 108
SOUTH CAROLINA, 7-9 17 23 32 34-36 46-47 51 53 55-57 77 81-83 97 101 104 107-108 115 117 136 139 159 161 174 191 194 210 277 280 283 288 307 324 333 336-337 379 Adjutant Of Regiment 8 Army Of 138 Camden 204 Charleston 1 Claims Occupation Of Fort Sumter First Act Of Hostility 46 Columbia 22 Columbia First Baptist Church Convention Gathering Place 22 Commonwealth Of 22 Congressional Delegation 13 38 Convention 36 Convention Qualifications To Vote 22 Convention To Secede Union 21 Customs House Seized 38 Customs Post Office Seized 38 Dates Of Occupation 93

SOUTH CAROLINA (cont) Declaration Of Justification For Secession 24 Declaration To Be Independent 25 Declares Sovereignty And Independence 37 Declares War Against US 45 Draft Authorized 135 Edisto Island 202 First Federal Property Gained 29 First To Secede 50 Forms It's Own Government 23 Forts Seized 68 Governor's Offer Of Meat And Vegetables Declined 137 Harbor Activities Of Secessionists 41 High Commitment To Secession 49 Inspection By Confederate Forces 140 List Of Supplies 137 Many Felt Had Started A War 44 Military 33 Militia 4 134 137 Militia Description 135 Militia Requests Return Of Forty Muskets 18 Minute Men Formed 135 No Longer Represented In US Senate 21 Ordinance Of Secession 36 Ordnance Board To Purchase Munitions And Equipment 135 Port Royal Sound 201 Preventing Transfer Of Munitions 33 Secession 30 Secession From Union 20 Secessionists In Possession Of All US Property Except Fort Sumter 35 Secretary Of State 180 See Removal As Breach Of Buchanan's Commitment 28 Seizes Three Forts And Arsenal 40 St Andrew's Hall Convention Gathering Place 22 Treats With US Gov For Federal Property 36 University 101 US Arsenal Defense Of 33 US Arsenal Losses In 34 Vigilance Committees Formed 135 Volunteer Forces 142

SOUTH CAROLINA (cont)
  Volunteers To Serve For Six
  Months 136 Vote To Secede 22
  War Threatened 37
SOUTH CAROLINIANS, 151
SOUTHERN, Nation 23 96 States
  192
SOUTHERN STATES DEMANDS
  FROM NORTHERN STATES
  IF NOT MET THEY WOULD
  SECEDE, 51
SOUTHERNERS, Belief They
  Would Prevail 105
SOUTHPORT, 78
SPAIN, 172 397 Attacks Mexico 361
  Ferrol 396
SPANGLER, Edward 394
SPANISH, Viceroys 362
SPANISH FORT, 204 292-295 297
SPEED, 384 Capt 385 Frederic 383
SPENCER, 301 311 Christopher
  300
SPRAGUE, 349 351-352 John A 348
SPRING HILL, 320
SPRINGFIELD, Rifles 194
SPRINGFIELD RIFLES, 161
STANTON, 266 282 286 381 386-
  387 389 392-394 Edwin M
  Attorney-gen Replaces Black 35
  Secretary Of War 235 253 268
  385 396 Secretary Of War
  Orders End Of Draft 267
  Secretary Of War Reward For
  Capture Of Davis 337
  Suggestions In Reply To
  Commissioners 37
STARKE'S LANDING, 293 298
STATES, Take Federal Forts Before
  Secession 56
STEAM TUG, The Freeborn 177
  The Uncle Ben 177 The Yankee
  177
STEAMBOAT, Pauline Carroll 383
  Sultana 383 Yankee 76

STEAMER, Catawba 189 John S Ide
  254 Joseph Whitney 71 Pawnee
  152 USS Brooklyn 40 USS
  Brooklyn Capable Of Dealing
  With Secession Batteries 40
  USS Mohawk 69 USS Pawnee
  170-171 USS Pocahontas 171
  USS Powhatan 172 USS
  Wyandotte 63
STEAMSHIP, Atlantic Arrives In
  Florida 174 Atlantic Leaves
  New York With Troops And
  Horses 173
STEELE, 294 Frederick 293 Gen
  364
STEPHENS, 233 Alexander H
  Confederate Vice-president 209
  Alexander H Provisional Vice-
  president 100 Vice-president
  392
STEVENS, Atherton 223 P F 32
  Vice-president 339
STEWART, A P 257
STOCKS, And Bonds Terms Of
  Described 121
STOCKTON, 294
STONE, Charles P 48
STONEMAN, Gen 266 George 208
  277 300
STONEMAN'S, Union Forces 263
STONY CREEK, 252
STORESHIP, Supply 63-64
SULLIVAN'S ISLAND, 1-2 31 182
SULLIVAN ISLAND, 141
SULTAN OF ZANZIBAR, 400
SUMMERVILLE ROAD, 316-317
SUPPLY SHIP, Illinois 174 Laura
  398
SUPPLY VESSEL, Baltic 185-186
  The Baltic 190
SUPPLY VESSELS, 183
SURRATT, John H Reward Posted
  253 Mary E 394
SUTHERLAND'S STATION, 221
SUTHERLIN, William 243

SWAIN, 259 Davis L 258
SWASH CHANNEL, 2 179
SWEETWATER RIVER, 371
SWITZERLAND, 385
SYDNEY, 400
TALLADEGA, 323
TALLAHASSEE, 50 311 326 329-331 335-336
TARIFF LAWS, Of US Adopted By Confederacy 120 Of US Government 120
TAYLOR, 209 244 298 310 312 338 341 357 360 373 397 Gen 243 302 336 Lt-gen 309 Richard 208 293 308 Surrender 307 Surrender Of 367 Zachary 293
TAYLORSVILLE, 356
TENERIFE, 396
TENNESSEE, 49 101 121 196-197 202-203 207-208 267 278-279 286 300 336 355 384 Convention Called 131 Fort Pillow 203 Knoxville 203 Murfreesboro 203
TENNESSEE RIVER, 300
TERRILL, 357
TEXAS, 52 70 85 87 89 101-102 107 116 168 173 188 191 194 197 244 282 291 320 330 343 348 350 354 359-360 366 368 373 Committee On Public Safety Formed 86 Coriscana 365 Dates Of Occupation 94-95 Department Of 88 District Of 364 Exempted From Tariff Laws 120 Galveston 203 395 Houston Asks Legislature Not To Consider The Secession Convention 53 Last Federal Troops 91 Marshall 340 Mounted Volunteers 158 Occupation Of By Sheridan 363 Officer Hanged In Raleigh 260 Opposed To Secession 52 Postal Map 125 Prisoners Of War 92

Secedes From The Union 53 Secession 85-86 90 State Of 84 Washington 340
TEXAS-MEXICAN BORDER, 362
THEARD, Paul 76
THOMAS, 182 208 302 Gen 382 George H 207 277 299 Lorenzo Adjutant-gen 180 Louis 41 Philip F Secretary Of The Treasury 35 William M Letter To President Lincoln 191
THOMASVILLE, 325 330
THOMPSON, 346 Jacob Secretary Of The Interior 35 M Jeff 344-345 347 Resigns 35 West Point 320
THREE OILCLOTH FACTORIES, 319
TIN, And Zinc Sulphur And Nitrates Scarce 106
TOBESOFKEE, 321
TOBESOFKEE CREEK, 320
TODD, Col 75
TOMBIGBEE RIVER, 298-299 310
TOOMBS, Robert Secretary Of State 101 Secretary Of State 102 128 Secretary Of State Suggestions To Diplomats 129
TORTUGAS, 70
TORTUGAS HARBOR, 70
TOTTEN, 71 77 139 Capt 80 Explains He Has No Course Of Action Given By Government 81 Gen 138 James 79 Joseph G 57
TOUCET, Secretary 65
TOUCEY, 37 64 66
TOUCHEY, Isaac Secretary Of The Navy 35
TRANS-MISSISSIPPI, 353 Surrender 364
TRANS-MISSISSIPPI DEPARTMENT, 351 358 Rolls 209
TRANSPORT, General Banks 298

TRANSPORT STEAMER, Baltic
177
TREATY OF, Ghent 244
  Guadalupe Hidalgo 244
TREDEGAR IRON WORKS, 115-
  116 Set On Fire 222
TRESCOT, W H Asst Secretary Of
  State 36
TRINIDAD, 100
TROOPS, Federal 88
TROUGH SPRING, 312
TUCKER, Gen 344
TUGBOATS, 185-186
TURNER, W F 344
TUSCALOOSA, 303-304 306 314
  322 386
TWIGGS, 85-86 88 David E 84 89
  Gen 87 Surrendered 95
TWO POWDER MAGAZINES,
  319
TYBEE LIGHTHOUSE, 179
TYGART RIVER, 252
TYLER, Chairman Of Virginia
  Peace Conference 132 John 131
  Robert C 315
UNDERWOOD, John 30
UNION, 49 51 72 177 Breakup Into
  For Confederacies Proposal 12
  Casualties 298 313 316 324
  College 101 Federal Position Of
  South Carolina In 21 Imminent
  Danger Of Disruption By
  Secession 12 Losses 306 Navy
  373 Preservation Of 23
  Prisoners 325 Vessels 342
UNION COLLEGE, 147
UNION SECESSIONS, South
  Carolina 20 22
UNITED, States Constitution
  Repeal Of 22 States Forces 402
  States Government 402 States
  Law 98 States Olympic Teams
  402 States Passports 402 States
  Seven States Seceded From 53
  States Sovereignty 31

UPTON, 305 319 337 339 Emory
  301 Gen 303
UPTON'S, Division 316-317 Fourth
  Division 314
US, Army Ambulance 242 Army
  Buying Weapons From England
  117 Army Composition 1861
  158 Army Maximum Strength
  198 Army Officers No Guidance
  64 Army Officers Who
  Resigned To Join Confederacy
  115 Army Strength Of 89 Army
  Weakened By Losses Of
  Munitions 197 Cabinet 36
  Cabinet Discussion On Fate Of
  Forts Sumter And Pickens 168-
  169 Cabinet Resignations Over
  Secession Policy 35 Cabinet
  Says South Carolina Would Not
  Attack Federal Forts 38 Cabinet
  Suggestions In Reply To
  Commissioners 37 Capitol Trial
  Begins 386 Congress 154 272
  Congress Little Time To
  Debate Recommendations 133
  Congress Power To Make War
  131 Congress Right To Make
  Laws 48 Congress Southern
  Democrats Abandon Seats 147
  Congress Southerners Prevent
  Army Growth 158 Congress
  Virginia Peace Conference Final
  Report Given 132 Congress
  Virginia Resolutions Submitted
  131 Constitution 129 272
  Constitution Amendment
  Forbidding Congress Power To
  Interfere With Slavery 143
  Constitution Proposed
  Amendments 131 Constitution
  Tenth Amendment 402
  Constitution Thirteenth
  Amendment Described 132-133
  Constitution Thirteenth
  Amendment In Effect 401

US (cont)
  Constitution What
    Amendments Necessary 52
  Consul 400 Customs Duties
    Primary Source Of Public Funds
    154 Customs House 70 Federal
    Property Dispute With States
    55 Forts In Seceded States
    Remained In Federal Hands 150
    Government 105 194 280-281
    309 Government Policy On
    Militia 114 Government Postal
    Service To South 124 House
    Committee Military Affairs
    House 25 House Of
    Representatives 97 263 House
    Of Representatives Pass
    Resolution 39 Militia Adjutant
    And Inspector Gen 154 Militia
    Bureau 154 Militia Men On The
    Rolls 160 Militia Northern
    Defects 160-161 Mint 60 Mints
    Taken By Secessionists 95 Navy
    151 Navy Composition 13 Navy
    Department 69 Navy Officers
    No Guidance 64 Pacific
    Squadron 398 Post Offices
    Taken By Secessionists 95
    Quartermaster Corps 69
    Secretary Of The Navy 258
    Senate Appointed Special
    Committee Of Five To Consider
    Report 133 State Forces
    Organization 193 Sub-treasuries
    Taken By Secessionists 95
    Terms Of Surrender In Georgia
    59 War Articles 112 War
    Department 70-71 160 War
    Department Bureaus Of 158
US ARMY, Chief-of-staff 247
  Composition 192 Only Enlarged
  By Two Regiments 192
US CONSTITUTION, 244

US MINTS, Necessary To South As
  Source Of Nitric Acid 120 Not
  Necessary To South 119
US NAVAL ACADEMY, 341
US NAVY, Dept Bureau Of
  Provisions And Clothing 146
US POSTAL SERVICE, 166 Mail
  Service Suspended In Seceded
  States 127 Will Continue In All
  Parts Of The Union 127
UTAH, 158
VALLEY OF MEXICO, 363
VANCE, 259-261 Gov 276 291
  Zebulon B 258
VANDORN, 92 Earl 90 Gen 91
VEATCH, 294-295 368 James C 367
VEATCH'S, Division 297
VERA, Cruz 361
VERA CRUZ, 365
VERMONT, 146
VESSEL, Alabama 398 Barracouta
  400 Brooklyn 66 166 Clyde 392
  CSS Alabama 398 CSS Florida
  398 CSS Shenandoah 397 CSS
  Virginia 222 Denbigh 396 Fort
  Jackson 360 Harriet Lane 185-
  186 Henry James 383 James
  Murry 399 Jerah Swift 399
  Joseph Whitney 72 Laurel 398
  Mohawk 72 Nina 30 Olive
  Branch 383 River Queen 256
  Sea King 398 Shenandoah 399-
  400 Star Of The West 42-43 45
  48 62 90 138 Stonewall 397
  Sultana 384-385 The Brooklyn
  178 The General Clinch 31 The
  Nina 31 Titanic 385 USS
  Brooklyn 65 163 USS Kearsarge
  398 USS Saginaw 399 USS
  Wachusett 398 Webb 342-343
  Wyandotte 64
VESSEL ISLAND, 77
VICKSBURG, 98 194 203 382-383

VICTORIA, Queen Of England Reluctant To Recognize Slave State 116
VIRGINIA, 4 30 35 40 48-50 79 107-108 112 184-185 197 203 207-208 213 216 244 253 263 265-266 277 283 293 297 345 390 398 City Point Grant's Headquarters 256 Convention Called 131 Fort Monroe 26 339 Fortress Monroe 329 Fredericksburg 203 Harpers Ferry 79 Joins Confederacy 196 Militia Ordered To Seize Harpers Ferry Arsenal 195 Peace Conference Closed To Public 132 Petersburg 204 329 Port Royal 254 Rebuilding Of 249 Requests Troop Withdrawal From Fort Sumter 132 Resolutions Try To Pull North And South Together 131 Richmond 115 Secession 116 Unionists Form Separate State 196 University 100-101
VIRGINIA PEACE CONFERENCE, 142-143
VODGES, 168 176 326-329 331-332 334-335 Capt 175 Gen-in-chief 174 Israel 163 Israel West Point 1837 325 Letter To Washington 164
VOLUNTEERS, 48 160 Military 158
WADDELL, 399-400 James I 398
WAITE, 88-89 92 Carlos A 85 Col 86-87
WAKEFIELD, James H 356
WALDO, 332
WALKER, 114-115 140-141 184 263 364 Gen 262 H H 261 Leroy P 100 Leroy P Secretary Of War 100 Ordnance Sergeant 57 Secretary 117 Secretary Of State 113 Secretary Of War 183

WALTER'S CHURCH, 237
WAR, Materials Of Supplied To Southern Army 115
WAR OF 1812, 157 244
WARM SPRINGS, 252
WARREN, K 219 Relieved Of Command 220
WARRINGTON NAVY YARD, 61 Description Of 61
WARSHIP, Harriet Lane 171 Merite 341 Missouri 341 Pawnee 177 185 Pawnee Offers To Go To Rescue Of Fort Sumter 186 Pocahontas 177 185 Powhatan 174 177 185-186 The Brooklyn 175 Wyandotte 176
WASHINGTON, 2 9 41 47 66 70 80-81 84 88-89 105 148 164 171 175 177-178 180-181 191 193- 194 240 254 267 278-279 286 291 337 352 369-370 380 386 392-394 Artillerists 193 George 157 401 In Danger Of Secessionist Seizure 48 Lincoln Lies In State 253 Military District Of 394 Militia 48 Peace Conference Held 134 Pennsylvania Avenue Guarded In Case Of War 143
WASHITA RIVER, 367
WATIE, 367 369 Stand 366
WATSON, Josiah 63
WAYNESBORO, 217
WEITZEL, Accepts Mayo's Surrender 224 Godfrey 223
WELLES, 165-166 168 170-171 174-176 Gideon Secretary Of The Navy 146 Secretary Of The Navy 396
WEST POINT, 5 105 192-193 204 322 390 Fort Tyler 324
WEST VIRGINIA, 250-251 384 388 Admitted To Union 1863 196

WESTERN VIRGINIA EAST
TENNESSEE AND
WESTERN NORTH
CAROLINA, Rolls 209
WHEELER, 261 285 339 Joseph
  260
WHITAKER, 354
WHITE, 321 Frank 320
WHITE'S RANCH, 363 374-375
WHITE HOUSE, 13 36 49 169-170
  172 327-328 Beseiged By Men
  Seeking Office 151 Town Of
  217
WHITE OAK ROAD, 218
WHITING, 58 Maj 140 W H C 139
  William H 57
WIGFALL, 189 Col 188 Louis T
  186
WILCOX, 355
WILDER, John T 301
WILLARD'S HOTEL, 131
WILLIAMS, 384 Capt 385 George
  A 383 M H 311
WILLIAMSBURG, 202
WILMINGTON, 77-78 185 196 204
  208 255 382 389 395
WILSON, 299 301-306 313-314
  320-322 324 330 332 335 337-
  339 Gen 385 James 284 James
  H 208 James H West Point
  1860 300
WINCHESTER, 202 246 251
WINDER, John H 379
WINSLOW, 318 337 Edward F 301
WINSLOW'S, Brigade 317
WINTRENGER, Nathan 383
WIRZ, 386-387 Henry 385 Henry
  Capture Of 386
WISE, Henry 195
WISMER, Moses 162
WITTSBURG, 346
WOOD, Fernando Democratic
  Mayor Of New York City 53
  John T 264
WOODS, Charles R 41 Lt 42-43
WORDEN, John L Carries
  Instructions To Adams 175
  Prisoner Of War 175
WRIGHT, Horatio G 220
YADKIN, 262
YADKIN RIVER, 288
YALE COLLEGE, 293
YALE UNIVERSITY, 101
YANCEY, William L 116 128
YAZOO CITY, 203
YEOMAN, Joseph 337
YORKTOWN, 202
YULEE, David L 335

www.ingramcontent.com/pod-product-compliance
Lightning Source LLC
Chambersburg PA
CBHW050424240426
43661CB00055B/2261